The Stern Trawler

The Stern Trawler

Peter Hjul (Editor)

*G. C. Eddie, P. D. Chaplain, N. M. Kerr,
J. J. Waterman, John Burgess*

Fishing News (Books) Ltd, 23 Rosemount Avenue, West Byfleet, Surrey, England, and
110 Fleet Street, London EC4A 2JL

© Fishing News (Books) Ltd, 1972
23 Rosemount Avenue, West Byfleet, Surrey

Printed in Great Britain
by W & J Mackay Limited, Chatham

Contents

Introduction	1
The Development of the Modern Stern Trawler *G. C. Eddie and P. D. Chaplin*	3
Mechanisation of Trawl Gear Handling Aboard Shelter-deck Stern Trawlers in the Atlantic Fisheries *N. M. Kerr*	30
Handling and Processing the Catch in Stern Trawlers *J. J. Waterman*	87
Notable Small Stern Trawlers *John Burgess*	122
Shelter-deck Stern Trawlers Built Since 1963 *Peter Hjul*	140

Canada	140	Poland	176
France	144	South Africa	179
East Germany	150	Spain	183
West Germany	153	United Kingdom	192
Italy	157	USSR	203
Japan	160	Stern Trawler-type Research Ships	209
The Netherlands	166	Other Countries	213
Norway	168		

Introduction

PETER HJUL, Editor, *Fishing News International*

In September 1963, a technical conference was held in the British trawler port of Grimsby. It was organised by the White Fish Authority and its purpose was to review the progress up to then of stern trawling. Fishing News (Books) Ltd published the proceedings of the conference in May 1964 in a 100-page volume titled "Stern Trawling". The demand for this book revealed the wide interest around the world in one of the most significant post-war developments in fish capture and in the handling of fish at sea. The demand a few years ago caught up with our supply; and the changes in the design and operation of the stern trawler, its spread into the fleets of more than 30 countries, the huge number of different vessels being designed and built all indicated that a mere second edition of the original book would not be adequate.

We decided, therefore, on a completely new and much enlarged review of this vessel type, drawing on sources linked with the 1963 Grimsby conference and concentrating on the ship itself.

Reporting as a consultant to the Committee for Fisheries of the Organisation for Economic Cooperation and Development (OECD) in April 1968, the late Mr. E. R. Gueroult, the French naval architect, noted that for some years very few side trawlers had been built in Western Europe and that "today the demand for this type of vessel is practically non-existent". Meanwhile, in western and eastern Europe, the Soviet Union and Japan, stern trawlers were being built in increasing numbers.

He saw this as not just a fashion but as a trend that had spread right through the world's fishing industry with many major consequences. "By the end of this century," he added, "1960 will probably stand out as the year when the fishing industry went over once and for all from side to stern trawling."

The exact year is difficult to pin point but there can be no doubt that the decade of the 1960s was, for commercial fisheries, the momentous decade of the stern trawler with its profound influence on the whole conduct of catching operations, fish finding, handling, and transportation to the ports. The impact effects of this vessel type on the industry are already well known; the longer term dynamic effects on fishery economics, technology and science will become better known as we move through the 1970s.

We have, however, reached a stage where it is possible to trace the evolution of the stern trawler, to record it as a remarkable success story and to suggest how it might continue in the years immediately ahead. Eventually this might be done in a detailed, definitive work which would evaluate the results of the most successful stern trawlers after ten years or more in service. It is too early yet for such a work. There is no typical stern trawler, although there are signs that several standard types might find applications well beyond their original countries and fishing areas.

In the first chapters of this book, the two authors draw on their considerable experience to examine the stern trawler in the wide context of the industry it serves. Through much of a distinguished career in the engineering aspects of the fishing industry, Mr. Gordon Eddie has been involved in the stern trawler. He is now technical director of the White Fish Authority, and his co-author, Mr. Peter Chaplin, is chief naval architect of its Industrial Development Unit.

From its base in Hull – the main port of the British fleet of stern trawlers – the IDU has been an active participant in trawler design studies both in Britain and abroad, and in the experimental and development work which has helped to transform the techniques of gear handling aboard British vessels.

Dr. Norman Kerr, who contributes the substantial chapter on gear handling, is chief development engineer of the IDU. He deals with this subject in considerable detail because this is one of the features of stern trawlers where guidance, based on accumulated practical experience, can be given to the owner contemplating a new trawler or seeking ways of improving the performance of an existing vessel.

The handling of gear aboard and the processing of fish at sea are two of the main features of the stern trawler which distinguish it from other fishing craft and ensure its permanent place in modern fishing fleets. A pioneering part in processing at sea was played by the Torry Research Station in Aberdeen. Its research work over many years led, through the *Fairtry* trawlers, to the factory stern trawler producing sea-frozen fillets; and, through the *Lord Nelson*, to the whole fish freezer.

In his chapters on processing, Mr. John Waterman, industrial liaison officer at Torry, draws on the collective experience of his organisation to describe how the various systems have been applied to stern trawlers, and to advise owners how to get the finest quality products from their fish.

The two final sections of "The Stern Trawler" describe and illustrate many of the ships built since 1963. Lieutenant-Commander John Burgess, technical correspondent of the publications "Fishing News" and "Fishing News International", deals with the smaller vessels, most of them under 100 ft. long.

For the large stern trawlers, we have made a selection from more than 300 ships described and usually illustrated in the monthly magazine "Fishing News International". This is done to show the variety of ships which have been introduced in a relatively short period, and it will give the reader of this book some idea of the extent to which the stern trawler has taken over in the fleets of the main trawling countries.

Our selection of the 13 main countries now operating stern trawlers is an arbitrary one. Some of the countries not included, such as Cuba and Iceland, have made important recent moves towards the ownership of stern trawlers. Among the 13, countries such as South Africa and Italy, have only a small number of ships. But all of those included have contributed to the rapid evolution of the stern trawler – as designers, builders and owners.

The Development of the Modern Stern Trawler

G. C. Eddie, B.Sc., C.Eng., F.I.Mech.E., M.I.Mar.E., M.Inst.R., Technical Director, White Fish Authority
P. D. Chaplin, B.Sc., C.Eng., F.R.I.N.A., Chief Naval Architect, Industrial Development Unit, White Fish Authority

Mankind's ability to harvest the riches of the ocean has increased greatly in the second half of the 20th century as a result of advances, great and small, in almost every branch of fisheries technology. One of the innovations of crucial importance was the large shelter-deck stern-ramp trawler, which was developed to facilitate processing of the catch at sea. Fishing over the stern is now being adopted in all trawling fleets, irrespective of size of vessel. The introduction of the stern trawler together with other innovations has given a big impetus to technical investigation and development, in order to ensure that the new methods and equipment can be employed economically and effectively. This has led in turn to a general advance in the arts of fishing vessel design and operation. Thus although, for many fleets, the economic environment has become more harsh in recent years, the world fishing industry has been able to meet greatly increased and more onerous demands for its products.

Between 1950 and 1970 the catch rose from about 20 million tons to about 60 million tons a year. Although this was made possible partly by the increasing adoption, in the developing countries, of mechanical propulsion and of other techniques already well-established in the more advanced fishing nations of the northern hemisphere, it was also due, in large part, to new developments which made their first appearance in the late 1940s and 1950s. These included electronic navigation systems, more effective echo sounders and sonar, and also the power block for hauling purse seines, all of which increased the ability of the fisherman to find and catch the fish.

The range of operation of the fleets was, however, still restricted by the means available for preserving the catch and the acceptability of the resulting product to the consumer. In many fisheries the uncertainty caused by alternating glut and short supply, together with the limited methods of preservation practicable aboard ship, continued to inhibit investment and technical development. This situation was completely changed with the advent of modern techniques of quick-freezing which could be employed on board relatively small ships. It then became possible to contemplate the construction of fishing vessels capable of exploiting the most distant grounds, of staying out until they were full, and of landing their catch in virtually imperishable form.

The first modern factory trawler was also the first shelter-deck stern trawler. Her construction inspired intensive development of smaller stern trawlers for the near and middle distance fisheries as well as for distant water fisheries, because of the advantages in crew comfort, safety, and mechanisation that the concept of stern trawling was seen to offer. The consequent increased activity in the field of technical development has since led to many other improvements, the benefits of which are enjoyed by the operators of vessels of many types, prosecuting fisheries which in some cases are very different from the North Atlantic distant water cod fishery for which the factory trawler was conceived.

The origin of the new concept

The pioneers of the modern factory trawler found that they had to adopt a method of processing the catch which involved the filleting of such fish as cod, partly because acceptable means of quick-freezing such large fish whole had not yet been developed, and partly because their philosophy, in any event, was to land fish in a form that would require little subsequent handling and re-processing. Freezing fillets at sea had become feasible because of the development, in Germany, of automatic machine tools for filleting cod and certain other species. It did mean, however, that a large factory deck would be required, and this was not practicable in a ship of the size and type of the classic wet fish side trawler of the late 1940s. Thus the pioneers of the modern factory trawler were forced to consider a new concept of trawler design.

The idea of fishing over the stern was not new; indeed this was standard practice in many fisheries, and had been employed to a limited extent in the pioneering days of the development of steam trawlers in the 19th century. Nevertheless, the building of *Fairtry* (Ref. 1), the first modern factory trawler, does represent an historic landmark: she inaugurated the modern era of freezing at sea; she was the first shelter-decked fishing vessel; she was also the first example of the adoption of the practice of handling the trawl over the stern to facilitate the use of new methods and equipment aboard. There are other new developments which are difficult or impracticable to introduce or employ on a side trawler, and which are not connected with freezing or other sophisticated methods of processing the catch.

Following the building of the first modern factory trawler, means were developed whereby it is possible to freeze cod aboard ship in the whole, gutted form, with very little labour, and the *Northern Wave* experiment in 1956 demonstrated that this operation was feasible in a single-decked side trawler (Ref. 2). It is significant, however, that with one or two exceptions all freezer trawlers built since then have been of the shelter-deck stern-fishing type.

The classic single-decked side trawler indeed seems to be the ultimate of its kind, not capable of much further evolution or development. The stern trawler lends itself much more readily to the introduction of modern equipment and methods intended to save labour, increase productivity and improve the quality of the catch, and it is usually safer and more comfortable.

Early attitudes

Not all of these points, however, were self-evident in the eyes of the majority of trawler builders and operators in the late 1940s and in the 1950s. In the view of many, stern trawling was a technique which those who wished to invest in factory trawlers were forced to develop, make a success of, and accept the limitations and disadvantages of, simply because, otherwise, the factory trawler was not feasible. To them, stern trawling, as a concept, was not obviously superior to conventional side trawling.

It was by no means a case of having had to wait upon the technology of the second half of the 20th century in order to realise certain obvious advantages. On the contrary, the method would have been perfectly feasible with the technology of the late 19th century, but few people had ever seen any point in expensive experiments in stern trawling, and although some owners and builders had studied possible designs, none had been built. The side trawler seemed adequate; its defects and limitations, and the real advantages of the stern trawler, became apparent only in the years following the appearance of *Fairtry*. Indeed, it was not until 18 years after *Fairtry* was built in Aberdeen that a shelter-deck stern trawler – *Ben Lui* – joined the Aberdeen trawler fleet.

Advantages, of course, must be paid for. The disadvantages, real and imaginary, of stern trawling, were often much more apparent in the early 1950s than the advantages, some of which were yet to be realised and others of which were in doubt. Any account of the technical evolution of the modern stern trawler, both the large shelter-deck type and the small single-deck type, is therefore bound to be very largely an account of how the disadvantages were overcome or discounted, and the advantages realised and made apparent, by processes of trial and error, and by practical research and development.

Such an account must therefore be to some extent of an historical nature if the way in which the stern trawler evolved is to be understood, and how it came to be accepted that this type of ship is a substantial improvement over the side trawler, the limitations of which will be briefly indicated. An attempt will also be made to indicate some possibilities for the future.

EVOLUTION OF STERN TRAWLERS FOR DEEP SEA FISHING

Historical

In 1948 a number of ideas on the development of fishing vessels and trawl gear were put forward by Sir Charles Dennistoun Burney, who had been closely connected with the development of the minesweeping paravane, with the design and building of airships, and with several other innovative enterprises. His ideas in the fisheries field included the development of a trawl with a much larger mouth opening, using adaptations of the minesweeping paravane to provide the spreading force; freezing fillets at sea, and landing the catches in seaports close to main centres of population; and the design of spherical cold stores to minimise the costs of insulation and refrigeration.

It was recognised from the start that freezing fillets at sea would require the development of a shelter-deck type of vessel trawling from the stern. Burney, with the support of Sir James Lithgow and others, put his ideas to practical trial in a converted 200-ton steam yacht, *Oriana,* and subsequently in a converted frigate of the Black Swan class re-named *Fairfree,* which was based on Aberdeen. Appropriately enough, *Fairfree* was berthed opposite the Torry Research Station and near to the shipyard

Fig. 1. Built in Aberdeen in 1953 for Chr. Salvesen of Leith, the 80-metre long "Fairtry" was the first ship to be designed from the keel up as a factory stern trawler.

that was to design and build her successor, *Fairtry*. An account of the *Fairfree* project, from the point of view of the development engineer, was given by Lochridge (Ref. 3).

Full advantage was taken of the advice available from Torry on the requirements for quick-freezing and cold storage of fish. An elegant design of high-performance quick-freezing plant, the "Fair-freezer" (with fixed horizontal refrigerated shelves on which the trays of produce rested, and between which the air was force-circulated over the trays and continuously refrigerated by cooling fins depending from the lower surfaces of the shelves), was designed, built and tested. This part of the concept was therefore validated.

Fishing over the stern was shown to be practicable, but the paravane trawl was not. Burney and his associates subsequently persevered, over many years, in attempts to develop trawls but the setback was not allowed, at the time, to prejudice the development of the idea of the factory trawler. This might easily have been the case if the programme had been in the hands of people less confident in the soundness of the basic idea. Existing designs of trawl would have to do – and, although this may have limited the economic success of the early large factory trawlers, it does not seem to have put a heavy brake on the rate of development. Subsequently, Germans, Russians and Japanese have developed new types of trawl capable of absorbing the full power available in large stern trawlers.

When *Fairtry* was built, the concept of by-passing the existing distribution system, and landing and marketing the catch in or near the large centres of population, was also put aside. Twenty years later the freezing of consumer packs at sea must still be regarded as experimental, although there has been some production of consumer-sized cans of fish products.

The knowledge and experience gained in the operation of the low-endurance steam-propelled *Fairfree* were put to practical use in 1953 in the design and building of *Fairtry* by John Lewis and Son Limited of Aberdeen for Chr. Salvesen and Company of Leith. Salvesen's were a large and well-known family company owning and operating Antarctic whaling factories and merchant shipping fleets. Like Burney's original group, Salvesen's had no previous experience in the fishing industry. It might be remarked that, as operators of Antarctic whaling enterprises, they had the advantage of familiarity with the concept of large factory vessels. The mother-ship concept, however, was already familiar to, and used by, the fishing industry: indeed in the 1930s there had been pioneering enterprises in freezing at sea using mother-ships in association with catchers of traditional type.

The mother-ship operations of the 1930s were only one manifestation, albeit a novel one in some respects, of a long tradition of distant water operations on the part of the deepsea fishermen of north-western Europe. The French were already fishing at

Newfoundland in summer-time in the early 16th century; the Portuguese were still using sailing schooners and dories there in the 20th – and dories were used in the mother-ship operations in the 1930s. Also used earlier in this century in the salt-cod fishery of the north-west Atlantic were some very large side-fishing steam trawlers, so large they had two Scotch boilers back-to-back. In the late 1940s builders of this class of vessel were producing designs for side-fishing motor trawlers of no less than 220 ft. (67m) long b.p., and such vessels as the multi-engined diesel-electric *Cap Fagnet III* show how there was no reluctance to accept technically-advanced ideas in this fishery.

It is interesting to speculate that a steam-propelled shelter-deck stern-fishing factory trawler, producing salt cod or stock-fish, would have been technically feasible, and perhaps acceptable, 60 years or more before *Fairtry* first appeared on the north-west Atlantic grounds; after all, trawl fishing over the stern was known in the 19th century. That such a ship was not built in that era may therefore be due not so much to technical considerations as to economic and social factors: the fishing industry was not yet organised into sufficiently big and complex units to make the idea attractive, and there were still plenty of skilled fishermen with strong preferences for traditional methods engendered by life in small closed communities.

The continued preference for the side trawler well into the 1950s – and Hunter and Eddie felt constrained to put forward a proposal for freezing the early part of the catch on board a side trawler, of otherwise conventional design, as late as 1959 (Ref. 4) – is less easy to explain. It was probably due not so much to lack of willingness to accept new ideas as to the inevitable inhibitive effects on initiative (financial and technical) resulting from the small size of the average fishing enterprise, in relation to the resources required to take an entirely new departure in deep sea fishing vessel design. Moreover, in the aftermath of war, fish was in good demand, and was relatively plentiful and easy to catch with ships of conventional design. Most owners and operators of the long-distance trawler fleets of the world had concentrated their energies on re-building along conventional lines, and in coping with the problems of converting from steam to diesel propulsion.

Trawl fishing over the stern of the ship was of course already standard practice in many parts of the world, for example, in the small stern-draggers of North America, long before the advent of *Fairtry*. The advantages of stern trawling will be apparent from what we have already said and what follows, and it may be asked why it had not been adopted as the standard method when deep sea trawling with steam-powered vessels was developed in England in the second half of the 19th century. Some of the early steam trawlers were side-paddle vessels, adapted from tugs, in which, presumably, it was more convenient to handle the fishing gear from the stern.

Detailed information on the practice of those days is very difficult to come by, but one or two points are fairly clear. The first is that, in the early days of steam trawling, the beam trawl was still in favour. The beam itself, with its heavy trawl heads, must have been much easier to handle by two well-spaced gallows on the side of the ship, and over a low freeboard, than over the stern, and in the case of the sailing trawler the gear was presumably towed with the ship proceeding more or less beam-on, and making much leeway.

It might have been expected that with the adoption of the otter trawl, consideration would have been given, once again, to trawling over the stern. The otter trawl, however, seems to have been developed in fishing fleets familiar with the beam trawl, rather than in those deploying a bottom seine off the stern of the boat. Nevertheless, in some areas, as already noted, stern dragging has long since been the conventional practice. That side trawling continued to be the standard method in the deep sea fishing fleets of north-western Europe, and in those other fleets who derived their methods from this source, even after otter trawling was introduced, may be attributed to the force of tradition in the field of deep sea fishing vessel design and development, and to reluctance to risk the sacrifice of the seaworthiness of proven designs of vessel. There is a clear unbroken line of development from the English sailing smack designed for beam trawling to the latest British side trawler, which the adoption of steam propulsion did not interrupt.

The traditional method of fishing vessel development was always slow, step-by-step evolution, in which each small change is long contemplated and thoroughly tested by practical trial before general adoption. When developing small ships for work in the North Sea and North Atlantic, and on which operations have to be carried out on the open deck, there would be no better strategy of development than this, if time were always available, and if evolution did not sometimes arrive at a dead end. Then it is necessary to risk capital, and perhaps even lives, to make a fresh start.

The sail-powered fishing vessels of north-western Europe in the late 19th century were fast, good sea

Fig. 2. Highly mechanised stern trawlers designed to work North Sea grounds from Grimsby, the "Ross Daring" and her two sister ships were built in the early 1960s. They were not a success and have since been sold out of the British fishing industry.

boats and well adapted to the particular fisheries in which they were used. It so happened that many types had a pronounced rake of keel, a deep draught at the stern and the fullest hull section well aft; such a hull is well adapted to the installation of an engine somewhat aft of midships, and there are still many motor fishing vessels in N-W Europe that began life as sailing craft. In the size of vessel common at the turn of the century, the installation of an engine aft of amidships, and especially of a steam engine and boiler in that position, made it convenient to confine as many as possible of the fishing and fish handling operations to the foredeck, and this would have required the least changes from previous practice with the beam trawl.

In N-W Europe, the sail-powered fishing vessels had normally handled their own gear, and there was continuity in the method of fishing during the change from sail to power. By contrast, the Grand Banks schooner, for example, one of the most highly-developed and successful types of sailing vessel ever built, did not. Perhaps, therefore, in some areas of the world, the idea of towing an otter trawl from a powered vessel was so great a departure from previous practice that it was possible to look at the problem afresh. The resulting solution was what appears to be the obvious one of towing the trawl from the stern of a vessel with engines forward. Be that as it may, the introduction of the large stern-fishing deepsea trawler did not take place until over half-a-century after the general adoption of the otter trawl.

The process of change from side to stern trawling, in the fleets which had preferred the side trawler during the first half of the 20th century, was not without its difficulties, real and imaginary. Yet it is only too easy to envisage what objections would now be raised against a change from stern trawling to fishing over the side, had the former been the time-honoured method and the latter was now being advocated for the first time.

With the net drum developed sufficiently to handle any type of trawl, it is now possible to envisage a very large shelter-deck side trawler with high freeboard. Will anybody ever bother to experiment with this idea?

The later 1950s

There were other experimenters in stern trawling in the 1950s, besides Salvesen's, although it must be supposed that they were stimulated by the success of *Fairtry*. Some of the significant developments in large stern trawlers which took place in Germany, Norway and other countries will be described later.

The small stern trawler

A quite different line of development is represented by the *Universal Star*, a 104ft. (31.5m) long overall single-decked stern trawler completed in 1960. This vessel lacked both the shelter-deck and

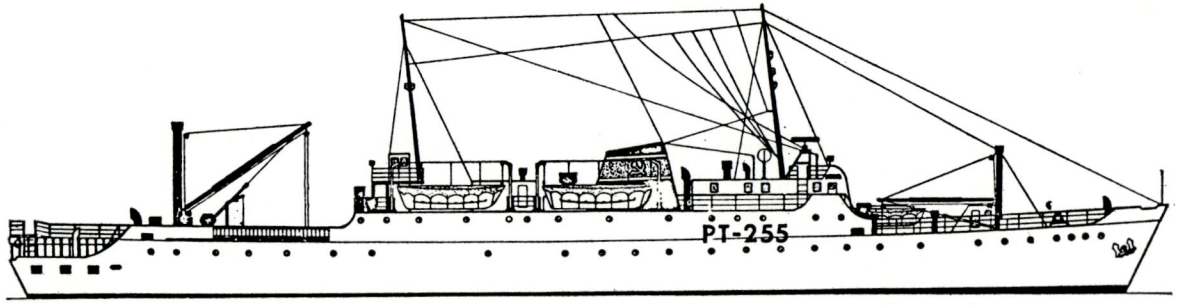

Fig. 3. The "Fairtry" concept of stern fishing and filleting and freezing at sea was incorporated by the Soviet Union in its "Pushkin" class ships. These trawlers are 84.5 metres long and 24 of them were built in West Germany between 1954 and 1956.

the stern ramp which were the main features of the *Fairtry* design. The ramp was considered too space-consuming and possibly dangerous in this size of ship; instead, a patented moveable gantry was fitted (the ramp on other vessels was also the subject of patents). *Universal Star* was therefore very different in concept as well as in size from *Fairtry* and attracted considerable attention.

Unfortunately the design was compromised, unnecessarily as it can now be seen, by imposing as a condition of financial support a requirement that the vessel be capable of being converted into a twin-screw tug. *Universal Star* therefore had an unorthodox propulsion arrangement, the choice of which owed little to considerations of the operation of stern trawling. Nevertheless, there is a class of small single-decked deep sea stern trawlers of which *Universal Star* can be considered in some respects

Fig. 4. From the "Pushkin" class ships, the Soviet Union developed the larger and higher capacity "Mayakovski" class. Several hundred of these trawlers have been built by yards in the USSR.

the precursor, and of which *Ross Daring* and *Ross Delight* were other early examples.

Although the small stern trawler or stern-dragger of less than 80ft. (25m) has for long been a familiar vessel type in North America, its acceptance in N-W Europe, for example in Scandinavia and the British Isles, has been slow. Indeed in 1970 less than three per cent of all British vessels in this size range were equipped to fish over the stern. However, vessels such as *St. Adrian*, incorporating a net drum, have recently appeared and there is increasing interest in small stern trawlers.

Further Developments

When Salvesen's built *Fairtry* in 1953, there was no immediate rush to build factory trawlers on the part of others in Britain or in Western Europe as a whole. The USSR, however, inaugurated a programme of modernisation and expansion of her fishing fleets, and this included the building of large numbers of shelter-deck stern ramp trawlers. The earliest classes of BMRT – the *Pushkin* class (built in Germany), the *Mayakovski* class (built in USSR), the Polish B-15 class – bear a remarkable resemblance in size and external appearance to *Fairtry*, but they employed air blast freezers in preference to the horizontal plate contact freezers with which *Fairtry* and most other north-west European factory trawlers have been equipped.

By 1970 there were about 900 freezer trawlers and factory trawlers over 1,000 tons in the world's fishing fleets, of which about 400 belonged to the USSR, 125 to Japan, 75 to Spain (including some vessels of 100m LOA) 50 to Western Germany, 40 to France and 40 to Britain. Whether the Eastern European nations, and later the Spaniards, would have embarked upon the building of large distant water fishing fleets, had it not been for the development and building of the first shelter-deck stern-ramp factory trawler in Scotland, it is not possible

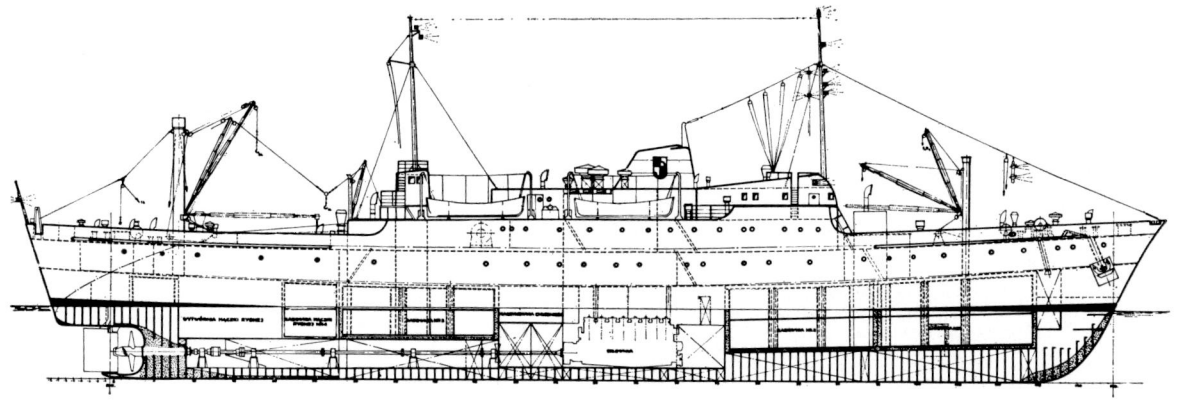

Fig. 5. Profile of the B-15 class BMRT type stern trawler built by Polish yards for the Soviet Union.

to say, but undoubtedly the *Fairtry* pointed the way that they should go.

With displacements of about 3,000 tons, lengths between perpendiculars of 240 ft. (73m), crews of 75 to 100 and capital costs at 1953 prices in the region of £0.75m ($ 3m.) the *Fairtry* and B-15 were very much larger and more costly than the typical conventional distant-water trawler of their time, which displaced roughly 1,000 tons, had a length of around 180 ft. b.p. (55m), a crew of 20 to 30, and cost £0.25m ($ 1m.).

The philosophy which led to *Fairtry* being so much bigger will be discussed later. What was clear was that the trawler owners of Western Europe, North America and Japan would be much more receptive to the idea of the stern-fishing shelter-deck trawler if it could be shown to be a feasible proposition at a much smaller size. This was by no means immediately obvious: costs, ship motion, stability, manoeuvrability, and general arrangement of the ship all presented possible problems.

The Germans and the Japanese were among the first to examine these questions in a practical way, by building smaller shelter-deck stern-ramp trawlers, although the Germans first of all made a few attempts to gain the advantages of a shelter-deck while retaining low free-board and continuing to fish over the side: e.g., *Hans Pickenpack*. Such gambits were obviously of limited benefit and by 1958 the shelter-deck stern-ramp trawlers *Carl Kampf* (not the present vessel of that name) and *Sagitta* were in service, the latter being propelled originally by a gas turbine fed by a free-piston gas generator, but subsequently re-engined in an orthodox manner. These and other German vessels demonstrated that the shelter-deck stern-ramp concept was valid for trawlers at least as small as 180 ft. LOA (55m).

The most significant fact about the early German stern trawlers, however, was that these included the first stern-ramp trawlers that were not equipped for freezing at sea or other advanced forms of processing. They were built in the belief that fishing over the stern, and the provision of a shelter-deck, might be advantages worth having in their own right, and it was the German owners, skippers and crews, and the German builders, who demonstrated convincingly that for long-distance deep sea fishing, the shelter-deck stern-ramp trawler was superior to the classic side trawler, irrespective of the method of preservation of the catch.

During the later 1950s, there was much speculation as to how small a shelter-deck trawler would be practicable. With the design and building of *Hekktind* in 1961, the Norwegians showed that shelter-deck stern-ramp trawlers were a practical proposition at least down to 150 ft. LOA (46m).

Obviously there is a size below which the shelter-

Fig. 6. The "Hekktind" was the first Norwegian shelter deck stern trawler. She was built in 1961 and supplies a freezing plant at Melbu in the Vesteraalen.

Fig. 7. Norway's first factory stern trawler was the "Longva", built in Aalesund in 1962.

deck becomes impracticable. The minimum acceptable head clearance in the shelter-deck is obviously something over six feet (2m) in order to allow men to stand erect and move freely. In the smaller vessels, therefore, the shelter-deck becomes proportionately higher in comparison with the length of the vessel, and there is proportionately more weight at a greater relative height; in turn this demands greater beam in order to maintain adequate lateral stability. As the overall length decreases, the problems of producing a shelter-deck design of reasonable proportions and layout become steadily more severe.

Opinion varies as to the practical minimum limit of size for a shelter-deck stern trawler, but it seems to be somewhere in the region of 120 ft. to 135 ft. LOA (37m to 42m). However, it is possible to retain some of the benefits of the shelter-deck type in single-decked stern trawlers, e.g. gutting under cover, if some care is paid to the layout. This has been done, for example, in a number of single-decked British stern trawlers in the region of 130 ft. (40m) LOA designed and built in 1970–71 and referred to later.

Salvesen's built two more large factory trawlers in the late 1950s, *Fairtry II* and *Fairtry III*, but the general adoption of shelter-deck stern-ramp trawlers did not come in the British distant-water fleet until the early 1960s. The first of these, *Lord Nelson* and *Junella*, were of 240 ft. LOA (73m) and incorporated in their design much of the German experience with this size of vessel; *Lord Nelson* was designed and built in Bremerhaven but *Junella* also incorporated German experience. In one important respect, however, these vessels represented a new and significant departure: they were the first successful commercial trawlers equipped to freeze the catch in the whole, gutted form in vertical-plate freezers specially developed for the purpose, rather than as blocks of fillets. The total crew on these vessels was only 25 or 26, and in terms of manpower they set a new standard of productivity in the distant water cod fisheries.

The majority of large distant-water vessels built for British owners in the 1960s were freezer trawlers, although one factory trawler was also built of a size similar to the freezer trawlers. Norwegian owners developed and perfected small factory trawlers of less than 200 ft. (60m) LBP, e.g., *Longva*. One British owner put similar ideas to practical effect in the *Ranger Ajax* and her sister ships, and this approach is described later in the discussion on techno-economic matters.

Yet other British owners have since built wet-fish shelter-deck stern-ramp trawlers in the length range 150 ft. to 200 ft. (45 to 60m) as the Norwegians did earlier with the *Hekktind* class and as also have Canadian, Dutch, Icelandic, French and South African owners.

Besides their fleet of large shelter-deck stern trawlers already mentioned, the French played a prominent part in the further development of the small single-deck stern trawler concept of which *Universal Star* was one of the earliest examples. Among the more recent single-decked vessels are those built for Lowestoft owners incorporating a high degree of mechanisation and with the sorting, gutting and stowage of the catch down below under cover.

This brief historical sketch will serve as background for the main theme of this chapter. Some of the technical and techno-economic problems faced during the last 20 years will now be described; the advantages of the stern trawler will be enumerated and contrasted with the limitations of the side trawler, and some possibilities for further development will also be mentioned.

TECHNICAL AND OPERATIONAL CONSIDERATIONS

Since *Fairtry* was obviously operationally effective, much of the early debate centred round the questions of whether the large factory trawler was economically viable, and whether the stern-trawling concept would be valid not only for the very large factory trawlers, which did not interest the majority of owners and specialist trawler builders in the 1950s, but also for smaller vessels. The doubts and objections related to practical aspects of trawling operations as well as to economics. The technical and practical difficulties will be described first.

Facilities for development

The protagonists of stern trawling often had less practical experience than the doubters, and hence their claims did little to allay the doubts, especially since in some instances they tended to attach greater importance to some theoretical advantages than was eventually justified by experience, and to ignore the difficulties. Such a situation is not uncommon in the marine field and is best resolved by practical trial. But, with such a large departure from conventional design as is represented by the stern trawler, this could be done only by an organisation with access to considerable resources, both for capital investment and for carrying the project through the stages of development and teething troubles. Also, money alone could not guarantee success: an enthusiastic and capable team of practical fishermen and engineers was needed, with the development of the new ship as their sole function, and without too many innovations combined in one project.

This is illustrated not only by the history of the development of various successful classes of stern trawler, but also and more pointedly by other instances where these fairly obvious requirements were not satisfied and where, in consequence, the chances of success were less than the enterprising designers and owners imagined. What happened only too often was that a prototype stern trawler failed to achieve success for reasons which had little to do with the fact that she was a stern trawler. All too often, however, to the industry at large she was yet another stern trawler that had failed. This was particularly the case with small stern trawlers.

Some examination of the financial resources available, the nature of the tax laws in relation to experiment, the government support available and the size and quality of the technical effort deployed in various of the stern trawler projects of the 1950s and early 1960s, might throw some light on why, ten years after *Fairtry* went into service, the approach to stern trawling on the part of many owners (as illustrated in the predecessor of this book) was very cautious, and why the general introduction of stern trawlers into some deep sea trawling ports is only beginning 20 years and more after the *Fairfree* experiments. What is reasonably clear is that doubts might have been resolved much sooner had the pre-conditions for high probability of success, mentioned above, been satisfied more fully in a number of early projects, especially in the case of the smaller, single-decked vessels.

Fishing operations

Among the fears expressed in the early days was that fishing over the stern would increase the chance of fouling the propeller; in practice the frequency of this occurrence seems to be no higher, if as high, as with side trawlers. To reduce the risk, it was foreseen that it would be advisable to keep the propeller running at all times when the gear was outboard; with many types of diesel engine the minimum speed of steady rotation would however still produce considerable thrust, resulting in extra load on the gear and winch and a need for much sea-room. The alternative seemed to be to adopt the controllable-pitch propeller, with which many owners were unfamiliar, or some other complication in the propulsion system.

Those owners, such as the Germans and Icelanders, who had experimented in the early 1950s with c.p. propellers, diesel-electric systems and other flexible forms of propulsion, were therefore at an advantage. In the event, these more sophisticated propulsion systems have been adopted in many instances for quite different reasons. From the point of view of handling the ship and the fishing gear, direct coupled fixed-pitch propellers do seem to be acceptable, at least in the larger vessels, provided, of course, that there is independent control of propeller and winch.

The impracticability, in the stern-ramp trawler, of bringing a heavy catch aboard in several lifts, was also regarded as a potential disadvantage. Some Dutch and British stern trawlers (e.g. *Ross Daring*) were arranged to handle the cod-end over the quarter, in a fashion similar to a side trawler. In practice, with suitable strengthening of the net, this difficulty has not turned out to be a real one, except when the catch is so big that the bag jams on the ramp. Hauling the cod-end over the quarter is still common practice in stern fishing vessels of under 80ft. LOA (25m). On this size of vessel space is very restricted and handling of the trawl over the stern becomes really practicable only if a net drum is fitted.

A more serious difficulty, encountered in some of the early stern trawlers, and not foreseen, was that of getting a large bag of fish over the edge of the stern ramp when the ship was pitching in a seaway. One manoeuvre which was found to assist in overcoming this problem, and which also helped to prevent the ship from over-running the gear, was to haul stern-on to wind and seas. However, there are well-authenticated cases when a wave came up the ramp and swept everything lying loose on the weather deck, and everybody on that deck, 60 or

70 feet forward, to end up in a heap around the winch; one vessel took a sea in such a way with the fish hatch open, with the result that the main hull was flooded in the area of the aft accommodation – a space which in some layouts would have contained the main machinery.

In some situations, such as fishing in confined areas or among icebergs, as is described by Drever (Ref. 5), it is not possible to turn stern-or head-to-wind to haul, however desirable or undesirable these practices may be. The solution to the problem of getting the bag on to the ramp has instead been to arrange and dispose sufficient tanks for ballast, fuel or water, as to allow the ship to be trimmed well down by the stern when fishing, so that the ramp is sufficiently immersed to obviate any difficulty in hauling the cod-end over the edge.

A source of much doubt, among owners and fishermen, as to the practicability of stern trawling, was the fact that the fishing gear, when on the bottom, is attached to the side trawler at a single point – the towing block – and in such a way that the vessel can still be manoeuvred in yaw reasonably smartly; moreover the point of attachment of the gear to the ship is low down so as to reduce the chance of inadvertently developing serious overturning moments if the vessel comes beam-on to the line of the warps. To those who laid emphasis on these considerations, it appeared that the stern trawler, attached to the gear at two separate points, relatively high, would be dangerous and insufficiently manoeuvrable, if, for example, the gear came fast on the sea bed. (It would also be costly in gear.) There also seemed to be a great deal more surface above the waterline to catch the wind, which would further reduce manoeuvrability. These difficulties have not been serious in practice, and in any case can be resolved by suitable arrangements of towing blocks if it is considered necessary to take them into account. The people who foresaw these difficulties, incidentally, usually also imagined that a stern trawler's gear always lies dead aft, whereas in practice the ship can find itself, in some circumstances, at a noticeable angle to the line of the warps.

What is slightly surprising, however, is that there appear to have been few difficulties in steering stern trawlers, or, to be more precise, in manoeuvring them in yaw, when towing bottom trawls, in spite of the usual arrangement whereby the points of attachment of the two warps are some distance apart and symmetrically disposed with regard to the fore-and-aft centre line of the ship. In side elevation, these points are, as it happens, very near in most cases to the vertical line through the centre of pressure of the rudder. The protagonists of mounting the screw propeller forward, to eliminate long shafts in ships with forward-mounted engines, have to consider the problem of manoeuvring, if problem it is. The German stern trawler *Heinrich Meins* was originally built with twin side-by-side Voith-Schneider propellers forward and it would be interesting to have an account of how the vessel behaved.

One more practical difficulty, again not foreseen, arises when towing through floating ice. The warps then tend to catch on pieces of ice, which collect until they constitute a danger to the propeller and are in any case a nuisance when hauling and in other ways. The solution of this problem was the adoption of the arrangement of tackle known as the Polish rig, which allows the warps to be lifted out of the farthest aft set of sheaves – which would normally act as towing blocks – and to be dropped on to the ramp during the tow, so that they enter the water where it is clear of ice immediately astern of the ship.

Warp tension meters

A problem of a more fundamental kind, that was much less widely recognised and appreciated by the shipbuilders, the owners and even the skippers, was that of ensuring that the trawl was being towed at such a speed that it was fishing effectively. This may have had an unnoticed effect on fishing performance and hence on the economic success of early stern trawlers. The difficulty arises because most commercial instruments for measuring ship's speed are not very accurate at the speeds associated with bottom trawling, and were not in general use for this purpose in the side trawlers, nor were shaft torsion meters common. Only in the diesel-electric vessels could shaft horsepower be indicated reasonably accurately.

The most usual practice in the side trawlers, therefore, was for the skipper to call for a standard value of propeller rev/min which seemed to produce good results, and to vary the engine settings intuitively from this standard according to depth of water, weather conditions and season. "Three-quarters full" were typical standard towing rev/min in British steam trawlers. Moreover, in the side trawler the skipper had a check on trawl behaviour, insofar as he could see, and roughly estimate, the angle between the warps as they diverged from the towing block, and he could, and did, sense certain things by putting his hand on the fore warp.

A skipper who transferred into a stern trawler

found himself in a ship that was probably more powerful, bigger and heavier, and had more windage. It might well be equipped with a c.p. propeller. He would probably find himself standing higher above the waterline, and he was unable to discern the angle of divergence of the warps, or to put his hand on to them. In these circumstances, his previous experience would give little guidance in helping him decide upon the power settings that would result in the trawl being towed over the sea bed at such a speed that it was fishing effectively. The best skippers quickly managed to sort things out, but observations at sea suggest it is likely that many stern trawlers were less successful in the early years than they should have been, because the skippers failed to adapt successfully in this respect.

The development of various forms of warp tension meter during the 1960s was therefore a significant step towards ensuring that the change to stern trawling did not result in a reduction in fishing performance. At the same time, the greater power and weight of many stern trawlers, compared with the vessels they replaced, has meant that, if and when the trawl does come fast, damage is likely to be much greater. Any warning that the gear has come fast, by way of the behaviour of the ship, will be less prompt and less clear. In these circumstances the warp tension meter has saved money and time which would otherwise represent extra costs associated with stern trawling. It has other uses – for instance it helps to avoid excessive warp loads and loss of time when shooting and hauling the gear, by providing a parameter which can be used in controlling the speed and direction of the ship during these manoeuvres.

Warp tension meters are now in use in other classes of fishing vessel, including side trawlers, and the performance of the fishing fleets as a whole has benefited accordingly.

Bridge control

In order to ensure the degree of precision and speed of response in the manoeuvring of a big stern trawler that is required, it is very desirable, if not absolutely essential, to have bridge control of propulsion and preferably also of the winch. These features are in any case necessary in order to reap full advantage from the provision of warp tension meters (and of telemetry from trawl to ship) and are therefore also becoming standard requirements in many other types of fishing vessel. Another very desirable feature is for the entire fishing deck to be visible from the bridge, and for the propulsion and winch controls on the bridge, and the fishing instru-

Fig. 8. Wheelhouse indicators of Kelvin Hughes warp tension meters can be seen (left) on this console in the wheelhouse of the Greenland wet fish stern trawler "Pamiut". The "Pamiut" was built in Denmark in 1971.

ments, to be mounted accordingly. Such considerations were not always given the importance they deserved in early designs, but more recently a great deal of attention has been paid to visual and voice communication between the bridge and fishing deck.

Quality of the catch

As has already been remarked, in the majority of stern trawlers the cod-end is brought aboard with the entire catch; it is not possible, or convenient, to divide a large catch into a number of smaller lifts, which in any case would waste time. Among the early objections to stern trawling was the fear that hauling a large catch up a stern ramp, or over a transom, and subsequently dropping it through a hatch on to the deck below, would damage the fish. This has proved much less serious in practice than was originally feared. In a side trawler the catch is subject to exposure and to damage from trampling on deck. The facility for installing speedier and more sophisticated methods of handling the catch in a stern trawler means that it should be easier to ensure maintenance of high quality aboard her than in a side trawler.

Design of stern trawlers

Many of the early protagonists of the stern trawler were naval architects or people from the world of shipbuilding, who were often not equipped by their own knowledge and experience to appreciate the practical problems we have so far discussed, and who were usually in no position to investigate them and produce answers. There were also naval architects and shipbuilders who saw disadvantages in the replacement of conventional deep sea trawlers by stern trawlers. Among the early objections was one already touched upon – the need to keep the propeller running while the fishing gear was in the water, with consequent extra costs. Another was the increased resistance of a hull form which involved the provision of a stern ramp. The second of these objections was serious only for vessels operating at considerable distances from their home ports, and was overcome by the provision of moveable ballast as already indicated.

A more serious objection was the extra cost of construction of a shelter-deck vessel, as compared with a single-deck vessel of low freeboard. Another was the difficulty of achieving a workable layout, economical of space, if an engines-aft arrangement were chosen; this difficulty increased as the size of the vessel decreased. The alternative was to accept a long propeller shaft and tunnel, or split diesel-electric machinery, and it was felt by some that the degree of motion and accelerations to which the engines would then be subject would give rise to problems.

Some of the disadvantages foreseen turned out to be real enough, and require trade-offs in the form of some of the gains from improved costs and earnings and other advantages that can be obtained by adopting stern trawling in the right circumstances. Others have been overcome by the exercise of a good deal of thought and ingenuity on the part of owners and naval architects. Some have proved, in the end, to be less serious difficulties than forecast. There is no doubt that some of the opposition on the part of shipbuilders arose because particular yards did not have facilities suitable for the construction of the new types of vessel, especially if, as was often the case, these were much larger than the previous generation of trawlers.

Propulsive requirements

Surprisingly little attention was given by naval architects in the early days to aspects of the design of stern trawlers on which neither they nor the owners had sufficient information to be sure of achieving the hoped-for fishing performance. The most important of these was a knowledge of the power required at the propeller when fishing or, to be more precise, of the propulsive thrust required, at the speeds of advance being obtained in various fishing situations and at various stages of the fishing operation. In the case of the early large, distant-water stern trawlers, the problem was not immediately apparent. The vessels themselves were much larger than the conventional side trawlers they replaced, and they thus happened to have ample reserves of power to tow what, after all, was very much the same size and type of trawl, as well as being able to overcome the extra wind resistance. These vessels were therefore, as a rule, operationally effective, although the power installed might not be the economic optimum.

It was very much otherwise with some of the early small stern trawlers, several of which could not tow the type of gear intended, or fish on the grounds familiar to the skipper in weather conditions that should have been tolerable, because they lacked sufficient propulsive power in the towing condition. One early experimental class of small stern trawlers was powered, not with a type of propulsive system known to be adequate from experience in side trawlers, but with an installation incorporating a high-speed engine, a c.p. propeller and a control system, all of which had characteristics different from those of the machinery commonly used in the fishery in question, and which, it was found, did not produce adequate thrust in the trawling condition. This class of vessel therefore failed to demonstrate convincingly what advantages there might be in stern trawling. Had the first vessels been fitted with machinery of conventional type and power, small stern trawlers might have found readier acceptance in the North Sea fisheries.

Lack of sufficient knowledge of propulsive requirements when fishing can therefore be identified as one of the factors that delayed acceptance of the small stern trawler in some fishing fleets ten to fifteen years ago. From about 1963 onwards a considerable improvement has come about in this situation, through the mounting of programmes of measurement of the performance of commercial fishing vessels and their machinery in a wide variety of fishing situations.

Among the leaders in this field have been the Industrial Development Unit of the White Fish Authority, who have developed techniques of measurement suitable for the continuous recording, or automatic data-logging at intervals, of such parameters as thrust, torque, and rev/min of propellers, warp speed and pull on winches, ship's speed, wind speed and direction and so on. By such means, designers can now be provided with comprehensive information on what is required of the propulsion system and deck machinery in many types of fishing and classes of vessel, and on many different fishing grounds in various weathers (Refs. 6, 7, 8 and 9). Some of this information is of a statistical nature, e.g. a histogram of the maximum power used when shooting the trawl on each of a large number of occasions on a stern trawler of a certain type operating in the North West Atlantic (Fig. 9).

In the specification of a fishing vessel it is necessary to ensure not only that it is operationally effective, but that capital and other costs have not been unnecessarily inflated by over-design. The correct choice of installed power, throughput of freezing plant, and so on, are all important to the commercial success of the vessel.

Ship layout

One very practical point which has exercised owners in certain ports is that in a shelter-deck trawler the hatches for the discharge of the catch, if in the weather deck, will be much higher in relation to the quay than those in a single-decked trawler. This may even delay the adoption of stern trawlers, because of the necessity to modify the quay or to provide new equipment to facilitate discharge. Some owners have built equipment into the ship, which is an expensive solution. In any case there are likely to be fewer hatches, and here again some owners have provided mechanical conveying systems within the fish hold to bring fish directly below the discharge hatch.

Such problems have called for much thought, discussion, negotiation and experiment – and they are only one small sector of the vast range of problems that an owner may have to solve when building his first stern trawler; but because they involve other organisations, including the labour force which lands the catches, they can be a fruitful source of trouble and worry and so they require a good deal of careful consideration.

They also represent a problem for the ship designer – accommodating the mechanical handling systems, if any, and in every case arranging the shelter-deck and weather deck so that the discharge operation is reasonably straightforward, while preventing this consideration from leading to a layout that is awkward or uncomfortable at sea. Sometimes a discharge hatch trunking has to pass through accommodation.

Similar problems have faced the vessel designer in those general arrangements where the main machinery space and its casing, trunkings, ducts and funnels lie between the area where the fish is brought aboard and the hold where it will finally be stowed. Arrangements with engines forward give rise to fewer problems in this respect, but they are

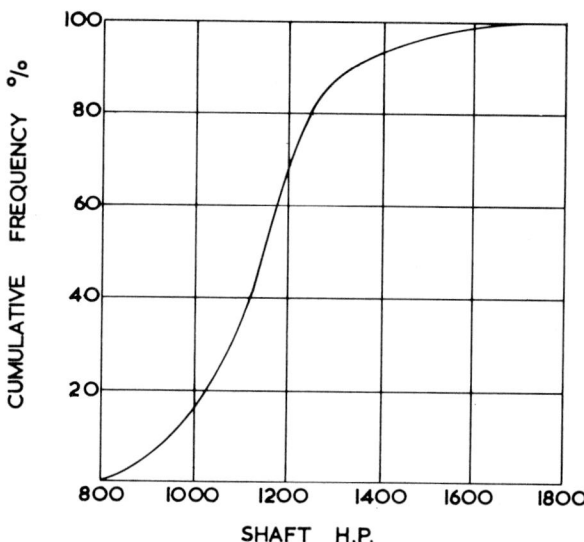

Fig. 9. Statistical record of propulsive power demand when shooting Granton trawl on N.W. Atlantic grounds, obtained by data-logging.

not always feasible, or the owner may not favour them. The problem is more acute in the smaller vessels, and care has to be exercised when considering hull form and trim.

A less well-recognised requirement in the arrangement of shelter-decks and accommodation is that the access from the accommodation to the decks where fish is to be handled should be limited, and should ideally be through a room where the crew can wash and change.

Yet other problems for the designers of stern trawlers arise in achieving a long trawl deck (slip deck) without putting the deckhouse so far forward that there will be too much motion and spray, or producing a profile that tends to make the ship fall off the wind in a beam wind. A figure is often quoted of 75 ft. (23m) as desirable between the top of the ramp and the winch, with a minimum of 60 ft. (18m). There are of course, stern-ramp trawlers with fishing decks shorter than this, while small single-deck stern trawlers have very much shorter fishing decks, and even a length of 75 ft. (23m) is not anything like sufficient to be able to bring the entire net on board in one pull.

Various designs have been evolved in efforts to produce the longest possible fishing deck, with the winches for hauling the net placed as far forward in the ship as possible. These arrangements included asymmetrical positioning of the bridge house, as in an aircraft carrier (*Colonel Pleven*) and building the bridge house with a fore-and-aft tunnel through it at

Fig. 10. A feature of the French stern trawlers "Colonel Pleven" and "Pierre Pleven" is their offset wheelhouse to give a long fishing deck.

time when handling the net. The use of powered net drums is another answer.

A shortening of the fishing deck might lead to a significant improvement in economy of design, since the same overall requirements might then be met on a shorter waterline. So far, however, this idea has been pursued only in research vessels where a large amount of deckhouse accommodation is always needed.

In many stern trawler designs it is difficult to avoid the siting of the crew accommodation well forward in the ship. Since in many fishing fleets in recent years it had become the practice in side trawlers to accommodate all crew amidships and aft, this might be seen as a retrograde step, and neither ILO nor IMCO favour forward accommodation in ships in so far as this may increase the risk of injury or death in a collision. However, some points should be made. First, in the larger side trawlers, and especially in those built to operate at a maximum free-running speed equivalent to a $V/\sqrt{L}$ of 1.0 or higher, the after accommodation was by no means always as comfortable as might be supposed, because of the noise and vibration that occurred at full power. Second, there was always propeller noise. Third, it is by no means certain that it is not

fishing deck level (*Ross Fame*). Such layouts have not become standard, and it is clear that with appropriate auxiliary winches and other arrangements, a fishing deck of 60 to 75 ft. is quite workable and need not involve an unacceptable loss of

Fig. 11. The British trawlers "Ross Fame" and "Ross Fortune" were designed with fore-and-aft tunnel through the bridge superstructure at fishing deck level. These ships were sold in 1971 to a Newfoundland fishing company.

preferable, at least in the larger ships, and when working hours are so long, to work in relative comfort and under protection, and sleep forward – rather than sleep aft, and work in exposed conditions on the forward deck.

Ship motion

At one time it was thought that the siting of the galley might be a special problem, if the accommodation and mess decks were forward. Apparent vertical accelerations of well over 1.0g, due to a combination of various ship motions, have been measured in the farthest forward accommodation of a 240ft. LOA (73m) stern trawler when on passage in the North Atlantic. Experience has shown that this does not give rise to any problems provided some thought is indeed given to the siting of the galley.

When fishing, and especially when hauling the gear, pitching motions of up to 30 degrees amplitude can be experienced in a 240ft. LOA (73m) stern trawler. These cause peak loads on the warps, fairleads and supporting structure, and on the winch, that require to be taken into consideration when designing these pieces of equipment. (Ref. 10). Such extreme pitching, together with a large heaving motion, can result in vertical movement at the ramp which makes gear handling dangerous in this area in such conditions. This is in contrast to the side trawler where rolling is the limiting motion so far as gear handling is concerned.

Rolling motion has less direct effect on the design of stern trawlers but may in some circumstances be the factor limiting the fishing operations, at any rate in so far as it may increase the difficulty of working on the fishing deck or factory deck, or reduce the speed of working. Anti-roll systems are theoretically feasible in all types of ship, but it is probably no accident that in the fishing industry they have been tried out mainly in large stern trawlers, because it is much easier to accommodate existing designs in these relatively big vessels. An account of an assessment of the value of anti-roll systems in large stern trawlers, which included practical measurements in operational conditions, is given in Reference 11.

The current tendency to build even larger ships could result in ships with uncomfortable rolling motion in cases where maximum beam is restricted, for example by the width of lock gates. Generally speaking, however, as regards ship motion, especially rolling motion, and transverse stability, the stern trawler is potentially superior to the side trawler.

Stern trawlers of less than 80ft. (25m)

This account of the reasons, well-founded and otherwise, for the reluctance to adopt the stern trawler would not be complete without some special reference to the smallest class of vessels – those under, say, 80ft. (25m). As already noted, there has been reluctance in N-W Europe and the British Isles to adapt vessel design and fishing methods so as to operate over the stern, despite the experience with stern draggers and trawlers of very similar size in other parts of the world. There is a number of good reasons for this. One is that the pattern of ownership is for the working skipper to own the vessel or to share the ownership of a single vessel with other fishermen; thus all of each individual's working capital is tied up in one ship and it is a very big decision to make major experiments in vessel design and fishing method.

Some of the caution arose from the fact that many of these vessels use the otter trawl only part of the time, the other most popular method being the use of the seine net for bottom fishing, either Danish (anchor-seining) or Scots (fly-dragging) fashion. It is widely believed that this requires a canoe-type or pointed stern to present a smooth continuous support to the fishing ropes; stern trawling, on the other hand, requires so much deck area aft that a transom-sterned boat is desirable. In seine-netting, moreover, the gear is shot by deploying first one warp, then the net, then the other warp, whereas in trawling the net is shot first, to be followed by both warps, so that the gear is at all times symmetrical. For this reason, the seine net could not be handled by a conventional trawl net drum; hence power-blocks have been widely adopted.

These questions were only partly resolved by the building of the transom-sterned stern-fishing trawler/seiner *Constellation* in which trials of the use of a powered net drum were carried out. The experience was, however, put to good effect in the design and building of the transom-sterned *St. Adrian*. This vessel has a split net drum which makes it possible to use the drum to haul and shoot a seine net as well an otter trawl; fishing by bottom seine from a transom-sterned vessel with net drum is now seen to be entirely practicable. Until the advent of *St. Adrian*, it was very common practice to haul the cod-end over the quarter, even if the gear was towed from the stern, and thus the advantages of mechanical hauling could not be fully realised. Now, however, vessels of under 80ft. LOA (25m) can be designed and equipped to handle both otter trawl and bottom seine over the stern by powered net drums.

Fig. 12. The small British transom-sterned fishing trawler "Constellation".

Like the deepsea trawler owners, the skipper-owners of the under 80ft. (25m) class of vessel have also been worried about the problems of safety and of steering the ship when towing from two well-spaced points astern. Again, like the owners of the larger vessels, they have not looked with favour on the vessel layouts with accommodation forward, and it is not easy to design stern-fishing vessels of this size with accommodation in the traditional areas amidships and aft. For the crew of a vessel under 80ft. LOA (less than 25m) fishing in the northern North Sea and Western approaches to the British Isles, on trips from two to four days to as much as three weeks, this is a very serious consideration.

Nevertheless, in various ways, many of the fears and objections expressed regarding stern trawling have been discounted in the light of experience or overcome by development, while the real disadvantages have also been overcome or accepted because they are outweighed by the advantages. It is now time to examine what the most important of these advantages are.

THE ADVANTAGES OF THE STERN TRAWLER

Advantages are rarely won without paying for them in some way; many of the benefits that can be gained by replacing side trawlers with stern trawlers are neither automatic nor certain. What follows is therefore by no means a simple list of those points where the stern trawler is superior. Many potentially beneficial features have their dangers, or can be realised only in certain circumstances, and by giving careful attention to design, and may require the acceptance of some disadvantages. This will become clear in the discussion of some of the advantages listed below.

Reduced exposure

One of the most important advantages, clearly seen by the protagonists of the stern trawler from the beginning, is the reduction in the degree of exposure to wind chill, spray and immersion in green seas, suffered by the crew. The ship can usually be manoeuvred so that the men on the weather deck are at least partially sheltered by the bridge house; in any event high bulwarks are feasible. The weather deck of a shelter-deck ship is much higher out of the water and shipping green seas is much less frequent. Moreover, in the shelter-deckers, and also in some of the latest designs of single-decked stern trawlers, the washing, sorting and gutting of the fish, and its subsequent handling and stowage, are carried out under cover, so that the fishermen are exposed on the weather deck for much shorter periods of time and for a smaller fraction of the working day. These advantages of course are greatest in cold and rough weather at temperate and high latitudes. In the tropics, the shelter deck will act as an awning and provide some shelter, but may require insulation and air conditioning to make it tolerable for the men in extreme conditions as well as to prevent rapid spoilage of the catch awaiting stowage.

Motion

As was appreciated by the early protagonists, the stern trawler can in many circumstances be manoeuvred until she is head-on to wind and sea when hauling and shooting the gear, whereas the side trawler is forced to carry out the same operations when stopped, beam-on to wind and sea, and rolling violently. Besides reduced exposure, the stern trawler therefore also offers increased comfort through reduced severity of motion.

Even the biggest stern trawler, however, suffers a higher degree of motion than most merchant ships, because of her relatively small size and the hostile seas in which many fishing vessels have to work. Hence the interest in anti-roll devices, already mentioned. One doubt was whether men, working in the confines of a shelter deck, and requiring the free use of both hands, but unable to see the waves, would be able to keep their feet and work effectively in severe sea states. This has turned out to be no problem.

According to at least one British owner, the increased degree of comfort and reduced exposure has enabled the fishermen to continue an active seagoing life in the deep sea fisheries to a higher age

Fig. 13. Fishing deck scene aboard a Cape Town freezer stern trawler working hake grounds in the south-east Atlantic.

than heretofore, despite the fact that the stern trawlers in that owner's fleet, being the newest vessels, are commanded by the best skippers, and therefore the catches are large and so is the work load.

Safety and fatigue

Stern fishing also lessens the chances of men on deck being injured, or swept overboard, because of the reduced motion and much less frequent occurrence of taking seas on board. Moreover, the men do not have to heave the net aboard (note however that powered net drums performing this function are feasible in side trawlers) nor do they have to lean over the rail to attend to the hanging blocks or towing block (note again, however, that automatic latching and unlatching devices for otter boards, and remotely-operated towing blocks, are presumably feasible and usable on side trawlers).

Occasionally, but very rarely, a man has to go down the ramp on a stern trawler, but not as a routine operation. Again, in nearly all existing side trawlers, the men must carry out much of their work on deck in close proximity to and danger from trawl warps under tension, and under gilsons and lifting tackles suspended from the main mast. There is the ever-present possibility of a warp breaking or a sheave or bollard coming loose from its supporting structure, and the men in a side trawler are often unavoidably in positions where they are exposed to risk of injury in such an event. The chances of this sort of accident are much reduced in a stern trawler and it is much easier to arrange the layout of the fishing deck, the run of the warps and the siting of lifting tackle and auxiliary winches, so that the men are not exposed to the same degree of risk.

Moreover, it is relatively easy to arrange the layout of a stern trawler so that everybody on the fishing deck is simultaneously visible to the man (or men) at the controls of the winches and the controls of the ship; this is not easy to achieve, and is not usually achieved, in side trawler layouts.

For these reasons the future seems at present to lie with the stern trawler, if the safety of the men working on the fishing deck is a prime consideration. That does not mean to say that the same objective is impossible to attain in side trawlers, especially in the smallest classes, also in the very large ones that would be now feasible as a result of the development of the powered net drum.

Seaworthiness

Safety has many aspects. Besides the safety of the individual fisherman there is the safety of the ship as a whole. Here the situation is a good deal more complicated than some of the early protagonists of stern trawling would have had us believe. It is true that it is possible to design stern trawlers with static transverse stability and freeboard very much superior to any existing side trawler, but this does not come about without careful design, and it may be necessary to accept certain complicating features that introduce other hazards by their presence. Large shelter-deck stern trawlers have been built which, in certain conditions, had no more transverse static stability than many side trawlers, and in which the effective freeboard was also no greater. On the other hand, there are designs which, in theory, will right themselves after lying over on their beam ends. Generally speaking, there should be no difficulty in achieving a high standard of static transverse stability if the owner's requirements are not conditioned to too great an extent by the width of dock gates or by a desire for very high speed.

Most shelter-deck stern trawlers can carry substantially more ice on the superstructure and rigging than a comparable side trawler and still meet the IMCO stability requirements. This of course can have its disadvantages in that a skipper of a stern trawler may decide to delay taking action to avoid or combat the accumulation of ice.

The apparent freeboard of a shelter-deck stern trawler, measured to the weather deck, is very much greater than that of any side trawler. The freeboard measured to the deck below the weather deck is also very adequate, by side trawler standards, in some designs, but in other designs it may be only a few inches. Which of these measurements it is more appropriate to regard as a true measure of the freeboard, depends of course on the attitudes of Governments, statutory authorities and classification societies, but as a general statement it would be true to say that it should depend mainly on the steps taken to maintain full water-tightness up to the weather deck. Since the shelter deck is where the fish is processed, this introduces the problems of disposing of offal, unwanted fish, stones and other objects brought up in the trawl, and the large quantities of water used for washing and fluming the fish, as well as the water used in pre-chilling tanks, the effluent from liver boilers, the water from fish-working machine tools and so on. There is a similar problem in those single-decked stern trawlers where the handling of the catch is performed under cover below decks.

If the freeboard is great enough, the water and rubbish can of course be allowed to go overboard from a shelter-deck through normal freeing ports, provided care is taken to keep them clear. However, it will be more satisfactory, indeed necessary in many cases, to adopt more elaborate arrangements. These may consist of specially-designed openings in the shelter-deck that operate so as to allow water and rubbish to be discharged but not to allow the sea to enter. There is a danger of these failing to close in a watertight fashion. The alternatives are to handle solid rubbish by elevator to the level of the weather deck, and to pump the water overboard, or to pass everything through a suitable pump. Dump tanks or sumps below the main deck level are a feature of certain systems. In any of these cases there is a danger of the ship flooding through malfunctioning of some mechanical device or another, which either allows the sea to enter or fails to cope with the flow of water from hoses, fish-working machines, etc.

Since the processing deck is not always occupied, and water supplies to hoses, machines, etc., can be left turned on, these are very real dangers, especially when the ship is on passage. Some of the various systems lend themselves to the fitting of alarms to indicate rising water level in sumps, or equivalent features, but there is no doubt that frequent inspections by the engineer-on-watch are desirable to ensure that the arrangements for removing water and offal from the shelter-deck, and for preventing the ingress of the sea, are working properly.

Any hatches and doorways in the deck below the weather deck should obviously be fitted with coamings, and indeed this is usually necessary to satisfy classification societies. On the weather deck itself this is not always feasible, because the handling of the fishing gear demands a smooth deck and any hatches must therefore be of the flush type. This is accepted by statutory authorities and classification societies, provided that the exposed space below is suitably protected by coamings – except in those cases where the hatch in question will not be opened at sea.

Fishing performance

Because of the greater seaworthiness of many stern trawler designs, the reduced motion and exposure, and the removal of the need to put the ship beam-on to wind and seas when handling the gear, and also because of the general attitudes of fishermen and the conditions of deep sea fishing, it would be surprising if the opportunity were not taken, when paying quantities of fish can be caught, to continue fishing in rather worse weather than would be tolerable in a side trawler. This advantage, while a real one in some fisheries, was perhaps made too much of by the early protagonists of the stern trawler, especially as regards the gains to be obtained in those fisheries where the small single-decked vessel would be the appropriate choice.

Perhaps more important is the shortening of the time taken to haul and shoot the gear, resulting from the opportunities offered by the stern-fishing layout to introduce improved methods of gear handling, the ultimate in this line, so far, being the powered net drum. The incorporation of a powered net drum in a side trawler can interfere a great deal with other operations on the fishing deck, except in the cases of very small vessels using light trawls and perhaps also in the case of very big vessels. Certainly the use of twin net drums, which can further improve the gear handling time, is more feasible in small vessels if they are stern trawlers. Providing for the mechanical handling of the gear may also, of course, lead to reductions in the number of crew required.

Handling the catch

Gutting machines are on the market which can be used on the open decks of side trawlers, with suitable designs of conveyor, as has been demonstrated by Aberdeen trawler owners. It also appears feasible to use machines for sorting and orienting fish and grading them for size on the open deck. It is probably true, nevertheless, that the cost of such systems, and the difficulty of operating them and keeping them properly maintained, would be much less were they installed in a shelter deck. Moreover, it would then be possible to use electric drives directly, instead of having to adopt hydraulic power transmissions.

Again, as already mentioned, certain German trawlers of the 1950s, and also the *Narfi*, demonstrated that some types of freezing plant could be installed and operated in a shelter deck in an otherwise classic single-deck side trawler. Other types of processing plant, however, including filleting machines, weighing machines and packaging lines, and horizontal plate freezers, really require the space and shelter offered by a large shelter-deck if they are to be used to good effect and properly maintained. This, as our thesis began by pointing out, was why the pioneers of the factory trawler found it necessary to develop stern trawling from a shelter-deck stern-ramp ship.

In the single-deck classic side trawlers, all operations are carried out in the same area of foredeck, and it is extremely difficult to achieve a workable layout if it is intended to instal net drums, sorting, grading, orienting and gutting machinery, and pre-chilling tanks, all of which are already, or soon will be, standard requirements in some fisheries. This is so even when the side trawler is equipped to fish only from the starboard side, as is often the case nowadays. The acceptance of this limitation, by the way, probably helped to bring about a more favourable attitude to the stern trawler, where likewise only one trawl was available for use at a time. Nowadays, twin net drums or some other arrangement provides the stern trawler with the same standby facility as in a side trawler equipped to fish from both port and starboard.

There is no doubt that the stern-trawling concept has made it much easier for the designer to accommodate the growing number of mechanical aids and of processing machinery that are now beginning to be provided in the modern fishing vessel in attempts to reduce the number of crew and to make the tasks of the remainder less physically fatiguing. Thus, in this way also, the stern trawling concept leads to better conditions for the crew as well as improving the economic situation of fleets where labour is scarce. It can also allow the vessel to land a more valuable product, either because it is possible to process the fish to a greater degree, or because the crew have more time and energy to devote to the proper care of the fish, or both.

Multi-purpose vessels

Dual-purpose and multi-purpose fishing vessels are not new. The drifter-trawler, for example, was a well-known vessel type in the English North Sea fleet until recently. As already noted, many Scottish vessels of under 80ft. LOA (25m) change from trawling to fly-dragging, and perhaps to long-lining or two-boat trawling, or ring-netting, or purse seining, as circumstances may dictate. Larger vessels of the side-trawler type can be successfully converted to deepsea long lining, or to purse-seining (and converted back again), as has been done in Scotland, Iceland and Norway.

In all these cases, however, the vessel has normally been equipped to prosecute only one method of fishing at a time, and changing to another method meant a visit to the home base and a conversion taking days, sometimes several days, rather than hours. Here again the stern-fishing vessel seems more flexible and versatile. This facility has been most fully exploited in the so-called combination vessels that have been coming into service in the Canadian fleets for a number of years and are now adopted in other fisheries as well. Another example of the multi-purpose stern fishing vessel is to be found in the catchers with which the Russian

Fig. 14. The "Nadezhda-1" is the prototype of 14 RP-hull combination stern trawler-purse seiners specially built in the USSR to supply the giant factory mother ship "Vostok".

mother-ship *Vostok* is equipped. The advantage of versatility, and the ability to change quickly from one method of fishing to another, without having recourse to dockyard facilities, must be especially attractive in such a case.

The ability to change quickly from one type of trawl gear to another may be important on certain fishing grounds, such as those in the North Atlantic where the gadoids may be found either on or off the bottom, and the other important species – herring – is pelagic. The classic side trawler equipped to fish from both port and starboard sides was undoubtedly superior in this respect, if the crew were well enough trained. However, the size of some of the pelagic trawls now in use makes them much more suitable for stern trawlers, either with plenty of space on the fishing deck, or else equipped with a powered net drum. Although as Schärfe points out (Ref. 12) the single-boat mid-water trawl with netzsonde is workable from quite small side trawlers, the larger gears now in use are probably much more conveniently handled from stern trawlers.

Improved technology

Factors such as the development of larger and more effective types of fishing gear like the single-boat mid-water trawl with netzsonde, the need to go far afield, and the need to pay more attention to the preservation of the catch, are producing a trend towards fewer and larger units; the capital cost of the vessels is growing with their fishing potential. It has been necessary to develop more refined methods of design, and new fishing aids, in order to ensure as far as possible that the investment will be profitable. Warp tension meters, for example, are found to be necessary; however, they are also found to improve the average fishing performance.

No doubt the same will be found to be true of the introduction of telemetry from trawl to ship. Satellite navigation may yield the same benefits as did Decca in the coastal fisheries. None of these items, or various other developments in knowledge and in methods and equipment of the last 20 years, is specific to stern trawling. Yet it may be doubted whether some of them would have yet been introduced into the fisheries if the need to make the large stern trawler an economic and effective fishing tool had not stimulated the necessary experimental work and technical development. Thus the introduction of the stern trawler has stimulated a rapid development in fisheries technology in general, to the benefit of the industry as a whole.

Ship-board computers

An example of the increasing sophistication of fishing vessels is the development of the use of computers on board. Again, this is not specific to stern trawlers, but it is not surprising that the first application has been in a large distant water stern-fishing freezer trawler, because the complexity of the ship as well as the size of the capital investment is bound to be a great stimulus to development of automation and of means of improving performance and reducing costs. There is no reason, however, why the principles developed in this case should not be applied to other classes of vessel, as and when small, compact and relatively cheap computers become available – always provided that the benefits can be clearly identified.

The primary purpose of the installation in *Saint Jasper* (Ref. 13) is to enable the machinery space to be operated unmanned, 24 hours a day, on voyages lasting several weeks. It is hoped, however, to develop other applications. First, the computer should be capable of being used to relieve the skipper of much of the need to monitor, more or less continuously, a growing mass of instruments, including warp tension meters, echo sounders, and telemetry; and it is hoped to develop the use of the computer for signal processing and recognition as well as for simple alarm functions and the like. Catch estimation by counting relevant echoes is already under development; this involves the use of computing circuits and is obviously a suitable function for a central data processor, as also is satellite navigation, and head-up chart displays.

The use of a computer to monitor various instruments also suggests the possibility of on-line control of ship and winch in certain fishing operations: either in order to ensure the minimum expenditure of time and fuel, as in the systems that have been proposed for automatic shooting of the trawl; or to manoeuvre the ship and gear when pelagic trawling or when fishing on the sea bed along contours of constant depth or perhaps even contours of constant water temperature. Finally, the computer may be used as an aid in decision making: whether to shift ground, or return home, or continue to fish on the present location, all according to the information received about the way in which catch rates are varying on other fishing grounds, the current state of the ship as regards fuel and stores and unfilled hold capacity, and the costs-and-earnings situation to date.

Training

The need to improve fishing performance because of the growth in size and complexity of the ships consequent, very largely, upon the introduction of the large stern trawler, will not have been fully discussed without some reference to training. It is not only necessary to give the skipper more instruments and other aids to ensure effective use of the capital investment represented by a modern fishing vessel, but also to ensure that the skipper is well trained in their operation and interpretation. At least one passive training aid is already in use, in which the trainee skipper can be put into a mock-up wheelhouse, where the instrument displays reproduce recordings of real fishing situations, with commentary.

In very many fisheries the range of performance between the top ship and the poorest performer is as much as three to one, the greater part of which is attributable to variations in ability between skippers. The potential benefits of better training are clear. There is little doubt that the industry would be more certain of securing maximum benefit if fully-active training simulators, driven by computer, were developed, such as are already in use in the armed forces and airlines. Sophisticated training aids of this type, will, it is hoped, be in use by the mid-1970s.

When we look back at the fisheries technology of the later 1940s, this is perhaps the most striking expression of the resulting impetus given to the development of fisheries technology by the innovations of that time, of which the introduction of the large stern trawler and freezing at sea undoubtedly provided the greatest stimulus to engineering investigation and development.

Major benefit

Another and more direct benefit of the introduction of the large stern trawler should be recalled at this point, to make the account reasonably complete. This is the increased capability it conferred on the fishing nations to harvest the sea, because it allowed the use of large vessels of great endurance and seaworthiness, able to fish almost anywhere in the world's oceans at any season of the year. Since, as the demand for fish grows, it is reasonable to suppose that we shall have resort to stocks more and more remote from the centres of population, the use of long-distance fleets is likely to continue to increase.

The development of the factory trawler has thus led to the possibility of a fuller and more effective use of the food in the oceans. Some conservationists would find this trend deplorable; one must hope that it will not lead to general over-fishing and depletion of stocks, which is avoidable, but to development and implementation of rational and effective means of control.

TECHNO-ECONOMICS

In the early days there were as many doubts about the economic viability of the stern trawler as about its operational effectiveness. Shelter decks, gantries and other new features represented extra costs, and it was not obvious that these would be offset by reduced costs in other directions or by increased earnings. The sheer size of *Fairtry* and the early Russian vessels was daunting.

Lochridge described the design and operation of *Fairtry* in a paper read in 1956 (Ref. 1). *Fairtry* was the first fishing vessel to be comprehensively-equipped with filleting machines; the machines for demersal fish were comparatively new and there was little relevant experience. The success of the enterprise was dependent on them and on the freezing plant. It is clear enough that the designer's policy was so to equip the ship that there would be the minimum possible risk of fishing having to stop because the right type of processing facilities had not been provided on board, or, if provided, were temporarily out of action.

The factory was therefore equipped to be capable of handling most species likely to be caught in quantity by bottom trawl in the north-west Atlantic and many machines were duplicated in case of breakdown. However, the factory deck was not so compact or highly mechanised as to destroy flexibility or make modifications in layout difficult and expensive – a wise policy at that stage of factory trawler development. The filleting lines, freezing plant and associated equipment therefore occupied much space and needed a comparatively large number of men to operate them at full throughput, and to maintain them.

A ship had therefore to be built big enough to accommodate all these men and all the equipment, as well as a low temperature hold and fuel and water tanks for a long voyage. The attempt to develop a special trawl and so to improve catching performance had failed. The hold therefore had to be large enough to allow voyages of sufficient duration to offset the extra costs represented by the factory, the large crew and the large size of the vessel: only by achieving a high proportion of time on the fishing grounds would it be possible to produce high enough annual earnings. The result – a ship in the region of 3,000 tons, and 240ft. LBP, with 2,000 horsepower on the shaft, far bigger than any previous fishing vessel – was therefore the inevitable consequence of the conservative approach to the design, which was undoubtedly the correct one in the circumstances.

To some extent the extra costs were balanced, but only in the early years, by the high catch rates enjoyed on the relatively unexploited grounds of the N-W Atlantic and by the ability of the ship to continue fishing in bad weather. These advantages must have been offset by the relative lack of familiarity with the fishing grounds, and the inevitable lack of refinement of a prototype venture.

Broadly speaking, no premium was obtained for the high quality of the fish – the price received for sea-frozen fillet blocks was roughly the same as for the same product frozen ashore – and to this day, the higher quality of sea-frozen fish does not generally command a premium. Moreover, the product of the factory trawler was not, and is not, a consumer pack, but a larger block suitable for the catering trade or for further processing ashore. Because of difficulties arising from phenomena associated with *rigor mortis*, thawed sea-frozen fillets may not always be acceptable for retail sale in the raw state, and it was generally admitted that it was difficult to make first-quality cold smoke cures from frozen fillets. For all these reasons there were doubts regarding the economic soundness of the *Fairtry* concept, reflected in the continuing efforts to develop systems for freezing whole fish at sea in Britain, the United States and elsewhere, and which, in the case of the British efforts, have since reached the stage of large-scale commercial adoption.

However, the dominant factors in the costs and earnings of the *Fairtry* type of vessel were the size and cost of the vessel and the number of the crew, in relation to the fishing performance. Since then, the potential fishing performance of large stern trawlers has been improved, as a result of the development of trawls, especially pelagic trawls, capable of absorbing the full available power, and by many other less spectacular improvements.

The third line of attack that was followed with the aim of improving on the doubtful commercial viability of large factory stern trawlers was to reduce the size and cost of the ship, and this was also pursued vigorously, as already described. As experience grew, the policy of carrying a full range of filleting machines – as like as not in duplicate – to deal with all species, was modified, and a calculated risk taken on the probability of machine breakdown in order to achieve a smaller and less costly ship and a smaller crew. Such vessels as *Ranger Ajax* have shown what can be done in this direction; there is a deliberate acceptance that it may be necessary to stop fishing sooner than the large vessels, in times when heavy catches can be taken.

In contrast to the comprehensive equipment on the processing deck of *Fairtry*, provided in order to enable most eventualities to be met, the specification of *Ranger Ajax* called for a single Baader 188 filleting machine, together with a heading and a skinning machine. Speed on trials was to be 11.5 knots. Horizontal plate contact freezers were employed. Thus equipped, *Ranger Ajax* had to carry a crew of only 28 of all ranks, and with a hold capacity of 13,000 cu. ft. (370 cu. m) the length overall was only 161 ft. (49.5m). Thus the acceptance of the lack of capacity to cope with very high catch rates or with fish of a size or species unsuitable for the simple processing facilities on board, led to greatly reduced capital and running costs. Nevertheless, when bottom trawling, the gear used by *Ranger Ajax* would be much the same as in *Fairtry*.

This approach does, of course, also require that the skipper, crew and owners accept such limitations as the small size and low speed of the vessel, her more limited range of operation, weather tolerance and flexibility of deployment. With limited mechanisation, they also have to accept that there may be many more occasions when fishing has to stop temporarily in order to clear away the accumulated catch. The approach also requires considerable confidence in the reliability of the processing plant.

Considering her size, *Fairtry*'s free-running

speed, like that of *Ranger Ajax*, was low in comparison with that of the orthodox wet-fish trawler. Since each trip of *Fairtry* might last anything up to four months, there was little or no economic advantage in high speed with its concomitant extra costs in fuel, maintenance and capital. This was the first practical demonstration of a design philosophy, for vessels equipped to freeze at sea, strongly advocated by Hunter and Eddie (Ref. 4) and implemented in a number of freezer trawlers and factory trawlers by the early 1960s. Another school of thought held that a reserve of power would always be an advantage. In so far as trawls have now been developed to absorb powers of 2000 shp and more, which is greater than that available in some of the smaller freezer trawlers and factory trawlers, there is a wider range of options regarding choice of propulsive power for this size of vessel than hitherto. In the larger vessels, however, say 3,000 tons and upwards, a power adequate for fishing by any standards will still be relatively modest in terms of speed on passage.

The owner contemplating the building of a freezer trawler or a factory trawler is therefore faced with a range of choices in various areas. Nowadays, displacement may be anything from 1,000 to 8,000 tons, power may be as little as that just adequate for fishing with a small Granton bottom trawl, up to double that power or more; the criterion of choice may be speed on passage or ability to use large pelagic trawls effectively. There is the question of whether to freeze fillets or whole fish, whether to freeze all the catch or only the catch taken on the early part of the voyage. There is a wide range of choice of maximum daily throughput of the processing plant, which depends in turn on the estimates of future catch rates, the attitude regarding the extent to which peak catch rates should be catered for, and the decision as to whether all or most fish should be frozen pre-rigor, or not (besides all this, the various time limits imposed by the food technologists on the handling of the fish must be adhered to.) There can be varying degrees of duplication and redundancy in the provision of processing plant. The limits of duration of voyages acceptable to the crews may vary in the course of time. Most of these considerations affect the likely size of the catch and capacity of the hold.

In comparison with this bewildering range of choices, the planning of a new wet-fish trawler in the earlier part of the century, or even in the 1950s, had been a very much simpler task. In those days, the possibility of improving productivity by transfer of catches, rotation of crews or in any other way,

Fig. 15. The "Ranger Apollo", one of three sisters in the "Ranger Ajax" class of small factory stern trawler. She was built in Lowestoft in 1966.

received less consideration than it might. The limiting time after the first fish was caught, at which it would normally be rejected as unfit for human consumption, was pretty well fixed and known. The owner's area of choice of design parameters of direct techno-economic importance was thus confined to speed and power; both had not only direct effects on costs and earnings, but also psychological aspects which allowed much scope for personal preference and style.

It is not surprising, therefore, that in, for example, the British distant-water trawler fleet of the 1960s, a number of stern trawlers appeared greatly differing in size, speed, hold capacity and throughput of processing plant. One was a part-freezer, some were freezer trawlers, some factory trawlers. They varied widely in capital cost, and more especially in the ratio of capital cost to hold capacity. This was due partly to different choices of other parameters, partly to variations in quality of design: for instance, some designers made more effective use of space in the shelter deck than others. Some part of the cost variation was, of course, the usual difference between one shipyard and another and one contract and the next.

Profitability could obviously be affected by choice of hold capacity, service speed and throughput of processing plant, and in the early days owners had little to guide them in making the correct choice except their own intuition. The Government were still seeking assurance that the new big stern trawlers were economically viable, but with such a wide range of choice before the owners, it was not at all certain that the early vessels would represent convincing demonstrations of the potential of the large stern trawler concept. Evolution, by trial and error, was obviously going to be too slow to cope with the large number of variables. More sophisticated techniques of investment appraisal were required which could narrow the multi-dimensional field of choice open to the owner to a useful extent, and indicate the sensitivity of his favoured solution to such eventualities as changes in catch rates, fuel costs, labour costs, etc. Thus the adoption of the stern trawler gave rise to a much increased need for, and interest in, the techniques of Operational Research. Up to that time only a few small, pioneering efforts had been made in this field in the fisheries, notably in Britain, Poland and Germany.

The first investment problem, relating to large stern trawlers, to be tackled by Operational Research, was to determine the optimum size of the processing plant for a freezer trawler, taking into account the likely rates of catch and the way in which the duration of the tow and the size of the catch varies from haul to haul, and with due regard to the time limits on bleeding, gutting, holding and freezing the fish, imposed by the food technologists. This queuing problem was solved by simulation techniques using a digital computer. Sufficient information by way of detailed logs of fishing operations was obviously a pre-requisite of any realistic and statistically-valid solution of this kind. Fortunately this was available.

Later the technique was extended by Chaplin and Haywood (Ref. 14) to allow estimates of the likely relative costs and earnings, over several years, of a series of freezer trawlers of similar design but varying in speed and hold capacity. The same technique also showed the effect on the economics of the vessels, and on the correct choice of vessel, of the skill of the skipper – whether he was an outstanding fisherman, a fisherman of medium skill, or a relatively poor performer. The published paper gives examples of estimates of the profitability of various designs, which were based on realistic data, but the main intention of the project was to develop a technique. This is embodied in a computer program, into which any owner can feed his own data and assumptions. As already indicated, the method should not be regarded as giving a unique answer, but as a means of usefully narrowing the field within which the owner exercises his flair and intuition, and of indicating to him the implications of his assumptions.

Following pioneering work by Swiecicki, the Polish United Shipyards developed a technique in which a stochastic model of a fishery is used to determine the optimum ship speed, hold capacity, type and size of the processing plant, and endurance.

Similar techniques have since been developed for investment appraisal in the case of wet fish vessels. They differ in power and purpose from the earlier work by Doust and Hayes (see Ref. 15) which was limited to ascertaining the optimum combination of design parameters from within the envelope of a number of already existing vessels. This technique is obviously more applicable to a mature technology than to the pioneering stage of rapid development which fishing vessel design entered with the advent of stern trawling.

Here, therefore, we see the development of more powerful and rational techniques of design of fishing vessels and investment appraisal arising out of the introduction of the stern trawler. They had to be developed in order to ensure that the full potential of the stern trawler could be realised and so that the doubters' fears could be put at rest.

The techno-economic studies mentioned above have shown clearly that for stern freezer trawlers the largest vessels give the best return on investment. However, one cannot continue to increase the size of vessel without considering the effect on trip length and the associated sociological problems. Speed has been shown to be an expensive feature and it is now becoming recognised that adequate power for fishing operations is the prime need.

For the wet fish stern trawler the position is somewhat different. Here there is still a time limit imposed by the acceptability of the fish at the time of marketing. In the past, this concern about spoilage of the catch led to an emphasis on high speed in the design of wet fish side trawlers which was inevitably accompanied by a trend towards increased vessel size. Owners often justified such vessels on the grounds that speed and size were favourable factors in recruiting and retaining the services of the best skippers and crews and there was certainly a great deal of truth in this proposition. However, this policy overlooks the fact that large, fast wet fish vessels can often be made to pay only by top skippers and may become unprofitable in later years when they are in the hands of less successful skippers.

Crews will continue to be attracted to the highest-earning vessels, but in future these are likely to be the vessels in which the fish handling and processing methods are most highly-mechanised and in which multi-gear handling systems are installed. These features are most easily provided in stern trawlers and their development was given the necessary impetus by the advent of the stern trawler. It should now pay owners to invest in mechanisation and crew comfort rather than in speed, and in this sense the development of the stern trawler has widened the options open to the owner in his continuing struggle to adapt to changing economic circumstances

A new series of stern trawlers will soon be operating from Lowestoft which have the features mentioned above. These single deck vessels, 128 ft. (39m) LOA will have twin net drums with fish processing carried out below the main deck. For a fuller discussion of the economic considerations behind the choice of design of wet fish stern trawlers and a description of the features of the Lowestoft vessels the reader is referred to Insull and Hopper (Ref. 16.)

FUTURE TRENDS AND POSSIBILITIES

One trend of recent years is towards the dual purpose or multi-purpose fishing vessel. In future, therefore, we may have more vessels equipped to fish by stern trawling and also capable of very rapid changes to other methods rather than separate and distinct vessel types such as stern trawlers, purse seiners, and so on.

As regards stern trawling, one fairly obvious imminent development seems to be the provision of facilities for avoiding loss of fishing time due to the need to mend the net, and for changing from one type of trawl to another. Systems are now coming into use whereby the skipper can deploy either of two types of trawl at will, and designs are in hand for systems with a spare trawl of each type ready to deploy as soon as the other is aboard. Such systems will probably incorporate net drums.

Some designs of shelter-deck stern trawler are less efficient in the use of the space in the shelter-deck than others. If the advent of powered net drums results in a shortening of the fishing deck, designers may be forced to pay increasing attention to this area. Some designs already use part of the shelter-deck as hold space. On the other hand, with the advent of processing systems that include bleeding, pre-chilling, gutting, and chilled buffer storage or temperature-conditioning, with sorting, size grading and orienting of the fish at appropriate points, and probably automatic weighing also, there will be much more equipment to fit into the processing deck, even if the vessel does not freeze her catch. The tendency to haul the gear less frequently also means bigger individual catches, but it is hoped that the use of twin net drums will reverse this trend.

The processing systems just envisaged will have to be highly mechanised and may involve continuous-flow rather than batch processing at certain stages, e.g. freezing. Specialised vessels, equipped to handle herring in this way, are already in service, and more versatile ones are to be expected. The need to achieve workable and efficient layouts on such ships may well force the preference for engine-forward layouts, in order to leave a clear uninterrupted processing deck or decks and achieve an optimum flow of fish from net to hold, perhaps with alternate paths according to species, intrinsic quality and product demand.

Other considerations altogether, such as the possible effect of machinery noise on catches, about which little is known, may influence choice of type of machinery in the direction of light, resiliently-mounted high-speed engines and slow-running propulsion motors. Developments in a.c. propulsion systems may in any case make such machinery attractive on cost, as well as facilitating the introduction of the concept of a single central source of a.c. power for all purposes. Taken together with the previous forecast, this could lead to unorthodox vessel arrangements: for example, siting of the generating station forward in the shelter deck, where the engines would be easily removeable for servicing. This would leave the main part of the hull entirely free for handling and stowage of the catch.

Be that as it may, it is clear that the imminent adoption of a very much higher degree of mechanisation on both the fishing deck and the processing deck – and probably also in the holds of wet-fish trawlers – means that the general arrangement of the shelter-deck stern-ramp trawler should be looked at anew. It is not axiomatic that the optimum layout of the kind of highly-mechanised stern trawler already possible will be achieved merely by adding mechanical aids to a classic stern trawler design. The optimum layout may be so different that the first vessel will be highly experimental. What is certain is that there will be a great deal more quantitative information, and more powerful techniques of appraisal, available to its designers, than was available to Lochridge and his collaborators when designing *Fairtry*.

In examining such possibilities, it would be as well not to exclude the possibility of a large shelter-deck high-freeboard side trawler, with powered net drums on the rail amidships, in case this has, after all, some advantages in layout over the vessel equipped to haul the gear over the stern. Another possible direction of development, already under practical examination in a number of coastal fishing craft and in the Russian deep sea trawler *Experiment*, is the twin-hulled fishing vessel. All that can

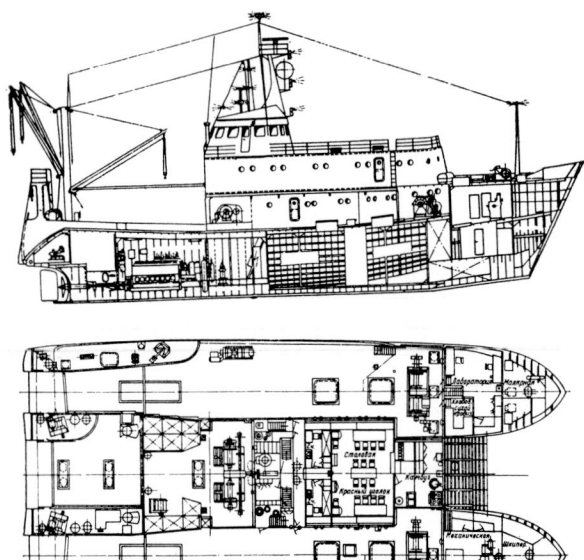

Fig. 16. Profile and general arrangement of the Soviet catamaran stern trawler "Experiment".

ing more powerful methods, but by stimulating engineering research and development which has resulted in a general advance in fisheries technology. It has also resulted in improvements in safety and comfort and has facilitated the mechanisation necessary if catching power is to be maintained and improved in spite of a decline in the availability of fishermen.

The introduction of stern trawling was not without considerable difficulties and doubts, some of which were avoidable and many of which were inherent in the organisation and economic structure of the fishing industry as it had existed until the mid-20th century and which are still inhibiting its development to a significant extent. Others were unavoidable, and illustrate the general difficulty of technical development in the marine environment.

In this account of the technical evolution of the stern trawler, little by way of detailed technical description or quantitative information has been given. This will be found in the references, many of which themselves contain lists of valuable references, and in the succeeding chapters of this book.

be said at present is that although the single-hulled deep-sea stern trawler, of both shelter-deck and single-deck stern-ramp and single-deck types, has proved to be superior in most important respects to the side trawler, it is by no means established as the last word in deep sea fishing vessel design.

The advent of the modern stern trawler had a great impact on the ability of the fishing industry to reap the harvest of the oceans, not only by facilitat-

REFERENCES

1. Lochridge, W. – Mechanisation in Fishing Vessels. Trans. I.E.S. 1955–6 *99*, 511.
2. Report on an Experiment into the Freezing of Fish at Sea. White Fish Authority 1957.
3. Lochridge, W. – FAIRFREE Trans. I.E.S. 1950.
4. Hunter, A. and Eddie, G. C. – Fishing Vessel Development. Trans. I.Mar.E. 1959 *71*, 175.
5. Drever, C. – Cod Fishing at Greenland. White Fish Authority 1971.
6. Hearn, P. J. and Chaplin, P. D. Data logging on deep sea trawlers BSRA T.M. 159, 1967.
7. Bennett, R. and Hatfield, M. Development of strain gauge techniques for measurement of propeller torque in distant water trawlers J. Strain Analysis 1966 *1* (No. 2) 102.
8. Bennett, R., Chaplin, P. D. and Kerr, N. M. Controllable pitch propellers in large stern trawlers. Trans. I.Mar.E. 1968 *80* (No. 8).
9. Chaplin, P. D. and Foster, J. F. Performance of a propeller nozzle fitted to M.T. *Ardenlea* Proc. Int.Tug.Conf. 1969 (Ship and Boat International.)
10. Specification for Deck Machinery for a Distant Water Stern Trawler, White Fish Authority, 1971.
11. Chaplin, P. D. The effect of ship motion on the economics of fishing vessels. Univ. of Southampton Seminar on the application of Ship Motion Research to Design.
12. Scharfe, J. "The German one-boat mid-water trawl." *Fishing News International*. Vol. 8, Nos. 7–12, 1969.

Fig. 17. A US Coastguard photograph of the "Experiment" on north-west Atlantic fishing grounds.

13. Hatfield, M. – The introduction of computers into British stern trawlers. Proc. CAMFI 70. Canadian Fisheries Reports No. 15, 1970. Queen's Printer for Canada.
14. Chaplin, P. D. and Haywood, K. H. – Operational Research Applied to Stern Freezer Trawler Design. Trans. I.Mar.E. 1968.
15. Doust, D. J. – The relative importance of trawler design to fishing economics as a whole – FAO meeting on Business Decisions in Fishery Industries 1964.
16. Hopper, A. G. and Insull, A. D. – North Sea Trawling: Choice of Vessel size, Power and Type. NORSPEC. 70.

Mechanisation of Trawl Gear Handling Aboard Shelter-deck Stern Trawlers in the Atlantic Fisheries

N. M. KERR, Ph.D., C.Eng., M.I.Mech.E., Chief Development Engineer,
Industrial Development Unit, White Fish Authority

1. INTRODUCTION

Those operations of fishing that have to be performed on deck and which are the prime tasks of the deck crew are the handling of the fishing gear and the catch. With the performance of these tasks occupying a relatively small proportion of the working day, the deck crew are also heavily involved in the subsequent processing of the catch prior to its stowage in the vessel's hold. Except in factory vessels there is no supplementary crew to assist in processing the fish. Therefore, in discussing the degree of mechanisation necessary to handle the trawl gear, it is essential to consider also the degree of mechanisation required to process the catch and to strive to achieve a reasonable balance of manpower requirements between the two.

The advent of the stern trawler has permitted the development and adoption of a higher degree of mechanisation than previously and has thus helped to meet the growing problems of rising costs and increased scarcity of labour.

When labour is both plentiful and cheap, little attention is given to manning scales and consequently the tasks to be performed, in any industry, are relatively un-mechanised. While this situation was, at least partially, true for the fishing industry in the first half of this century, labour costs have now reached a level at which they cannot be ignored, and they are rising fast. In the United Kingdom, for example, on all classes of vessel, crew cost at between 35 per cent and 40 per cent of the total operating costs is now by far the largest of the separately identifiable costs: all others, including depreciation, fuel, etc., are now individually less than 15 per cent.

Similar proportionate levels of labour cost obtain in many fishing nations. In the absence of improvements in catch rates or prices, one of the most rewarding approaches in any attempt to improve profitability is to increase the degree of mechanisation aboard with the aims of reducing unproductive time on the grounds and reducing the number of men required. This economic argument is supported more strongly with the passing of each year by the difficulty in recruiting crews of high calibre when shore-based industries offer well paid employment with mechanical aids to perform the heavier work.

The forward-looking vessel operator must have not only an open mind to new developments, but must also realise that considerable changes may be required in the layout of working decks, and even in the vessel design itself, if trawlers, crewed by a smaller number of highly skilled and highly paid men, are to be evolved. What is probably the most significant change in both attitude and vessel design has already been made in the deepsea trawler fleets. This is, of course, the change from trawling over the side to trawling over the stern, which during the 1960s saw the former method completely eclipsed. In the British distant water fleet the catching power of a stern freezer trawler is approximately 50 per cent greater than for a side trawler, while the crew complement has only increased by 25 per cent, from 20 to 25 men.

In side trawlers, whose design has evolved over nearly a century, methods are extremely well established and are highly optimised within the constraints imposed by the vessel design. In fact, any attempts to alter methods radically in a side trawler are liable to end in failure because improvements in one aspect invariably lead to unacceptable handicaps in the performance of some other operation.

This point was illustrated most clearly in one experimental installation aboard the British side trawler *Ross Kelvin* (50 m long) when a net drum, to haul the net under power, was fitted. While the net drum itself worked satisfactorily, its presence on the foredeck resulted in a loss of 40 per cent of the

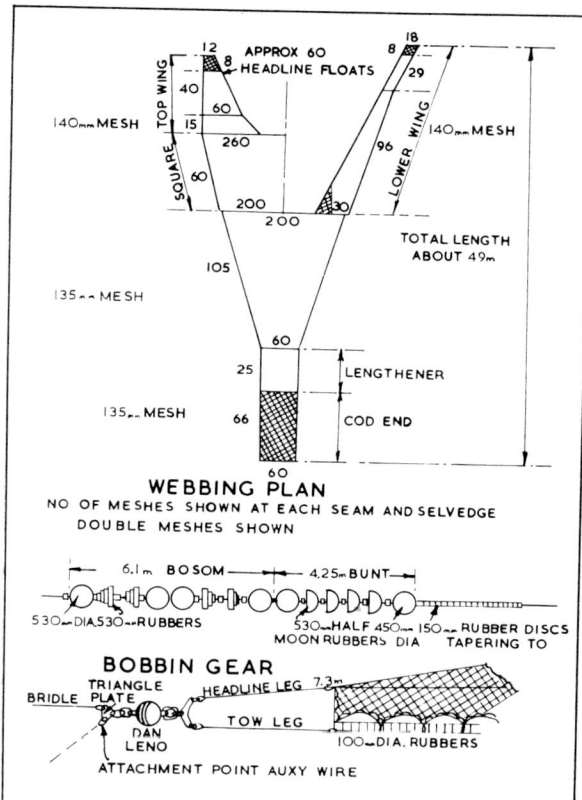

Fig. 1. Standard Granton trawl (1.9 metres headline height).

stern working deck than on the fore deck of a side trawler.

Thus at present there exists both a climate which is favourable to the advancement of fishing technology and a concept of vessel design which provides a framework within which technical enterprise can be exercised. Vessel owners and operators are receptive to change, but they are at the same time keenly concerned with their vessels' profitability. New ideas, methods and equipment are required, but so are thorough studies of service performance from which detailed equipment specifications can be written and cost/benefit analyses attempted to assess the relative merits of the schemes projected.

Since the developments in mechanisation to be described are relatively recent – indeed most of them have arisen out of the development of the stern trawler – the technical requirements are not widely known and understood. Some space will therefore be devoted to specifying the requirements, so far as they are known, for the deck machinery of large trawlers fishing the North Atlantic. The information

deck area available. This in turn so reduced the fish pond space available that the vessel had to stop fishing earlier in times of high catch rates, which proved commercially uneconomic. In addition, the deck area available for net mending was adversely affected (resulting in more awkward work for the crew) and free and rapid movement of men was hindered.

While it is true that the working deck arrangements for virtually all side trawlers over 25 m long are basically identical, this is certainly not the case for stern trawlers. The latter have not been sufficiently long in service for a standard pattern to be evolved, but this is not the most important reason for the variety of layouts already in service. Essentially the stern trawler design affords greater flexibility regarding layout and methods because it permits the main activities of warp and trawl handling to be separated completely from fish processing by moving the latter to a different part of the ship. Even in vessels smaller than about 35 m, when it is not possible to arrange fish processing below decks, these activities can still be better separated on a

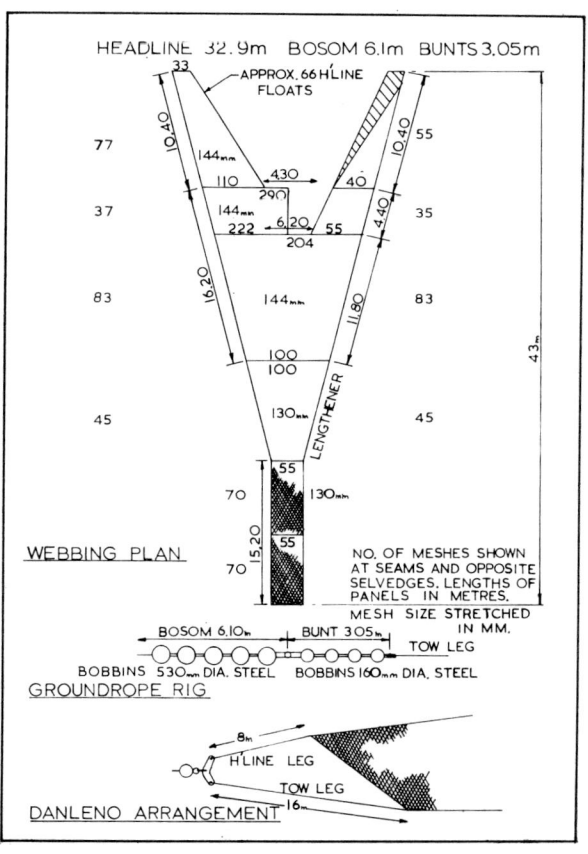

Fig. 2. Fécamp high headline bottom trawl (4 metres headline height).

should not of course be applied without careful assessment as to whether it is relevant to the fishery under consideration.

When working on new developments, it is only too easy for the designers to become too closely involved with the immediate problem, so much so that sub-optimal solutions are achieved. It is essential that the trawler is considered as a complete fishing tool, with alterations to one system examined, not in isolation, but in conjunction with the other systems which might be affected and perhaps simultaneously improved.

2. FISHING METHODS

Before discussing mechanical equipment, layouts and methods for handling gear and catches in stern trawlers, it is necessary to describe the operations in order that what is required of the equipment, and the conditions in which it is used may be defined. Design and rigging of trawl nets is in itself a subject worthy of a whole book. In this chapter, discussion of the subject is limited to a brief description of the principal types of gear worked, their main components and the way in which they are towed. This is to provide some understanding of the on-board handling and deck layouts required

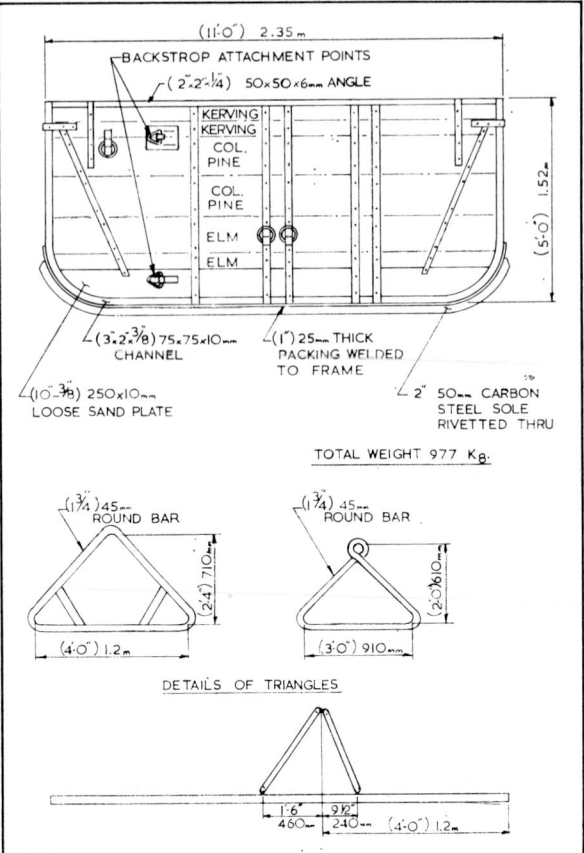

Fig. 4a. Standard trawl board (Granton).

for the different types of trawl, especially when more than one type is to be worked from the same vessel.

2.1. *Fishing gear employed*

Deepsea trawlers make use of two main classes of gear. These are the demersal, or bottom fishing, trawl and the pelagic, or mid-water, trawl.

The demersal trawls used by stern trawlers are virtually identical to those traditionally used by side trawlers for the past 50 years. There are many different trawl types in this class, for example the Granton trawl (Fig. 1) used by the majority of the British distant water fleet and the Fécamp high headline trawl (Fig. 2) (sometimes referred to as a semi-pelagic trawl) popular with the Boulogne fleet.

Pelagic trawls became of major economic significance in the 1960s, with the Scandinavians developing pair boat operation for the smaller vessels and the Germans developing the one-boat trawl (Fig. 3) for larger vessels (Ref. 1).

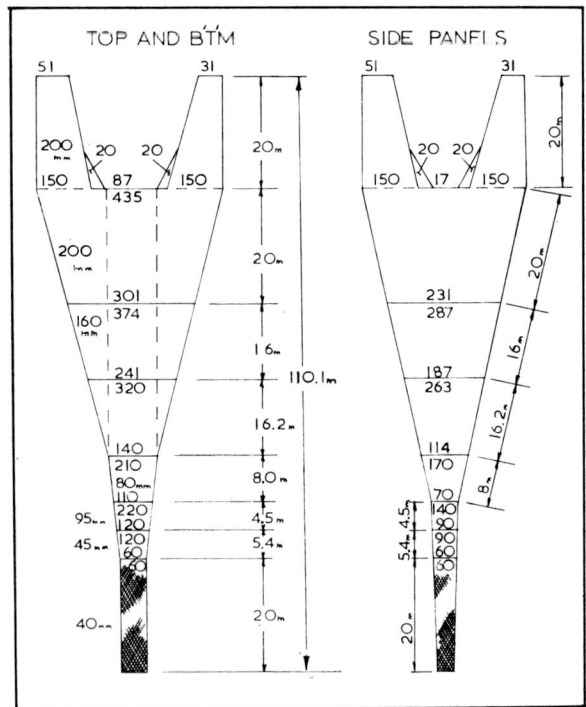

Fig. 3. Pelagic trawl (1600 mesh by 20 cm.).

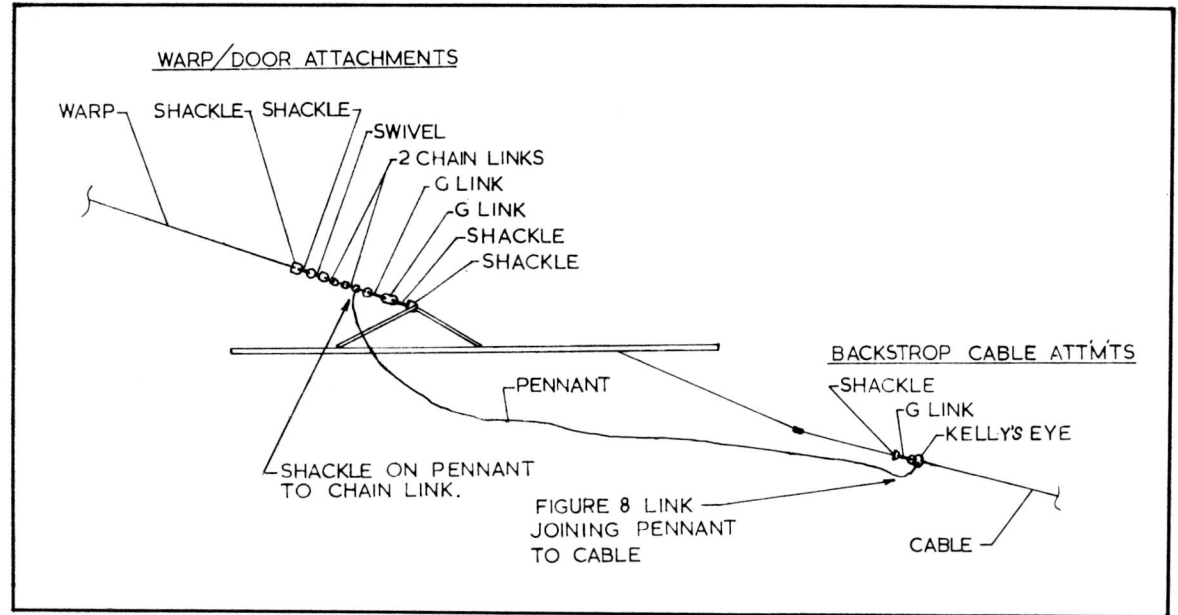

Fig. 4b. Standard side trawler door rigging (distant water vessel) with modifications for stern trawler. Dimensions on associated wires: Side Trawler – *Backstrops 4 m. (28 mm. dia.) and pennants 6.4 m. (19 mm. dia.).* Stern trawler – *Backstrops 6 m. (28 mm. dia.) and pennants 12 m. (19 mm. dia.). N.B. Chain is increasingly used for backstrops and bridles in lieu of wires.*

In Iceland, many side trawlers have been converted to purse seining, and the Russians have built a number of vessels which are basically stern trawlers but which are stated to be capable of purse seining also. They have recently been experimenting with trawl and purse seine fishing using a large twin-hulled stern fishing vessel (Ref. 2).

As the types of net to be handled have a considerable influence on the layout of the trawler's working deck, it is important to discuss the design and construction of the nets and their associated rigging before discussing the layout of the working deck itself.

Trawls are essentially flexible bags of netting which require spreading forces to hold the mouth of the net open. The horizontal force is generated by a pair of otter boards (alternatively called trawl doors) acting as kites. These boards are connected to the end of the main trawl warps. There are various methods of connecting the boards to the trawl, typical arrangements being illustrated in Figs. 4a and 4b for demersal and pelagic trawls. The vertical forces are provided by the addition of floats to the headrope of the net and weights either directly to the footrope as for the demersal trawl, or on the lower spreading wires joining the footrope to the otter board for the pelagic net. For both trawl types the otter boards themselves contribute significantly to the sinking forces.

From Figs. 1, 2 and 3 it can be seen that the pelagic nets are very much larger than the demersal or semi-pelagic nets, and also require larger and heavier trawl boards to generate the greater spreading forces required (see Figs. 4a and b).

2.2. Fishing operations
  2.2.1. Demersal trawling (includes semi-pelagic, or high headline trawls)

The trawl is towed along the sea bed for a period of between one and four hours depending on the catch rate prevailing. At the end of this period the trawl gear is hauled aboard, the fish emptied from the cod-end, any damage to the gear repaired and alterations to its rig made as required by the skipper, before it is returned to the sea bed. The time the trawl is off the sea bed is lost fishing time and the hauling, deck handling and shooting operations must therefore be kept to a minimum. With operations taking place on a 24 hour basis, the gear is generally hauled on six to eight occasions daily with a loss in productive fishing time of between four and six hours.

There are several changes that can be made to the rig of the trawl. The ground gear, or footrope, can be exchanged for one with larger or smaller bobbins, or a different mix of bobbins and rollers, to suit the roughness of the terrain being worked. The length of the cables between the trawl doors and

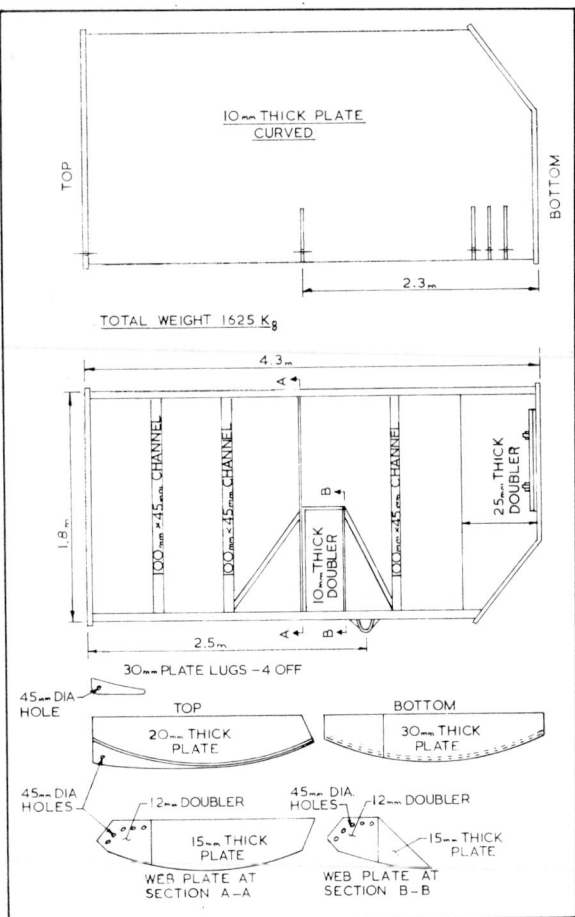

Fig. 4c. Süberkrüb pelagic trawl door (starboard).

the dan-leno bobbins can be altered; longer cables increase the catch rate by shepherding more fish into the path of the net, the greater the length of wire the greater the risk of damage and loss of time on rough ground. Each vessel generally has several standard variations to the rig of the trawl, all of which can be effected relatively quickly.

Demersal trawls, being used to scrape the sea bed, are very prone to damage and on occasion, to complete loss. Thus all skippers like to have a spare trawl fully rigged conveniently stowed on deck so that it can be shot away speedily once it becomes apparent that the working trawl is so damaged that it cannot be repaired in a shorter time than is required to exchange the trawls.

While fishing, the skipper has continuously to build a mental picture of the fish distribution and how it is moving, using his echo sounders and knowledge of the catch from the previous tow(s). In addition to the obvious desire to maximise catch rates, this mental activity on the part of the skipper is essential on trawlers freezing the catch, as bringing on board too large a quantity of fish at one time creates delays in processing the fish, with subsequent loss of quality in the product. Electronic aids (Ref. 3) are being developed to relieve the skipper of much of this strain of mentally integrating the echo traces and deciding when sufficient fish have been caught. Demersal fish, such as cod, generally do not occur in dense concentrations over large areas of sea bed: for example, catching one fish of 2 kg weight for every 15 metres travelled, at four knots, would result in a daily catch of 20 tons, which is above the 1970 average for the North Atlantic cod fisheries.

It is not possible, on the other hand, to extend the duration of the tow at times of low catch rate beyond a limit set by considerations of the effect on the subsequent quality of the fish caught early in the tow. Thus only limited improvements in productivity can be looked for by the simple expedient of carrying out fewer tows of longer duration in each 24 hour period.

2.2.2. *Pelagic trawling*

In pelagic trawling the net can be towed from just above the sea bed, to virtually on the surface. Positioning the net correctly in depth is vitally important both to achieve good catches, and to avoid snagging when fishing close to a ragged sea bed. It has been found essential to fit a telemeter, usually of the cable type, on the headline of the net to transmit this information directly to the skipper.

The depth of the net is controlled by its speed through the water and by the length of warp out. Thus during fishing, for shoals of herring or of roundfish (cod, etc) swimming close to the sea bed (but too high to be taken by a demersal trawl) the depth of the net has to be adjusted frequently and is generally done by varying propeller power, or if large changes in depth are required, by hauling in or paying out on the trawl winch. The tow times vary considerably, depending on whether the fish are in shoals or are widely dispersed, and can be as little as half-an-hour, or as much as ten hours (for red fish).

2.3. *Propulsion and winch power requirements*

For a 75-metre stern trawler, a propulsive power of 1500 kW (2000 hp) gives a free running speed of approximately 14.5 knots. Increasing this power by 50 per cent to 2250 kW (3000 hp) is unlikely to raise the free running speed above 15.5 knots. Thus if the

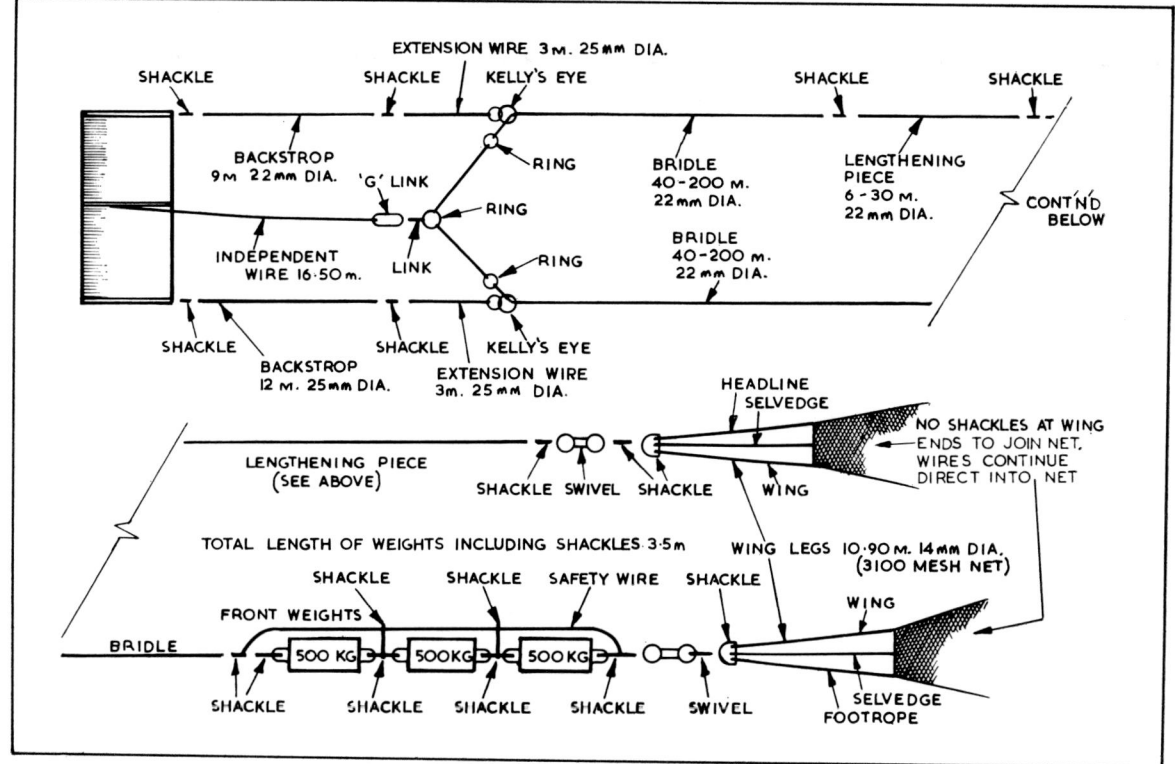

Fig. 4d. *Rigging for 3100 mesh pelagic trawl.*

propulsive power were to be determined from considerations of free running speed and fuel economy only, 1500 to 1800 kW (2000 to 2400 hp) would probably be selected for a North Atlantic trawler of this size.

When working with a demersal trawl, the highest power requirement occurs when the trawl is being shot during bad weather. For a Granton and other demersal trawls this maximum is approximately 1200 kW (1600 hp) which is often considerably less than the free-running power available. Larger demersal trawls which could make fuller use of the 'excess' power are not yet common, and indeed it may not be possible to develop them.

Pelagic trawls on the other hand, can be enlarged to make maximum use of the propulsive power available. If the winch and propeller are driven from the same engine, it is important to note that the maximum power requirement occurs when it is necessary to raise the trawl (e.g., to avoid a sea bed obstruction) either by increasing vessel and net speed or by heaving in on the winch while maintaining constant power on the propeller. With an allowance of around 450 kW (600 hp) for the winch drive, main engine power of 2700 kW (3600 hp) and more can be used beneficially in pelagic trawling and thus the installed power level is determined by the fishing, and not the free-running requirement. Details of winch operating specifications are given in Section 6 of this Chapter.

Although purse seine fishing is not discussed in this chapter, it is worth noting that the power requirements for this type of fishing are less than for either demersal or pelagic fishing. Thus a vessel designed initially for the latter methods would not be precluded from purse seining, at a later date, on the grounds of inadequate power, but the winch arrangements and deck layout would probably not be so adaptable.

3. LAYOUT OF THE TRAWL DECK ON EXISTING SHIPS

3.1. *Defining the function of the trawl deck*

Before a shipyard can propose designs to prospective vessel owners, their naval architect has to formulate the operations that have to be performed. This on the face of it may sound very simple for shipyards long connected with the building of side trawlers. If this argument were true, then all stern trawlers of the same general size would have very similar working decks, as was the case with side trawlers.

One fundamental difficulty confronting the shipyard naval architect is that he cannot be spared from his other duties for sufficiently long a time to make a detailed assessment of the operational functions under service conditions. He has, therefore to rely heavily on advice and information provided by the vessel owner. For the side trawler, the evolutionary process over the best part of a century had provided a highly optimised system (within the constraints imposed by the overall vessel design) and had resulted in a well trusted specification which was known to meet the operational requirements. These requirements however were themselves not necessarily full and explicitly defined. In this sense there was, therefore, insufficient understanding of the requirements in detail, and no formal procedures for ascertaining them and for proposing design solutions.

Thus, despite the obviously significant design alterations in towing from the stern, the designers and operators of the first stern trawlers were not prepared to depart from side trawler practice in the handling of the trawl and this was employed wherever it was still valid. As experience with the new vessels grew, their operators realised that there was scope for improvement, a process which is still continuing, especially as new requirements, such as the ability to be able to work both demersal and pelagic trawls, are being introduced.

In a side trawler, the functions listed in Table 1 were carried out on the trawl deck.

TABLE 1 Trawl Deck Functions for a Side Trawler

1 Shooting and hauling the main warps.
2 Handling the trawl boards.
3 Handling the net.
4 Mending and changing the net.
5 Sorting the catch and rejecting unwanted material.
6a Bleeding the fish, if required.
6b Gutting the fish.
7 Washing the fish.
8 Loading the cleaned fish into the fishroom.

In a large stern trawler, that is one over about 40 metres long, it is possible to provide two working decks above the water line in the stern section. By this means, the functions listed above can be divided between the two decks with the fish processing operations (i.e. items 5 to 8 in Table 1) being transferred to the lower deck. Besides providing welcome shelter for the crew during the frequently lengthy gutting periods, this arrangement has the considerable merit of simplifying the layout of the upper deck, by confining its function to that of handling the trawl and its associated gear (items 1 to 4 in Table 1).

Before considering trawl deck layouts adopted for existing stern ramp trawlers, it is worthwhile examining the necessary functions in greater detail than listed as items 3 and 4 in Table 1 (items 1 and 2 are sufficiently explanatory). This is done in Tables 2 and 3.

TABLE 2 Net Handling Operations in a Stern Ramp Trawler

1 Disconnecting the cables from the trawl doors.
2 Hauling the cables.
3 Hauling the tow legs.
4 Hauling the netting from wing ends until the cod-end is at the foot of the stern ramp.
5 Hauling the cod-end.
6 Spilling the fish to the lower (fish processing) deck.
7 Outhauling the cod-end and netting under winch power.
8 Paying out the remainder of netting by moving the vessel ahead against the drag of the netting already in the water.
9 Paying out the tow legs and cables.
10 Connecting the cables to the trawl doors.

TABLE 3 Mending the Net on a Stern Trawler

Includes
1 Minor repairs to the net.
2 Complete change of net when damage is too extensive for rapid repair.
3 Change of ground gear.
4 Change of cables.
With 3 and 4 being necessitated either by damage to the original or because the skipper wishes to work a different rig.

When subsequently discussing improved methods of net handling (Section 4), it is important to know the work content of the present operations. The on-board handling time is the time taken to handle the trawl gear starting when the doors reach the towing blocks and finishing when the doors are payed away, less (because of its variability) the time taken to empty the cod-end.

That is, the on-board handling time is for operations 1 to 10 (except item 6) in Table 2. Recorded times from two vessels, one 55 metres and the other 70 metres overall length, and the frequency of occurrence, are given in Table 4 for the Granton trawl.

From this table, it appears that the larger vessel, the one with the longer trawl deck, has a higher proportion of the shorter handling times (63 per cent

TABLE 4 Granton Trawl. On Board Handling Times (i.e. time elapsed from doors up to doors away less time to empty cod-end).

On-board handling time (min)	55 m.o.a. Vessel		70 m.o.a. Vessel	
	Frequency	Cumulative Frequency (%)	Frequency	Cumulative Frequency (%)
8	0	0	0	0
9	2	4	2	2
10	7	20	13	17
11	6	33	27	47
12	7	49	14	63
13	5	60	9	73
14	8	78	7	81
15	4	87	9	91
16	3	94	2	93
17	1	96	2	95
18	0	96	1	97
19	1	98	0	97
20	0	98	2	99
21	0	98	1	100
22	1	100	0	100
Sample Size	45		89	
Average Time	13.0 min		12.1 min	

determine how great is the advantage of trawl deck length. Similar data for handling the Granton trawl cod-end is presented in Table 5: these times do not include any delays caused by net mending.

TABLE 5 Granton Trawl. Cod-end handling times.

Time (min)	70 m.o.a. Vessel	
	Frequency	Cumulative Frequency (%)
2–3.9	6	8
4–5.9	14	27
6–7.9	18	51
8–9.9	7	60
10–11.9	13	77
12–13.9	4	83
14–15.9	5	89
16–17.9	3	93
18–19.9	2	96
20 and over	3	100
Sample Size	75	
Average Time	8.8 min	

less than 13 minutes compared with 49 per cent) although the range of times is identical; however, other factors such as rigging details of the handling equipment and the crews themselves influence this result and data from more vessels is required to

Delays due to net damage, change of trawl or its rig are very much dependent on where the vessel is fishing. On smooth ground, such as in the Barents Sea and off South West Africa, damage is a rare occurrence, but on others mending, frequently extensive, is required after every tow. Time losses due to net damage were measured in a vessel of 70

TABLE 6 Granton Trawl. Delays Caused by Net Damage, 70 m o.a. Vessel

	Area	Number of Hauls	Number of Times Damaged	Number of Net Changes	Time Delay	
					min	% Fishing Time
First third of trip	North Hamilton Bank	33	22	6	1213*	20
Second third of trip	South Hamilton Bank	27	9	2	341	7
Final third of trip	Woolfalls	29	7	2	216	4
Total		89	38	10	1770*	11
Average (per haul)					20**	11**

(Note:—The above times do not include repair work on spare trawls)
  * This value is inflated as on five consecutive tows the net was damaged and had to be repaired as no spare was available. With spare trawls to hand, this time would have been reduced by approximately 300 minutes and the average time ** would be 16 minutes, 8.8 per cent.

metres overall length during a trip to the Hamilton Banks and Woolfalls, and are given in Table 6. Similar analyses of other voyages in several large stern trawlers indicate that, on average, the loss in fishing time in the North Atlantic due to repairing or changing damaged Granton trawls is eight per cent.

British experience with pelagic trawls is relatively limited and therefore handling times have been obtained from a German vessel, working Engel trawls. The handling operations are essentially as listed in Table 2: with the greater length of netting, several pulls are necessary to bring it aboard. Also, great care has to be taken to fleet the net when hauling to ensure a smooth payout on the subsequent shoot. Typical times for on-board handling of the net (i.e. doors-up to doors away, less cod-end handling time) are given in Table 7 along with average cod-end discharge times for 10-ton catches (equivalent to 250 baskets).

TABLE 7 Pelagic Trawl (Engel). Typical On-board Handling Times in Good Weather. 63 m.o.a. German Vessel

Net Size	1114 × 56 cm	948 × 56 cm
Equivalent net size	3100 × 20 cm	2700 × 20 cm
Doors up to cod-end aboard	19 min	18 min
Cod-end away to doors away	8 min	7 min
On-board handling time	27 min	25 min
Cod-end handling time (10 tons)	43 min	39 min

To control the deck activities listed in Table 2, the skipper, winchman and deck crew have to work together and thus there is need for a good communication system. As far as the man on the bridge is concerned, this requirement is more pronounced in stern trawler than in a side trawler: working in a stern trawler, the skipper has a greater role to play by manoeuvring the vessel ahead at varying speed while the net and its associated gear is being hauled aboard and again while it is being payed away. This is discussed more fully in Para 6.11.

The adoption of the stern fishing layout also calls for fresh thought to be given to the protection of the crew when handling the gear.

3.2. Existing trawl deck layouts and methods of working

3.2.1. Length of the trawl deck

By the early 1960s, stern trawling had made a considerable impact on the fishing industry. Progress in vessel design and gear handling methods developed are very well presented and discussed in the proceedings of the Conference held in Grimsby, UK, in 1963 (Ref. 4). By then, the stern ramp trawler was accepted as the vessel type for the distant water fisheries. The ramp was regarded as an essential feature, allowing large catches (20 tons and more) to be taken aboard in a continuous operation, without the need to divide the catch into multiple "lifts". The length of the working deck from the ramp head to the winch needed for handling bottom trawls was

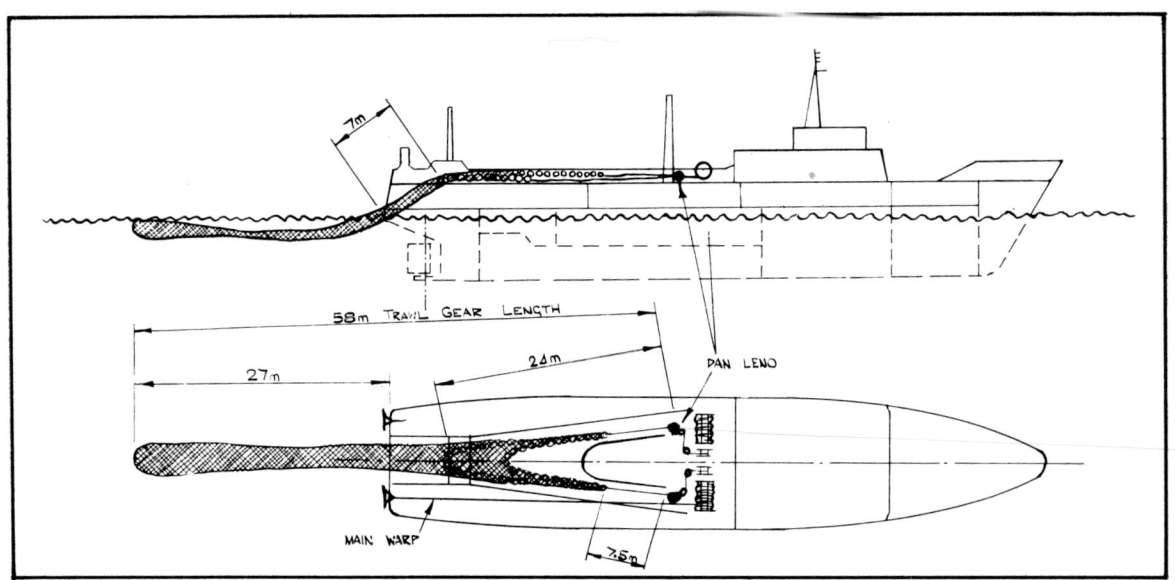

Fig. 5a. Granton trawl hauling sequence. First pull, bringing dan-leno bobbins to winch, using auxiliary barrels. Note that trawl doors are supported on main warps.

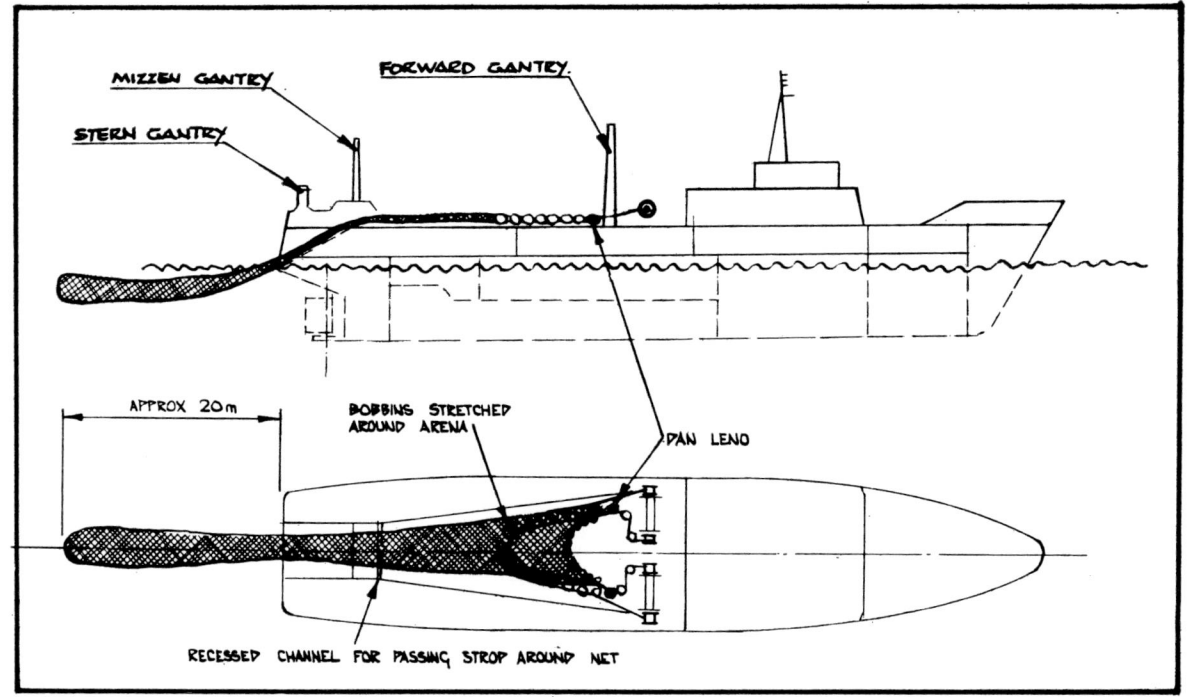

Fig. 5b. Second pull, bringing lead bobbin up to dan-leno bobbin, using whipping ends on main winch.

agreed by the various contributors to be approximately 23 metres.

Moller described the handling procedure for this deck length which allowed a trawl 50 m long from dan-leno to wing end, to be brought aboard in three pulls;

   i). The dan-leno bobbins to the winch.
  ii). The leading bobbins to the winch.
 iii). The pull from high up on the forward gantry drawing the netting forward until the cod-end is inboard of the ramp.

These operations are shown diagrammatically in Figs. 5a, 5b and 5d. He further stated that, to reduce the number of pulls to two, it would be necessary to site the winch further from the ramp head. This would eliminate the second pull. It would require a minimum deck length of 40 metres forward of the ramp head, a distance which is somewhat impracticable even with split winches positioned on side decks and the superstructure extending well aft into the central arena. This arrangement is shown diagrammatically in Fig. 6.

It had not, in 1963, been put into practice; deck arrangements were as shown in Fig. 7 for the 73 m long o.a. diesel-electric *Junella*. In practice, British vessels working the modified Granton trawl 58 metres from dan-leno to cod-end have found it necessary to introduce an extra pull (Fig. 5c) making four in all, to take in a bight of netting while leaving the cod-end still in the water at the foot of the ramp. The working deck length on these distant water vessels varies from 19.6 m in the *C. S. Forester* (56 m l.o.a.) and in the *Gavina* (46 m l.o.a.) to 26 m in the *Junella* (73 m l.o.a.) and in the *Ross Intrepid* (69 m l.o.a.) excluding the ramp slant length of approximately seven metres.

Even with the longest deck of 26 metres, the cod-end knot is still approximately 30 metres aft of the forward end of the hatch, when the footrope is around the arena. Only those vessels with the support sheave for the cod-end gilson wire mounted well forward of the ramp, have the facility to heave the cod-end sufficiently far forward in one pull. Most British vessels have gilson heave lengths (i.e. from the ramp head to the support sheave) of 18 to 25 m and only four have a 30 m length.

There are advantages in making a fourth pull. Firstly, the double mesh of the cod end and lengthener pieces of netting does not extend sufficiently far forward of the cod-end to provide a strong attachment point for the main gilson pull. Secondly, the first gilson pull is a single purchase and therefore rapid, compared with a multiple purchase frequently used when bringing the bag aboard.

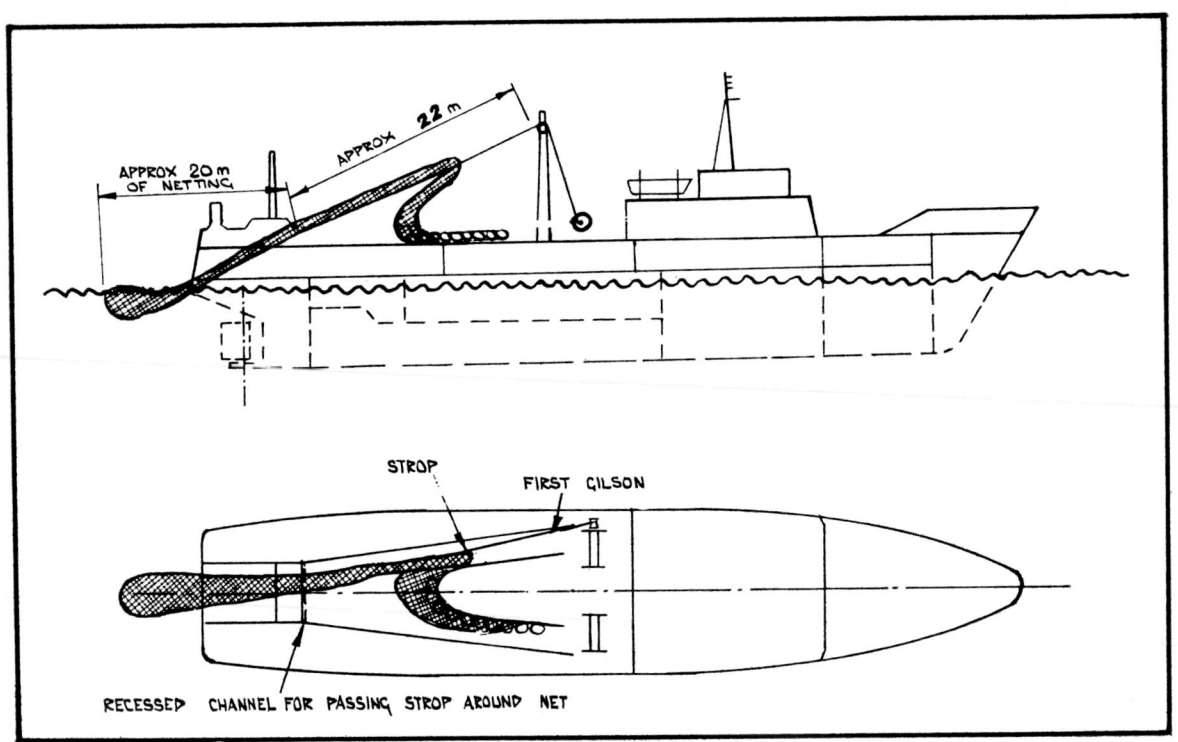

Fig. 5c. Third pull, taking in approximately 15 m. of netting to bring bag of fish to foot of ramp, using whipping end of auxiliary barrel.

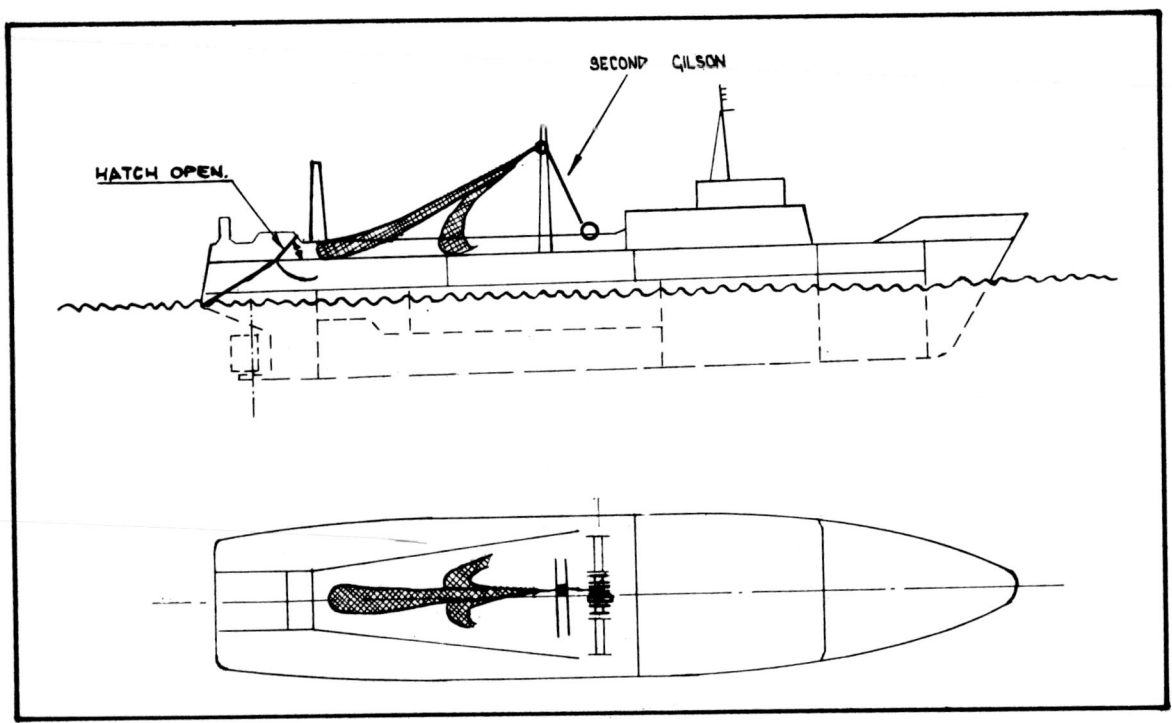

Fig. 5d. Granton trawl hauling sequence. Fourth pull, bringing cod-end aboard and forward of hatch, using fifth auxiliary barrel.

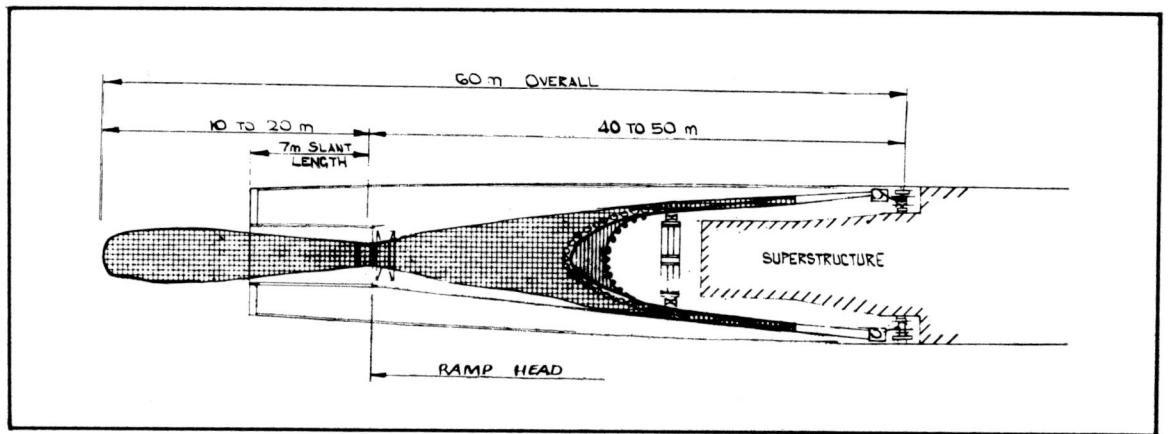

Fig. 6. One example of an extended trawl deck layout designed to reduce the number of pulls during hauling (by eliminating the second and possibly third pulls shown in Figs. 5).

Thirdly, this pull serves to dry up the catch to show whether a single or multiple purchase tackle is required for the cod-end. Certain vessels with the forward gantry positioned well aft of the winch giving a reduced gilson heave length have found it necessary to have three gilson pulls to bring the bag aboard.

Inner bulwarks or coamings (Fig. 7) are fitted the full length of the trawl deck, from the ramp head to the sides of the winch, to restrain the trawl and its heavy ground gear in the centre section of the deck. An arena (see Fig. 7), of similar construction to the inner bulwarks, is fitted aft of the winch; the length around its perimeter is slightly greater than the length of the ground rope so that the latter is secured in position once hauled to the winch.

3.2.2. *Winch arrangements*

Although it is possible to handle the trawl warps and net using a two-barrel winch and its whipping

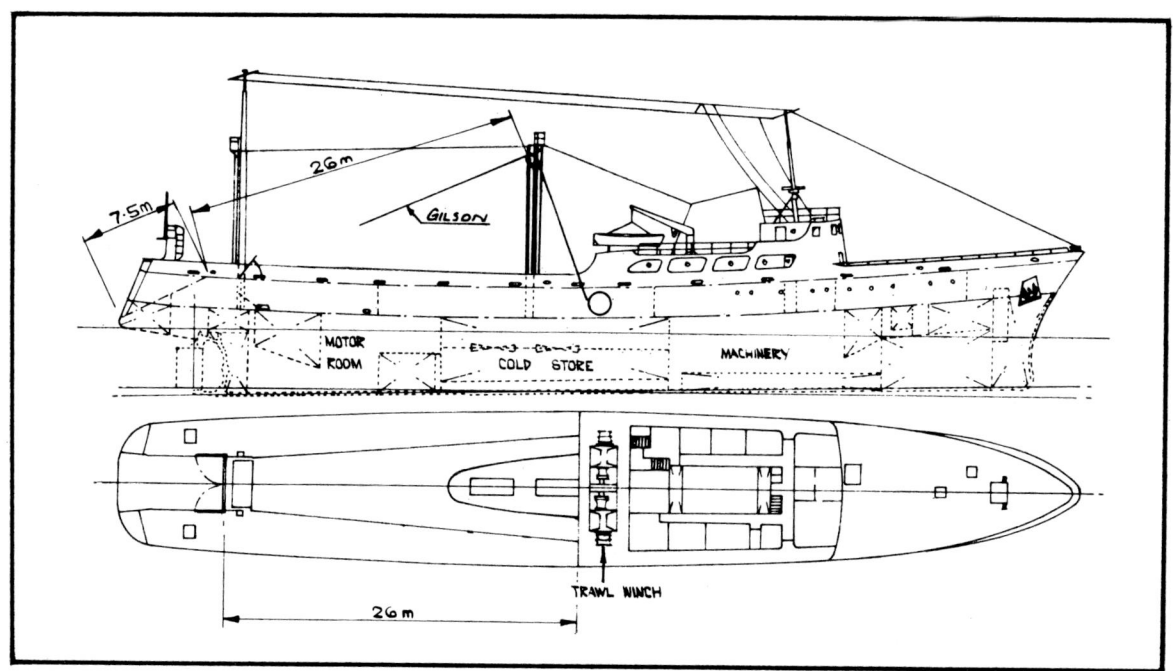

Fig. 7. General arrangement of the diesel-electric stern trawler "Junella", a 73 metres long overall vessel built in 1962.

ends, as is done in side trawlers, this results in a large number of loose wires which are potential hazards in operation. Most stern trawlers are therefore equipped with main winches having four, five or even six barrels.

The procedure generally adopted when hauling is to bring the trawl doors to the stern gantry and lock them in position there, by maintaining tension

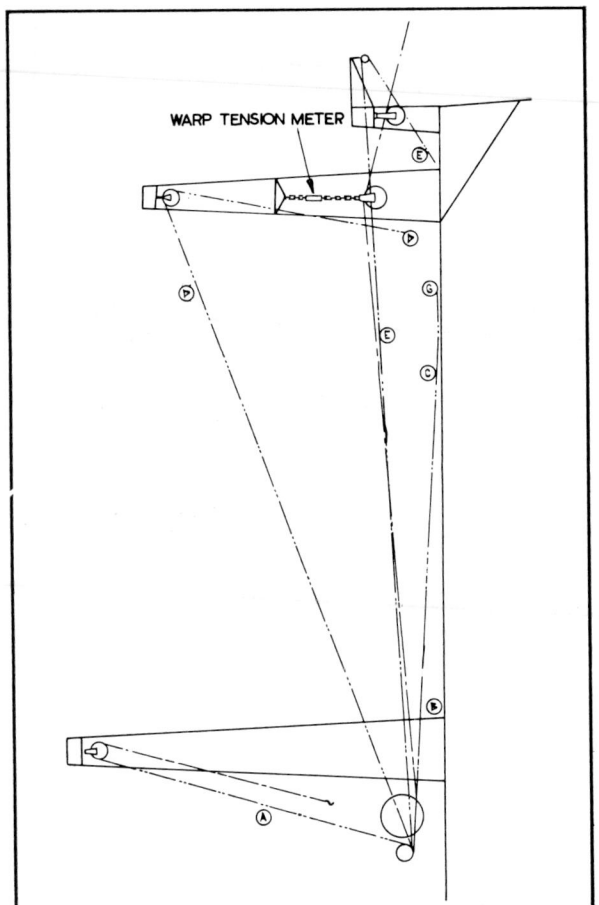
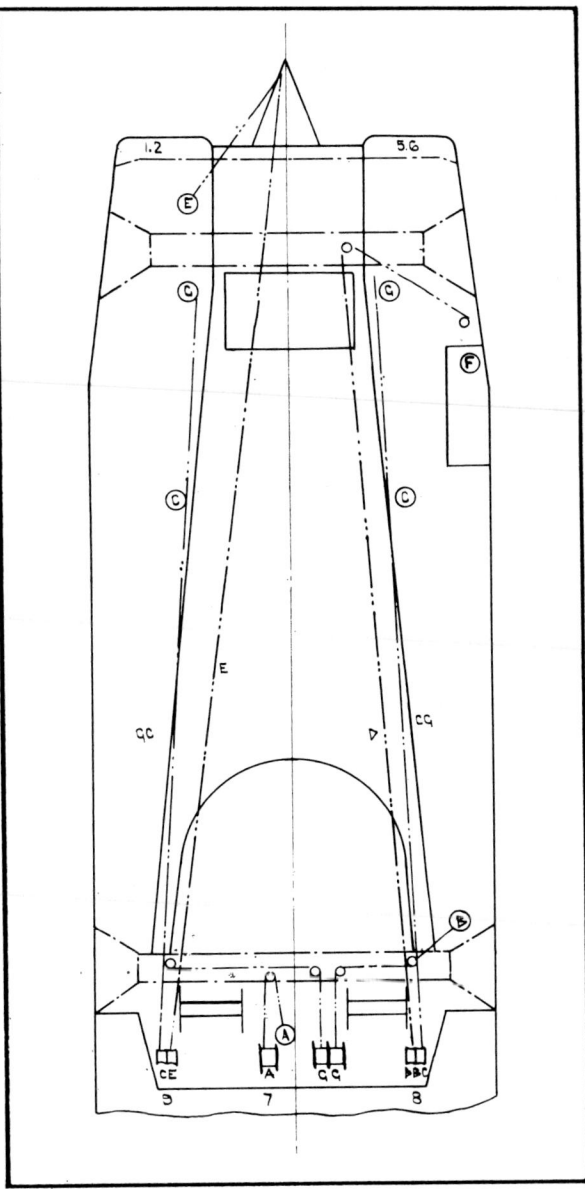

Fig. 8. Layout of auxiliary wires. Not to scale. Key. Numbers 1 to 9 indicate position of men at "doors up". Stowage position of equipment: A. Stowage of second gilson. B. First gilson. C. Inhauler wires. D. Bag lifting wire. E. Outhauler. F. Strops. G. Auxiliary messenger wires.

in the main warps. Messenger wires from two auxiliary barrels (Fig. 8) are then connected to the pennants and the doors disconnected from the cables by using backstrops sufficiently long to be disconnected at the ramp head. The cables are then wound on to the auxiliary barrels until the dan-leno bobbins are drawn up to the winch. In some stern trawlers, notably those built in Poland, the doors are chained off in the normal side trawler manner,

and the cables are hauled on to the main winch barrels.

While removing the need for the two auxiliary barrels already mentioned (or freeing them for other duties), this method requires special towing blocks (Fig. 9) which can be traversed in-board on the stern gantry to tip the warps, under the load imposed by the net, into the ramp. It also introduces a further operation in shooting the gear when the warps, again under load from the net streamed astern, have to be raised into the towing blocks by means of auxiliary wires. The ability to drop the warps into the ramp is advantageous when towing among ice, as by entering the water so close to the vessel, it is virtually impossible for ice floes to wedge under warps. If the floe provides support for the warp, and if it is dragged further and further astern of the vessel, this alters the warp length to depth ratio, to the detriment of fishing.

Once the dan-lenos are at the winch, in-haul wires are attached to the leading (or bunt end) bobbins which are then pulled in until the ground gear is stretched around the arena (Figs. 5 and 7). These auxiliary wires are usually operated from the whipping ends. During this operation, the headline has to be lifted over the coaming into the arena.

A strop is then put round the netting at the ramp head: a small channel recessed across the deck at this point facilitates this operation. The first gilson pull, from one whipping end over a block on the forward gantry, takes in about 20 metres of netting and brings the bag to the foot of the ramp, but leaves it still supported by the water.

The final pull which brings the cod-end up the ramp is a heavy one as the bag of fish is brought aboard in one lift. As it cannot safely be done from a whipping end, a fifth winch barrel is employed. This fixed wire is led upwards from the winch through a block hung from the forward gantry before being attached to the cod-end becket either directly for small catches, or through a multiple purchase block for larger bags.

In some more recently built vessels, the addition of a sixth barrel to the main winch allows both gilson pulls to be provided by fixed wires. This arrangement has the merit of confining the use of the whipping ends to heaving the in-haul wires and avoids confusion over choice of loose wires as only one wire is worked from each whipping end.

To eliminate this remaining whipping end operation, requires the provision of two additional barrels. This has been achieved on the *Othello* class British freezer stern trawler (Fig. 10) by installing two small auxiliary winches, on either side of the main winch. (By working a shorter net, these vessels require only one gilson pull, and consequently the main winch has only five barrels.)

Eight winch barrels are used aboard the Aberdeen wet fish stern trawler *Ben Lui* (50 m.o.a.). The main winch, situated on the deck above the trawl deck, has four barrels, while two, two-barrel winches are positioned further forward on the trawl deck. These smaller winches are used 1) to haul the

Fig. 9. Towing blocks at stern and on quarter, Polish-style tipping blocks at stern.

cables, and 2) to haul the bobbins to the arena. The 3rd and 4th barrels on the main winch are used for the two gilson pulls.

Twin (port and starboard) outhaul winches are frequently fitted aft of the mizzen gantry. Each winch has one barrel and one whipping end. The wires from the barrels are used to outhaul the trawl, the cod-end outhaul wire being lead through the A-frame derrick mounted on the stern gantry and the ground gear wire being led through a block on the stern gantry above the ramp. These winches are conveniently situated for spilling the fish down the chute to the fish processing deck: a wire is lead from the whipping end on one winch through a block on the mizzen gantry. In addition to the fishing operations, these winches are also used in mooring operations.

In vessels not provided with separate outhaul winches, the two outhaul pulls, and the spilling of the cod-end, can be made using the whipping ends on the main winch. With a five-barrel winch, this results in the whipping ends being used for five

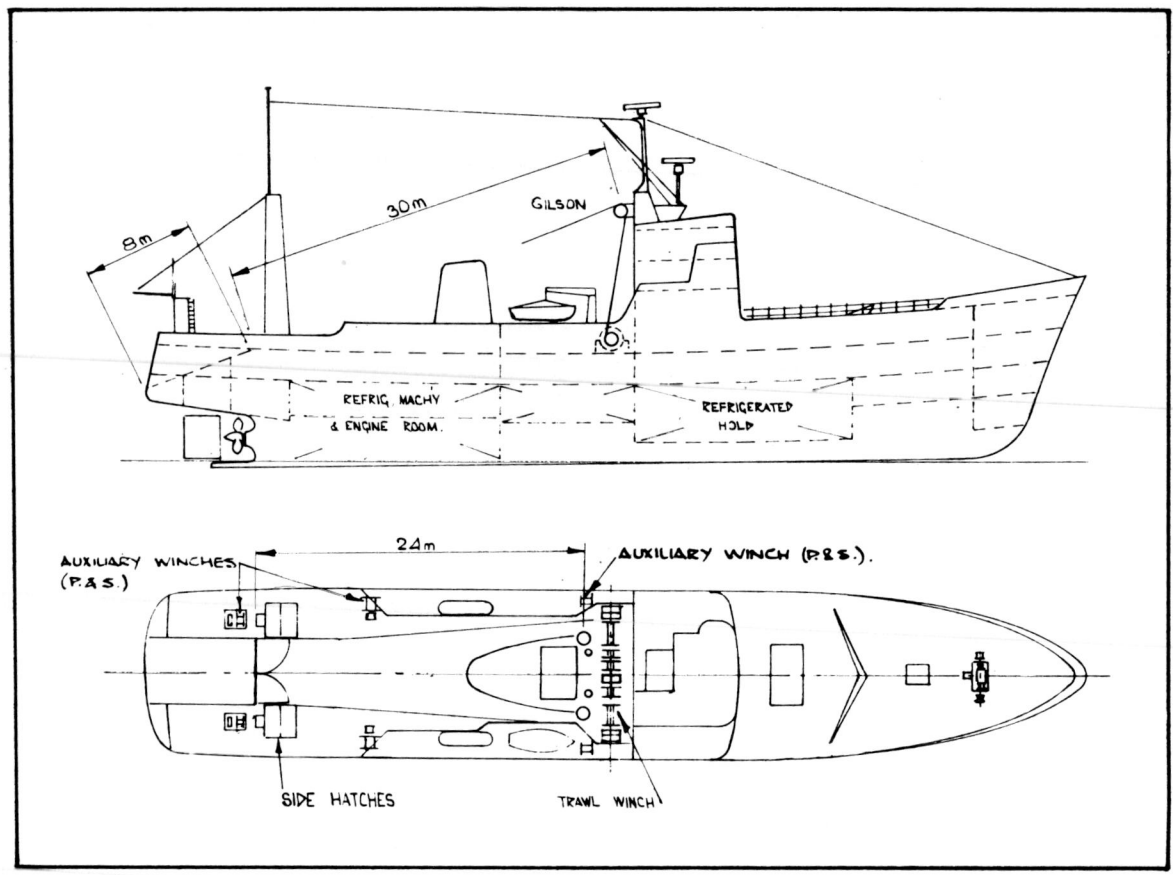

Fig. 10. General arrangement of the 69 metres long overall stern trawler "Orsino".

different wires, which can lead to mistakes in operation.

The *Ben Lui*, with her eight hauling barrels, does not have additional outhaul winches. Two wires, permanently run and supported by a series of rollers above head height and along the side of the vessel, are clipped to the messenger wires from the barrels also used for pulling the bobbins around the arena.

Pelagic trawls are considerably longer than demersal trawls (Figs. 1, 2 and 3) and consequently require several pulls of netting before the cod-end is reached. The procedure developed by the Germans (Ref. 1), is to work two wires alternately, one from each whipping end. As a bight of netting is being hauled by one wire, the second wire is being walked aft and hooked in so that the haul can proceed almost without interruption. When hauling this type of trawl, with its large meshes, it is essential that all surfaces (deck, inner bulwark and arena) are completely free from obstructions, even as small as bolt heads, to prevent meshes snagging. The forward corner edges of the recessed hatch cover, unless well-rounded, are prone to catching the meshes which occasionally fall into the narrow recess around the hatch.

3.2.3. Gantry Design

In earlier paragraphs reference has been made to three different gantries – the stern, mizzen and forward gantries (Fig. 5).

The stern gantry is positioned fully aft and over the ramp. The towing blocks are hung from it and it also serves as the 'gallows' structure for handling the trawl doors. With the Polish style of towing block (Fig. 9), this gantry is used to support the rails along which these blocks are traversed inboard, to position them over the ramp, before tipping out the warps. The outhaul bracket, which provides a purchase point aft of the foot of the ramp, is supported from this gantry.

When hauling the cod-end up the ramp, which has an angle of approximately 27° from the horizontal, it is desirable to have the pulling wire parallel to the ramp. This wire, which is attached to an auxiliary barrel, must have sufficient length to bring the cod-end from fully in the water to just forward of the hatch leading to the processing deck, a distance of around 30 metres. Thus the cod-end gilson wires are led through a high point well forward on the working deck, usually supplied by a forward gantry positioned slightly aft of the main winch.

In one class of vessel, the *Othello* class (Fig. 10) the need for this gantry is removed by providing a very stiff superstructure with the lifting block mounted centrally on the aft side of the bridge. One disadvantage of the arrangement is that, because of the stiffening in way of the block, it is not possible to provide the bridge with the central aft-facing window favoured by many companies. In fact this fault was corrected when the *Othello* was damaged by fire. During repairs and reconstruction, the gilson block was lowered to bridge deck level, allowing good aft vision from that deck to be incorporated: the angle of the gilson pulled was reduced, but the ramp-head roller provided a satisfactory fairlead. With the forward gantry just aft of the main winch, the heave length on the gilson wire is 22 to 25 metres. In the *Othello* class this length is increased to 30 metres. A few vessels, however, have this gantry relatively far aft reducing the heave length to less than 20 metres, which in one or two extreme cases results in a third gilson pull being required for the Granton trawl (i.e. five pulls in all).

The mizzen gantry is primarily required to support the wire used for spilling the cod-end into the hatch. With the fish hatch positioned centrally forward of the ramp head, the spilling action is literally so, the fish being poured down the chute as the cod-end is raised slowly off the deck. A pair of side-mounted hatches, outboard of the inner bulwarks, have the advantage, in fish processing, of keeping consecutive catches separate by working the hatches alternately. As in practice it proved essential to have continuous inner bulwarks from the ramp head forward, this arrangement necessitates lifting the cod-end bodily over the inner bulwark. This pull is taken either from an auxiliary winch aft, or, if the catch is heavy, from the main-winch's fifth barrel, through the gilson tackle, which presents the crew with a tricky operation, especially when the vessel is rolling, and extends the cod-end handling time. The mizzen gantry also serves as a convenient lifting point for handling trawl doors up and down the ramp, when they have to be changed.

With the introduction, in 1964, of warp tension meters (Ref. 3), which are nowadays regarded as standard equipment in UK stern trawlers, the mizzen gantry was conveniently positioned to support the additional hanging block in each warp run (Fig. 8). Loadcells inserted in the chain length supporting these blocks measure the tension in the warps by deflecting the warp run by a small amount, a mere 12°, which has no noticeable effect on warp wear. In addition to the valuable information presented by the meters to the skipper about the behaviour of his trawl gear, this alteration to the warp run has the merit of lifting the warp above head height over the major part of the deck, especially the region around the ramp head and stern gantry where most of the deck handling operations take place.

Up to 1969, UK stern trawlers were designed to handle only demersal trawls based mainly on the Granton. The success of the Germans (Ref. 1), the French and the Norwegians in catching cod in pelagic trawls at certain times of the year has led to many trawlers being equipped to fish with both types of trawl. As the skipper cannot with certainty decide which trawl to rig before reaching the grounds, he is at times of necessity forced to change both nets and doors with the attendant loss in fishing time. This loss is considerable if the doors have to be changed over by bringing the first set inboard (up the ramp) and then lowering away the second set and hoisting them into position on the stern gantry.

Existing vessels are, therefore, being adapted by fitting a second pair of towing blocks, hung on the quarters from a beam welded between the mizzen and stern gantries (Fig. 11). With two sets of doors hung ready, there is little time lost in transferring the warps if the pelagic gear is to be towed from the quarters. Changing the nets over is discussed in Section 5, Multiple Gear Handling.

If it is desired to retain the normal warp run, (towing from the stern blocks) which allows the conventional warp tension meter hanging blocks to be kept in use, the main warps have to be passed outboard of the stern gantry before being coupled to the pelagic doors. In either case before the pelagic gear is shot, auxiliary wires are used to heave the Granton doors either round to the quarters, or up on to the extension 'gallows' built on top of the stern gantry (Fig. 9).

Moveable gantries, such as the Unigan, have been tried out, with mixed success, in some smaller stern trawlers. To the author's knowledge none has been fitted to deepsea vessels, which with the handling methods previously described, do not

Fig. 11. Towing a Granton trawl through stern blocks, pelagic doors hung ready.

require a tiltable stern gantry for lifting the catch forward and aboard.

4. IMPROVED NET HANDLING

4.1. *Extensions to existing practice*

For a demersal trawl handled in the general manner described in Para 3.2., improvements in method are confined, for those vessels not already doing so, to drum winding all the wires. This can require up to twelve barrels:

Wire	Number of Barrels
Main Warps	2
Cables	2
Bobbin inhaul	2
Gilsons	2
Cod-end emptying	1
Cod-end outhaul	1
Bobbin outhaul	1 or 2
	12

This number can be reduced by two, if the cables are taken on to the main barrels, in side trawler fashion. To achieve this, the towing blocks must be of the open type and arranged to be traversed inboard to drop the warps into the ramp, once the doors are hung off. When shooting, a pull is required to lift each warp back into the hanging block, this usually being taken from the whipping end on the auxiliary winches aft. If fixed wires are to be used, the number of barrels required returns to 12, but with a much lighter pull and travel required.

Provision of permanently run wires, as in the *Ben Lui* (see Para 3.2.2.), can allow the two outhaul wires to be operated from the same barrels as the bobbin inhaul. It is generally accepted that the degree of control required in spilling the fish from the cod-end (i.e. the heave, pause, slack-back sequence) is too fine for the winch drives currently employed. Thus it is better to continue to use a whipping end, unless a more sophisticated speed and direction control, incorporating braking and holding, is fitted.

In the least mechanised of the arrangements described above, at least eight men are required to handle the trawl. With the hauling and shooting routines performed entirely by drum-wound wires, there is no need for the two deckhands who formerly worked the whipping ends. Providing these men are not required to operate the new auxiliary winches, the deck crew can be reduced to six men. Further reductions are not possible without new trawl door handling methods: two men are required to handle each door, one man controls the winch and the mate is in charge of the operations.

Increased fishing time can be gained if the handling of the trawl gear can be made more rapid. With so many stern trawlers now in operation, handling procedures are very slick and the crews highly skilled in performing them. Unproductive fishing time is from knock-out to all-square (that is, it includes hauling and shooting the warps as well as the on-board trawl-gear handling times). The efficiency of the net handling operations, therefore, can only be assessed by taking the time from doors-up to doors-away (less the time to spill the fish from the cod-end which is governed more by the quantity of fish, and the conditions on the processing deck, than by the efficiency of the deck operations).

With a Granton trawl this on-board handling time (see Para 3.1.) varies from a minimum of about nine minutes up to approximately 20 minutes for normal hauls with an average of 12 to 13 minutes. The time delays in handling the cod-end, and repairing damage, are nearly as great, being respectively approximately eight minutes and 16 minutes on average. (The latter depends considerably on the grounds being fished.) Thus the total average time from doors-up to doors away for a Granton trawl is 36 minutes, which is three times the minimum time of 11 minutes for a slick, trouble free handling sequence.

In discussing gear handling times, it is often said that a minute is neither here nor there, and if one views these operations on only a few occasions one can readily accept this statement. However, it is worth while examining the facts to see what can be gained if, for example, each and every on-board handling time could be reduced by just one minute. Taking an average of six hauls a day, each haul losing 36 minutes on-deck handling time plus 15 minutes for hauling and shooting the warps means that the trawl is fishing for 18 hours and 54 minutes a day (24 hours less 6 × 51 minutes). Thus the gain in fishing time $= \dfrac{6 \times 1 \times 100}{18.9 \times 60} = 0.53$ per cent. (If an average of 8 hauls a day were made the increase would become 0.77 per cent).

The only additional expenses in gaining this bonus are the equivalent increases in gear costs and in fuel consumption while towing. Taking £300,000 as a round figure yearly grossing for a British distant water stern trawler, then the economics shown in Table 8 indicate a clear margin of profit of over £1,000 for each minute saved, in the conditions of the North Atlantic cod fishery prosecuted by the British, in 1970.

TABLE 8 Increased Profit for a Reduction of One Minute in On-Board Trawl Handling Time (Granton Trawl)		
Vessel annual gross		£300 000
Increase in annual gross 0.53%		£1590
Less, increase in gear costs	£220	
increase in fuel costs	160	
increase in maintenance	110	
		490
Hence nett annual increase		£1100

Clearly it is desirable to reduce on-board handling times and in an average clear-gear handling time of 12 to 13 minutes, there still appears to be room for improvement: the longer delays resulting from cod-end handling and net repairing offer greater potential for reduction which would require a radical change in approach to achieve, see Section 5. With the handling procedure as described in Section 3 already involving high line-hauling speeds, the scope for improvement is limited to 1) eliminating one of the two gilson pulls and, 2) eliminating the separate pull which brings the bunt-end bobbins up to the dan-leno bobbins.

Both these possibilities would require the trawl deck to be lengthened, the former by about five metres and the latter by nearly 20 metres: potential time savings are of the order of one minute and half-a-minute respectively. To increase the length of the trawl deck it may be necessary to increase the length of the ship; or, as indicated in Para 3.2.1., the superstructure could be brought aft into an elongated area (Fig. 6), or a passage made through the superstructure as done in the case of the *Ross Fame* (40 m l.o.a.), or the superstructure could be offset as in the French trawler *Pierre Pleven* (78 m l.o.a.). To lengthen the ship, unless the extra length can be put to good use by increasing the fishroom volume (Ref. 5), is to incur a cost penalty of around £3,000 per metre of length. Thus, the maximum gain of approximately £1,500 a year has set against it the additional depreciation resulting from the enlarged ship, or the additional cost of other methods of achieving a longer trawl deck. Depreciating over 16 years, a probable length extension of six metres

Fig. 12. A Granton trawl, with heavy ground gear, wound onto a net drum.

gives an annual charge of £1,250, which makes this option of little commercial attraction.

Greater deck length would of course be beneficial in handling a pelagic trawl, but due to inadequate data presently available for cod fishing it is not possible to quantify the benefits with meaningful accuracy. However, in the author's opinion at least, a superior solution for handling either a demersal or a pelagic trawl is to install a net drum.

4.2. *Net Drum for winding on demersal or pelagic trawls*

Mechanisation of handling trawl nets, including those rigged with heavy bobbin ground gear, has been achieved by winding on to a large diameter drum. That this method works (see Fig. 12), which to the uninitiated generally seems a doubtful proposition, was first proved in the small (25 m) stern trawlers on the west coast of Canada (Ref. 6). This method was extended to larger vessels, to larger trawls and to heavier ground gears by both the Canadian Fisheries Service and the British White Fish Authority.

The net drum is essentially a very large winch barrel. To minimise stretching or bending components of the ground gear the core diameter is large; the length and flange diameter are then chosen to suit:

    i) the volume of netting to be handled,
    ii) the torque capability of the most suitable drive motor,
    iii) the space available to accommodate the bed plate,
    iv) the visibility from the winchman's position.

Some provision has to be made at the outer ends of the core to restrain the cables when wound on, so that the wing ends are kept well apart. This can be provided by:

    i) stepping the core to provide recesses,
    ii) fitting inner flanges,
    iii) providing guide-on-gear.

The method of working with a net drum is as follows. Once the trawl doors are up and hung off in the normal manner, messenger wires from the net drum are attached to the independent wires. The net drum is then set to haul until the Kelly's eyes reach the head of the ramp when the drum is stopped and the long backstrops are disconnected from the cables. The operations up to this point are identical to those normally carried out in transferring the cables to the auxiliary barrels of the main winch (see Para 3.2.2.). The messenger wires and cables are then wound on to the outer sections of the drum, to keep the wing ends as widely spaced as possible when they reach the net drum. Hauling continues until the bunt end bobbins are on the drum.

Unless the drum is mounted well forward, two gilson pulls are necessary to bring the cod-end aboard in the conventional manner. With the heavy ground gear on distant water nets, it is inadvisable to take the centre of the footrope over the top of the drum, as this bight may fall clear and require lifting, by another wire, back over the drum when outhauling. There is no problem in taking the bobbin groundgear of smaller trawls or the lighter ground rope of pelagic trawls fully on to the drum. Small catches can be hauled by the net drum, but larger catches would strain netting when passing over the ramp head and put undue compression on the volume of netting already wound on to the drum.

Used in this manner for demersal trawls, the net drum combines the following standard operations:

    i) the hauling of the cables, bringing the danlenos to the main winch,
    ii) hauling the bunt end bobbins to the danleno bobbins,

and also, but only if the net drum is mounted sufficiently far forward,

    iii) the first gilson pull, bringing the cod-end to the foot of the ramp.

It thus effectively replaces for distant water vessels four (or five) of the eight winch barrels required for conventional hauling (see Para 4.1.), and reduces the requirement on the main winch to the two warp barrels and two (or possibly one) gilson barrels.

For a pelagic trawl, the net drum combines all the operations from the time the cables are disconnected from the doors till the cod-end is at the foot of the ramp. Thus the number of winch barrels required is reduced to the two main warp barrels, plus the gilson barrels: two of the latter are required to bring aboard large catches.

Retaining the auxiliary barrels on the main winch has a distinct advantage when it is necessary to change cables. Note that if the maximum cable length used is stored on the net drum, and links fitted at the shorter length positions, it is only necessary to change the cables when damaged. The replacement cables are wound on to the auxiliary barrels (attached to messenger wires as at present) and the trawl hauled off the drum until the dan-lenos are accessible.

The shooting procedure is very similar to the conventional method, as two outhaul pulls are necessary with the drum being reversed under power. Once the bobbins are on the ramp the procedure is identical, with the net drum acting as the pair of auxiliary barrels on which the cables are wound.

If a pelagic net is being drum wound, the heavy weights attached to the lower tow legs have to be disconnected when they clear the ramp in hauling. Both this operation and the re-attachment when shooting require the drum to be halted for the same length of time as the winch in conventional handling. The drum has also to be stopped for removal and re-attachment of the headline transducer for the telemetry link essential for working this type of net efficiently: lashing a locating frame to the headline speeds up these operations.

4.2.1. *Some experiences with net drums*

The White Fish Authority has designed and tested net drums aboard the following vessels:

1. *Constellation*, a 20m stern trawler in 1966 (Fig. 13).
2. *Ross Daring*, a 30m stern trawler in 1967 (Fig. 14).
3. *Ross Kelvin*, a 50m side trawler in 1968 (Fig. 15).
4. *St. Adrian*, a 15m stern trawler in 1970 (Fig. 16).
5. *Orsino*, a 68m stern trawler in 1971 (Fig. 17).

The *Constellation* trial was a very simple one, merely repeating the Canadian west coast experience (Ref. 6), using a Lowestoft No. 2 trawl rigged with 22 × 200 mm floats and 12 × 350 mm rubber rollers. The net drum itself was driven by a rope drive from the main winch and the equipment, which was somewhat too crude, was removed after a month's trial. It proved however that time savings were possible (see Table 9), and that the work load was reduced both in terms of physical effort and number of crew (five to three men).

The *Ross Daring* trial lasted a year (until the vessel was sold abroad) using a hydraulically driven drum controlled by the skipper from the bridge. The net used was a North Sea trawl rigged with 34 × 200 mm floats, 6 × 300 mm bobbins and 11 × 460 mm bobbins.

As with the *Constellation*, time (see Table 9) and labour savings were possible. A 90 metre long herring trawl was also tried out. Although found to be slightly too bulky for the volume available, drum hauling was seen to be extremely useful with nets of this length.

TABLE 9 On Board Gear Handling Times for Demersal Trawl With and Without a Net Drum

Vessel	Constellation (20m)	Ross Daring (30m)	Ross Kelvin (50m)	St, Adrian (15m)
Without drum (minutes)	19.0	17.0	24.0	+
With drum (minutes)	14.5	11.0	21.0	8.3 (i) 4.6 (ii)
Time saving	4.5	6.0	3.0	+

+ This vessel has never worked without the net drum
 (i) Lowestoft C3 trawl
 ii) Stuart 480 trawl

In the *Ross Kelvin* the net drum system, as explained in the introductory Section 1, was not a success because of the problems of working in a side trawler. This trial is only included in this chapter as it provided the full design data for hauling and handling the Granton trawl (Fig. 1), and proved the hydraulic drive system.

Two different trawls were used aboard the *St. Adrian*:

i) Lowestoft C.3 trawl, 22 m headline with 15 × 180 mm floats and groundrope of 90 mm rubber discs and 50 m of chain.
ii) Stuart 480 bottom trawl, 42 m headline, 7 × 200 mm floats, 20 × 125 mm floats, and 6 × 360 mm bobbins.

drum was to be retained as a permanent feature aboard his vessel.

In the *Orsino* (an *Othello*-class trawler), the net drum was installed in May 1971 primarily for handling the larger pelagic trawl (the 1600 × 20 cm mesh Engel trawl). Although insufficient experience had been gained at the time of writing this chapter, certain preliminary results from the first voyage using the drum were sufficiently encouraging to warrant inclusion here.

A glance at Figs. 13 to 17 shows the development stages that the drum concept has undergone. Firstly in the *Constellation* a plain core was used with no provision to separate the cables. Then for the two *Ross* vessels large diameter intermediate flanges were fitted, which necessitated a break in the hauling sequence while the wires were transferred to the central portion through radial slots. This undesirable break was eliminated for the *St. Adrian* and the *Orsino* installations either by fitting small inner flanges, or by stepping the shaft, to provide sufficient volume to store the cables. Commercial usage has shown that these methods are considerably superior to large inner flanges.

In the small Canadian trawlers (Ref. 6) and in the *Constellation*, the net drum was mounted close to the transom stern and the net was hauled over the top of the drum. This hauling procedure was repeated in the *Ross* vessels, although the drums were mounted eight metres inboard. In *St. Adrian*, by coincidence also with an eight metre length of deck between drum and transom, the direction of winding was reversed, the net being taken underneath the barrel: this method resulted in a smoother haul and neater, tighter winding on, especially when bobbins were used. The *Orsino* net drum mounted 15 m forward of the ramp head was designed to haul in either direction, and the arena was suitably modified (Fig. 7), to provide clear access from the ramp to the drum.

The considerable care taken in designing the *St. Adrian*'s deck layout (Fig. 16) to provide this clear access has been proved well worthwhile in commercial service. It included off-setting the hatch to the fishroom, a most unusual feature for fishing vessels, where designers virtually invariably specify centre line hatches: in an inshore vessel, the offset hatch does not introduce the problems of discharging the cod-end mentioned in Para 3.2.3. for distant water vessels processing below decks.

The actual net hauling worked very well on all installations and once sharp projections had been eliminated from the dan-lenos, etc., no net damage was caused by the drum operations even when very

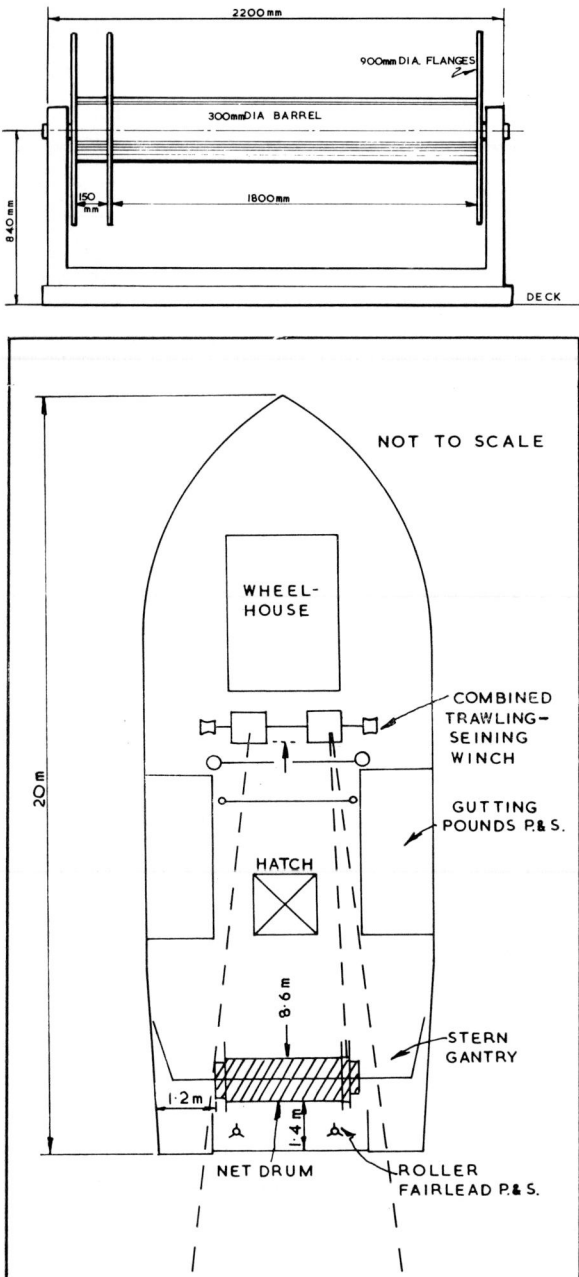

Fig. 13. Net drum (top) and its installation (bottom) aboard the 20 metres long small stern trawler "Constellation".

This vessel differed from all the others by being designed and built with the net drum and was therefore free from the conversion problems encountered in varying degrees on the other installations. Although installed for trials purposes, the skipper/owner of the *St. Adrian* soon decided that the net

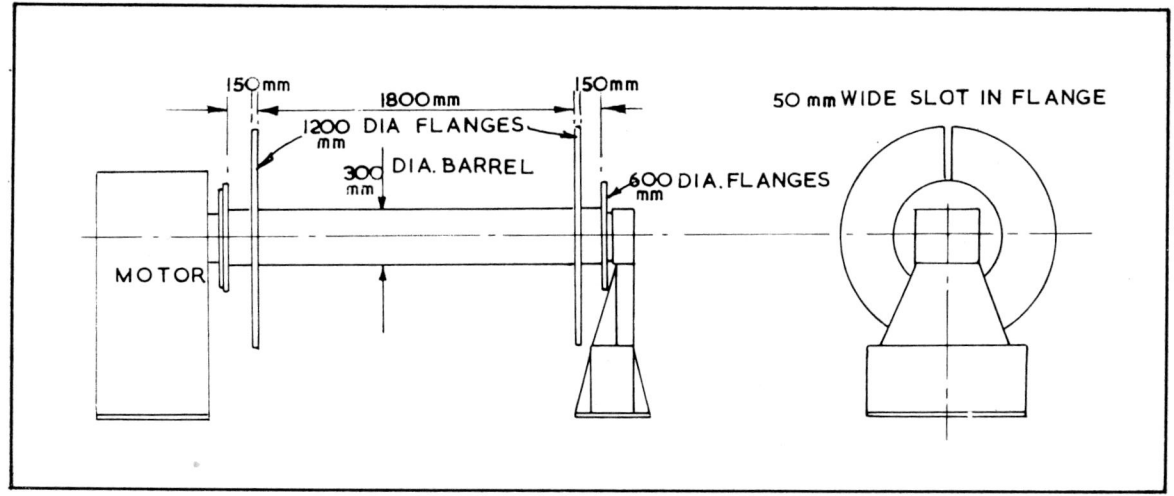

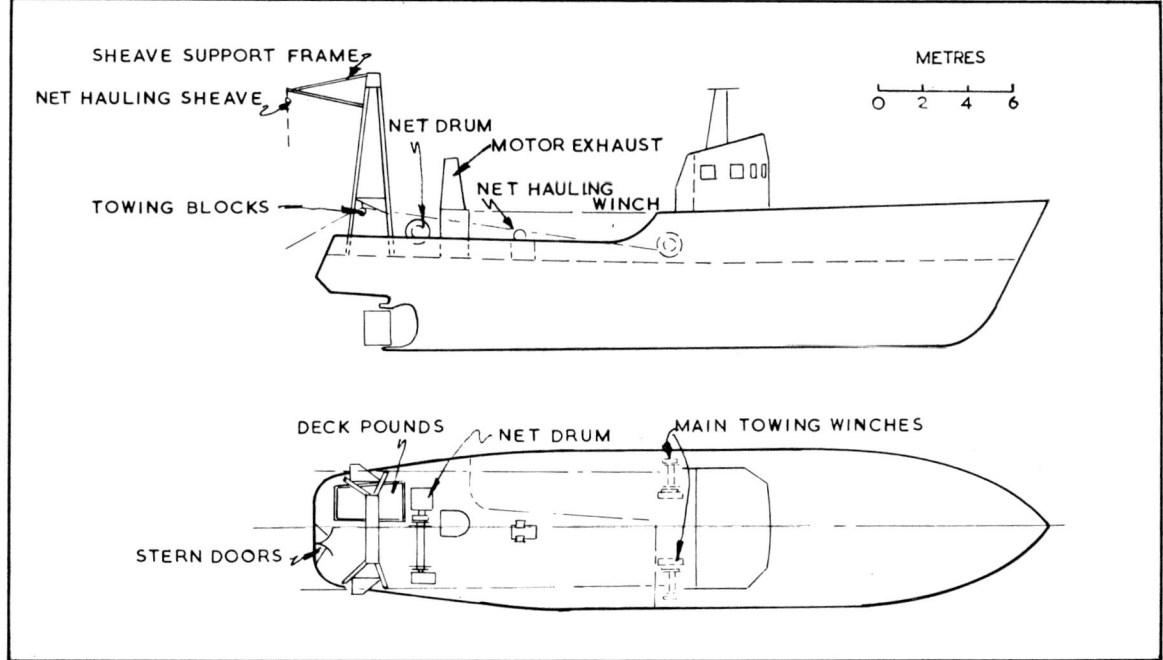

Fig. 14. Net drum (top) and its installation (bottom) aboard the 30 metres long overall stern trawler "Ross Daring".

large bobbins were being used. For pelagic trawls, floats have to be sheathed in groups in smaller mesh netting like sausages, to prevent their snagging the large meshes round the mouth of the net.

When the net is damaged, this can be seen reasonably well during hauling and certainly can be seen during the slower paying out operation. Minor damage can be repaired by paying away, or hauling aft, sufficient netting to expose the damaged section(s). In this context, hauling over the top of the drum has the advantage of partially raising the netting above the deck, which eases net mending.

If the trawl is badly damaged, or has to be replaced, it is quicker to shoot the spare net in more or less the conventional manner and then to remove the damaged one from the drum, before the next haul is started.

It has been found advisable to have the net drum mounted sufficiently far from the stern to be properly under the winchman's eye and control. A

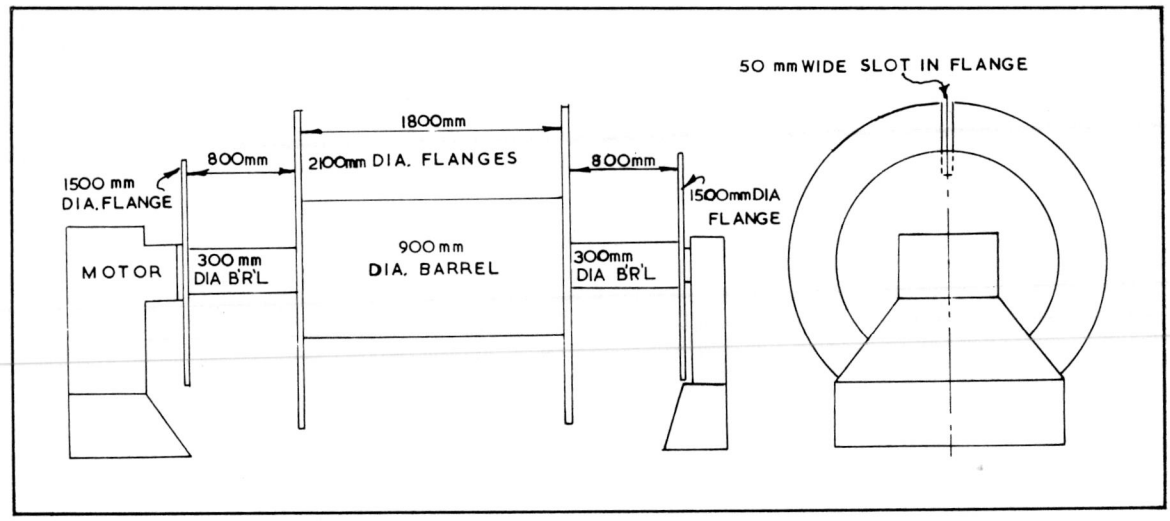

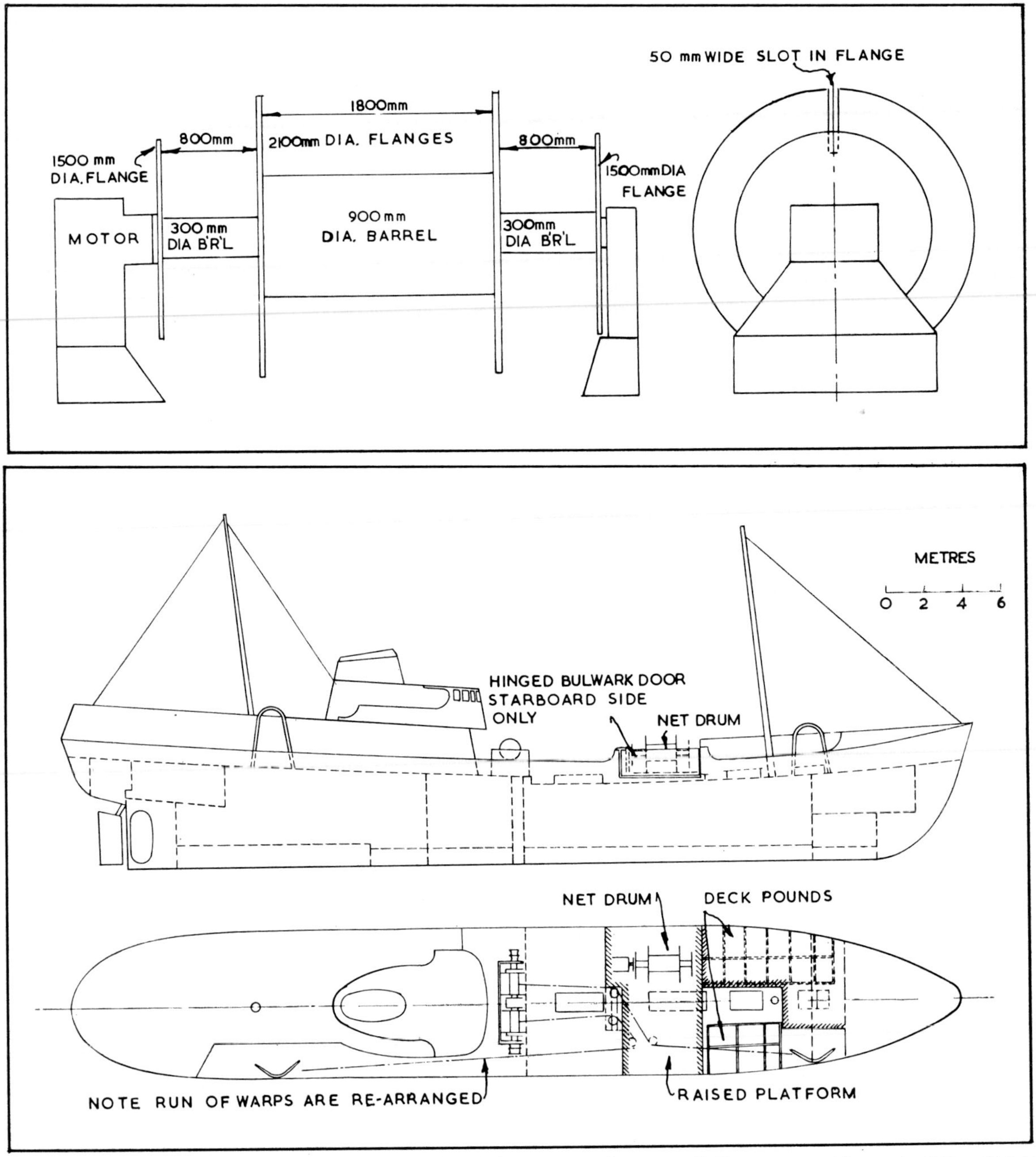

Fig. 15. Net drum (*top*) and its installation (*bottom*) aboard the 50 metres long overall distant water side trawler "*Ross Kelvin*".

minimum clear length of deck of six metres is advisable, to provide access for the crew when mending: the trawl is wound off and either hoisted aloft or streamed astern until the damaged panel is exposed. Mounting the drum near to the stern may appear to sacrifice this facility, but the netting can be lifted (by gantry pull) forward of the drum where it is more accessible for repair. Sited aft, the drum would, in large vessels, obstruct the working deck and hinder the discharge of large catches, which must be hauled up the ramp and along the deck until the cod-end knot is forward of the hatch to the processing deck.

In smaller, single-deck vessels without a ramp,

larger catches are lifted over the stern, or sometimes the side, in a series of lifts, and put into deck pounds aft of the drum. This layout leaves the large centre area of the deck clear for fish processing and mending the nets. Shooting the net is simpler as the bobbins can be dropped overboard directly without outhaul. Inspection of the net is more difficult as it is in view for a much shorter period during hauling and shooting, than when the drum is mounted further from the stern.

When the gear fouls, the vessel's ability to clear it is considerably improved by the installation of a net drum, and can reduce delays by as much as half-an-hour. This was demonstrated on all the installations.

As far as the crew are concerned, hard physical effort is eliminated and their safety enhanced by the reduction in the number of operations they have to perform. Further, the number of men required to haul the net is reduced by two for all sizes of stern trawler. Whether or not this potential reduction in deck crew can be realised depends on the size of the trawl doors and the access between the port and starboard towing blocks.

In the two inshore vessels (the *Constellation* and the *St. Adrian*) each door could be handled by one man and thus the full trawl gear could be shot and hauled by two men on deck, plus the winchman and skipper (in the *St. Adrian* the winch and net drum controls sited in the wheelhouse allowed the skipper to undertake the winchman's duties). The doors in the *Ross Daring* were larger and required two men to work on each door. As there was reasonable access between the towing blocks, the same two men could handle the doors in series thus allowing two men on deck, plus the skipper at the wheelhouse winch controls, to work the trawl. With the serial handling of the doors there is obviously a time penalty, but against this has to be set the saving of two men from a former total of five or six (see also Section 8).

In the *Orsino*, as in all distant water vessels, the time men take to move from one towing block to the other, because of having to move forward round the ramp, makes it unattractive to reduce the deck crew by handling doors serially. This highlights the need to develop an improved method of handling the trawl doors to allow one-man operation of each (see Section 8).

During the preliminary trials in the *Orsino*, the net drum showed no noticeable improvement in time when handling the Granton trawl. This situation may improve with practice, but because in the *Orsino* (see Para 3.2.2) all gear-handling wires are drum wound, the time savings are likely to be marginal. However, large savings in time and effort were apparent when handling the pelagic trawl, and in changing from Granton to pelagic or vice versa. Typical times for the *Orsino* with drum (on first voyage) and for the (63 m) German vessel *Jochen Homann*, handling the gear in the conventional manner, are given in Table 10.

TABLE 10 Pelagic Trawl Handling Times, With and Without Net Drum		
Doors up to doors away (excluding cod-end handling)	*Orsino* With pelagic net on drum (minutes)	*Jochen Homann* Without net drum (minutes)
Pelagic up, pelagic away	25 to 30*	25 to 35
Pelagic up, demersal away	36	55
Demersal up, pelagic away	45*	—
* With the pelagic net shot over the top of the Granton, some time was lost in clearing snags, and in stowing Granton neatly around arena. These times should be improved on subsequent voyages, when the Granton trawl is to be covered with a heavy plastic shroud when stowed.		

Once the doors were disconnected, three men (including the winchman), could haul the entire net on the drum. The removal of the physical effort and of the need to run across the deck with several wires were welcomed by the crew.

With the exception of the *St. Adrian* installation, the net drums previously referred to are of single piece construction. The two-piece, or split drum, with both halves driven separately, offers additional operational benefits. With a single piece drum, it is essential that the skipper maintains the vessel on the course which streams the net square to the drum during hauling, otherwise the cables and netting do not wind on evenly. Once the haul becomes uneven, it may be necessry to stop heaving and manoeuvre the vessel, or to back off a few turns. With a split drum, this situation is resolved by declutching the side which is too far advanced until the cables, or wing ends are again square. The split facility is also useful in dealing with fouled gear and single-ended hauls. As these benefits are of secondary importance to the presence of the drum itself, they may be overlooked by owners considering drum hauling of nets for the first time. However, recent Canadian experience, with large drums for pelagic trawls (Fig. 18) and the *St. Adrian* trials,

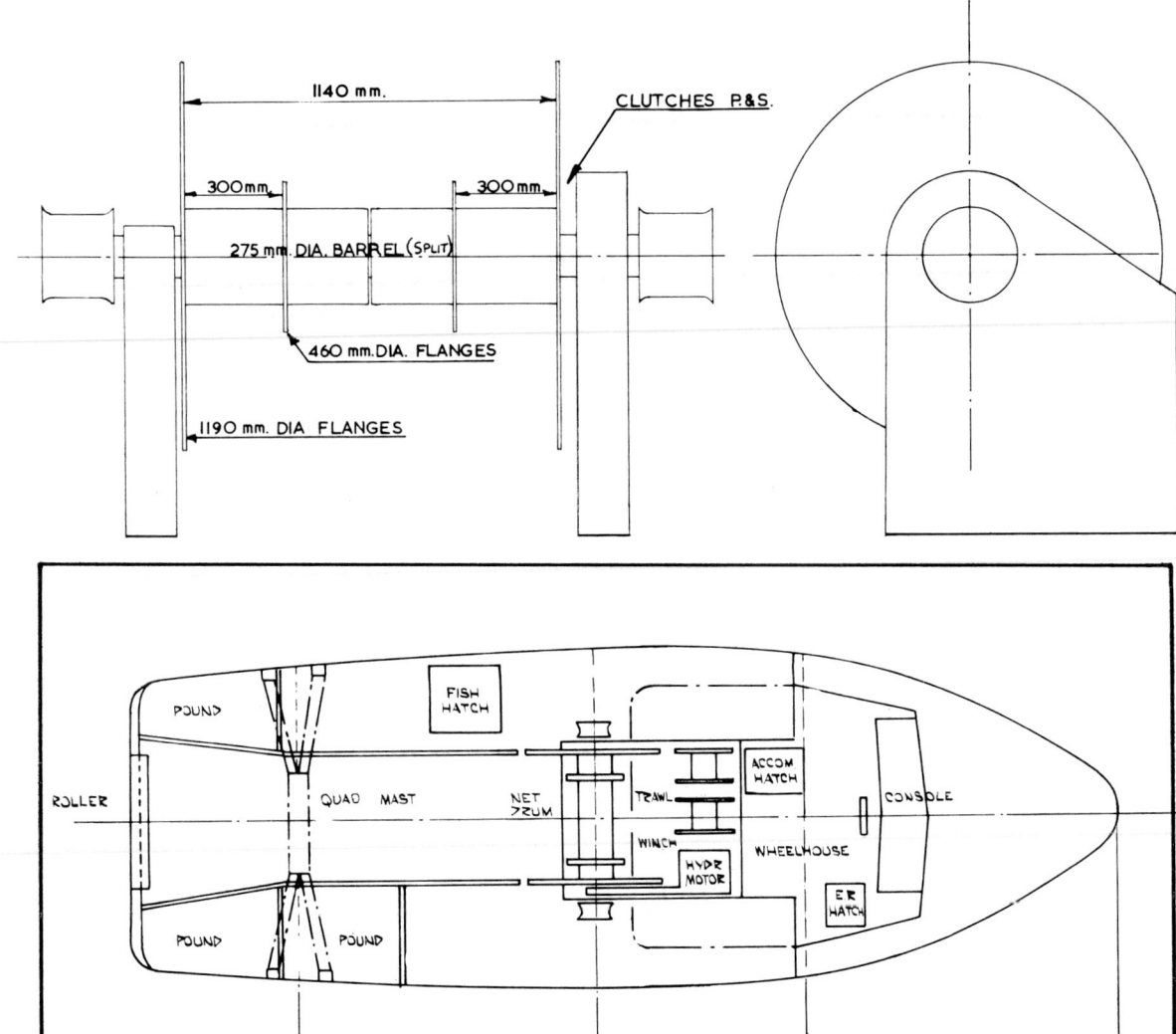

Fig. 16. Net drum (top) and its installation (bottom) aboard the 15 metres long small stern trawler "St. Adrian".

suggests that a split drum is well worth the increased cost.

Pelagic trawling, mainly for herring, has become a major fishing method in Dutch stern trawlers. The specifications for new vessels, the first of which is now in service, show that Dutch owners have accepted the net drum as a primary piece of deck equipment. The Dutch Sea Fisheries Institute has carried out detailed studies of the net drum and winch requirements. In collaboration with the owners, these have resulted in a new design of winch which incorporates two net drums, two main warp and two auxiliary barrels. The net drums are mounted one above the other with the upper one being slightly further aft. This design has proved successful in service allowing a pelagic trawl (of size equivalent to a 1736 × 20 cm net) to be worked from the upper drum and a demersal trawl (rigged with chains and not bobbins) to be worked from the lower drum. The core diameter, at approximately 400 mm is smaller than used for trials in British vessels of similar size and consequently the drive has to be capable of working over a wider speed range (see Para 6.2.). The author, as discussed above, is in favour of a larger core diameter.

The Norwegian stern trawler type research

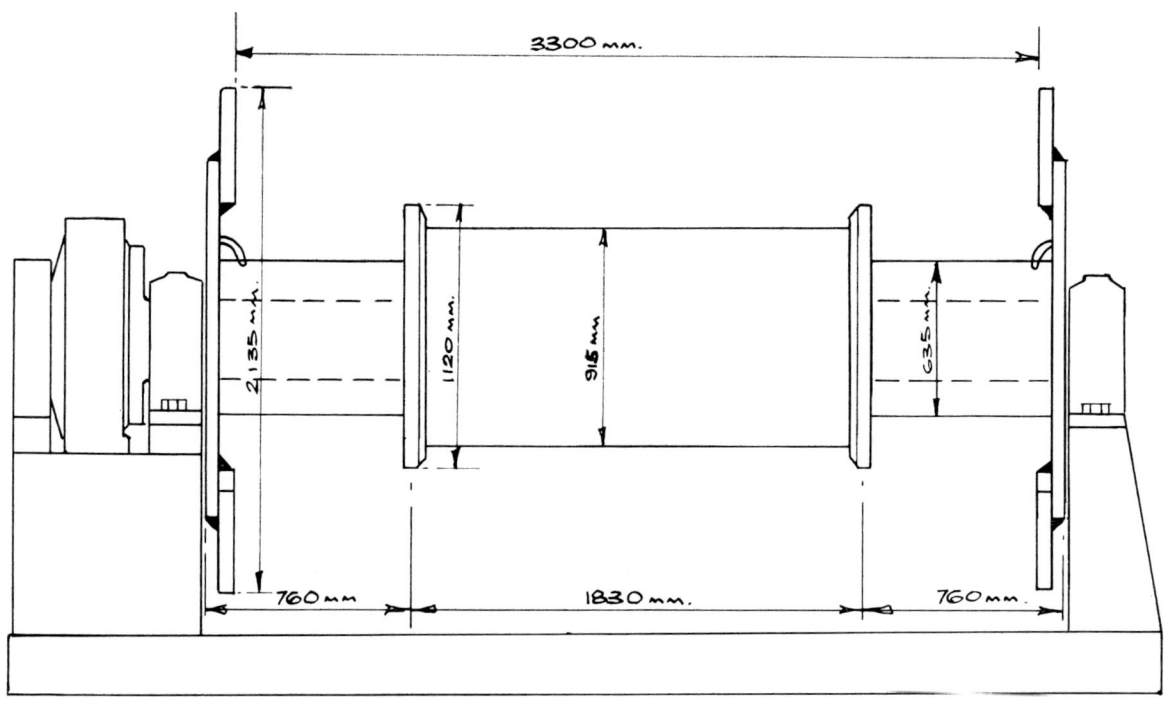
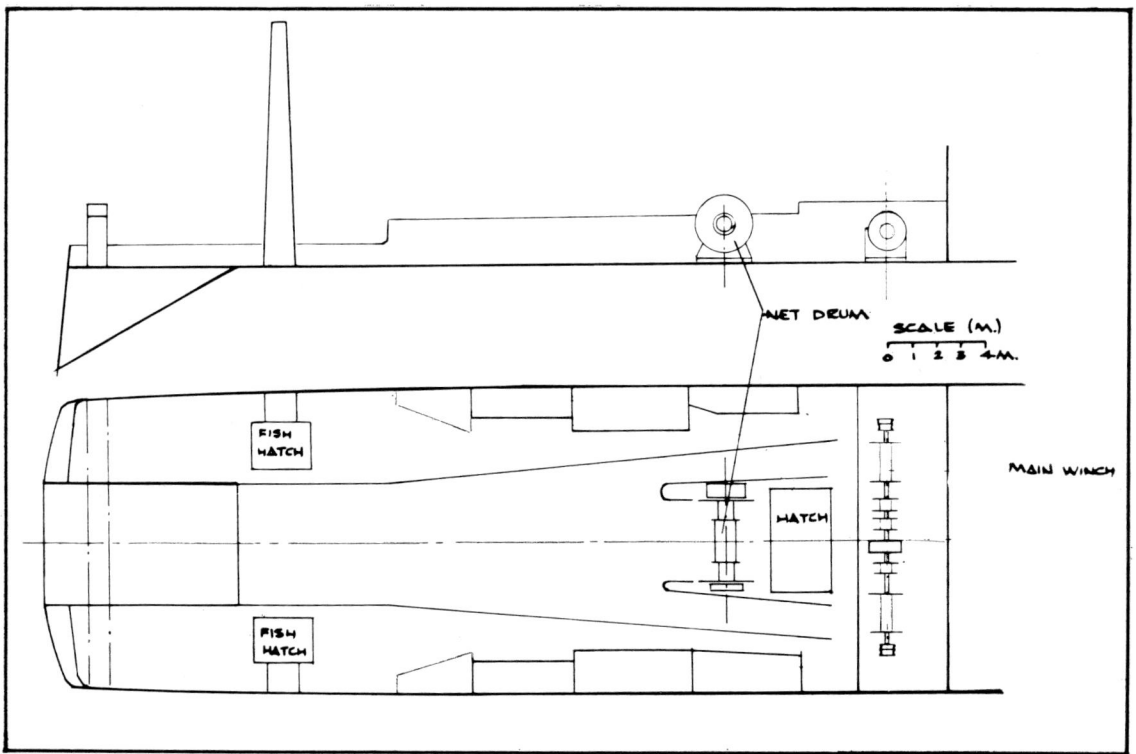

Fig. 17. Net drum (top) and its installation (bottom) aboard the 63 metres long overall stern trawler "Orsino".

Fig. 18. A net drum made by Fish and Ships Gear A/S of Norway for a large pelagic trawl.

vessel *G.O. Sars* (70 m l.o.a.) is equipped with three net drums one upper and two lower (side by side) mounted between the legs of the forward gantry. The design of these drums has recently been altered and at mid-1971 the upper drum had a three-section barrel of similar construction to that used in the *Ross Kelvin* trials (Fig. 15b) with one major difference—the outer sections were of larger diameter than the central section, to provide a high line hauling speed for the cables. The inner flanges, as in the *Ross Kelvin* experiment, require the drum to be halted while the wires are transferred to the central section before hauling the net. The larger outer section has the merit of being able to wind on the heavy (600 kg) weights. To suit the drum, these weights are small and round, in the form of a string of beads, and two strings are attached side by side on each lower bridle. The lower drums are used to handle a small pelagic trawl and a high-headline bottom trawl.

5. HANDLING MORE THAN ONE TYPE OF GEAR

In the previous sections of this chapter mention has been made of fishing time lost due to delays in handling the cod-end and in repairing net damage. Furthermore, the time lost in changing from one type of trawl to another (for example, demersal to pelagic or vice-versa) can be sufficient to deter the skipper from trying the alternative type, unless he is assured of higher catch rates.

To emphasise the last point in particular, a vessel designed purely to handle a Granton trawl, requires the following operations to be undertaken, when changing over from a Granton to a pelagic net.

The cables on the auxiliary barrels of the main winch have to be taken off. This is a slow operation as the wires have to be coiled down, by hand, in a convenient location, usually on the boat deck. Then the longer, double cables for the pelagic gear have to be wound on, with manual guidance from open coil stowage. The Granton net has then to be lifted inside the arena and the pelagic net, which is generally too large for storage on the working deck, has to be taken from the net store and flaked out in a manner which will give a clean shoot: it is common practice to lash the loose netting at intervals, like a string of sausages, to prevent fouling in the store, and these lashings have to be cut free. The Granton doors have to be unshipped and brought aboard up the ramp, and the pelagic doors lowered down the ramp and then lifted to the towing blocks. This procedure has resulted in the loss of two hours after some practice, and as much as nine hours on the first attempt – a considerable deterrent to acquiring experience and familiarity with the pelagic trawl.

These problems are very closely interlinked and are therefore discussed together in this section. In each case the solution is to have another trawl ready-rigged to be shot away as soon as practicable after hauling the first. Multiple gear handling can therefore be defined as specially designed deck layouts permitting simultaneously two, or more, trawls to be ready-rigged for shooting.

5.1. *Advantages of multiple gear handling*

The benefit of saving one minute a haul, for a vessel fishing purely with a Granton trawl has been quantified, in Para 4.1. and Table 8, as at least £1,000 a year in the conditions of the British North Atlantic cod fishery; improvements in the handling times of other demersal trawls in other fisheries should give broadly similar increases in profitability. If now the time lost in net mending could be eliminated by shooting the second trawl if damage is observed in the first, there is a potential increase in profits of £16,000 a year (See Table 6).

It is unlikely that the full saving, of 16 minutes a haul on average, could be made, because part of this mending time will have been employed to advantage on at least some occasions either to turn the vessel back on to the previous tow or to manoeuvre it so as to pick up previously-observed fish marks or in successful searching for new fish marks, or steaming towards another trawler. The fraction of the total mending time which is really wasted time is not known with accuracy, but it is extremely unlikely to be less than half – worth at least £8,000 a year.

Trawl repairs carried out immediately prior to shooting are often hurried and consequently the repair does not hold or the net is distorted. Thus, the ability to shoot only trawls known to be in good repair, should reduce the incidence of damage and may even improve catches.

By working two identical trawls alternately, the net mending benefits could be supplemented by a reduction in the cod-end handling times. This could be achieved by pulling the first cod-end to one side to be discharged once the second net was fishing. From Table 5, the average cod-end handling time is around 8.8 minutes of which perhaps half could be reclaimed, with a yearly increase in profit of say £4,000.

In pelagic fishing, catch rates are generally higher than in demersal fishing and fewer hauls are made in a day. Also the larger catches frequently mean that the vessel has to lay to, at least while the fish are being discharged into the processing deck (see Table 7) a very much wider deck would be required to allow a second net to be shot away, with a full cod-end aboard. Thus there is less urgency to reduce on-board handling times, though from Table 10 the use of a net drum offers a saving of two to five minutes a handling.

When pelagic fishing, there are times when a change to a larger or smaller net could produce better catch rates. Consequently the facility to have a spare trawl ready-rigged would save delays of over an hour when the change-over becomes necessary. This facility could also prove advantageous for identical trawls for vessels fishing only with pelagic nets, as, when these large nets are damaged (an infrequent occurrence), they cannot be repaired satisfactorily aboard.

In German vessels only small repairs are made aboard. When serious damage occurs, for instance if the net comes into ground contact, or is fouled when shooting, or becomes weakened by bad mending imposing an uneven strain on the meshes, whole sections can be split and the usual method of repair is to cut out and replace the complete panel. The damaged panels are repaired ashore by the manufacturers to whom the complete nets are returned at regular intervals for overhaul.

For vessels wishing to exploit both demersal and pelagic trawls on the same voyage, the time losses in changing from one type to the other have to be set against the improved catches once the change has been made. During the early trials of pelagic nets in British vessels, using the deck layout designed for the Granton trawl supplemented by some extra sheaves, the change-over times were seldom less than three hours, which proved a considerable deterrent to changing.

The simple addition of a net drum (described in Para 4.2.), provided the *Orsino* with a two-gear facility and reduced the change-over time (doors-up to doors away) to around 40 minutes (See Table 10) including changing the doors, which is only 15 to 20 minutes longer than the normal time for handling a Granton trawl (13 minutes gear handling, plus nine minutes cod-end handling) with no net mending. It is doubtful if this sort of facility could be provided in a side trawler, except a very large vessel equipped to fish from either side.

Multiple gear handling systems are much more practicable in stern trawlers. The advantages to be gained can be summarised as:

1. Working one trawl, with identical trawl on standby, to eliminate delays caused by repairing damaged gear.
2. Working identical trawls alternately, to reduce delays in discharging the cod-end, in addition to net damage delays. It should be noted that if the catch is large, it will be difficult or impossible to shoot the alternative net, until the first cod-end has been cleared.
3. Working one trawl, with another type of trawl as standby for rapid change-over when dictated by change in fishing conditions.

5.1.1. *Double-gear system*

With a deck layout designed to handle two trawls, advantages 1) or 2) in Para 5.1. above can be obtained when working one type of trawl. When a change in fishing pattern is anticipated and a different trawl type fitted to one section of the system, the vessel in effect reverts to single gear handling until the changeover is made. (This change-over facility will, for many vessels, be the most important advantage.) Thus the full benefits cannot be realised with a double-gear system.

5.1.2. *Triple-gear system*

Much greater flexibility of action is possible with a triple facility. Two sections can be rigged with the trawl type in use and the type most likely for changeover can be rigged on the third section. This arrangement would be the most probable when working a demersal trawl, with either a pelagic or semi-pelagic trawl on standby. However, when working with pelagic trawls a variation which could be advantageous is to rig two sizes of net and to have either a demersal or semi-pelagic on standby. Alternatively, if the fishing pattern is variable, the best overall catch rates might be obtained by rigging three different trawl types and accepting any delays arising from damaged nets.

5.1.3. *Higher-order systems*

While the triple-gear system virtually reduces on-board gear handling times to a minimum, it may require the crew to change the standby trawls to other types on numerous occasions. To eliminate this need would require the system to cater for six trawls, two of each of the three main types, simultaneously. At this stage in the development of multiple gear handling a sextuple system is not considered to be practical, even if a suitable deck layout could be designed. A quadruple system, however, is considered both to be within practical bounds and to make a worthwhile reduction in the number of changes to the standby trawls. It would then be possible to work one pair of trawls with either a second pair, or two different trawl types, on standby. In all schemes discussed in this paragraph, it is assumed that the stern gantry arrangement is capable of handling two sets of trawl doors (see Para 5.3.).

5.2. *Possible deck layouts*

5.2.1. *Double gear systems*

There are four main arrangements, depending on whether one, two or no net drums are incorporated. These are:

a) double arena,
b) central arena and net drum,
c) offset arena and net drum,
d) twin net drums,

and are illustrated in Figs. 19a to d.

The simplest arrangement (Fig. 19a) is to provide two arenas and four auxiliary winch barrels for winding on the two sets of cables. These four barrels need not be on the main winch as small auxiliary winches could readily perform the same task: in fact it is better to retain two barrels on the main winch for the gilsons. If both auxiliary winches are fitted with two barrels, the bobbins can be pulled to the arena using the second barrels, as discussed in Para 3.2.2. Retractable, or removable bollards are desirable to keep the port and starboard trawls apart. This arrangement has been proved aboard the Hull trawler *Arctic Raider* (70 m l.o.a.) to be very practical for handling two Granton trawls, but it does suffer from the disadvantage of insufficient storage space for a pelagic net—Fig. 19e.

The second arrangement, of a central arena and net drum, is equally well suited for incorporation in existing vessels. The net drum provides rapid and convenient storage for the pelagic net, and thus this solution is superior to the double arena if both demersal and pelagic nets are to be worked on the same trip. This arrangement has been proved in the Hull trawler *Orsino* (68 m l.o.a.). With both sections working on the same centre-line, the net on the drum has to be hauled over the one around the arena. On the initial trials (May 1971) in the *Orsino*, some snagging was experienced, but the provision of a heavy duty canvas or plastic cover would vir-

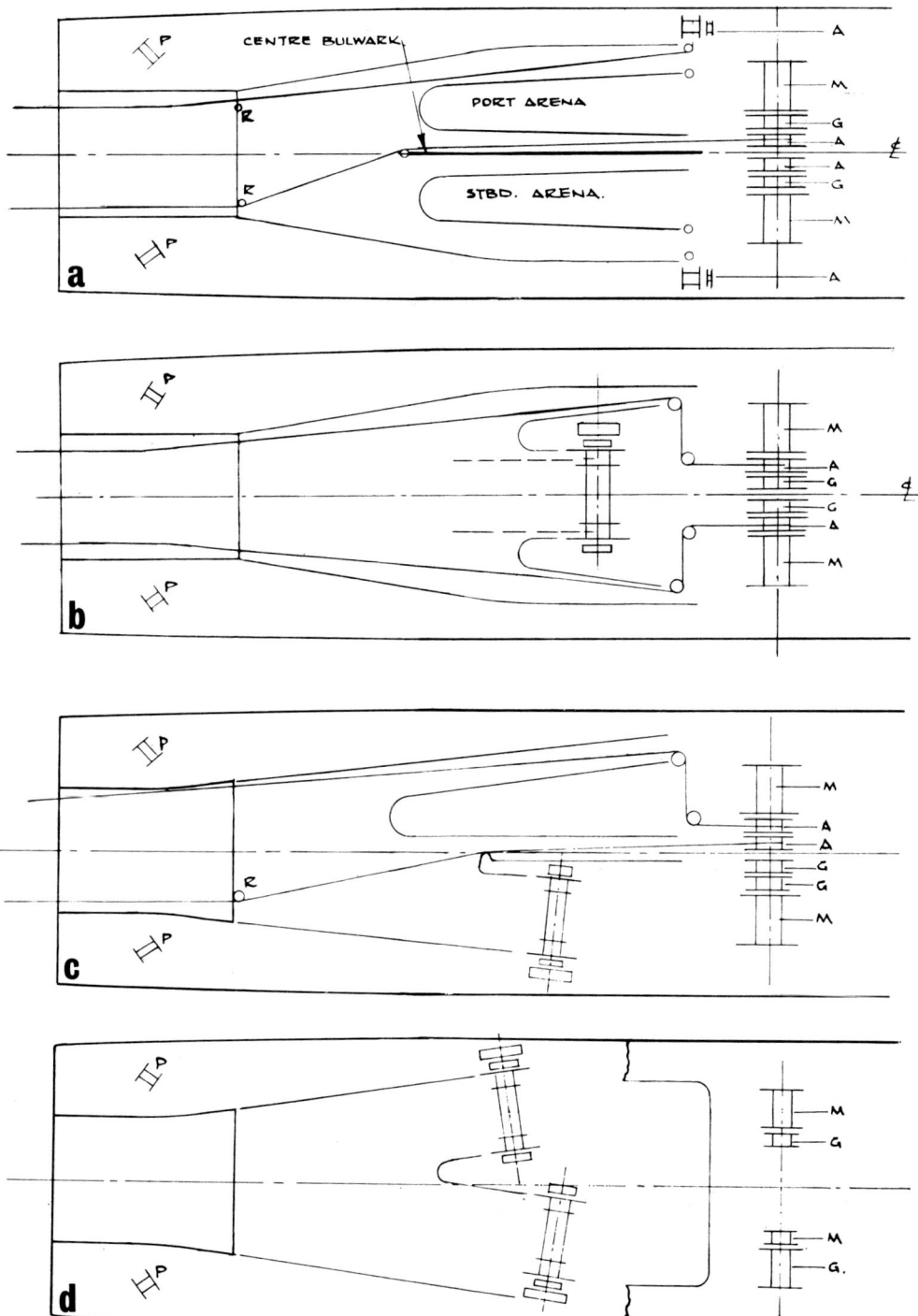

Fig. 19. Double gear handling systems. Key. M. Main barrel R. Retractable or removable bollard G. Gilson barrel A. Auxiliary barrel P. Outhaul barrel.

(a) *Double arena with four auxiliary barrels.* (b) *Central arena and net drum.* (c) *Offset arena and net drum.* (d) *Twin net drums (the main and gilson winch barrels are on the deck above).*

Fig. 19e. Twin arena layout in Arctic Raider *(70 m loa). Deck rigged for pelagic trawl. Vessel normally works two demersal trawls side by side.*

tually eliminate this fault: a hinged ramp might provide a more permanent solution. When costs are considered, the net drum installation is only slightly more expensive than the double arena conversion which involves the installation of two auxiliary winches and preferably two retractable or removable bollards.

Placing the net drum and arena side-by-side has the benefit of separating the hauling paths of the two nets, which is probably of second order importance, but makes the lead of the main warp difficult to arrange over the net drum, without drastically increasing the fleet angle to the spooling gear. Furthermore, it is necessary to provide one, or possibly two, retractable bollards to keep the arena net clear of the net drum.

The twin net drum arrangement is only suitable for new vessels, because, to provide a clean layout, the main winch has to be fitted on a deck above the trawl deck. This scheme (Fig. 22) is being incorporated on four (40 m) vessels building in 1971 for a Lowestoft owner, who wishes to exploit the option of reducing the cod-end handling time which, in fishing for flat fish, is exacerbated by the presence of considerable quantities of weed in the cod-end.

If a catamaran vessel is considered, the twin hull arrangement provides an ideal double gear handling facility, as has been proved aboard the Russian prototype trawler *Experiment* (Ref. 2) with one ramp in each hull.

5.2.2. *Triple gear systems*

There are three main arrangements, involving the use of one, two or three net drums, and these are illustrated in Figs. 20a to c. It is possible to design a triple arena arrangement, but the deck width required for such a scheme is considered impracticable for vessels of less than about 16 metres beam which is three or more metres greater than the beam of most existing distant water vessels.

Up to the middle of 1971, only the Norwegian research vessel *G.O.Sars*, had been designed with a triple gear handling system (see Para 4.2.1.). This system, involving three drums, is operating to the satisfaction of the Norwegian scientists, and therefore proves, at least on new tonnage, that a triple gear facility is a practical proposition.

The simplest arrangement is to take the double arena system (Fig. 19a) and add a net drum centrally between the arenas. The centre walls of the arenas must be tailored to give a clear access to the drum from the ramp and, as with the single arena/net drum combination in the *Orsino* (Paras 4.2.1. and 5.2.1.) provision must be made to cover the arena-held trawls to prevent snagging when using the net drum. This arrangement allows the two arenas to be used for handling the demersal trawls while the net drum provides excellent handling and storage for the pelagic net. As neither arena provides sufficient storage volume for a pelagic net, it is awkward to work two pelagic nets alternately.

If more emphasis is placed on flexibility of choice of pelagic net, to permit say a large and a small net to be available at the same time, it is necessary to install two (or three) net drums. The arrangement shown in Fig. 20b also provides a central arena for handling a demersal trawl. Alternatively, when demersal fishing predominates, one net drum can be used to handle a demersal trawl allowing alternate shooting of this type of net. If the skipper considers it unlikely that the pelagic net will be required for some time, both drums could be used for the demersal duty: with the arena being too small to store the pelagic net, this option means that some extra time, probably approaching one hour, will be lost when it is necessary to rig the pelagic net again. As with the double systems c) and d) (Para 5.2.1.) there are problems in running the main warps unless their barrels are sited one deck higher.

A much more elaborate installation is required to overcome the restrictions of the twin net drum system, and requires the siting of a third net drum on the deck above the trawl deck, with a roller fairlead on the after edge of the upper deck. It would also be possible to support the net drum

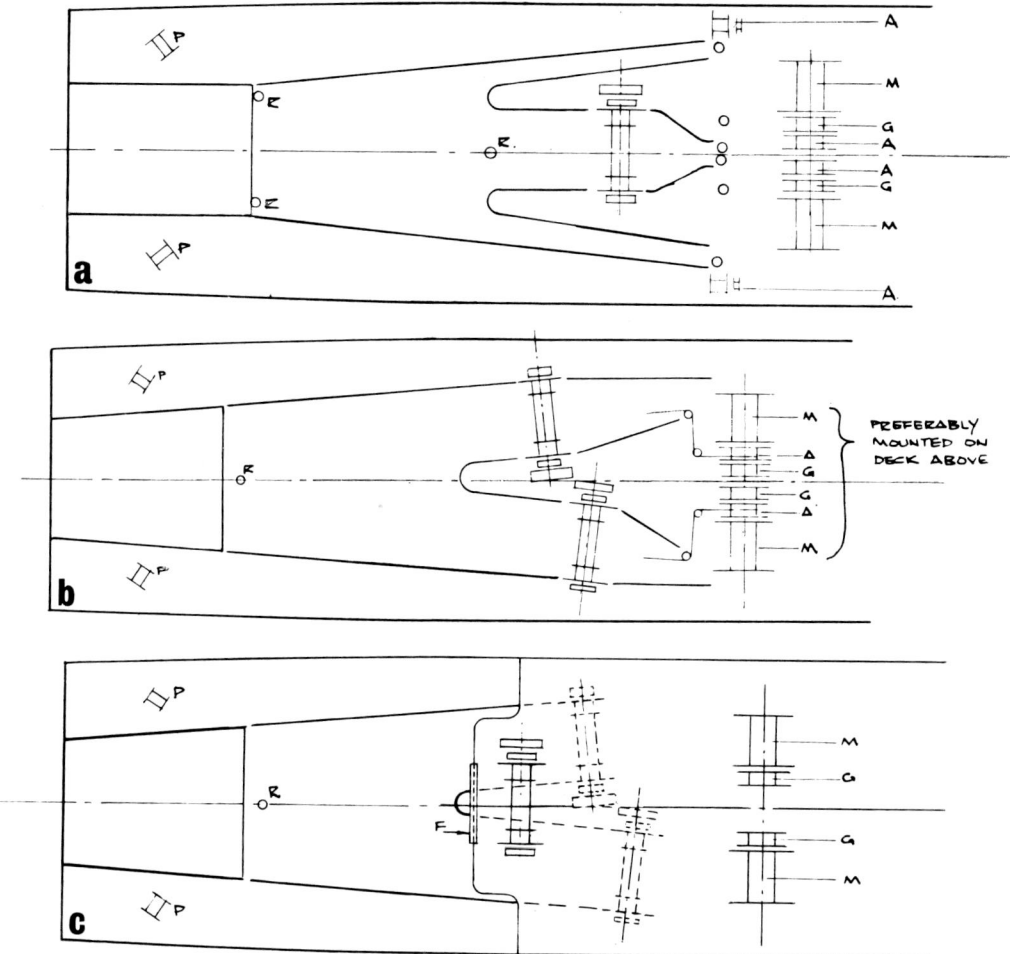

Figs. 20. Triple gear handling systems. Key. M. Main barrel R. Retractable or removable bollard. G. Gilson barrel A. Auxiliary barrel P. Outhaul barrel F. Roller fairlead.

Top to bottom: (a) Double arena with four auxiliary barrels and central net drum. (b) Single arena with two auxiliary barrels and twin net drums. The main, auxiliary and gilson barrels would be better mounted on the deck above. (c) Triple net drum arrangement on two deck levels. The third net drum and main and gilson barrels are mounted on the deck above.

between the legs of the forward gantry. The positioning of the three net drums will require careful detailed design, in relation to visibility of the trawl deck from the bridge and in access to the lower drums for maintenance.

Although the triple net drum system offers the greatest flexibility, it is a very much more sophisticated solution which, at the present stage of multiple gear fishing, does not seem justified in comparison with the simpler double arena/single net drum arrangement. Until more experience is gained with double-gear handling systems, and realistic requirements are established regarding the degree of flexibility of choice of gear and need for standby gear, it will not be possible to assess properly the relative merits, and cost-benefits, of the three schemes discussed above.

5.2.3. *Quadruple gear systems*

At present such layouts can only be conjecture, as triple gear systems have yet to be evaluated in practice. However, as it is possible to design schemes which could be incorporated in vessels of the size presently in service, it is felt worthwhile to include two feasible layouts (illustrated in Figs. 21a and b).

To obtain a four-gear capability, it is necessary to work on two deck levels. The two net drums on the upper deck, fitted with roller fairleads on the

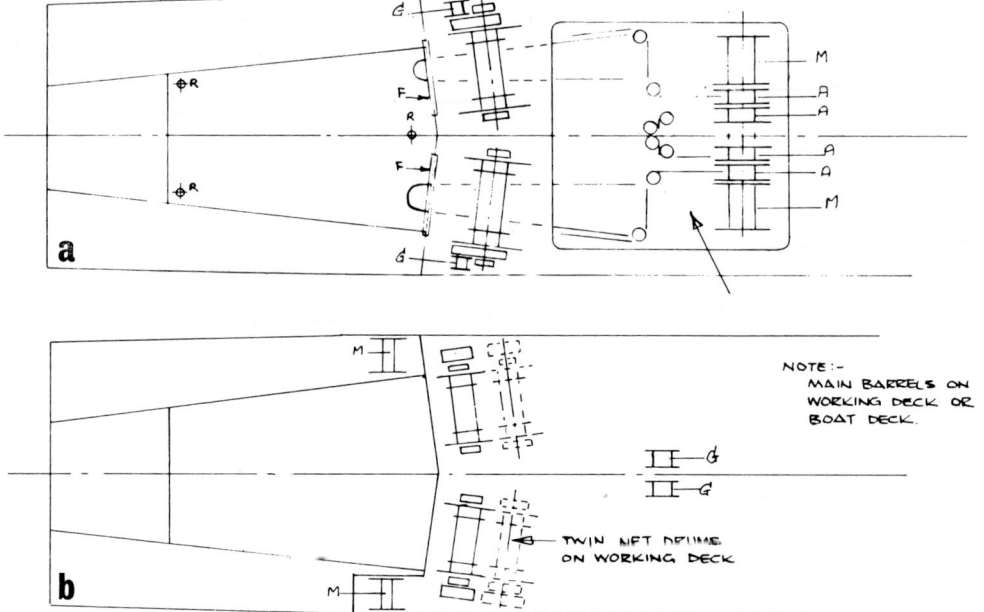

Figs. 21. Quadruple gear handling systems. Key. M. Main barrel R. Retractable or removable bollard G. Gilson barrel A. Auxiliary barrel P. Outhaul barrel F. Roller fairlead.
Fig. 21a. Double arena with four auxiliary barrels and twin net drums. Arrow indicates open area (overhead).
Fig. 21b. Quadruple net drum arrangement.

latters' after edge, handle the pelagic nets, while the demersal trawls are handled on the lower deck, either by double arena or by double net drum.

A conventional main winch may be used with the double arena layout, and auxiliary winches fitted as in the schemes shown in Figs. 19a and 20a. A variation (shown in Fig. 21a) is to employ the four auxiliary barrels of the six-barrel main winch to haul the cables for the demersal trawls, and to obtain the gilson pulls from auxiliary barrels incorporated in the net drums, as is done on the net drums supplied to east coast Canadian vessels by Fish and Ships Gear A/S of Norway (Fig. 18).

With the two schemes shown here, the upper deck, which is situated relatively far aft, will cause visibility problems for the skipper in observing trawl deck operations. The importance of the control function is discussed in Para 6.11 below.

5.3. Stern gantry design for multiple gear handling

In working more than one type of trawl, it is generally necessary to work two different sets of trawl doors. There are proprietary doors commercially available which can operate both on and off the sea bed, but the disparity in spreading forces required for demersal and pelagic nets means that the doors must be re-rigged in changing their duty.

There is also the worry that the reduced angle of incidence necessary to 'balance' large doors when working with a demersal trawl may make it difficult to shoot the gear.

If two sets of doors are to be operated, the gantry must be designed to allow easy handling of either and rapid change-over between them. The system already evolved (see Para 3.2.3.) of working two sets of towing blocks seems well suited to the duty. Because of better access to the cables, it is easier to handle large Süberkrüb doors (Figs. 4c and d), used in pelagic fishing, on the quarters than on the stern. With the demersal doors handled on the transom, both sets are effectively separated. The pelagic doors are stowed on the quarters, when working the demersal net, but the latter's doors must be moved from their hauled position on the transom, to provide access for wires between ramp and quarters. Two solutions have already been tried out successfully. One is to raise the demersal doors on to extension gallows mounted on top of the stern gantry (Fig. 9) and the other is to lead a wire through a second block on the quarter, forward of the pelagic towing block, and use it to pull the demersal door into stow on the quarter. The extra time to bring the change-over set into service, and to stow the previously used set, is in the range of five to ten minutes and is done in parallel with the operations to change the nets over.

With the present design of stern gantry it is difficult to pass wires outboard round its legs as they are positioned flush with the vessel's sides. This difficulty is caused mainly by the doors, when hung on the quarters, lying hard against the gantry leg. It would therefore be advisable to design future vessels with the gantry legs slightly inboard to provide access for wires but not necessarily for men. To achieve the latter, might require the leg to be moved so far inboard that it is detrimental to the access to the demersal towing block on the transom.

6. WINCH SPECIFICATIONS

It will be clear from the above discussion of equipment, layout and methods of handling the fishing gear in modern deep sea trawlers that the advent of the stern trawler has facilitated a number of advances in the state of the art. Indeed, it is difficult to envisage how the systems already in use, or now contemplated, could be incorporated in a classic side trawler, except a very large one.

Before discussing the handling of the catch (Section 9) some information regarding performance requirements and other details of the specification of winches for stern trawlers will be given in Sections 6, 7 and 8. Since, as already noted, designs and methods have as yet by no means crystallised, and since much quantitative information is not yet widely available, it might be helpful to put on record some of the performance figures and other technical requirements gleaned from observations and measurements made during commercial voyages of British and German stern trawlers by staff of the White Fish Authority.

The operations that the various winch barrels and net drums are used for have been described in Sections 3, 4 and 5. In this Section, the torque and speed requirements of each individual barrel are discussed, being based on the results of detailed instrumented performance trials aboard the *Junella* (73 m l.o.a.), the *Orsino* (68 m l.o.a.), the *Ross Valiant* (70 m l.o.a.) and the *Arctic Freebooter* (75 m l.o.a.) for the Granton trawl and aboard the *Orsino* (68 m l.o.a.), and the *Southella* (72 m l.o.a.) for pelagic trawls. Simpler trials involving only warp tension and speed measurements, during both shooting and hauling, have been made aboard at least eight other vessels, using one or both types of trawl.

6.1. *Convention for specifying winch requirements*

There is one general point which must be dealt

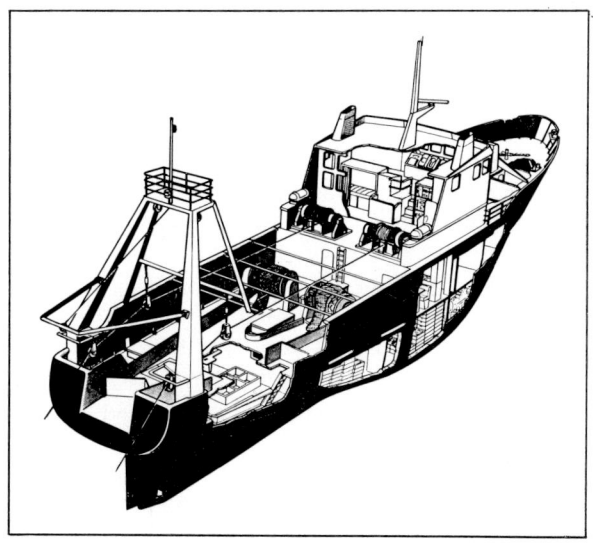

Fig. 22. Artist's impression of a double net drum arrangement aboard a 40 metre long stern trawler.

with first, and that is the convention for specifying the output capabilities of a winch. Some manufacturers unfortunately use the imprecise convention of describing a winch as having so many tons pull, without stating at what radius this pull can be developed. Others state, or imply, that the rated pull is developed at mid-barrel. But do they mean halfway between inner and outer barrel diameters, or the diameter at which the drum holds 50 per cent of the warp capacity? Take, for example, a barrel of outer diameter 1.2 m and core diameter 0.2 m, then the half-way diameter is 0.7 m while the half-warp capacity is 0.86 m, a difference in radius of pull – and hence in the torque developed by the motor, which largely governs its size and cost – of 23 per cent. Even if the mid-barrel diameter is stated, the information is still misleading, as the vessel owner is thinking in terms of the tension in the warp and not the pull from the barrel.

If a steady haul is made in calm weather, then the tension (or pull) remains constant throughout the haul, and the maximum diameter at which the pull is required occurs when all the warp is wound on to the barrel. In this case, taking the rated pull at mid-barrel as the design requirement, results in the winch having a pull which is inadequate at full barrel by 42 per cent if the pull at half-way diameter is quoted and by 28 per cent if the pull at half-warp capacity is quoted as reference. From high-speed recordings of warp tensions on distant water trawlers, it has been established that transient loadings can be up to 100 per cent greater than the mean, or steady state, loading. As owners generally over-specify their winch requirements, the operational requirements have usually been met, but the loadings upon which gear-box calculations have been based may be only one-third of the peak conditions – a factor which may explain the high maintenance and replacement costs for winch gearing.

Throughout this sub-section the following convention has been adopted:

1. Warp conditions are specified as tension (tonne) and line speed (m/min).
2. Winch conditions are specified as torque (kNm) and revolutions (rev/min).

The two sets of conditions are linked by the formula:

$$9.81 \times L(\text{tonne}) \times v(\text{m/min}) = 2\pi N(\text{rev/min}) \times T(\text{kNm})$$

or $\quad L \times v = 0.64\, N \times T \quad$ (1)

$$\left[\begin{array}{l} \text{or } L(\text{ton}) \times v(\text{ft/min}) = 0.0028 N(\text{rev/min}) \\ \qquad\qquad\qquad\qquad\qquad \times T(\text{lb ft}) \end{array}\right]$$

The power output from the winch is obtained from the formulae:

$P_0(\text{kW}) = 0.164\, L(\text{tonne}) \times v(\text{m/min})$ —(2)
or $P_0(\text{kW}) = 0.105\, N(\text{rev/min}) \times T(\text{kNm})$ —(3)

$$\left[\begin{array}{l} \text{or } P_0(\text{hp}) = 0.068\, L(\text{ton}) \times v(\text{ft/min}) \\ \text{or } P_0(\text{hp}) = \dfrac{0.19\, N(\text{rev/min}) \times T(\text{lb ft})}{1000} \end{array}\right]$$

Note that the power required from the engine is greater than the warp power (or output power) as there are sizeable losses in the winch bearings and in the power transmission. These losses, which must be assessed separately for each winch and its chosen drive, are seldom less than 35 per cent, and can be as much as 80 per cent of the winch output power.

6.2. *Barrel dimensions – general comments*

If, in specifying a winch, an owner merely asks for so many metres capacity he may, in addition to the line tension problems referred to in Para 6.1., encounter difficulty in service in achieving adequate hauling speeds, especially when working long warps. Take again the example of a barrel of 1.2 m full diameter and 0.2 m core diameter, hauling at steady tension and line speed. To achieve constant line speed, this barrel will have to rotate $\frac{1.2}{0.2}$ = six times faster when all the warp is out than when the barrel is full. Note that the torque requirement goes down in the same proportion as the revolutions increase. Thus a winch drive which provides the correct line tension and line speed at full barrel, may not have sufficient rotational speed at empty barrel. The ratio of full barrel diameter to core diameter is therefore important, and should be considered in conjunction with the winch drive. Although many winches have full to core diameter ratios of 5:1 or even 6:1, this is too high for the winch transmissions and is the reason most skippers carry a considerable proportion of 'dead' warp on their barrels, to increase the core diameter to a size which gives an acceptable hauling speed.

As a guide, with existing winch drives, the barrel should be so designed as to accommodate the maximum *working* length of warp specified at a full barrel to core diameter ratio not exceeding 3:1. Note that the outside diameter of the barrel flange should be greater than the full barrel diameter (by about 0.2 m) to allow for loose spooling of the last layers.

Once the diameters are fixed, from winch drive considerations, the barrel length is calculated to give the required volume for the necessary length of warp. The efficiency of the spooling has a noticeable effect on the barrel volume required. With ideal spooling, where each layer lies smoothly on top of the one below, such as can be obtained with the Lebus system, up to 90 per cent of the barrel volume can be filled with warp (note that there will always be air gaps between coils). Trawl winch spooling seldom reaches this ideal, and a more conservative efficiency for spooling is 70 per cent. With an outside to core diameter ratio of 3:1, the barrel length L becomes:—

$$L = 1.6\, \frac{d^2 l}{D^2} \text{ for average spooling (70\% efficient)} \text{—(4)}$$

or $L = 1.25\, \dfrac{d^2 l}{D^2}$ for ideal spooling (90% efficient)—(5)

where D = outside diameter of barrel (m)
l = length of warp (m)
d = diameter of warp (m)

As an example, for 1800 m (1000 fathoms) of 25 mm diameter ($3\frac{1}{4}$ in circ.) warp on a barrel 1.2 m (4 ft) diameter requires a barrel length of 1.25 m (4 ft 2 in) for average spooling.

To avoid distortion or buckling of the barrel flanges, their thickness requires careful design, especially at the root junction with the core. This subject is too technical for further discussion here, but is very fully discussed in Ref. 7.

6.3. *Main barrels*

The maximum loading conditions on the main barrels occur at the end of the haul, when the barrels are virtually full. The warp tensions and

TABLE 11 Main Winch—Hauling Preferred Minimum Design Conditions for One Barrel (of 1.2 m diameter)

Trawl	Steady State Warp		Barrel Torque			Barrel Revs at Steady State Torque (rev/min)	Barrel Revs at Light Load (rev/min)	Steady State Barrel Power (kW)
	Tension (tonne)	Speed (m/min)	Steady State (kNm)	Overload				
				Frequent (kNm)	Occasional (kNm)			
Granton	6.0	140	36	65	72	37	50	140
Pelagic 1600 mesh × 20 cm	12.0	80	72	130	144	20	37	152
Pelagic 1114 mesh × 56 cm	15.0	80	90	162	180	20	37	186

N.B. 1 kNm = 735 lb ft

speeds quoted in Table 11 have been obtained from records taken aboard several distant water vessels, and are referred to a maximum-spooling (full-barrel) diameter of 1.2 metres. Steady state conditions and transient overloads, which arise mainly from the pitching motion of the vessel, are also given: the transient overloads frequently reach 80 per cent and occasionally 100 per cent of the steady state tension. For larger winch barrel diameters the torques must be increased, and the revolutions decreased proportionately, and vice versa for smaller winch barrels (warp tensions and line speeds are not altered).

As the barrel must be capable of higher revolutions at light loads, an additional column is given in Table 11 to cover this requirement. Tensions during shooting are lower than those during hauling, and despite the higher payout speeds the power to be absorbed in braking the barrel is less than the power required to drive it when hauling (see Table 12).

TABLE 12 Main Winch—Shooting Preferred Minimum Design Conditions for One Barrel (of 1.2 m full diameter)

Trawl	Barrel Torque (kNm)	Barrel Speed (rev/min)	Brake Power (kW)
Granton	18	70	132
Pelagic 1600 mesh × 20 cm	30	37	116
Pelagic 1114 mesh × 56 cm	45	37	175

1 kNm = 735 lb ft

Note that the hauling powers quoted in Table 11 apply to the power to be transmitted to the warps: the power requirement from the engine is greater by between 35 per cent and 80 per cent to cover losses in the winch bearings and the winch drive. Note that if lower winch powers have to be used, this can only be achieved by reducing the hauling speed and *not* the torque at the barrel.

From Table 12 it can be seen that the Granton trawl has a low torque/high speed requirement compared to the pelagic trawl, although both have approximately the same power requirement. Thus it is highly desirable that the winch should have a drive which has an essentially constant-power characteristic, otherwise the drive machinery will have to be oversized for the combined duty. If it is not possible to provide the constant-power characteristic, a two-speed facility should be considered for incorporation in the drive.

It is desirable that the high braking powers developed when shooting (see Table 12), which can endure for up to 15 minutes, should be absorbed within the winch drive or transmitted through it back to the prime mover. The quoted loads are capable of being absorbed by conventional winch brakes but the high wear rate and time-consuming replacement of brake shoes at sea has resulted in most recent distant water vessels being fitted with regenerative braking systems. Conventional brakes are still required for towing, and as a standby for the regenerative system. When towing, the brake must be capable of being set to slip at a predetermined torque, from virtually zero up to a value somewhat in excess of the maximum torque of 180 kNm quoted in Table 11. To cater for manoeuvring when the gear comes fast, and for possible subsequent developments in trawl gear, a design value of at least 200 kNm is suggested.

The warp capacity of the barrel will be to suit the owners requirements, but recent experience of working in deeper water on the edge of the continental shelf shows that 2500 m is a reasonable minimum. If the cables are to be wound on the main barrels in Polish (or side trawler) fashion, then allowance should be made for a further 100 m of warp.

With such a large warp capacity, good automatic spooling is essential. Most winches are supplied with mechanically or hydraulically driven spool gear which provides a reasonably even layering of the warp. Trials early in 1971 aboard the *Conqueror* (72 m l.o.a.) with Lebus International self-generating spooling proved that, despite warp marks and splices, this type of spooling gave better results than guiding-on gear adjacent to the winch. As most stern trawlers have adequate deck length to keep the fleet angle sufficiently narrow for the Lebus equipment to work properly, this system can readily be adopted, with the attendant benefits of:

1. Eliminating the spooling gear, and its maintenance.
2. Providing more space and better access aft of the winch.
3. Probably extending the life of the warp significantly. (This point is presently under evaluation aboard the *Conqueror*.)

6.4. Auxiliary barrels (for cables)

Each barrel requires to be able to hold the length of the longest cable to be worked, plus the length of the messenger wire to reach the trawl door. The capacity required for demersal nets is approximately 110 metres and for pelagic nets approximately 350 metres (there are two cables per barrel for the latter).

The stall load for each barrel, when full, should not be less than five tonnes and the hauling speed under load should exceed 40 m/min. With the normal working load being 2.5 tonnes or less, a minimum power, at the warp, of 17 kW should be provided. A higher hauling speed, of around 75 m/min, can safely be used when working at light loads.

Each brake must be capable of holding a load in excess of stall by at least 50 per cent, i.e. a pull of eight tonnes at full barrel is the minimum design condition.

6.5. Auxiliary barrels (for inhauling bobbins)

The heavier part of handling the Granton trawl is performed by the auxiliary barrels for the cables (Para 6.4.), as that operation brings the majority of the bobbins up the ramp. Note that if longer low legs are used, or if the trawl deck is shorter than about 22 metres, this statement will not be true and the specification for the bobbin inhaul barrel must be the same as for the cable auxiliary barrel (Para 6.4.).

If the reduced requirement is in order, the winch stall load for one barrel, at full diameter, is three tonnes. For the normal load of 1.5 tonnes the hauling speed is 40 m/min, giving a power at the warps of 10 kW.

The warp capacity is only that for the messenger wire and should at least exceed the deck length. The design requirement for the brake is to hold a pull of at least five tonnes at full barrel.

6.6. Gilson barrels

These barrels have to be capable of hauling small catches reasonably quickly as well as of bringing aboard the largest catch in a pelagic net. Multiple purchase tackles are generally used to handle the larger catches.

The actual specification will depend on how the gilson barrels are driven, as they are generally fitted on the same winch shaft as the main barrels (Para 6.3.). A minimum pull of 14 tonnes is therefore recommended for the stall condition and much higher values can prove useful if readily available. The gilson barrels fitted to many existing main winches and also those fitted on the net drums in Canadian trawlers (Fig. 18), have a rated pull of 30 tonnes. With a 14 tonne stall condition, the warp capacity required is about 160 metres, to allow for multiple purchase lifts. The brake on each barrel should hold a minimum of 21 tonnes at full barrel. A maximum light-hook hauling speed of 40 m/min is adequate for present methods of working.

In bad weather, with the vessel pitching heavily, a pull of 14 tonnes will bring aboard a catch of approximately 15 tonnes, though under average conditions this would be enough to handle 20 tonnes. The coefficient of friction between cod-end and ramp appears to be approximately 0.33.

6.7. Spilling fish from cod-end

This operation, for reasons of control with existing winches, is best performed using a whipping end. A stall load of 8.5 tonnes at a speed of 11 m/min and a light hook speed of 15 m/min are the minimum requirements.

6.8. Cod-end outhaul

The warp capacity is determined by the length of the messenger wire required (up to 80 m). A pull of 1 tonne at up to 50 m/min is adequate for this duty. Higher light-hook speeds are preferable.

6.9. Groundrope outhaul

As with the cod-end outhaul, the drum capacity is determined by the run of the messenger wire (i.e. up to 80 m). The minimum warp output requirements are a pull of 1.5 tonnes and light hook speeds of up to 50 m/min, with a warp power requirement of 6 kW.

6.10. Net drum

The net drum has to be designed to haul and store the cables tow legs, ground rope gear, floats and netting. To provide the required storage volume, a variety of diameters and lengths could be chosen. Such experience as the White Fish Authority has gained in the use of net drums (Para 4.2.1.), suggests that a diameter of about 2.15 metres is a reasonable maximum and this has been adopted as standard in calculating the other dimensions listed.

Additional information on net drum sizes for pelagic nets is given in Ref. 8 and in Table 13. The

TABLE 13 Suggested Dimensions for Net Drums

Trawl	A dia (m)	B (m)	C dia (m)	D dia (m)	L (m)
Granton	2.15	0.22	0.45	0.90	2.15
Pelagic 1600 × 20 cm	2.15	0.52	0.45	0.90	2.45
Pelagic 1114 × 56 cm	2.15	0.52	0.45	0.90	3.75

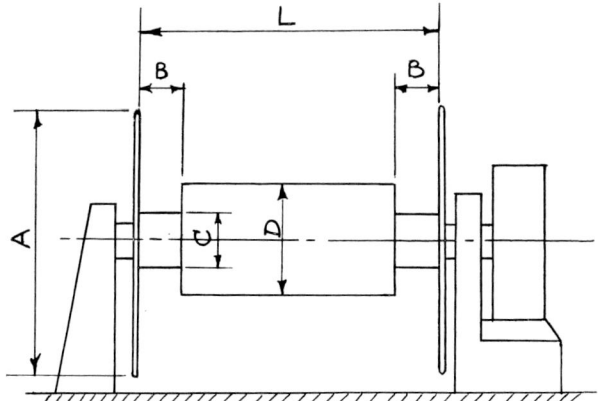

core of the drum has three sections, the outer two serving to retain the cables and tow legs; storage volume for a total wire length of at least 400 metres per side is required. The diameter of outer sections of the core should be at least 0.45 m and of the centre section, especially if bobbins are to be wound on, should be at least 0.90 metres.

As the catch is brought aboard using the conventional gilson, the highest load requirement occurs when hauling heavy bobbin gear up the ramp. With a Granton trawl, the required pull is about eight tonnes. The highest torque occurs as the dan-leno bobbins are taken on to the barrel, momentarily increasing the hauling radius by approximately 0.3 m, which, with a core diameter of 0.9 m, gives a maximum torque requirement of 60 kNm. If, instead of dan-leno bobbins, triangular junction plates, which lie more flatly when wound on, are used, then the torque requirement becomes 40 kNm.

High hauling speeds are neither necessary nor safe when winding on the cables, 25 to 45 m/min being quite sufficient. With an outer core diameter of 0.45 m, a rotational speed of up to 24 rev/min is required. Although this gives a corner power requirement of 100 kW, note that the highest torque is used at low speeds of approximately half the maximum so that the maximum power requirement at the net drum shaft does not exceed 50 kW. The highest power recorded (37 kW) during all the trials that have been carried out by the White Fish Authority was of short duration and occurred when hauling the Granton dan-lenos on to the centre section (0.90 m diameter) of the net drum in the *Ross Kelvin* (Fig. 15). Generally, the power levels were less than 25 kW for the Granton trawl. Even with the 1600 × 20 cm mesh Engel pelagic trawl used on the *Orsino* net drum (Fig. 17), the power requirements so far recorded have been less than 35 kW, but this figure is probably low for two reasons. Catches during trials were small compared to those that can be taken by a pelagic net, and the hauling speeds were lower than could be achieved with more experience in operation. A drive power of 50 kW at the net drum shaft is considered to be more nearly adequate; in any case, a lower rotational speed can be accepted on the few occasions that nearly full torque is required.

6.11. Control of deck operations

With the increase in the number of winch barrels, the importance of the control function cannot be over-stated. Localised control is wasteful of manpower and poor in communication. Several owners have already appreciated the need for centralised control and have provided a separate cabin, with a good view over the working deck, for the winchman. A good example of this is shown in Fig. 23, which shows the winchman's cabin built into the after gantry.

The winchman should have good communication with both the skipper on the bridge and the mate on the working deck. To ease the crew's task

Fig. 23. Winchman's cabin on the mizzen gantry of the Norwegian stern trawler type research ship "G.O.Sars".

in handling the gear, especially in making and breaking connections under tension when the loads are mainly due to drag from speed through the water, it is highly desirable that the skipper and winchman should work as a team. In this respect, if vessel design affords good visibility of all the deck operations carried out by the crew, (though not necessarily of all the winch barrels themselves), building the winchman's cabin on to the aft end of the bridge provides better communication than a voice-link to a separate cabin.

With bridge mounted controls, the skipper is able, when towing a pelagic trawl, to take immediate action if it is necessary to haul to avoid a sea bed obstruction, or if the fish marks change in depth, without having the winchman on constant standby. Communication between mate and winchman is traditionally by hand signals. Although adequate, it is felt that better understanding could be achieved by using modern light-weight radios with throat-pad microphones.

When handling the gear, the better the skipper's control over the vessel's forward speed, the easier is his task in adjusting the drag loads on the gear to assist the crew. The choice of the propulsion system should take account of this requirement, by providing a thrust which is continuously variable from zero, with fine control at low thrust in both the forward and reverse directions. Either diesel electric propulsion, currently out of favour because of its higher capital and running costs, or a controllable pitch propeller, will give the necessary degree of control, providing the lever is under the skipper's own hand, without the intermediate link of an engineer.

The controls necessary for each individual winch barrel are discussed in the following section.

6.12. *Winch controls*

Centralisation of the controls and suitable location for the winchman have previously been discussed in Para 6.11. We are concerned here with the narrower objective of defining the winchman's controls.

The winchman must have full control over every winch barrel, which means that he must be capable of selecting its drive, engaging the clutch (if necessary), adjusting the speed and applying the brake. The layout of these controls is important and here ergonomic design principles should be employed. Levers requiring a delicate touch should be placed in front of, and close to the operator (for example, the speed controls and brakes for the main barrels, and selector switches further away). Spatial distri-

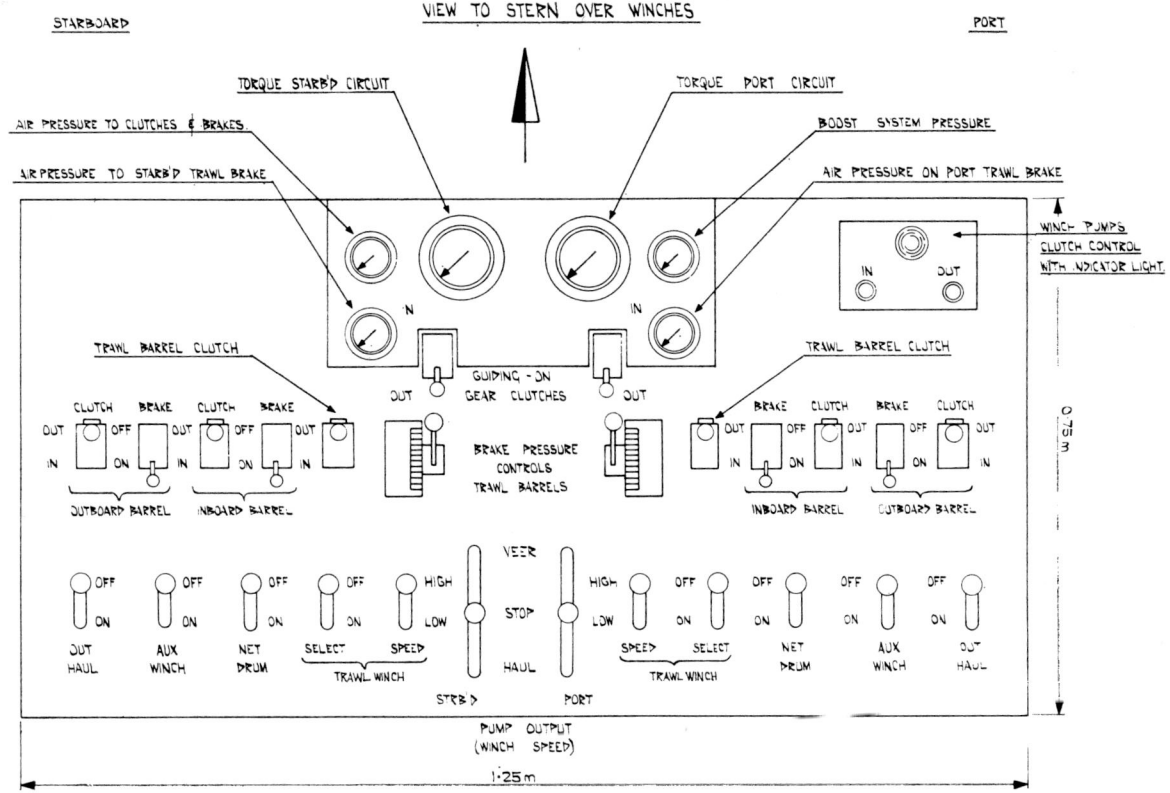

Fig. 24. Control console for hydraulic winches aboard a stern trawler.

bution of the controls corresponding to the layout of the barrels is helpful; and differently shaped handle knobs for speed controls, brakes and clutches means that the sense of touch can be used in addition to sight. Thought should also be given to the type of movement, and the direction or sense of movement, provided for each control, so that it corresponds to the operation being controlled. By using mainly a knowledge of approximate position, and the sense of touch to confirm that the correct lever is being held, the operator can keep his gaze on the trawl deck except when checking gauge readings.

Gauges or indicators should be provided for the following:

1. Torque (or load) on main trawl barrels, gilson barrels, and net drums.
2. Braking torque on main trawl barrels.
3. Main supplies not covered by above (e.g., air pressure line to operate clutches and brakes).

Obviously, the number and location of the barrels, and how they are driven, will affect the winch console design. In Fig. 24, one possible layout is shown for:

1. A pair of split winches, each comprising one trawl warp barrel, one auxiliary barrel and one gilson barrel.
2. Two small auxiliary winches at forward end of trawl deck.
3. Two outhaul winches aft.
4. Two net drums.

In this example, it is assumed that the port and starboard sets of barrels are separately supplied with power and that only one of the four port (and one of the four starboard) can be selected at any one time. (It is possible, with certain transmissions, to select two or more barrels simultaneously, see Paras 7.3. and 7.4.1.) A higher capacity is not necessary as the gear handling operations described previously can be met by selecting the requisite pair of winches, with the exception of bringing the cod-end aboard while using a net drum. In the latter case, the port gilson must be used with the starboard net drum and vice versa.

Winch Barrel	Maximum Torque (kNm)	At Radius (m)	Revs at Maximum Torque (rev/min)	Maximum Revs (Rev/min)	Warp Power Required at Max Torque (kW)	Input Power to Drive (at 75% efficiency) (kW)
1. Main Warp	90	0.6	20	50	186+	260
(on over-load)	180	0.6	<20	—	—	—
2. Auxiliary (cable)	20	0.4	10	40	21	28
3. Groundgear Inhaul*	12	0.4	8	40	11	15
4. Gilson	56	0.4	4	25	24	32
5. Codend Spill	26	0.3	2	10	6	8
6. Codend Outhaul	3	0.3	10	25	4	6
7. Groundrope Outhaul	5	0.3	12	25	6	8
8. Net Drum	40	0.45	12	24	50	67

TABLE 14 Winch Drive Specification (Minimum Requirements Per Barrel)

*See also Para 6.5.   +Veering requirement is slightly less (175 kW)
N.B. 1 kNm = 735 lb ft

If more than two power sources are provided, then the number of selectors is reduced, but the number of speed controls and load gauges goes up in proportion. Interlocking of certain controls to avoid accidental overloading may be necessary to protect the drive systems.

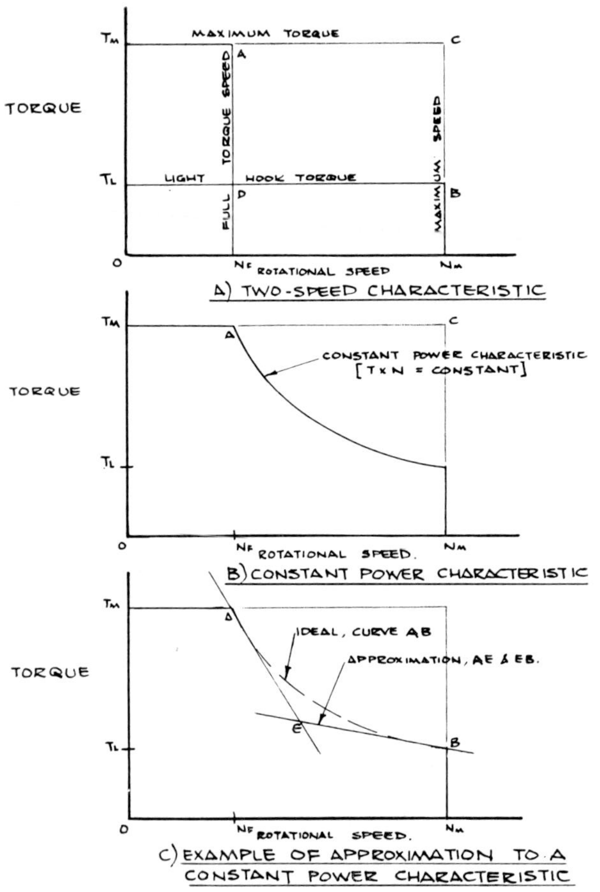

7. WINCH DRIVES

7.1. *General relationships between winch torque and rotational speed*

In order to specify the power transmission for the various winches, it is necessary to convert the warp tensions and line speeds quoted in Section 6, into torques and revolutions at the winch barrel shaft. This has been done and the requirements are summarised in Table 14, for individual barrels. Two rotational speeds are quoted, the lower being the speed at which full torque is required and the higher representing the light hook speed requirement. In each case, the maximum power required is derived from the maximum torque and its associated rotational speed.

The manner in which the torque capability is reduced as the speed is increased has to be considered in designing the transmission. The torque and speed requirements are shown diagrammatically in Fig. 25a, with the maximum power being developed at point A. The simplest manner in theory to achieve the higher speed is to fit a two-speed gear box, with the ratio chosen to allow the same power to be developed at point B. That is:

$$T_M \times N_F = T_L \times N_M$$

T_M = Maximum torque.
T_L = Torque at light hook speed.
N_M = Maximum revolutions.
N_F = Revs at maximum torque.

With this two-ratio system, the speed cannot be increased above N_F until the torque demand falls

Fig. 25. *Relationship between winch torque and rotational speed.*

TABLE 15 Number of Winch Motors Required for 11 Barrels, and Two Net Drums

Scheme	Number of Motors	1	2	3	4	5	6	7	8
A	Barrels Driven	(1,2&4(P) (1,2&4(S)	3(P)	3(S)	5&7	6	8(P)	8(S)	X
B		1,2&4(P)	1,2&4(S)	3(P)	3(S)	5&7	6	8(P)	8(S)
C		1&4(P)	1&4(S)	2&3(P)	2&3(S)	5&7	6	8(P)	8(S)
D		1,2&3(P)	1,2&3(S)	5&7	6	4&8(P)	4&8(S)	X	X
E		1(P)	1(S)	2&3(P)&6	(2&3(S) (5&7	4&8(P)	4&8(S)	X	X
etc									

Key:—
1. Main Warp
2. Auxiliary (cable)
3. Groundgear Inhaul
4. Gilson
5. Cod-end Spill
6. Cod-end Outhaul
7. Groundrope Outhaul
8. Net Drum

P = Port
S = Starboard
X = Not required

below T_L at point D, which means that the winch is generally working well below its full power. For example, if the ratio between the lower and maximum values of both torque and speed is 1:2, the power available at point D is one quarter of maximum. An operationally more satisfactory solution is to have a constant power characteristic (Fig. 25b), in which the torque is reduced in proportion as the speed is increased (to the law, $T \times N =$ constant), allowing the full winch power to be available over the operational speed range.

As it may be difficult or expensive for the designer to provide a true constant-power relationship, an approximation is generally acceptable. An example of how an approximation can be achieved even in hydraulic transmissions by means of two straight-line relationships is shown in Fig. 25c. Electric motors of the types used in trawl winches have an inherent characteristic whereby the speed falls as the torque rises. In the case of the constant current system, this characteristic is for all practical purposes a constant-power relationship. The characteristic curves for a Ward-Leonard system (Fig. 26) depart noticeably from this ideal, but still provide excellent operational control.

Recent developments by the Dutch firm of Smit-Slikkep Veer have resulted in an improved shape of the Ward-Leonard (it is called Kramer in Holland) characteristic curves (Fig. 26) with the result that the power delivered at the winch is almost constant over approximately half the speed range.

In certain applications involving relatively low powers, it may prove cheaper to design the transmission on the corner power, (point C in Fig. 25a), which means that the transmission is over-sized and is always run well below its maximum. Referring back to the example of point D providing only one-quarter of the maximum power required, the corner power is four times the maximum required, and hence the transmission equipment is effectively over-sized by a factor of four.

7.2. *Number and type of winch motors*

The number of motors required depends on the location of the various barrels to suit the gear handling methods chosen (see Section 5). Where possible, two or more barrels will be grouped to reduce the number of motors. As indicated in Table 15, which is by no means a complete list, there are many possible groupings, which are further influenced by the type of drive motor.

Both electric and hydraulic transmissions have been used successfully to drive winches, each providing slightly different advantages. The main advantages of the electrical drive are its higher transmission efficiency and its ability to accept torque overloads of about 50 per cent for short periods (approximately two minutes). Hydraulic transmissions offer smooth (stepless) speed control and motor sizes which are several times smaller than the electric equivalent.

Hydraulic transmissions are thus favoured for

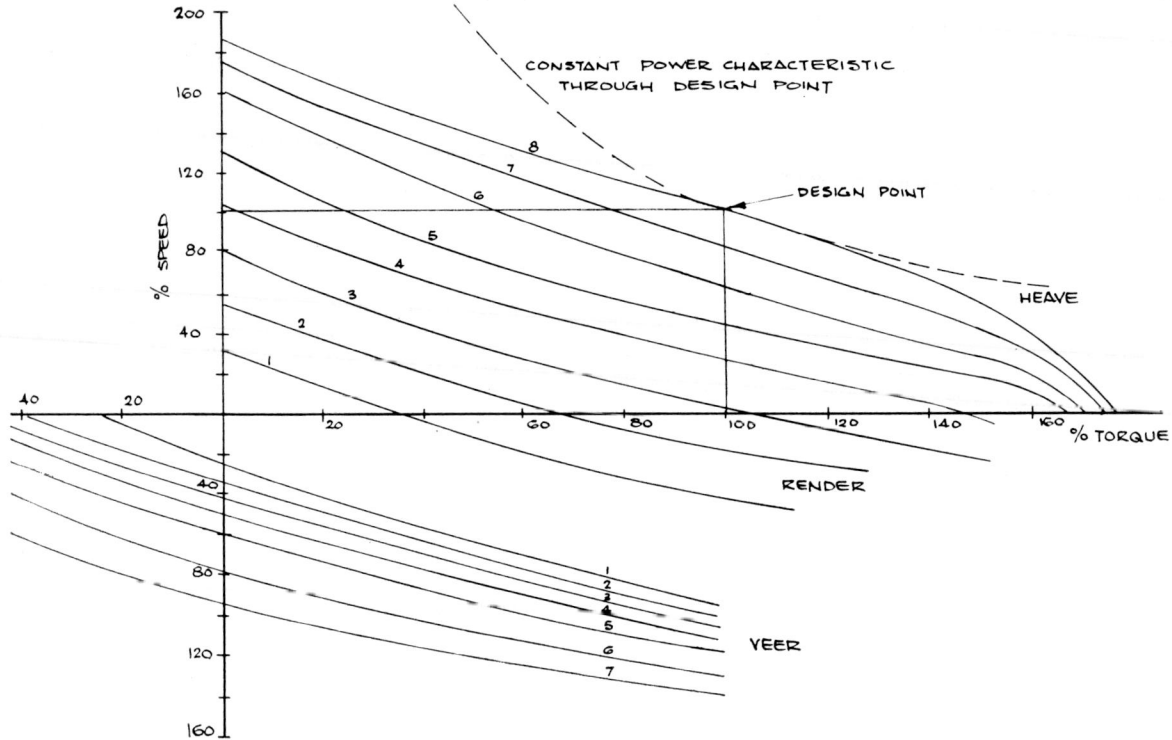

Fig. 26. Typical winch motor curves for Ward-Leonard electrically driven main winch.

the smaller deck winches, as the complete winches are smaller and therefore more readily sited. Also the stepless speed control is better suited to the relatively delicate deck handling operations required of these auxiliary winches. Hydraulic motors are considered essential for driving net drums where, firstly, smooth speed control is necessary to provide an even strain on the trawl netting and, secondly, the larger electric motors would probably have to be mounted below the deck as their presence on the trawl deck would prove too much of an obstruction.

If electric motors are to be used to drive the auxiliary winches, the constant current system is more flexible than the Ward-Leonard system. With the constant current system, many motors can be inserted into the loop, with no increase in the generating capacity (the maximum loading is caused by hauling the main warps). However, the Ward-Leonard system is much less adaptable, requiring in practice a matched motor and generator for each of the different power levels (see Table 14).

An electrical transmission is well suited to the main barrel duty as its greater efficiency makes a sizeable reduction to the engine take-off requirement. The large motor can readily be accommodated forward of the winch. Stepped control is quite acceptable, especially as on each 'notch' the speed can be arranged to reduce as the torque increases (Fig. 26). The greater efficiency of the electrical transmission is offset by the losses in the reduction gearbox between motor and winch. Typically, the overall efficiency between engine and winch might be 75 to 80 per cent for an electrical transmission and 55 to 70 per cent for a hydraulic one. With an output power of 380 kW for both main barrels, the input powers required would be 475 to 505 kW and 540 to 690 kW respectively, say a difference of 100 kW. These power levels are well within present design capabilities for electrical transmission, but are too high for individual hydraulic units, so that two or more have to be used in parallel. Thus, if the main winch is hydraulically driven, it is as convenient to have split winches (Fig. 27) as it is to have both barrels mounted on the same shaft.

7.3. Electrical transmission

As discussed in Para 7.2., electrical transmissions are better suited to driving the main barrels than to driving the net drum or auxiliary winches. A typical set of characteristic curves for a Ward-Leonard electric motor drive to a main winch comprising two main barrels (and two to four auxiliary barrels)

Fig. 27. Hydraulic split main winches aboard the Norwegian factory stern trawler "Longva II".

is shown in Fig. 26. The slope of these curves when starting to heave indicates that speed is built up slowly once the static friction is overcome. If the torque requirement increases excessively during heaving, the drive will permit over-hauling (i.e., the warp paying-out again). In the veering direction, the transmission provides very good control over the warp speed and tension, and prolongs the life of the brake linings by limiting their use to finally halting the barrel. To be used regeneratively, it is essential that the winch is driven from the main engine, so that a sufficiently large inertia is available to absorb the power fed back.

Suppliers of electrical drives are well aware of the control and overload protection requirements, so it is unnecessary to discuss these further. There is need, however, to examine the gear-box design, with particular attention to the selection of the reduction ratio.

For example, winches designed for demersal trawling are likely to have insufficient torque for pelagic trawling. In addition, many existing gear-boxes suffer from a high wear or damage rate because they are not designed to accept the high overload imposed by vessel motion. These overloads (see Para 6.3.) are frequently 80 per cent and occasionally 100 per cent in excess of the mean condition. Furthermore, the worm reduction gears used on many existing winches have a low efficiency of about 85 per cent.

Thus, when considering more highly powered winches for pelagic trawling, the ratio of the gearbox must be increased to provide a higher output torque, and its efficiency improved by using double or triple-reduction spur and bevel gears.

For a given electric motor size, an increased reduction ratio does not necessarily mean a corresponding reduction in winch speed. Reference to Fig. 26 shows that as the motor torque is reduced, the speed is increased, though not in the same proportion. This point is illustrated by taking, as examples a 370 kW and a 450 kW winch motor designed to drive both main barrels for Granton trawling and increasing the gearbox reduction ratio from the usual 17:1 to 25:1 and 34:1.

Using the line, on Fig. 26, for full power, (i.e. notch 8), the hauling speeds that can be achieved with the 370 kW motor which for these three gearbox ratios are presented in Table 16A for the range of trawling tensions (for both warps) that might be encountered with the winch barrels full and half full of warp. Table 16B is similarly constructed for the more powerful motor.

From these tables, it can be seen that, unless a gearbox ratio numerically greater than 17:1 is specified, the winch will be inadequate for pelagic trawling except with reduced warp length on the barrels for small nets in moderate weather. If the ratio is increased above 34:1, the warp hauling speed will never reach the 140 m/min recommended in Para 6.3. Even at 34:1, this line speed requirement is met only when the barrel is full of warp, and the intermediate ratio of 25:1 gives a better demersal/pelagic compromise for the more powerful winch.

TABLE 16 Effect of Gear Box Ratio on Main Warp Hauling Speed

Hauling Condition	Warp Tension (Both Warps) tonne	Maximum Warp Hauling Speed Available						
		Full-Barrel, 1.2m dia				Mid-Barrel, 0.85m dia		
		Barrel Torque kNm	Gear-Box Ratio			Barrel Torque kNm	Gear-Box Ratio		
			17:1 m/min	25:1 m/min	34:1 m/min		17:1 m/min	25:1 m/min	34:1 m/min
A) With a 370 kW, 975 rev/min Electric Motor Drive (Ward Leonard)									
Granton trawl—normal	8	47	242	184	141	33	192	141	104
Granton trawl—maximum	12	71	185	168	132	50	170	136	100
Pelagic trawl—normal	16	94	55	140	121	66	142	130	96
Pelagic (1600 mesh × 20 cm)—max	24	141	stall	15	88	100	creep	94	85
Pelagic (1114 mesh × 56 cm)—max	30	178	stall	stall	47	125	stall	59	74
B) With a 450 kW, 900 rev/min Electric Motor Drive (Ward-Leonard)									
Granton trawl—normal	8	47	253	188	143	33	194	140	106
Granton trawl—maximum	12	71	218	172	135	50	177	133	102
Pelagic trawl—normal	16	94	174	157	126	66	160	125	97
Pelagic (1600 mesh × 20 cm)—max	24	141	stall	116	109	100	114	108	89
Pelagic (1114 mesh × 56 cm)—max	30	178	stall	76	93	125	70	92	81

N.B. The hauling speeds are only approximate, and should be calculated from manufacturers rated curves.

With a 25:1 ratio gear-box, the less powerful winch has insufficient torque output for pelagic trawling unless the warp length carried is reduced: in this case the hauling speeds will be slower than recommended.

Electric motors may be used to drive the pumps for hydraulic transmissions. Although strictly speaking these cases are electro/hydraulic drives, the main design requirement is to specify the hydraulic equipment, as it is the latter which provides the required torque/speed and control characteristics: the electric motor merely has to run at constant speed and supply to the maximum input power demanded by the pump. Therefore these composite drives are adequately covered in Para 7.4., which describes the hydraulic drives.

7.4. *Hydraulic transmission*

7.4.1. *The different types of hydraulic equipment*

Before discussing the various applications of oil hydraulic transmissions, it is necessary to appreciate the main design and control features of the different types of equipment available.

As far as fishing vessel installations are concerned, the main classification is by pressure. There are low pressure (up to about 40 bar) (Ref. 9) and medium pressure (70 to 250 bar) systems (Ref. 10): high pressure (300 to 500 bar or more) systems, such as are used in the aircraft industry, are considered unsuitable for fishing vessels, owing to the extremely high standards of installation and maintenance required. As the power transmitted in the oil is proportional to the operating pressure multiplied by the volume of oil flow, the choice of pressure determines the size of pipes to be used. For example, a low pressure winch motor would require pipes of 10 cm diameter when its medium pressure equivalent would require pipes of only 4 cm diameter. Where the distance between pump and motor is large, the difference in the volume of oil to fill the system is appreciable, perhaps for the main winch being as much as 4500 litres (1000 imperial gallons).

Both pumps and motors can be either of the fixed displacement or variable displacement type. A fixed displacement unit is considerably simpler in construction, because for each revolution the same volume of oil is passed through it. As its name implies, a variable-displacement pump allows the volume of oil passing per revolution to be varied steplessly from zero to maximum, generally in both the forward and reverse flow directions without changing its direction of rotation.

The extremely good speed control provided by variable displacement pumps makes them very suitable for winch duties. There are few, if any, applications in fishing where a motor of continuously variable displacement is necessary. This is fortunate because to prevent overload, its control has to be linked to that of the variable pump, a difficult problem when the pump and motor are not immediately adjacent. Motors with two distinct displacements, however, have the merit of providing two torque/speed characteristics, that is they perform the same function as a two-speed gear-box in the drive between motor and winch. As the two-speed effect is obtained by running the motors' 'cylinders' in either series or parallel flow, the speed ratio available is normally 2:1. As seen from the previous paragraphs in this section, this is a choice of speed range well suited to the requirements of fishing with demersal and pelagic trawls in the same vessel.

A fixed displacement system is wasteful of power when the motor is running below its maximum speed. This is caused by the control over the motor speed being achieved by 'spilling' or by-passing a proportion of the oil delivered from the pump. The wasted power is proportional to the volume of oil by-passed, multiplied by the pressure at the pump delivery. The power-loss may be unimportant in terms of engine fuel consumption, but it greatly increases the cooling required, as this power re-appears as heat in the oil.

Hydraulic motors are smaller than electrical motors of the same power and can operate at very low rotational speeds. Radial piston motors and vane motors have small axial lengths, although their diameters are large. This allows a radial or vane motor to be incorporated into a winch design with minimum increase in overall winch dimensions, especially when the torque rating of the motor is sufficiently high to allow it to be coupled directly to the winch shaft without the need for an intermediate gearbox. Their large diameter is immaterial as it is likely to be smaller than the winch barrel diameter. Axial piston motors, with the cylinders lying parallel to the output shaft, have an overall length which is greater than the casing diameter. This shape is wasteful of deck space for direct coupling to the winch shaft, but may permit a neater design if a geared drive is to be employed.

Of the equipment presently in use in fishing vessels, low pressure systems are of vane construction with fixed displacement pumps, and motors with choice of two distinct displacements, while high pressure systems are of piston construction, with fixed displacement motors and, in the majority of cases, variable displacement pumps.

In addition to the equipment described above, gear pumps supplying the oil to gear motors, rams or actuators are suitable for certain applications, for example in driving fish processing machinery and conveyors (motors), or in traversing the tipping towing-blocks (rams), or in raising the fish hatch (actuators). These units generally operate in the pressure range 70 to 150 bar. Gear pumps and

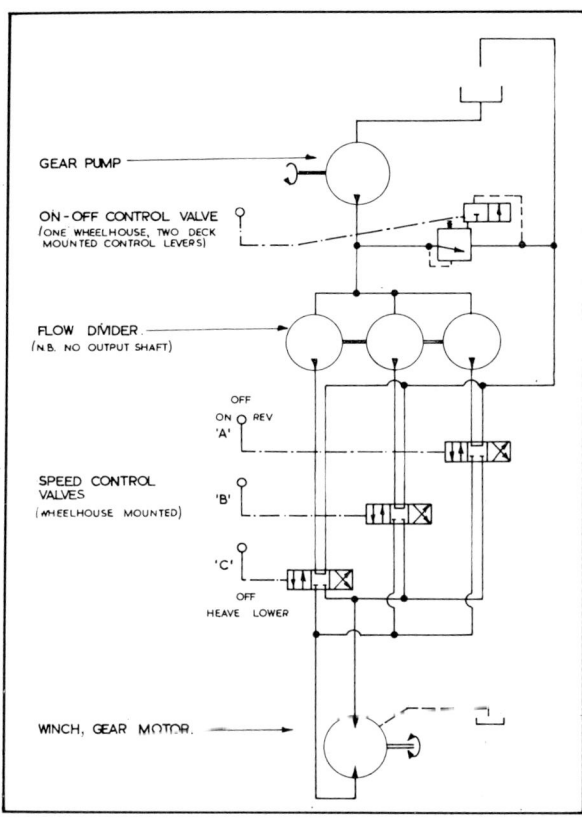

Fig. 28. A simplified winch circuit for speed control by flow divider aboard the small stern trawler "St. Adrian".

motors are fixed in displacement, simple to manufacture, and very cheap in relation to their power output. Gear motors generally suffer from a low starting torque of about half the running torque and therefore are not suitable for winch work where hauling has to be started under high load: vane and piston motors have satisfactory starting torque capabilities.

A rotary flow divider, which is essentially two or more gear motors mounted on a common shaft with no external shaft coupling, is a useful device for providing torque/speed control. The winch and net drum in the *St. Adrian*, were driven through a three-wheel rotary flow-divider, as shown in Fig. 28. Although the power output of such a transmission at around 30 kW is too low for main winch work, it is worthy of consideration for auxiliary winches. As an indication of its capabilities, the measured performance on the *St. Adrian* transmission is given in Table 17.

Wherever possible, having one motor driven by one pump gives greater reliability. This policy is, however, expensive and ring-main circuits comprising one pump and several motors can be oper-

TABLE 17 *St. Adrian* Hydraulic Net Drum Drive Trial Measurements

a) Stall torque

Valve Combination (See Fig. 28)	Nominal Ratio Relative to A	Stall Torque kNm	Pump Delivery Pressure bar	Motor Inlet Pressure bar
A	1.00	3.28	21	83
B	1.67	3.88	30	131
A & B	2.67	4.54	83	138
C	3.33	4.76	83	138
A & C	4.33	4.55	114	138
B & C	5.00	4.61	117	138
A & B & C	6.00	4.47	138	138

Note, running torque at 138 bar was approximately 8 kNm

N.B. 1 kNm = 735 lb ft 1 bar = 14.3 lb/in^2

b) Net drum speeds at light load

Valve Combination	Drum Speed rev/min	Actual Ratio Relative to A
A	7.7	1.00
B	12.5	1.62
A & B	20.4	2.65
C	25.0	3.24
A & C	32.0	4.15
B & C	37.0	4.80
A & B & C	44.8	5.81

ated satisfactorily, providing each motor can be separately isolated. Thus when a motor is selected the circuit effectively acts as a one pump, one motor system. Providing the combined power requirement is within the pump's capability, two motors can be run simultaneously: operated in this manner, neither motor can develop full torque, but both can achieve full speed.

Although ring mains running at constant pressure can be designed for medium pressure piston machines, the author does not believe that these are suitable, in terms of reliability and maintenance, for fishing vessel winch application. In this context, however, it is worth noting that the Royal Navy, which has a wide experience of sophisticated circuits, is, on new design work, adopting the one pump/one motor policy: this may not be a strict comparison as the Navy has on high priority the limitation of the vessel's disability in the event of damage to one circuit.

7.4.2. *Main barrels*

At the time of writing (late-1971), a single hydraulic pump and motor transmission is incapable of supplying the power required by a conventional winch with both main barrels driven from one input shaft. But hydraulic winches of this power do exist. Low pressure (30 bar) systems of Scandinavian design employ three or four motors mounted on the drive shaft, each motor being supplied from two pumps driven from the main engine through a multiple take-off gear-box.

If it is not possible to supply the power from one motor, then it is worthwhile considering the use of split winches which permit greater flexibility of deck layout (see Section 5). This has been done by a German firm using high pressure (250 bar) variable displacement pumps, each pump transmitting up to 165 kW to one half of a split winch (Ref. 10) and also by the Scandinavian manufacturers of low pressure systems (Fig. 27).

7.4.3. *Net drum*

Hydraulic drive is considered essential for this winch, on the grounds of requiring smooth, rapid speed changes, including starting and stopping, and the ability to creep at low speed. Furthermore, a high-torque, radial-piston motor, can be direct-coupled to the winch shaft with minimal increase in the overall dimensions of the equipment, as can be seen in Figs. 15, 17 and 29.

The hydraulic equipment, which was used for both the *Ross Kelvin* and the *Orsino* trials (see Para 4.2.1.), was based on a Dowty Dowmatic pump pack and the largest (in 1968 when the equipment was specified) Hagglund motor, developing a torque of 42 kNm at 18 rev/min: a two-speed facility was incorporated allowing half this torque to be developed at 36 rev/min. The hydraulic circuit (shown in Fig. 30) was designed to operate at a maximum pressure of 180 bar, the limit of the Hagglund motor rating at that time.

The winch brake, which was supplied by the manufacturer as an integral part of the motor, was arranged to be lifted off by a jack, actuated by applying the boost pressure when selecting drive to the motor. As well as providing safety protection, this feature allowed full remote control over the operation of the net drum.

This transmission has proved to be well-suited to the application, and has never been required to operate above 75 per cent of the rated maximum torque. It is for this reason that the design torque has been recommended as 40 kNm in Table 14.

7.4.4. *Auxiliary winches*

In common with the net drum, the excellent speed control and economy of deck space provided

Figs. 29. Handling a pelagic net and net drum aboard the stern trawler "Orsino".
Fig. 29a. Start of hauling cables.

Fig. 29c. Netting hauled sufficiently far to give access to cod-end.

by hydraulics, are the major reasons for their selection in specifying auxiliary winch transmissions. From Table 14, it can be seen that the auxiliary power levels are low, both in absolute terms, and in comparison with the main barrels and net drum. Thus, as discussed in Para 7.4.1. for medium pressure systems each motor is better driven by its own pump.

7.4.5. *Marketing hydraulic winch systems*

This sub-section is included to stress the need for a hydraulic winch to be marketed as a complete system, and not as separate winch and transmission units (Ref. 10). The Scandinavian manufacturers of low-pressure hydraulics have in fact made the complete winch system since their introduction in the 1930s. The delay of approximately 20 years in the appearance of higher pressure systems and their subsequent rapid acceptance by vessel owners was occasioned by several factors.

Firstly, and most significantly in the author's opinion, many of the early attempts with prototype transmissions failed, not because the hydraulic components themselves were inferior, but because the systems were not designed against adequate specifications of performance requirements in service. Secondly, if equipment passed the prototype stage, it was found difficult to maintain cleanliness standards in the many small engineering firms normally servicing fishing vessels and this gave reduced reliability in service.

Low pressure systems, with their larger clearances between moving parts, have a greater tolerance to dirt particles and were therefore less susceptible on this score, and this contributed to their success in Scandinavia. However, these two problems have, by

Fig. 29b. Cables fully wound on.

Fig. 29d. Complete net stored on drum.

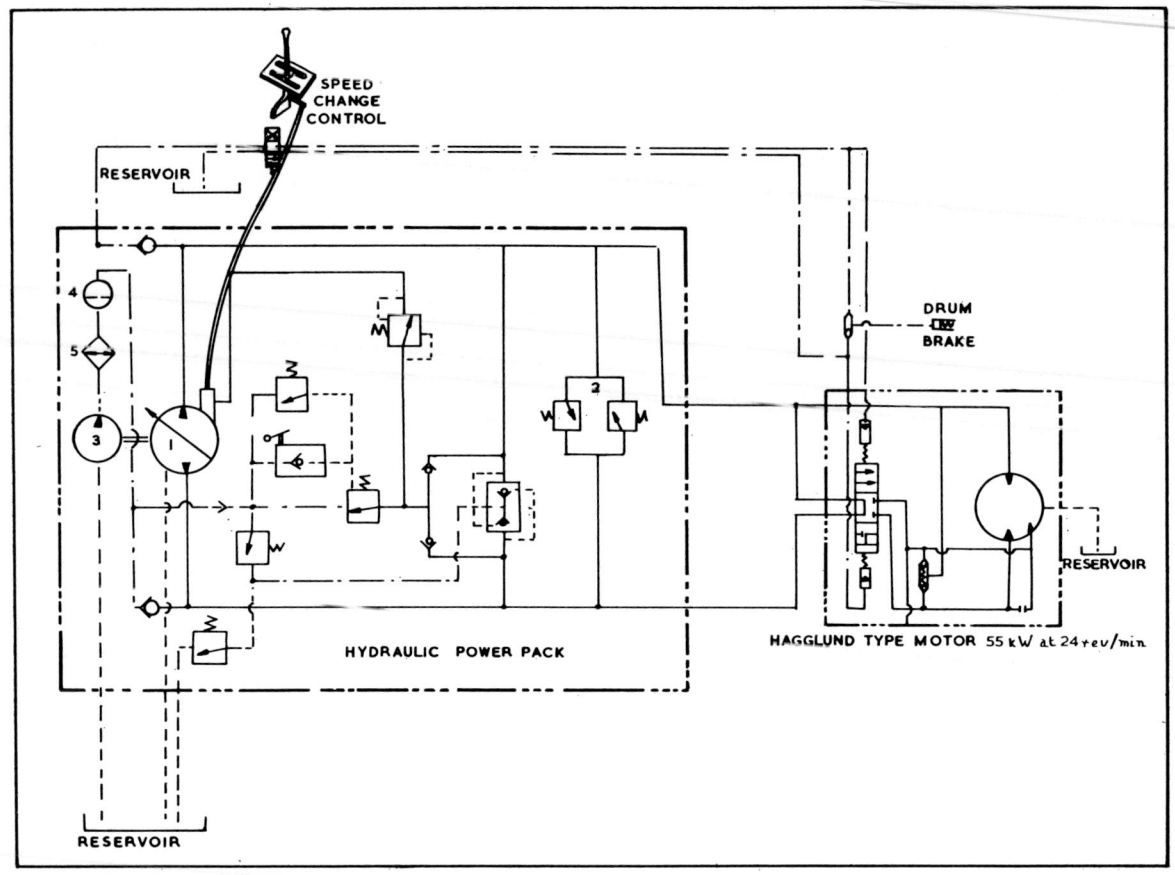

Fig. 30. Hydraulic circuit for net drum on the "Orsino" and the "Ross Kelvin". Key. 1. Dowty Dowmatic pump delivering 400 litres a minute at 2000 rpm 2. Cross relief valves 175 bar 3. Boost pump, 68 litres a min. at 21 bar 4. Filter 5. Seawater cooler, 300 k Cal/min.

and large, been overcome and are no longer acceptable as arguments against the use of medium pressure systems.

Although the technical problems of using medium pressure winch drives may have been overcome, the commercial aspects of designing, manufacturing, selling and servicing them may remain. This is quite simply understood when viewed from the vessel owner's standpoint: he wishes to purchase a winch which will meet his service requirements; several hydraulic manufacturers have suitable equipment to offer for the power transmission, but they do not sell winches, and many winch manufacturers offer winches only, requiring a separate firm to supply the drive. This division of responsbility leads to contractual difficulties over guarantees and maintenance and, unless one firm, which preferably is the one selling the winch, takes full responsibility, the vessel owner will stick to the devil he knows.

Electrical winch drives always incorporate reduction gearing with a ratio in the region of 20:1, and it may not be simply a matter of substituting a hydraulic motor for an electrical one, if the full advantage of hydraulics are to be realised. There may, therefore, have to be some re-design of the winch. In this context, it is very significant that low pressure hydraulic winches were offered as complete systems from their inception, which must have contributed greatly to their rapid acceptance in commercial fishing. Indeed, only those firms which have offered the trawler owner full systems have made a success of selling medium pressure winches. This was demonstrated initially by Marco in the United States (Ref. 11) in 1957 and in Germany in the same year by Mannesmann-Oelmechanik who both entered fishing operations from knowledge of hydraulic equipment and, later, by Brusselle of Belgium (1965) and Northern Tool and Gear of Scotland (1967) both of whom previously manufactured only the winch itself.

8. MECHANISATION OF TRAWL DOOR HANDLING

For distant water vessels, the size and weight of the wires and fastenings used to couple and uncouple the cables from the trawl doors (or vice-versa) is such that these operations require two men. Modern high tensile alloys are used wherever possible to reduce the weights that have to be handled, but this is insufficient to make operation possible by one man. When the handling operations at the doors are examined in detail, it is seen that the second man's function is to support the weight of components while the first man makes or breaks the connections. This statement makes the basic assumption that access to the connection points on and around the door is good, so that the second man is not performing the additional role of watching the safety of the first.

With centralised winch control (Paras 6.11. and 6.12.), it is possible for one man to control all the winch operations. With two men required to handle each door and the mate in charge of the deck operations, a total of six men is necessary to shoot and haul gear. This reduction from the present eight or nine men on many vessels is due to the centralisation of the winch controls and the use of drum wound wires for all operations (see Sections 5 and 6). Thus, if the deck crew is to be further reduced, then the doors have to be handled in a different manner.

One approach (mentioned in Para 4.2.1.) is to handle the doors in series, but this increases the onboard handling time by more than twice the time to handle one door, as the men have to move across the vessel. This practice is in fact adopted aboard some Norwegian stern trawlers (40 m l.o.a.) operating out of Hammerfest, and thus they work their gear with a deck crew of only four men, including the winchman.

It is interesting to consider the financial implications of this approach, as the saving of three men's wages (if the extra watch is included) has to be offset against the cost of the time penalty (see Para 4.1. and Table 8), and any other costs arising because of reduced manpower (e.g., fish gutting machinery, extra demersal nets to compensate for slower mending).

As the author does not have sufficient measured data on the range of times to handle the doors, the time penalty can only be estimated. The most rapid handling of one door, both in hauling and in shooting will be approximately $1\frac{1}{2}$ minutes, which could rise to around five minutes if pennants, etc., are fouled. Taking, pessimistically perhaps, three minutes as an average and adding one minute for the two movements across the deck from one towing block to the other, the annual loss in profits when demersal trawling is £4,000 (see Table 8). With each deckhand's basic wage amounting to approximately £2,000 a year, the maximum saving is £6,000, leaving a balance of some £2,000 a year to cover the costs of equipping the remaining crew so that they are able to cope with the proportionately heavier load of gutting and mending.

Another approach is to mechanise part of the door handling operations so that only one man is required at each door, with no increase in handling times. Applying the same financial considerations as for the first approach, the yearly wage saving would amount to some £6,000. To achieve, as before, a balance of £2,000 to cover the additional mechanisation elsewhere, the cost of introducing the mechanisation of door handling could be £4,000 a year multiplied by its expected life, less maintenance costs. In realistic terms, this means that the new equipment and its installation should cost less than £20,000, preferably considerably less, as the £2,000 a year allowed for the additional gutting and mending costs is not generous.

Some design work and practical trials have already been carried out in Britain, the United States and elsewhere into the mechanisation of handling demersal trawl doors. This work has not yet come to fruition, but the system so far tested in model form in Britain is worth a brief description.

This scheme required the vessel to be equipped with traversing/tipping towing blocks (Para 3.2.2.) so that the warps and cables could be handled in the side trawler, or Polish style. If on hauling, the door could be brought up to the transom in the same orientation each time, then it could be retained by a mechanically actuated claw, as illustrated in Fig. 31. In addition to installing this claw, alterations to the transom, to provide a guide, and to the triangle attachment would be necessary. When the door is pulled hard to the transom, with its upper edge supported against the lower edge of the stern gantry, the cam-shaped claw would be actuated by a power-assisted lever. As the claw slowly revolves it would pick up the cross-piece welded to the triangle on the door, locking the latter tightly to the vessel.

This operation would be readily achieved by one man, who next would have to disconnect the main warp from the door. At this point in present practice, the winchman slackens the warp and the second man applies his weight to that section of it between the door and the towing block to provide the first man with sufficient slack to break the con-

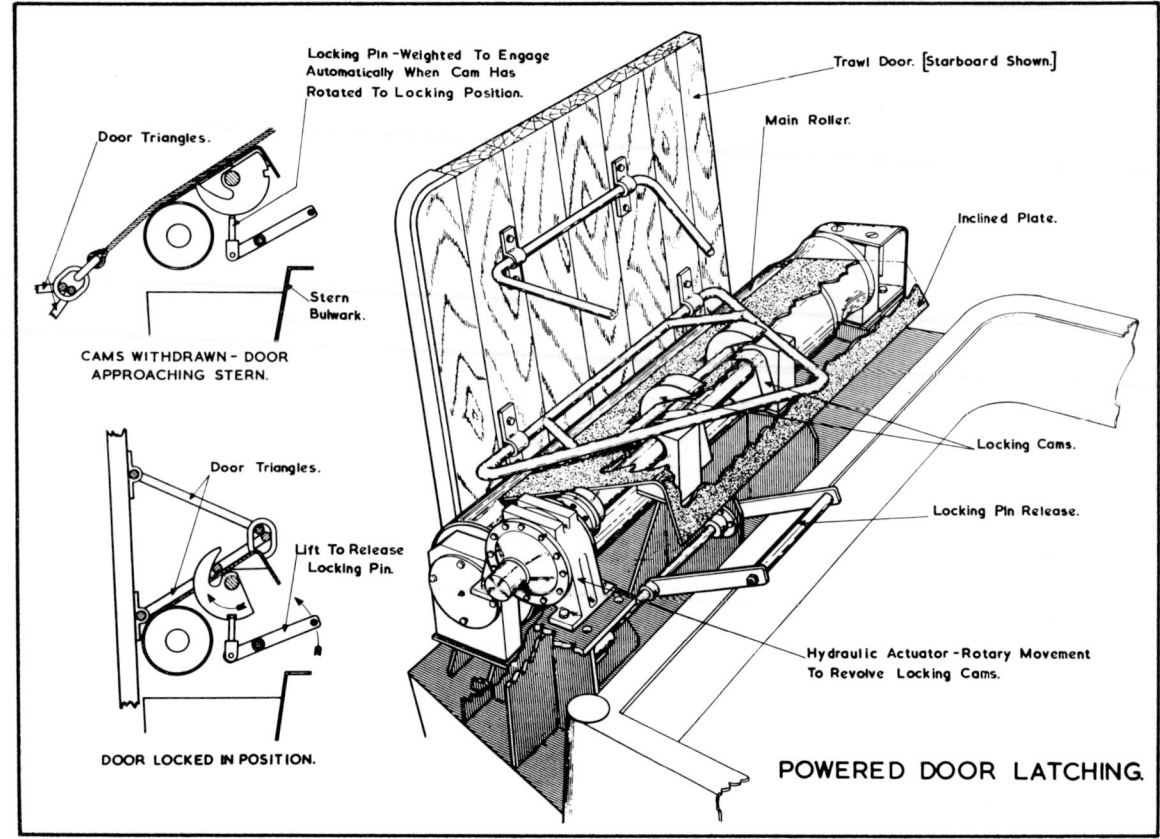

Fig. 31. Artist's impression of a powered door latching arrangement.

nection. This slack could be generated mechanically by introducing about three metres of chain, such that it lies over the towing block when the warp is slackened; if now the towing sheave were provided with gypsy indentations and were rotated under power, until sufficient slack was created at the door, and held in that position, then the second man would no longer be required.

Full scale trials have proved that a towing block with gypsy indentations is not harmful to the warp – the indentations were not even marked by the warp after ten weeks of shooting and hauling operations when a test sheave was substituted in a conventional towing block. A modified block, with an air-motor, reduction gearbox, and automatic de-clutching when not in use, was built and tried out in the *C. S. Forester* (55 m l.o.a.). This trial proved that one man could couple and un-couple the main warp while its weight was being supported by the gypsy block with the air-motor stalled.

It was estimated that the cost of altering the transom and stern gantry, supplying and installing the two motorised towing blocks, the two claw mechanisms and the power sources would be less than £10,000, at which price the project appeared attractive financially, providing demersal doors only were to be handled. It is likely that a system for handling the Süberkrüb pelagic doors, if such can be devised, would be more expensive. Thus if one man is to be capable of handling both a demersal and a pelagic door on his own, the equipment cost would probably exceed the economic maximum of £20,000.

Whether or not work is restarted with the aim of handling one door by one man, a door retention device, such as the claw mechanism proposed, does offer the possibility of making door handling less hazardous. The study had not progressed sufficiently far to propose a scheme for one-man operation of the replacement of the warp in the towing block when shooting.

Other work in a smaller vessel, the *Avenger* (22 m), Ref. 12, is also worthy of mention. Twin ramps were constructed, to a design evolved by the skipper/owner in conjunction with the White Fish Authority, to house the doors (Fig. 32). The ramps, inclined at about 30° to the horizontal are so shaped that the doors are always hauled into the same position by the main warp. The warp run is below this ramp, but as the door enters the ramp, and slides up it, the warp rises into a slot on its centre-line. When housed, the door is retained by the warp and its upper side, normally the outboard side, is easily accessible for detaching the backstrops, an operation readily performed by one man.

If the whole vessel is to be worked by a reduced crew, the manpower required for fish processing must also be taken into account. This is done in Section 9 for vessels bringing home wholefish, wet or frozen. If frozen fillets are the end product, the man-power requirements are greater, but the arguments here and in Section 9 are still more-or-less valid, because those crew involved in filleting and packing the catch, are not presently involved in the trawl deck operations.

9. MECHANICAL GUTTING OF ROUND FISH

In most vessels catching round fish, the number of men required to gut the fish is the same as the number of men required to handle the fishing gear. The progress described in the mechanisation of gear handling is such that the crews for this task could be reduced by at least three men in a large stern trawler, that is from nine to six men. With the handling of the trawl occupying approximately 30 minutes every three hours, the redeployment of these three men would increase the gutting throughput by only eight per cent. Although a worthwhile improvement in itself, this is insufficient to allow the reduction of the gutting crew by even one man: to do so it is necessary to mechanise the gutting process.

Many individuals and firms have attempted to design suitable machines but only two, to the author's knowledge, had succeeded by mid-1971 in introducing commercially available machines. The successful designs have originated from the German firm of Nordischer Maschinenbau Rud. Baader (Ref. 13) and from Mr. James Smith, MBE of the Shetland Isles, UK.

The firm of Baader is known throughout the fish processing industry for its very wide range of well-engineered filleting, skinning and packaging machines which are found aboard most factory trawlers and in factories ashore in most fishing countries. In fact, without filleting machines, factory trawlers could not have become a commercial proposition. These machines have been developed in the firm's own development department which

Fig. 32. Door handling ramps on the 22 metre long stern trawler "Avenger".

has more recently turned its attention to gutting machinery.

Three designs of gutting machine types have been produced, the main particulars being given in Table 18. The type 163 machine was tested by the White Fish Authority aboard the freezer trawler *Victory* in 1966 and was found to give a very high standard of gutting with a sustained throughput of 25 to 30 fish a minute. Unfortunately the manner in which the fish head is removed results in a fillet yield loss of approximately two per cent. As the *Victory*, in common with all UK wholefish freezer trawlers, was not equipped with a fish meal plant to process the heads, these two losses rendered this machine an uneconomic proposition. Both the type 165 and 166 machines have an optional head cut which is made after the gutting operation. The 165 machine has been on sale since late 1969 and several units are now in operation in Norwegian and Russian vessels. The 166 machine was expected to be in production at the end of 1971.

In 1967, Mr. James Smith, after years of experimentation, revealed his invention of the Shetland gutting machine. The White Fish Authority, whose engineers were at once impressed by the simplicity and compactness of the design, has since developed and tested it at sea and now considers it suitable for

	Table 18 Specification of Gutting Machine for Round Fish (Cod, Haddock, Saithe (Pollock), etc.)				
Manufacturer	Baader			Shetland (C. F. Wilson)	
Type Number	163	165	166	17	28
Fish Length (mm)	400–750	500–1200	350–700	270–440	380–710
Feeding Rate Per Minute	25–38	20–25	25, 35 or 40	30–45	25–35
Fish Heads Removed	Yes	Optional	Optional	No	No
Machine length (m)	4.83	2.49	1.2	1.09	1.40
breadth (m)	1.60	1.96	1.2	0.99	1.30
height (m)	1.63	2.26	1.9	1.22	1.65
Entered Service	1965	1968	Expected end-1971	1968	1970

use in all sizes of fishing vessel. The main particulars of the two machine types, which are being manufactured by C. F. Wilson Ltd. of Aberdeen, UK, are given in Table 18.

9.1. *Development of the Shetland gutting machine*

The type 17 machine developed from Mr. Smith's original prototype is illustrated in Fig. 33. It is extremely simple in both concept and operation, as well as being small in size. The fish are held in specially shaped boxes on the horizontal feed conveyor. Gutting is achieved by a circular blade with a very coarse tooth form and washing is done by circular brush and water jets. Adjustments for variation in fish size is automatically carried out by means of a pantograph assembly which descends on to the fish fractionally ahead of the gutting blade and which carries a stop to limit the depth of cut: this stop is the only setting required of the operator and occurs only occasionally. There are six operating stations on the feed conveyor – load, safety, gut, brush, flush and discharge.

The feed conveyor is advanced one station at a time with a dwell period of half the cycle; operating speeds are from 30 to 45 stations a minute for the Type 17 machine, and approximately 32 stations a minute for the Type 28 machine. The drives to the conveyor and to the gutting blade and brush lifting and lowering motions are obtained from the low-speed shaft on a two-output gear box, while the blade and brush themselves are driven from its high-speed shaft. Hydraulic power was chosen for the smaller machine, both to allow the good speed control necessary in matching the machine's speed to the operator's natural working rhythm and to suit the severe ambient conditions on the open decks of the smaller vessels likely to use this size of machine. Initially the larger Type 28 machine was also hydraulically driven. In service the feed rate preferred by the operators has been established as 30 to

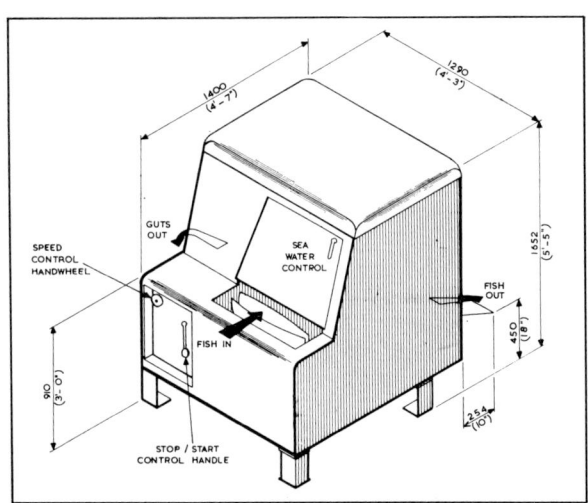

Fig. 33a. Type 28 Shetland gutting machine.

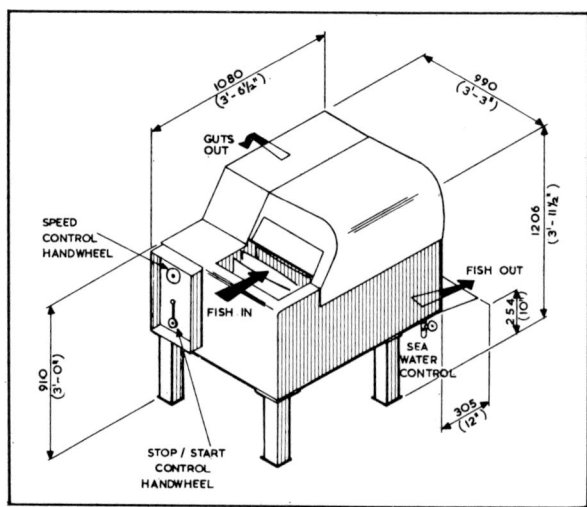

Fig. 33b. Type 17 Mark II Shetland gutting machine.

32 fish a minute, which effectively means that the hydraulic variable-speed drive is not required. As an electrically driven model would be considerably cheaper, the manufacturer introduced this in mid-1971.

9.1.1. *Experience with the Type 17 machine*

Although this experience has been gained in side trawlers and seiners, it is still relevant to stern trawlers.

Originally, the machine was designed to operate on whiting as there has in recent years frequently been an abundance of that species in Shetland waters. With over 99 per cent of whiting caught being less than 440 mm in length, this fixed the upper limit on fish size while the lower limit was fixed by the legal minimum size for landing (270 mm). This range of size was about the maximum which could be accommodated by the gutting blade mechanism and holding box shape.

In the course of shop trials, the machine design was altered in detail to extend its use to cod, haddock and saithe (pollock). These trials showed the importance of the blade tooth shape and set, the speed of the blade, the width of the brush and the length of its bristles, pressure and location of the water jets and the box shape. High-speed photography was employed in designing the blade. It was found that even with a large fish the guts were removed within 1.6 revolutions of the 230 mm diameter blade. At the conclusion of the shop trials involving the gutting of thousands of fish, the design had been evolved in which, irrespective of species, at least 90 per cent of the fish was gutted to a high standard and less than three per cent were poorly gutted or damaged. This performance compared favourably with samples of hand gutted fish of similar size taken at random from fish markets when six per cent to 15 per cent of the fish were found to be poorly gutted and up to 28 per cent had the fillet flesh damaged by a cut of excessive length. The machined fish never suffered fillet flesh damage unless they were (1) under-sized, (2) badly positioned when being fed in or (3) still lively.

At this stage in the development, the second prototype machine was taken to sea in mid-1968 and given full environmental testing for six voyages in the 33 m side trawler *Malcolm Croan*. As well as showing up some weaknesses in detail design of the machine, the sea trials revealed, more significantly, the difficulties in integrating a new tool into a well-established pattern of working and the need for conveyors to assist in moving fish even on a relatively small foredeck.

At the end of these trials, the machine, designated the Type 17 (the measurement in inches of the largest fish of the size range), was put into production. The first production machine was installed on the open foredeck of the 21 m seine net vessel *Onam*. As that vessel normally fished for small haddock, from 50 to 80 per cent of the catch was machine-gutted every trip, and in the first year of operation approximately 250 tons of fish were mechanically gutted. With the machine in operation the decks were cleared more rapidly and the crew were less fatigued.

The order of the increase in productivity can be seen from Fig. 34, which shows the gutting rates by machine and by hand for uninterrupted working. The most dextrous crew member aboard the *Onam* consistently achieved a feeding rate of over 40 fish a minute over periods of up to an hour; the average throughput measured over two voyages was 0.7 ton an hour of gutted fish of 340 mm mean length. The machine performance over longer periods is slightly better than might be expected as the machine operator is less tired and cannot slow down unintentionally as the machine determines his speed of working. Merchants have been eager to buy the *Onam*'s fish because of its high standard of cleanliness and because of the absence of damage to the fillet. Many other British and European vessels of from 15 m to 40 m in length have subsequently installed this type of machine.

9.1.2. *Experience with the Type 28 machine*

Once it was proved on the Type 17 machine that the circular saw principle could gut cod of 440 mm length, a test rig was built to determine whether this principle would work on larger cod and deal effectively with their very tough gullets. Initial results were encouraging and a fully designed gutting mechanism with a 380 mm diameter blade was built and tested. Maximum fish length of 710 mm was chosen as 90 per cent of the distant water fish landed in the UK over the previous three years were less than that length: to process the remaining 10 per cent of the catch, the machine would have to accommodate fish 1.2 m in length. The geometry of the gutting mechanism restricted the minimum size to 380 mm which gave a 60 mm overlap with the size range on the Type 17 machine. Using fish varying in size from 380 to 710 mm, the standard of gutting was checked and found to be as good as that achieved on the smaller machine. The full machine was then designed on the same general principle as the Type 17 machine, and the prototype after undergoing a short development trial in the Authority's

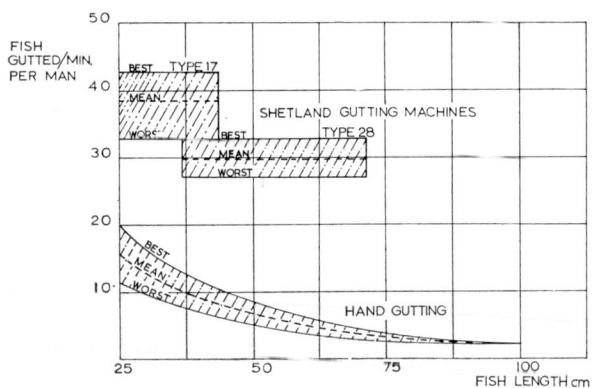

Fig. 34. Gutting rates by hand and machine with uninterrupted supplies of fish.

fish processing laboratory, was installed in the stern trawler *C. S. Forester* (55 m l.o.a.) in May 1970 (Fig 35).

On the first voyage, just over 100 tons of fish, approximately 60 per cent of the total catch, were machine gutted. In one day of very heavy fishing, just over 60 tons were processed in a 24 hour spell. The amount of fish processed on subsequent voyages has varied considerably as on certain trips the fish caught were largely above machine size. However, in nine months of operation well over 500 tons of fish had been processed. By May 1971, five other machines were in service in British vessels and the following comments refer to experience gained from all six machines.

From examination of several thousand fish that have been machine gutted, between 80 per cent and 90 per cent were found to be perfectly gutted and less than one per cent badly gutted or damaged. This performance is very similar to that achieved by a reasonably competent crew, but the machine has one distinct advantage over hand gutting in that it always removes the heart and the large blood vessels in the belly cavity. This is, in the long term, expected to show an improvement in the quality of fillets from wholefish frozen at sea.

To achieve a high throughput, it is essential that the operator should have a regular and sufficient supply of fish of the correct size for the machine. It is also essential that the gutted fish are automatically taken away from the machine. On almost all the installations, a feed conveyor has been employed to supply fish to a shallow holding bin, positioned at the operator's right hand. A discharge conveyor, or elevator, has been used to take the fish from the machine discharge into a washer. With these installations, most fishermen, including trainees, have been able to feed the machine continuously at about 30 fish a minute. With the inevitable occasional delays the long term rate is lower but not by much, and on average, in one hour approximately 1500 have been gutted, that is an average rate of 25 fish a minute. From Fig. 34, it can be seen that this is equivalent to the output of six men hand-gutting. However, the increase in productivity is not six times as the machine operator requires to have another man part-time to select suitable fish for him. Thus the true increase in productivity is approximately four times. The weight throughput of the machine depends very much on the size of fish being processed. With fish of a mean size of approximately 600 mm, a throughput of 1500 fish an hour is equivalent to about 2.7 tons an hour gutted weight.

The reduction in gutting manpower is of immediate benefit to the crew as several of them can be released for other duties such as net mending. If the vessel also has a mechanised trawl deck, then the owners can consider reducing the manning scale. There should also be an overall improvement in the fish quality as it is processed faster after catching. British distant water trawlers have in the past seldom retained fish of less than 500 mm length. With mechanised gutting making it easier to process the smaller fish, crews are now willing to process them, which can only be welcomed in present day conditions of under-supply of fish.

Liver retrieval is difficult with all the gutting machines discussed in this section, as in gutting the fish the liver is cut to a greater or lesser extent. In the Baader machines the liver is cut into several pieces which are discharged along with the guts. The situation is worse with the Shetland gutting machine as the gutting action of its blade shreds the liver and guts. It may be possible to reclaim a

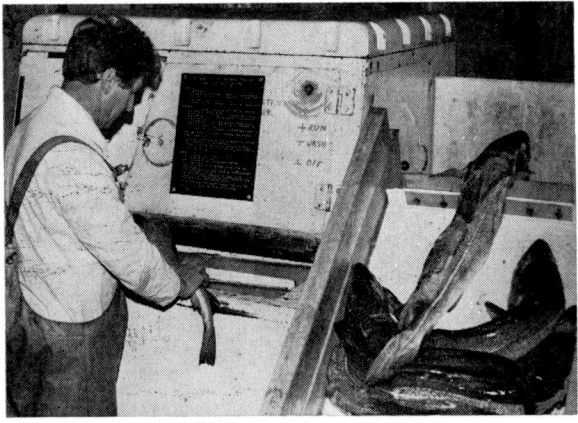

Fig. 35. Shetland Type 28 gutting machine in operation aboard the wet fish stern trawler "C. S. Forester".

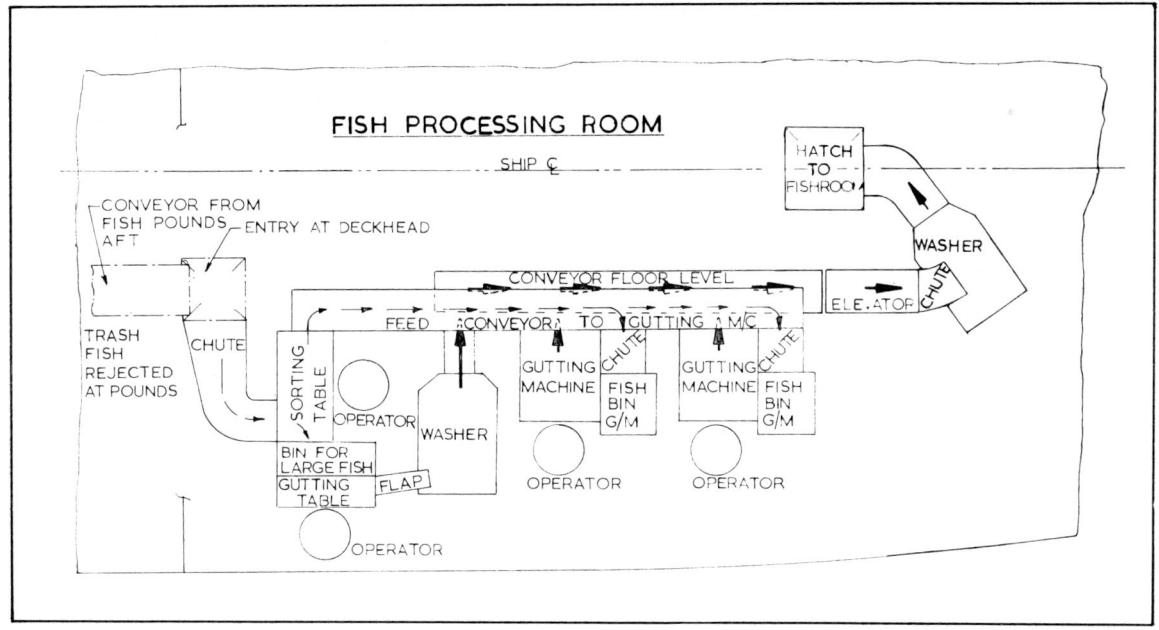

Fig. 36. Layout of gutting machines aboard the Aberdeen wet fish stern trawler "Ben Lui".

lower grade oil from this mixture, but further development work is required to ascertain whether this can be done commercially.

9.2. *The fish handling system*

In the previous paragraph, it has been stressed that it is essential to convey the fish both to and from the gutting machine. In fact, this has been done on all the Shetland gutting machine installations in UK vessels of over 30 m length. However, to design the equipment into the space available in existing vessels, has meant that the space at the input to the feed conveyor is somewhat cramped, as it has to compete with the normal requirements for hand gutting; the vessel owners so far wish to retain the facility to process the entire catch by manual means. There is thus insufficient room for rapid sorting of the catch and so the through-put of the gutting machine can suffer through interruptions in its supply.

This situation can be much improved when the fish processing space is designed around the gutting machine. The first new vessel to be equipped with gutting machines, is the *Ben Lui* (50 m l.o.a.) which has a sorting capability designed into the fish transportation system (see Fig. 36). Fish are mechanically conveyed continuously, or in batches as required, from the pounds to the gutting area. Before they reach the latter, they are split into two streams, those suitable for the gutting machines, and those to be hand-gutted. This layout has proved excellent in coping with any size and species mix of fish. From Fig. 36, it can be seen that a generous amount of space has been left in the sorting area. This is to allow for the later introduction of fish size grading machinery.

9.3. *Future developments*

The introduction of gutting machinery has provided a major part of the maximum improvement in productivity possible on the fish processing deck. Further mechanisation must therefore be carried out on a law of diminishing returns. After gutting, the next major workload is imposed by the grading of the fish into suitable sizes for machine gutting, Prototype grading machines have been undergoing trials (Fig. 37). The occasional wrong selection by the grader can be corrected by the gutting machine operator, but the rejected trash fish will have to be screened by a crew man to retrieve the smaller, but still marketable fish (e.g., flat fish, which will pass out from the grading machine in this stream).

The next stage is to feed the fish into the gutting machine automatically. The fish will have to be oriented in both planes, and then transferred to the gutting machine in correct synchronisation. Experimental equipment has been built by the Torry Research Station and it now seems quite feasible to

Fig. 37. Prototype size grading machine for round white fish.

achieve the aim of producing a hopper-fed gutting machine which automatically rejects over and undersized fish. It is unlikely that the automatic feed between grading and gutting machines can be justified economically for some years to come, but it is essential that this work should continue to be available for incorporation in the next generation of trawlers which will undoubtedly be worked by fewer men who will expect to undertake less manual work.

As in the case of the fishing gear, the provision of mechanical equipment for sorting, conveying, gutting and washing the catch is much easier in a stern trawler, and to provide the full complement of this equipment in a side trawler would be very difficult indeed.

10. CONCLUSION

Largely as a result of the advent of the stern trawler, there has been rapid development of mechanical equipment for handling the fishing gear aboard and also for handling and processing the catch. This development will continue for some time to come, and in the present state of the art, designs, layouts and methods are very fluid.

To incorporate much of this new equipment in a classic side trawler would scarcely be practicable. At the same time, it is not at all unlikely that, when systems for mechanically handling fishing gear and catches are developed to their ultimate potential, no doubt with at least some degree of automation, the vessels so equipped may not much resemble in layout the stern trawlers of today. Nevertheless, as first pointed out by Lochridge, the development and general adoption of the stern trawler have been essential steps in the mechanisation of fishing operations.

REFERENCES

1 'The German One-Boat Mid-Water Trawl' J. Schärfe, *Fishing News International*, July 1969.
2 'Trawler-Seiner Catamaran, its Commercial Features, Possibilities and Prospective Use' Y. V. Kadilnikoff. Conference on Automation and Mechanisation in Fishing Industry, Montreal, Canada, January 1970.
3 'Some Electronic Developments in the British Deep Sea Fishing Industry' R. Bennett, *Underwater Science and Technology Journal*, September 1969.
4 'Stern Trawling' Record of the Conference held in Grimsby U.K. in September 1963. Published by Fishing News (Books) Ltd.
5 'Operational Research Applied to Stern Freezer Trawler Design' P. D. Chaplin and K. Haywood. Joint Meeting of the Institute of Marine Engineers and the Grimsby Institution of Engineers and Shipbuilders at Grimsby, U.K., on 22nd March 1968.
6 'Small Stern Trawlers' W. M. Reid, *Fishing Boats of the World*, Vol. 3. Published by Fishing News (Books) Ltd.
7 'An Investigation into Flange Forces in Winch Drums' N. W. Bellamy and B. D. A. Phillips *Proceedings Institution of Mechanical Engineers 1968–69*, Vol. 183, Part 1.
8 'Deck Layout and Auxiliaries for Handling Mid-Water Trawls' W. Karger. F.A.O. Conference on Fish Finding, Purse Seining and Aimed Trawling, Reykjavik, Iceland, May 1970.
9 'Hydraulic Deck Machinery on Norwegian Fishing Vessels' *Ship and Boat Builder International*, October 1965.
10 'Hydraulics on Fishing Vessels' N. M. Kerr *Fluid Power International*, March and April 1971.
11 'The Marco Story' *World Fishing*, April 1969.
12 Door Handling on M.F.V. *Avenger*. *Fishing News International*, January 1971.
13 'Fifty Years of Baader Leadership' *World Fishing*, August 1969.

Handling and Processing the Catch in Stern Trawlers

J. J. WATERMAN, A.M.I.Mech.E., Head of Information Branch, Torry Research Station

INTRODUCTION

The development of stern trawling since World War II has run parallel to, and been closely linked with, improvements in methods of handling the catch, and it could be said that the interdependence of these two lines of development has resulted in the rapid evolution of the large freezer stern trawler as we know it today. Without a practical system of freezing the catch at sea, the design and development of trawlers for the distant water fishery would have been greatly hampered if not stopped altogether; without the more rational use of hull space and the logic of moving fish from aft to forward along a covered factory deck in a stern trawler, the concept of freezing fish at sea might have remained an impractical dream for very many years.

Although most large stern trawlers are particularly associated with freezing and cold storage of the catch at sea, a few large trawlers and many smaller ones below 50m in length that fish over the stern continue to preserve the catch by chilling it rather than freezing it, mainly by using ice. For small stern trawlers making voyages of only a few days, continuation of the traditional technique of chilling is perfectly satisfactory; quality of the catch remains good, and the limited availability of space, power and labour probably makes the use of more sophisticated systems of preservation economically unattractive, except for raw material of high value, for example shrimp, Norway lobster and some other shellfish caught by trawl. The continuance of chilling in large stern trawlers, however, has less to recommend it; ships that make voyages as long as, or longer than, the present pattern of the traditional side trawlers will land some fish of indifferent quality. The building of stern trawlers that perpetuate the shortcomings of their predecessors is a retrograde step.

Preservation of the catch in stern trawlers need not be confined to chilling or freezing; the factory deck can be used to accommodate other processing systems. The catch can be converted to dried, salted or canned products, or be reduced to fish meal and oil. There is nothing inherent in stern trawling as a method of capture that rigidly dictates the manner in which the catch should be handled and processed, but better layout and greater availability of space within the hull of a stern trawler give the operator more freedom of choice when designing the process and selecting the end product. Freezing at sea has become the predominant method of preservation of the catch in large stern trawlers. This is because the catch is destined largely for existing markets in developed countries, where the demand for high quality fish can best be met by supplying sea frozen fish which can either be distributed through the existing cold chain on shore, or be further processed at the ports in the same manner as best quality chilled fish.

The emphasis in this chapter will be on stern trawlers that chill or freeze the catch. For stern trawlers that stow the catch in ice or refrigerated sea water, the three main concepts of care, cleanliness and cooling apply in the same way as they do in side trawlers, and the recommendations made for good handling practice and good fishroom design remain virtually unchanged.

Of stern trawlers that freeze the catch and store it at low temperature, two principal types have evolved, those that freeze the catch as whole fish and those that process the catch further and freeze the fish as fillets. Some of the arguments for and against these two variants are discussed, but there is probably a continuing need for the development of both types to meet particular markets; certainly there is as yet no clearcut best design of freezer trawler. Methods and equipment for freezing at sea are described, and the problems of maintaining quality are discussed at some length; some recommendations are made for improving present practice. Some simplified calculations are given for determining the refrigeration requirements of shipborne freezers and cold stores, and a code of practice is given for crews on handling the catch.

Brief descriptions are also given of some of the

Fig. 1. Stacking blocks of frozen cod in the refrigerated fish room of a British wholefish freezer stern trawler.

mechanical handling, gutting, filleting and other processing equipment at present available.

Although some mention is made of stern trawler processing operations outside Europe, the main emphasis is on design and operation of vessels operating from European countries, and from the United Kingdom in particular. Brief mention is made of the problems of operation in tropical

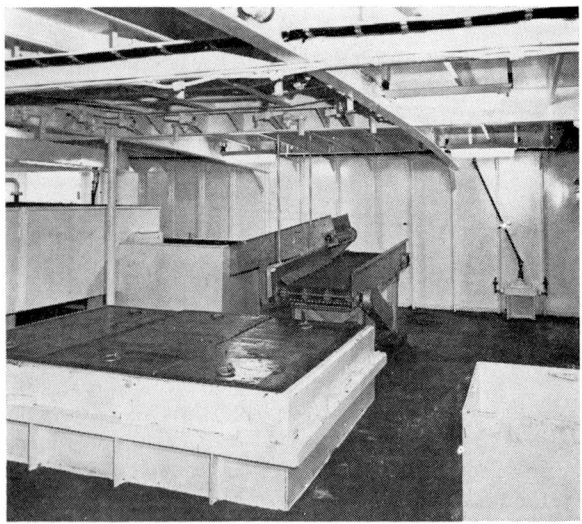

Fig. 2. Gutting, washing and conveying section and fish hold hatch top aboard the Grimsby-based wet fish trawler "Boston Beverley".

waters, but most of the information is based on experience of handling the catch, mainly of demersal white fish, in the North Atlantic.

Chilling the catch in stern trawlers

The practice of handling and stowing chilled fish in stern trawlers differs little from that in conventional side trawlers. The cod-end is winched up the stern ramp or, in smaller vessels, lifted inboard over the stern by derrick or gantry, and the contents are discharged either direct onto the fishing deck or to the aft end of a shelter deck below. The fish are then usually gutted, washed and transferred to the fishroom for stowage, typically in ice, either in boxes or in bulk, but less commonly in refrigerated sea water.

For most practical purposes, sea fishes can be divided into two main groups having markedly different spoilage characteristics. The first group, known as white fish, comprises those species in which the fat of the fish is contained almost entirely in the liver; these fishes are caught mostly on or near to the bottom of the sea, and constitute the bulk of the catch in the bottom trawl. Typical representatives of this group in the North Atlantic are the cod, the haddock and the flatfishes.

The second group, called fatty fish, includes those species in which the fat is distributed throughout the body structure; typical examples are the herring, the pilchard, the sprat and the anchovy. They are caught mainly near the surface of the sea, and constitute a large proportion of the catch of the midwater trawl. They are often caught in huge numbers during very short periods of fishing. In addition, there are some species that have a moderate amount of fat in the body tissues, and whose keeping quality falls somewhere between the two main groups; examples are redfish and mullets.

White fish from temperate and Arctic waters spoil fairly slowly at chill temperature. When the guts and liver are removed from cod for example immediately after capture, and the cleaned fish are quickly immersed in crushed ice, the flesh remains edible for 15 days or so, but is of poor quality after 10–12 days' storage. On the other hand, a fatty fish like the herring, taken at a season when the fat content is high, and stowed ungutted because of the large numbers caught, may keep only 4–5 days in ice before it becomes inedible, and may require processing within a day of capture to obtain a high quality product.

Chilled stowage of white fish

As soon as a haul is released from the cod-end of

Fig. 3. A fillet trimming line in operation at sea aboard a factory stern trawler owned by "Nordsee" Deutsche Hochseefischerei, West Germany's largest fishing company.

the trawl, the first essential is to gut and bleed the fish. Delay while the trawl is mended and shot again can mean some warming of the catch and consequent increase in spoilage. In addition, warm fish left ungutted long enough for the blood to coagulate will yield badly discoloured fillets. If a long delay is unavoidable, some attempt should be made to keep the fish cool either by sprinkling ice on them or by spraying them with cold sea water; this will reduce the rate of spoilage and keep the blood liquid until it can be released. The tedium of gutting large numbers of small white fish like whiting and small haddock can be alleviated by using a gutting machine and, where space on the processing deck permits, a wider range of sizes of round white fish can be gutted by adding a larger version of the machine.

Small fish should be gutted before large ones, because small fish spoil more quickly than large ones of the same species. Species that spoil quickly should be gutted first; for example haddock and whiting should be dealt with before cod, and flatfish after cod. In some European fisheries, white fish are bled as a separate operation before gutting begins, in order to give a whiter fillet, but experimental evidence in the UK indicates that the bleeding effect of gutting is just as satisfactory provided the fish are dealt with promptly.

Gutting benches can readily be provided on an enclosed processing deck, and robust conveyers can be used to remove offal and to move gutted fish to the washer, thus taking much of the effort of bending, lifting and throwing out of the job of hand gutting, and improving the hygiene of the operation.

Mechanical washing not only cleans the fish in a reasonably uniform manner, but also provides a means of delivering the fish to the fishroom in a fairly steady stream, thus making the job of stowage easier. The rotating horizontal drum is the most satisfactory type, because the residence time of each fish in the washer can be controlled reasonably well; the fish are moved forward by a helix on the inside of the perforated drum and subjected to sprays of clean sea water during their passage. The open bath type of washer in which the water is swirled by hoses is less satisfactory; the water in the bath is never clean, and some fish may remain in the water only for seconds before being slopped over the exit weir by the movement of the ship, while others may remain for long periods. This type of washer always requires clearing by hand when the last fish have gone in. Although bleeding may not be completed during washing, the fish can continue to bleed freely during stowage to give a product with white flesh. The shelter deck of a stern trawler lends itself well to the handling of fish through the gutting and washing stages to the fishroom; the raw material flows from aft to forward, and each step can easily be mechanised so that the cleaned catch goes into stowage very quickly after capture, with the minimum of labour.

Ice is still the most satisfactory medium in which to chill fish quickly and then keep them cool while stored aboard the ship. Although pure ice melts at 0°C, the temperature of fish stowed in crushed ice may be about $-1°C$, due mainly to the presence of salts in the fish flesh and of sea water on the surface of the fish. About 1 kg of ice to 2 kg fish is required on an Arctic trip of three weeks' duration. In tropical waters, a ratio of nearer 1:1 is usually necessary for voyages of more than a few days.

The ice has three main duties: to remove heat from the fish, to absorb heat coming in through the ship's structure, and to keep the chilled fish cool and moist by maintaining a steady flow of cold meltwater over the catch. Ice must therefore be distributed carefully throughout the catch; wherever possible fish should be in contact only with ice, and not with other fish or the structure of the fishroom. Fish touching one another do not cool as rapidly as they do when each is completely buried in ice, and when a fish is in contact with a smooth surface like a wooden or metal lining, air may be excluded; some of the spoilage bacteria inevitably present in spite of efficient gutting and washing will then multiply rapidly and produce foul smelling substances which can spread through the flesh. Additional ice must be placed against bulkheads and ship's sides to absorb heat coming in from warmer parts of the ship and from the sea and air outside.

The fish are cooled largely by cold meltwater flowing over them; in theory therefore the higher the surrounding temperature the faster the ice will melt and so the faster the fish will be cooled, but in practice the weight of ice required to ensure the fish remained covered and protected during two weeks or more in stowage would be far too high. Thus the fishroom temperature has to be kept reasonably low to avoid excessive wastage of ice; a temperature of $1-2°C$ is usually most suitable.

Mechanical cooling systems are sometimes fitted in fishrooms; a commonly encountered type is the deckhead cooling grid, consisting of a series of flat coils of plain pipe fitted close to the deckhead of the fishroom and cooled by direct expansion of refrigerant, typically refrigerant 12. Sometimes the grid is extended to cover one or both bulkheads. The cooling grid is of rather limited value for the chilling of fish in ice. It cannot be used as an alternative to ice; the grid alone will have little or no effect on the centre of a heap of warm fish. The thermal conductivity of wet fish is rather low, and the cooling medium must be in intimate contact with the product to achieve rapid cooling. Moreover, fish at the top of the stowage close to the grid may become partially frozen; the surface of the fish becomes dry and takes on an unattractive appearance.

The grids can be used on the outward voyage to cool the fishroom and its fittings, so that when stowage begins the duty of the ice will be largely confined to cooling the fish. Refrigeration on the outward voyage will also help to conserve the ice and keep it crisp and free flowing; the surface of a heap of ice in a warm fishroom will melt and then glaze over to form a hard crust which requires chopping with an axe when stowage begins. Once stowage starts – and this procedure may continue for 10 days or more in a large trawler – the grid will help to keep the fishroom air temperature low while hatches are continually being opened. Once stowage is complete, the temperature of the cargo will be governed almost entirely by the ice surrounding it and, if the fishroom is full, the grid should preferably be shut off.

When the grid is left on during the homeward run, the ice close to it is prevented from melting and thus cannot effectively do its job. When there are large spaces left empty in the fishroom at the end of fishing, the cooling grid will help to keep these air spaces cool, and to this end it is advisable to have more than one grid circuit so that the part of the grid close to completed stowage can be shut off, leaving the other part over the empty compartments to continue running.

The temperature of the fishroom should be indicated on the bridge by distant reading thermometers; the sensitive elements should be located so that they record an air temperature that is reasonably representative of the fishroom as a whole. They should not be located so close to the grid as to be unduly affected by it, nor partially buried in a mass of fish and ice; they should preferably be about midway between the hatch coaming and the ship's side, a little below grid level, with the bulbs shielded by a perforated cover. Where the condensing unit for the grid is controlled by a fishroom thermostat, its bulb should be similarly located, with the thermostat set to cut in at about $3°C$ and out again at about $1°C$.

Fan cooler units are sometimes used in fishrooms. The fishroom air is drawn through a refrigerated coil and blown around the airspaces in the fishroom; the same cautionary remarks apply to this system as to deckhead grids, but with the added proviso that fish exposed to rapidly moving air will become dried on the surface. The main value of ancillary cooling equipment of this kind is again during the outward voyage and during catching, rather than after the fishroom is full.

A variation of the fan cooler system which has been tried in some trawlers is the provision of a refrigerated air jacket between the insulation and the inner lining of the fishroom. The fan cooler unit is fitted in the airspace to absorb heat coming in through the insulation before it reaches the cargo space, after the manner of some shore-based cold stores. These installations have not been very successful in practice; the evaporator is inaccessible for maintenance and, since the lining is rarely moisture-tight, troubles have been experienced due to severe icing of the evaporator coils. More important however is the fact that the operator often misinterprets the purpose of the installation. A jacketed fishroom of this kind should enable the ice to be used solely for cooling the catch, but all too often the fisherman assumes that ice around the fish is no longer so necessary because the hidden equipment will in some way take care of things for him; the result is less careful stowage and poor quality catches.

Fishrooms in most steel stern trawlers are insulated; insulation in wooden vessels is less common and to some extent not so important. It is perfectly feasible to keep iced fish from Arctic waters in a fishroom that has only a 5 cm wooden lining with an airspace behind it, provided the ice is dispensed liberally and put in the right places; but the amount of ice required to combat the heat leak through such a structure in tropical waters would be excessive. In general, for any stern trawler making trips of more than a few hours, insulation is eminently desirable, even if only as insurance against inadequate icing or careless stowage. For northern waters, 5 cm of an expanded plastics insultant is usually adequate for ship's sides and deckhead; in tropical waters 10 cm is advisable for ships that are out for several days.

Insulating materials that readily absorb water are not very suitable for fishrooms, because linings are never watertight; slime and bacteria will eventually find their way into the insulation and become a source of contamination. Closed cell plastics are the most useful insulating materials for walls, either in rigid slab form or foamed in place behind the lining. Great care must be taken to ensure that wooden members of either the lining or the ship's structure cannot become susceptible to wet rot. Tanktops are often ignored completely when a fishroom is being insulated; considerable quantities of heat can come in from the sea through the ship's bottom, and insulation of the fishroom must be complete to be really effective. A denser grade of insulant is usually necessary on the tanktop if the surface is to be finished as a load bearing floor. The steelwork of slushwells is often directly connected to very warm parts of the ship, and heat leaks can be excessive; additional insulation around the slushwell is advisable.

Ice is reasonably cheap and plentiful at the principal European ports, and most vessels take their supply aboard before sailing. It is generally impracticable, except in very large factory trawlers, to consider manufacture of ice at sea. Somewhere between 2 and 4 kW are required to make a metric ton of ice a day, and large icing stern trawlers may require as much as 10 tonnes a day or more when fishing; there is not normally sufficient space available aboard to accommodate both a big enough ice-making plant and an adequate power supply for it without encroaching on valuable cargo space. It must be remembered that although there may be 100 tonnes of ice in the fishroom at the start of a voyage, that space gradually becomes available for fish, whereas space for an icemaking plant is permanently occupied.

In most cases, sea water would have to be used for making ice aboard the trawler; seawater ice is less suitable for the stowage of fish than freshwater ice for a number of reasons, but principally because the salt content is rarely uniform, and thus the melting point can vary; freshwater ice is its own thermostat, but with seawater ice the temperature of stowage is less easily controlled.

The form of the ice used for chilling fish is relatively unimportant, provided the ice is ice and not a mixture of ice and water. Most small ports and some large ones that have installed modern icemaking plant produce ice in forms other than large blocks; flake ice and tube ice are becoming more generally available. The cooling capacity of 1 kg of flake ice is the same as 1 kg of crushed block ice. Flake ice has the advantage that it marks the fish less badly, and pieces of flat shape usually make better contact with fish and cool it more rapidly. Crushed block ice on the other hand has a better stowage rate, and weight for weight takes up less room in the fishroom or in a box of fish. One tonne of crushed block ice occupies about 1.6 m^3 of fishroom space;

1 tonne of flake ice requires over 30 per cent more space and occupies about 2.1m³.

The fishroom in a stern trawler can often be located in a part of the hull that is roughly rectangular in cross section, so that better use can be made of the space for stowage. Boxing of the catch at sea is therefore a more attractive form of stowage in stern trawlers than in side trawlers, where a large part of the stowage space at the forward end of the fishroom is likely to be of unsuitable shape for boxes. Suitably designed boxes, properly used, make the best form of stowage for fish in ice; boxed fish are generally of better quality on landing than fish from bulk or shelf stowage, and can remain undisturbed in the same box right through to the port processor's premises.

A box must be properly designed for its job. It must have sufficient room in it for the amount of fish required plus room for enough ice to protect the fish until they are landed. The box should not be so deep that fish at the bottom are squashed, and it must be long enough to accommodate without bending most of the larger fish caught. At the same time it must not be so unwieldy that it cannot be handled comfortably by one or two men as required either at sea or at the port. The boxes should stack to a reasonable height when full without distortion or collapse of the bottom box, in order to reduce the number of supporting shelves in the fishroom, or to dispense with shelves altogether; this will keep down waste space in the fishroom and so increase stowage rate. The boxes should preferably nest when empty, so that there is sufficient room for stowage at the start of fishing.

The box should have drain holes so arranged that dirty meltwater does not drain onto the fish in the boxes below. It is difficult to design a nesting box that does this, and it may be necessary to compromise between these two conflicting requirements. The box should be of a material that is easily cleaned and kept clean, and that does not taint or contaminate the contents. It should be robust enough to withstand trawler working conditions and be suitable for use with mechanical handling equipment for rapid discharge of the cargo and its onward conveyance from the quayside; one of the important advantages of boxing at sea is that the catch can be landed and distributed without rehandling.

The box should have provision for marking on it the nature, quantity and date of capture of the contents; boxing facilitates the sale of fish by sample, because weight and quality of contents of all boxes bearing the same date of capture can be taken on trust after inspection of representative lots. Disturbance of the contents of every box on sale in order to inspect the quality defeats the main purpose of the method.

Boxes used at any one port, and preferably throughout a fishery, should be of standard design and size; the complete handling chain can then be made to suit the box. The fishroom dimensions will be multiples of the box dimensions, and conveyers, shore transport and storage facilities can all be designed around a standard unit container. Central cleaning, maintenance and distribution facilities for boxes can also be provided. Typical stowage rates for boxed fish are between 2.3 and 2.6m³ for a tonne of fish.

Chilled stowage of fatty fish

Fatty fish are typically of small size and of poor keeping quality, and are caught in very large numbers in a short period on voyages not far from the port of landing; they therefore present a serious handling and stowage problem and are all too often landed ungutted and unchilled, with disastrous effect on quality.

Boxing of the catch in ice is one solution, in the manner described for white fish. An alternative to ice for the cooling of fatty fish is refrigerated sea water; the method makes stowage of large numbers of small fish much easier, and makes it possible to transfer or discharge the catch by pump.

The sea water can be chilled in a heat exchanger by mechanical refrigeration, or ice can be added to the water. The recommended temperature of storage is $-1°C$, just above the freezing point of the fish, and three to four parts of fish by weight can be kept in one part of sea water.

Main drawback to the use of refrigerated sea water (RSW) is uptake of salt by the fish; ungutted fatty fish like herring, stowed in RSW for six to seven days, will take up about one per cent by weight of salt. This factor limits the outlets for which the fish are suitable, and the method is best applied to fish destined for canning or smoking, where some salt would normally be added during processing. The storage life of fatty fish in RSW is about the same as in crushed ice; lean herring for example will keep in good condition for up to a week, whereas fat herring that have been feeding heavily may keep for only one to two days.

An alternative to pump discharge of a catch stowed in RSW is the use of portable tanks that can be lifted from the ship onto shore transport, but this can introduce considerable problems in designing the ship layout; it may be difficult to provide a straight lift from the stowage area without interfering too much with the fishing deck and superstructure in a stern trawler. The use of ice instead of mechanical refrigeration for cooling the sea water makes the portable tank a more likely concept.

Stability can be a problem with a tank installation, and it is common practice to fit each tank with a narrow neck so that the free surface area when the tank is full is reduced to a minimum. It is preferable to fill one tank with fish and water before starting on another, because fish in partially filled tanks are readily damaged by the movement of the ship. Engineering design problems in RSW installations include provision of adequate water circulation to maintain even temperature distribution, adequate cleaning arrangements to prevent contamination of pipes and tanks, and sufficient refrigeration capacity to cope with high cooling loads if the method is to be any more rapid than stowage in ice.

RSW systems are as yet relatively untried in stern trawlers, except in shrimp vessels, but may well become accepted practice for catches of small ungutted fatty fish.

Summary of recommendations for handling chilled fish in stern trawlers

It is perhaps appropriate here to summarise the main design and operational requirements for good handling and stowage of fish in ice.

On the processing deck:

Provide adequate cleaning facilities, and design the deck and its equipment for easy cleaning; make full use of light alloys, stainless steel and plastics, and avoid the use of wood. Remember that fish is a food and should be handled as such from the time it is caught.

Provide some cooling arrangements for fish awaiting gutting; fit sprays of cold sea water or make it easy to move ice to the area.

Fit hygienic gutting benches or gutting machines; make it easy for the crew to reach the ungutted fish without trampling on them, and reduce the need for stooping and lifting.

Give clear instructions about the standard of gutting required, for example, insist on double naping, careful removal of all traces of gut and liver, avoidance of unnecessary wounds, and reporting of the presence of worms or other inherent defects in the fish.

Provide containers or conveyors for the movement of livers and guts, so that fish are not contaminated unnecessarily.

Insist that gutting starts as soon as the fish come aboard, and that all the fish from one haul are dealt with before the fish from the next haul are started. Lay down the order in which species should be dealt with.

Provide a continuous washer and where possible move the gutted fish to it by conveyor; bruising as a result of throwing fish about produces discoloured and damaged fillets.

Insist that the processing deck is cleaned down each time it is clear of fish.

In the fishroom:

Move the washed fish into the fishroom by chute or conveyor.

Install a boxed stowage system rather than a structure of stanchions and pound boards.

Insulate the fishroom completely and fit an impervious and hygienic fishroom lining.

Where the fishroom is very large, consider the provision of mechanical equipment for moving fish and ice to box filling points, and filled boxes to the stacking area.

Make sure that the design of box is appropriate for the species being handled and the stowage time required; the efficiency of the whole system depends on the suitability of the box.

Provide means of recording species, size and date of stowage on the box, and insist that this information is always accurately recorded.

Specify the manner of icing the fish in a box, for example by laying down the ratio of ice to fish, emphasising the need for ice in the bottom of the box, between the fish and on the top, and by banning overfilling of the box.

Provide mechanical cooling for the fishroom as a means of conserving ice on the outward voyage and of keeping the fishroom air cool, particularly when working in warmer waters, but provide precise instructions about the proper use and maintenance of the equipment.

Provide good access to the fishroom for rapid discharge by modern mechanical methods; make unloading hatches big enough, keep fishroom internal structure to a minimum, and provide accurate stowage plans.

Maintain a high standard of quality by limiting the length of the voyage; if it is likely that a stern trawler will have to land iced white fish more than 10–12 days out of the water, in order to make its operation economic, then consider more permanent methods of preservation like freezing and cold storage at sea.

The need for freezing at sea

There are distinct limitations to the practice of chilling fish at sea; white fish, no matter how well they are looked after, will eventually spoil at ice temperature after about 15 days, and fatty fish will spoil even more quickly, becoming inedible after about a week at the most.

It is possible, by using techniques like super-chilling, where the temperature of the fish is reduced to about $-2°C$, or by using antibiotic ices, to make some small extension of shelf life, but in general the length of voyage of a trawler that ices its catch is governed by the quality on landing of the first caught fish.

On many grounds the catching rate has decreased as increasing numbers of vessels have fished them, and operators have had to choose between bringing trawlers home with small and often uneconomic catches and staying out to fill the ship at the risk of spoiling some of the cargo. Inevitably, most European trawlers working a distant water fishery have to return from the grounds with their fishrooms far from full in order to avoid landing unacceptable fish.

The only method of long term preservation for fish that does not markedly change the nature of the product is freezing followed by low temperature storage. Properly frozen fish, stored at a temperature of $-30°C$ or lower for several months, is virtually indistinguishable in flavour and texture from fresh fish. It is essential however that the fish be frozen when fresh; freezing does not improve the product, but merely slows down or arrests the spoilage changes. It is obviously undesirable therefore to freeze at the port of landing fish that have been in ice for many days; in practice whole cod for example should be frozen within three days of capture, and be kept chilled while awaiting freezing, to give a product that when thawed can be treated like fresh iced fish. Other species like flatfish can be kept longer, five to six days after catching, and still give a first class frozen product. On the other hand haddock should not be more than two days old, and hake are sometimes too soft to stand up to the effects of freezing even after one day in ice. Fatty fish like herring should be frozen within 24 hours of capture, and preferably even sooner when full of food.

These limits on iced stowage before freezing are made on the assumption that the thawed whole fish must be suitable for further processing, for example filleting and smoking. When fillets are frozen and there is no intention to process them further after thawing, acceptable products can be obtained from fish that have been kept well iced for up to seven days after capture; it must again be emphasised however that the thawed product will be similar in quality to the original raw material and that freezing cannot improve a product. There is therefore a considerable incentive to freeze all fish as soon as possible after capture and this means in most distant water fisheries taking the freezing plant to sea.

The freezing of fish at sea leads to three very important benefits, a general improvement in the quality of fish from distant waters, greater utilisation of the fishing vessel by increasing the proportion of fishing time to steaming time, and the facility of stockpiling from times of glut to times of shortage.

The evolution of the modern freezer stern trawler is outlined in the following brief history of freezing fish at sea.

DEVELOPMENT OF THE FREEZER TRAWLER

Spasmodic attempts to freeze fish at sea were made as long ago as the second half of the 19th century, first by using freezing mixtures of ice and salt and later, as the art of mechanical refrigeration was developed, by immersing the fish in brine that had been cooled by using carbon dioxide as a primary refrigerant.

Although a number of patents appeared in the first two decades of the 20th century, and several isolated attempts were made to use brine freezing equipment in fishing vessels, the first serious attempts to freeze fish at sea on a commercial scale began in the 1920s.

The French operated a mother ship called the *Janot* in 1925, which was reported to be capable of freezing 12 tonnes of fish a day in a drum type, brine immersion freezer of a kind developed experimentally in the UK, The ship could carry 100 tonnes of fish in cold storage, and was fed by a fleet of trawlers.

The mother ship concept was tried in the UK in 1926, when a meat carrier named the *Helder* was converted to the brine freezing of fish. She was later renamed *Arctic Prince* and was subsequently joined in 1929 by another converted meat carrier, the *Arctic Queen*, on a series of voyages to Greenland. These two ships each made one fishing expedition each summer for several years, and were supplied with halibut from the catches of a fleet of lining dories. In the winter months the ships served as floating cold store depots at their UK base, and slowly discharged their cargoes of frozen halibut to meet market requirements.

Difficulties were experienced in transferring catches at sea in bad weather, the halibut stocks on the Greenland grounds became depleted, and the brine freezing plant proved difficult and costly to maintain properly at sea. The venture ended about 1935, and there is no doubt that the British market at that time was not geared to receive large consignments of frozen fish, nor prepared to pay an economic price; the quality of the frozen fish was not very good by present day standards, because the technology of freezing and cold storage of fish was not then fully understood.

A German trawler, the *Volkswohl*, was fitted with a brine freezer in 1929, and some effort was made to match freezing time to the product by sorting the fish for size before immersing them. In 1931 the French developed a freezer that combined spraying of brine with immersion in brine, and fitted two ships, the *Jean Hamonet* and the *Marie Helene*, with this equipment. The French continued to exploit freezing at sea by fitting out the *Vivagel* in 1936 and a number of other fishing vessels up to 1939.

Formal research of freezing at sea in the UK began in 1927–8 when the trawler *Ben Meidie* was used for a number of shipborne experiments. The results of this work emphasised the need for cold storage at a sufficiently low temperature, and it was quickly established that rapid freezing in brine at $-20°C$ followed by storage at $-24°C$ would keep fish as good as fresh for more than three months.

The economic advantages of freezing at sea to the distant water fishing fleet were being discussed in the UK as early as 1932. Numerous attempts were made to persuade British trawler owners to freeze the first part of the catch in the trawler, and thus bring back the oldest fish in good condition. But the prevailing economic climate was depressing, there was no established cold chain on shore, and shipborne freezing plant was still rather cumbersome and not very efficient. Further development of freezing at sea had to wait until after World War II.

In 1947 a very big advance towards the freezer trawler of today was made when, for the first time, the idea of trawling over the stern was linked with the idea of freezing the catch aboard. The *Fairfree*, a converted British minesweeper, was used as a floating testbed both for the development of stern trawling gear and for freezing equipment designed to handle fillets of fish; the freezer, known as the Fairfreezer, was of a hybrid type that combined air blast freezing with contact freezing, the fillets being laid on refrigerated plates while cold air was blown over them. This venture was sufficiently successful to encourage her owners subsequently to build the *Fairtry* and her two sister ships.

The *Fairfree* was conceived originally as a factory trawler rather than a stern trawler, but stern trawling became a necessity on the *Fairfree* and her successors because the inclusion of a factory deck increased the height above water of the fishing deck to such an extent that side trawling became impracticable. This interplay of catching and processing techniques and the resultant influence on ship design sparked off many years of valuable research work in both fields that led to the present designs of stern trawler. The *Fairfree* also demonstrated for the first time the logic of introducing the raw material at the aft end of the ship and directing its flow forwards through the factory.

Fish were emptied from the trawl through a hatch in the main deck to the factory on the shelter deck, where they were gutted, filleted by hand, packed in trays lined with cellulose film and frozen in the Fairfreezer, which had a capacity of one tonne an hour. The frozen blocks, weighing about 20 kg each, were taken out of the trays, glazed by dipping them in cold water, packed and sealed in plastic bags and stored aboard at a temperature of $-20°C$.

The *Fairfree*'s purpose-built successor, the *Fairtry*, was completed in Aberdeen in 1953; she was a factory stern trawler, 85 m long overall and 2,605 gross tons, equipped with heading, filleting and skinning machines, a Fairfreezer and horizontal plate freezers for freezing the fillets, and a fish meal plant for handling filleting offal and unwanted fish. She carried a crew of more than 80, had storage for 600 tonnes of frozen fillets at $-20°C$, and made voyages of about three months' duration. The *Fairtry* set the pattern for factory trawlers; not only did the same British company build the *Fairtry II* and *Fairtry III* in 1959 and 1960, but other European fishing nations also quickly copied the example almost in its entirety. Notably the USSR factory fleet began to develop its present form with the building of a series of stern trawlers closely modelled on the British pattern.

The three *Fairtry* ships were withdrawn from service in 1968; possible reasons for their early demise are discussed later, when the pros and cons of freezing whole fish or fillets are argued more fully.

Post-war pioneer work on freezing whole fish at sea

Pre-war work on the freezing of whole fish by immersing them in cold brine was seen to have its shortcomings; it was not possible to employ sufficiently low freezing temperatures, the product took up salt from the brine, thus making it unacceptable for some outlets, and the equipment was too bulky for shipboard use. In 1948 British research workers began practical experiments to develop simpler and

Fig. 4. Built in 1959, the factory stern trawler "Fairtry II" was laid up in 1968 and was sold in 1971 for conversion into an ocean research and submersible support ship.

more robust freezing equipment that would fit into the space available in existing side trawlers, and that would require little extra labour to operate. Contact freezing was judged the most likely method, and the first attempts simulated the traditional method for making blocks of ice, by freezing whole fish in water in a tapered metal mould immersed in cold brine; the contents expanded as they froze, and it was extremely difficult to remove the frozen mass without excessive thawing.

The next step was to eliminate immersion of the mould by making the walls of the mould hollow so that refrigerant could be passed through them. Two metal plates, one flat and the other embossed with a serpentine passageway, were welded together to make a suitable freezing plate, and defrosting was

Fig. 5. Baader fillet line for large fish in the pioneer factory trawler "Fairtry".

then simplified because hot refrigerant could be circulated through the mould wall. The block of frozen fish encased in ice still proved difficult to remove, and the need for freezing the fish in ice was reconsidered.

Experiment showed that any advantage of improved contact with the freezer plate gained by adding water to the fish in the mould before freezing was offset by the extra refrigeration capacity required to freeze the added water. Blocks of fish could be frozen just as rapidly without adding water, and so the requirement for a watertight mould disappeared. This made the problem of removing the frozen block much simpler; the one-piece freezing mould was replaced by a pair of vertical, parallel embossed plates, one of which could be moved away from the frozen block as soon as the plates were defrosted. This basic design for one block of frozen whole fish became the pattern for subsequent designs of plate freezer for producing numbers of blocks at a time.

The next experimental step was the building of multiple units. Four-station freezers were tried at sea on the 27 m research trawler *Keelby* in 1950, when the main emphasis of the work was directed towards investigation of quality of sea frozen fish, and determination of the conditions necessary for producing a high grade product. A processing specification for the freezing at sea of North Sea cod was gradually developed, by investigating factors like the time limit between catching and freezing, the need for bleeding or gutting, the speed of freezing and the temperature and time of cold storage. On the four-station freezer at this time the primary refrigerant, refrigerant 12, was fed to the plates through flexible hoses, the plates were defrosted by a hot gas system, and the plates were moved apart by pneumatic jacks to release the frozen blocks.

The extensive *Keelby* trials proved the ease and simplicity of operation of the freezer in all weather conditions, and established the acceptability of the product. The next big step was to demonstrate the system on something approaching a commercial scale. Although today it can be seen that the technique of freezing fish at sea is best applied in a new trawler designed for the purpose, and that the stern trawler is a most suitable type of ship, there had been considerable investment in the immediate post-war years in new side trawlers for distant water fishing, and most of these ships still had many years of useful life ahead of them in the 1950s. It was therefore decided to demonstrate freezing at sea in a manner that could be applied to the existing fleet.

A layout was prepared in 1953 that would fit into the part of a trawler fishroom that would normally remain unfilled, and with sufficient freezing and cold storage capacity to cope with the first three to four days' catch on an average voyage. Government and industry agreed to charter and convert an existing trawler to implement this plan, and the cost of the venture was shared by the distant water trawler owners, the White Fish Authority and the British Treasury. The steam trawler *Northern Wave* was selected and converted at Hull in 1955, under Government technical supervision, and between the end of 1955 and the autumn of 1956 she completed eight experimental voyages from Grimsby; some 30 tonnes of the earliest caught white fish were frozen and stored at $-30°C$ on each trip, probably the first time cargo had ever been carried at such a low temperature in a commercial ship. The blocks of fish were subsequently stored in shore cold stores, and then thawed and distributed through normal trade channels to assess their commercial acceptability.

The six-station freezers used in the *Northern Wave* were a modification of the type used in the *Keelby*; the refrigeration contractors improved the mechanical design of the prototype, making the new version more compact. The pneumatic jacks were replaced by spring jacks, and the movement of the refrigerated plates, the end plates and the bottom door of the freezer were all controlled by one large lever. Blocks of fish were discharged direct from the freezer into the cold store through the bottom door. The flexible hoses were replaced by synthetic rubber O rings in hollow trunnions, and refrigerant was fed through the trunnions to the freezer plates which hung in them. The refrigerant 12 was pumped through the freezers by means of a special pump driven magnetically through a stainless steel shroud; this solution was arrived at only after considerable experimental difficulty with sealing the pump shaft.

The freezing plant and cold store had to be built in the forward end of the fishroom, an unsatisfactory location, and the refrigeration machinery was on the foreside of the cold store. Despite the awkward position, the unsuitable shape of that part of the hull and the extraordinarily rough weather encountered in the early voyages, there was virtually no mechanical or electrical trouble at any time and the freezers withstood the rigours of rough handling by trawlermen without any difficulty.

This *Northern Wave* experiment demonstrated conclusively that freezing at sea was technically feasible on a commercial scale, and that sea frozen fish was generally acceptable to fish merchants, fishmongers and the public. But the scale of the

Fig. 6. Built in Germany in 1961, the Hull-based "Lord Nelson" was equipped to freeze part of her catch at sea.

experiment was still not big enough immediately to convince prospective owners of freezer trawlers that freezing at sea was profitable. None was prepared there and then to install and operate freezing plant at sea; apart from doubts about the economics, there were two other important reasons why the method was not immediately accepted. The cold storage chain from port to shop was still in its infancy, and the stern trawler, in spite of the example of the *Fairtry*, was still not a fully acceptable design of hull, at least in Britain, although the changeover had already begun in some European fleets, notably in West Germany.

One of the main controversies at this time concerning the design of a shipborne freezer installation was the freezer capacity necessary to cope with distant water catching rates. Many owners argued that the plant should be big enough to handle all of the catch immediately it came on board, and that the idea of keeping down the size of plant by re-handling fish in and out of chilled buffer storage was unworkable. To some extent this argument has been justified, and many of the existing freezer trawlers now have plants that almost always handle the fish within a few hours of catching, partly to keep down labour requirements, and partly to avoid the difficulties of fish going through rigor, an aspect which is discussed in detail later.

Economic studies were made to show how, from the pattern of typical wet fishing voyages, the introduction of freezing could have made the trips more profitable by increasing the proportion of time spent fishing and by reducing the amount of poor quality fish landed. In addition, a new layout was prepared in 1957 for a side trawler equipped for freezing part of the catch, using experience gained in the *Northern Wave*, a layout which looked remarkably little different from the 1953 proposals.

In 1959 a full design study was commissioned, using the hull lines of a recently completed side trawler, offering a number of choices of propulsion system, together with the argument that a freezer trawler need not be as fast as her wet fishing counterpart, and therefore the savings on engine space could be used to advantage to accommodate more frozen fish; it was estimated that a reduction in speed of one knot could provide enough cold storage for a further two days' catch.

The economics of freezing fillets at sea were also examined at this time, but only on the assumptions that gutting and filleting at sea could be fully mechanized at some time in the future, and that the crew need then be only a little larger than on a trawler freezing whole fish; on this basis, the freezing of fillets appeared to be competitive, provided there were no technical problems in producing an acceptable product.

In the late 1950s, the British trawling industry gradually accepted the idea that existing side trawlers were unlikely to be wholly suitable for conversion to freezing, and interest swung towards construction of new tonnage equipped for the job.

Fig. 7. Built in 1962, the "Junella" was Britain's first full wholefish freezer stern trawler.

The *Northern Wave* experiment, the subsequent design and economic studies, the growth of a shore-based freezing industry for fish and vegetables, and the appearance of new stern trawler designs on the European Continent all helped to heighten the interest in the possibility of building freezer stern trawlers for whole fish.

In 1959, the design of the British stern trawler *Lord Nelson* began; completed in Germany in 1961, she was in many ways the direct commercial successor of the *Northern Wave* as far as handling the catch was concerned; she was equipped to freeze the first part of the catch in vertical plate freezers; the same Government research workers acted as consultants throughout design, construction, and the early voyages; and the same refrigeration contractors built the freezing plant. The *Lord Nelson* was the first British commercial trawler, and probably the first anywhere, to freeze blocks of whole white fish at sea.

She was built with a cold store to hold about 180 tonnes of frozen fish, and a fishroom to carry about 150 tonnes of wet fish in ice. Sixteen six-station freezers produced about 25 tonnes of frozen gutted whole fish a day in 45-kg blocks. The freezer plates, made from extruded aluminium sections, were an improvement on their predecessors, but the O ring joints between trunnions and plates were a continual source of leaks. Laboratory experiments showed that the trouble was probably due to the frequent change of temperature between freezing and hot gas defrosting, and the O rings were soon replaced by coiled copper tubes as flexible connections to the freezer plates. The freezing cycle on the *Lord Nelson* was four hours, including time for loading and unloading.

The *Lord Nelson* was in many ways the trial horse for the British trawler fleet. Although she was the only part freezer to be built, and the only one to use a primary refrigerant in the freezer, the experience gained on her early voyages proved invaluable when her successors were being designed.

Another British trawler company had begun a series of experiments in 1958. Their first step was to install a single station freezer in one of their side trawlers, the *Marbella*. Research workers sailed in the ship and produced a range of experimental blocks of fish so that the owners could satisfy themselves that the quality was acceptable to them. A small cold store was then built in another existing side trawler, the *Junella*, and two six-station vertical plate freezers were installed. Government research staff and refrigeration contractors again accompanied the ship on a number of commercial voyages, and the experiment continued until the owners had acquired sufficient experience of handling and distributing sea frozen fish to be confident that a new freezer trawler could be a viable proposi-

Fig. 8. The wholefish freezer trawler "St. Finbarr" at her launching. Completed in 1964, she was lost at sea after a fire aboard at the end of 1966. But in her short career she had considerable influence on British freezer trawler design.

tion. The freezer used in this experiment was of different design, being a top loading, end unloading model based on a prototype developed earlier for the freezing of herring in blocks.

The name *Junella* was transferred to a new stern trawler built to freeze the whole of her catch when she was completed at Aberdeen in 1962. The ship differed in several important ways from the *Lord Nelson*, completed a year earlier. A secondary refrigerant, trichloroethylene, was pumped through the freezers and cooled in a heat exchanger by the primary refrigerant, R22. Wasteful and costly leaks of primary refrigerant from the freezers were thus largely eliminated, at the cost of some loss of efficiency as result of using a secondary system. Freezer plates were coated with a nonstick plastic, PTFE, and there was no hot defrost system fitted at that time; the frozen blocks were released simply by moving the plates apart. There were eleven 12-station freezers with a total capacity of 25 tonnes of fish a day, although the individual blocks were smaller and lighter than those made in the *Lord Nelson*.

Subsequent research showed that defrosting was necessary after every freeze; otherwise wet fish stuck to the cold plates while the freezer was being reloaded, and prevented compacting of the block. Thus the output of the freezer and capacity of the cold store were reduced. The *Junella* was later modified to incorporate a hot gas defrosting system, and this increased the cold store capacity from about 300 tonnes to about 400 tonnes because of the more compact blocks produced. The original freezers were also replaced by six 20-station freezers with a total capacity of about 50 tonnes of fish a day.

Although one existing side trawler, the *Ross Fighter*, was converted to freeze all of its catch at sea in 1963, the concept of adapting existing tonnage was never generally acceptable, and the *Ross Fighter* reverted to wet fishing after three years' work. Her owners had meanwhile adopted a policy of building new stern trawlers for freezing at sea, and built the first of a batch of four ships in 1964.

Another British trawling company introduced a rather different design of freezer stern trawler in 1964, the *St Finbarr*, a ship which was subsequently lost as a result of a fire at sea in 1966. The design was based to some extent on the argument made earlier that a freezer trawler need not be a very fast ship. The savings in engineroom space were used to give an improved layout; the engines were placed well forward in the hull, and the cold store, located amidships, was extended in height to the level of the fishing deck, thus giving a hold capacity equal to that of a vessel almost 10 m longer. This general layout was followed in a further three stern trawlers for the same company in 1968.

The British freezer stern trawler fleet at the end of 1970 consisted of 29 ships freezing whole fish at sea and six ships freezing fillets. There was a pause in the building programme from 1968 to 1970, and the three *Fairtry*s were withdrawn, but in late 1969 and 1970 a number of orders was placed that would bring the fleet total to over 40 ships. The most interesting feature of this period was the acquisition of fillet freezer stern trawlers, four being ordered new from British yards and two being bought secondhand from Germany. Since the size of crew on the new fillet freezer trawlers is likely to be about 30 men (that is closer in size to the 25 men on a whole fish freezer trawler than to the 80 or more that manned the *Fairtry*) it would seem that the fillet freezer trawler becomes a more economic proposi-

TABLE 1 Number of stern trawlers over 25 m registered length in the British fishing fleet on 31 December 1970

Method of preserving the catch	Based at the port of				
	Hull	Grimsby	North Shields	Fleetwood	Total
chilling in ice	1	3	0	1	5
freezing whole fish	22	6	0	1	29
freezing fillets	1	0	5	0	6
total	24	9	5	2	40

tion in British practice provided the number of crew is kept small, and the processing deck can be fully mechanized.

FREEZING AND COLD STORAGE EQUIPMENT IN STERN TRAWLERS

Types of freezer

Fish are frozen at sea either by surrounding them with a cold fluid or by placing them in contact with a cold surface, which in turn is in contact with a cold fluid. The fluid may be air or a liquid refrigerant. Three main types of freezer have been used in stern trawlers, the plate or contact freezer, the air blast freezer and the immersion freezer.

In the plate freezer, the fish is placed directly in contact with refrigerated metal plates. There are two kinds of plate freezer, the vertical plate freezer which was designed specifically for handling whole white fish, and the horizontal plate freezer. Plate freezers require less power than air blast freezers, freeze fish more quickly and take up less space, but they do not have the versatility of the air blast and may sometimes deform the product.

The vertical plate freezer as evolved in the 1960s is particularly suitable for the production of frozen blocks of whole fish such as cod and haddock, but has also been used for freezing small fatty fish like herring and sprat, for flatfish and for some packaged products. Fish are loaded between pairs of light alloy vertical plates through which the refrigerant is circulated in serpentine passages. The plates can be moved apart hydraulically or pneumatically. One multiple freezer unit has typically 12 or 20 stations, each producing a block of frozen fish measuring about $100 \times 50 \times 10$ cm and weighing 40–50 kg, the freezing time being about $3\frac{1}{2}$ hours for a block 10 cm thick. Although blocks of large white fish like cod are usually made without adding any water and without wrappings, the spaces in thinner blocks of small fish are sometimes filled with water to improve contact and to make the block less susceptible to damage during handling. It is normal practice to use wrappers or cartons for blocks of fillets.

In British practice, sea frozen fish are required to be stored at $-30°C$. This means that the mean temperature of the block must be $-30°C$ when it leaves the freezer in order to avoid overloading the cold store machinery, and this in turn requires a refrigerant temperature at the inlet of the freezer of between $-35°$ and $-40°C$.

The efficiency of the freezer depends not only on the refrigerant inlet temperature, but also on the rate of heat transfer from fish to refrigerant, which

Fig. 9. Conveyor, holding bins and vertical plate freezers on the processing deck of a British wholefish freezer stern trawler.

in turn is dependent on the manner of loading the fish to achieve good contact with the plates. The fish are normally loaded into the freezers through openings at the top and, provided the plates are not refrigerated, the fish can settle between them by means of their own weight to make a compact block with good contact between fish and plate. Loading is usually done manually, but hopper feeds have been used for small fish of uniform size. Contact is usually better in vertical than in horizontal plate freezers, and thus freezing time is shorter.

The plates should exert a slight pressure on the fish during freezing to maintain good contact, and this is usually achieved by a hydraulic mechanism. In some freezers the spacing between the plates can also be altered by the same means to accommodate changes in thickness of fish.

Regular defrosting of the freezer plates is essential during freezing at sea. Not only does this improve freezer performance, but it also makes loading and unloading easier. Either hot gas or hot secondary refrigerant is used, and the temperature at which the fluid is circulated is usually about 35°C. Defrosting typically takes one to three minutes after freezing is completed and is done before any attempt is made to remove the frozen blocks. The supply of hot fluid is shut off as soon as the plates are defrosted, but the plates are left warm until reloading has been completed. If the refrigerant is re-admitted to the plates while fish are being loaded, the fish will stick to the plates and will form a badly compacted block. Blocks of low density freeze slowly, break easily and waste stowage space.

Fig. 10. The discharge side of two of a battery of three large horizontal APV Clarke-Built horizontal plate freezers in the factory stern trawler "Ranger Cadmus".

The released blocks are removed from the freezer via the top, side or bottom; with bottom discharge, the blocks can be unloaded direct into cold store with the minimum of warming, but at the expense of some loss of storage space. Top unloading is useful where the space between plates has been divided during loading to produce more than one block of reduced size.

The design of freezer plates has been improved considerably during the last decade; the resistance of the plate itself to transfer of heat from fish to refrigerant is very low in most commercial models; plates built up of hollow sections of extruded aluminium have proved to be of high performance. Some mention has been made earlier of the problems encountered when designing flexible connections to freezer plates. The reliability of flexible hoses has also been much improved and most commercial plate freezers now employ these to link the plates to the refrigeration system; where plate movements are small, coiled copper pipes are still sometimes used, but O ring joints have generally been dispensed with.

The horizontal plate freezer is used at sea mainly for the freezing of blocks of fillets and thin blocks of small whole fish. It is particularly suitable for products of rectangular shape and with reasonably flat upper and lower surfaces. The packs or trays of fish are slid between pairs of horizontal refrigerated plates, and the bank of plates is closed up by means of a hydraulic jack to give good contact between plates and product. There are typically 12 or more plates with spaces of up to 8 cm between them. The horizontal plate freezer is often more difficult and dangerous to use at sea than a vertical one, particularly when loading or unloading in a rough sea. Heavy hinged doors have been replace by curtains on some models, making the freezer safer to use in bad weather. It is possible to provide mechanical loading and unloading systems for horizontal plate freezers, but these have not been used to any great extent in stern trawlers.

In a horizontal plate freezer, the packs are not always of the same thickness; there may be an air space at the top of the pack, or there may be ice on the plates. All of these factors can prevent the plate making good contact with all of the packs and thus extend the freezing time. An efficient defrost system is essential in order to prevent loading difficulties and to maintain high output.

The second main type of shipboard freezer is the air blast freezer. It requires more power than the plate freezer, mainly because of the requirements of the fans, but also because the temperature difference between the air and the primary refrigerant demands a lower suction temperature. The air blast freezer is versatile, in that almost any shape or size of product can be handled, limited only by the physical dimensions of the freezing compartment and the refrigeration capacity of the equipment; it is most useful therefore when handling large single fish which cannot be accommodated between freezer plates, or when freezing large quantities of small irregularly shaped fish that do not make good contact with flat plates.

Air blast freezers are generally more wasteful of space than plate freezers. Although they provide the main means of freezing on some very large European factory trawlers, their use in British stern trawlers is confined mainly to the freezing of oversize fish like halibut and very large cod, a special air blast freezing room often being provided for this purpose. Considerably more care has to be taken not to abuse the air blast freezer; it can easily be overloaded or underloaded in terms of refrigeration capacity when a change is made from the product for which it was designed.

Since air is a poor conductor of heat, forced convection by means of fans is essential; typical air speed is 5–7 m/second. The air temperature should be between −35° and −40°C for fish that are to be stored at −30°C, and this in turn means a refrigerant temperature of −40° to −45°C to give a 5° temperature difference between air and refrigerant in the heat exchanger.

The third type of freezer used at sea is the immersion freezer. Liquids hold and conduct heat much better than air, so that heat transfer can be rapid even with moderate circulation. Any shape or size of fish can be immersed in a cold liquid, and operation of an immersion freezer is comparatively simple. The immersion freezer is generally more compact than the air blast freezer, and consumes less power, but use of the method at sea has been limited because of the restricted range of suitable liquids that do not contaminate or taint the product, and because the fish are usually frozen individually and therefore have a poor stowage rate. Although some use has been made of the method in the tuna and salmon fisheries, using cold brine, the application of immersion freezing in stern trawlers has been limited to a few shrimp catchers, in which the fish have been frozen in brine or in a solution of sugar and salt. The method is not likely in the near future to become attractive for freezing white fish in large stern trawlers.

Cold store design

The recommended temperature for long term storage of frozen fish is −30°C, and this temperature is now widely employed in the British cold chain, both at sea and ashore. Shipborne cold store refrigeration plant is normally designed to maintain the frozen cargo at this temperature, with some quite small reserve of capacity in case the fish is insufficiently frozen before storage. However good the shipboard practice, some extra load will inevitably be imposed on the cold store from time to time, and reserve capacity will help to avoid undesirable rises in store temperature. The effects on quality of incorrect cold storage will be discussed in detail later in the chapter. Basically there are three methods of cooling that have been used in shipborne cold stores, forced air circulation over banks of finned coolers, finned cooling grids on the deckhead, and plain pipe cooling grids over deckhead and walls. Fan coolers are not very suitable; the evaporators require frequent defrosting, the evaporators and associated ducting take up valuable storage space, and the fans increase considerably the heat load in the store. In addition, forced movement of large volumes of air can cause considerable drying of the product in the store. Finned deckhead grids need defrosting at least at the end of each voyage if not more frequently, and it is sometimes necessary to defrost the whole store in order to allow meltwater to drain away; too frequent warming of the store is undesirable because insulation may be damaged and corrosion may be accelerated.

Erection of a large area of plain pipes over as much of the surface of the deckhead and walls of the cold store as possible is expensive in first cost, but the method has several advantages. Most of the heat leak is picked up close to the walls, so that large quantities of cold air do not have to be moved about; thus the temperature difference between grids and fish can be kept small, with resultant reduction in drying of the fish. Hot defrosting of the plain grids has been shown to be unnecessary even after very long periods of operation, and so the store temperature need never be raised above freezing point.

Insulation work for a cold store in a trawler has to be of the highest possible standard; space is at a premium aboard, and the thinner the insulation can be made without decreasing its resistance the better. Too little insulation, however, may impose an unacceptably high load on the refrigeration machinery, and may accelerate drying of the fish. Particular care must be taken to ensure sufficient insulation over the toes of structural members such as hull frames and deck beams, and insulation breaks must be provided wherever the insulation is penetrated by cold store metalwork.

Closed cell plastics, such as expanded polyurethane foam, are almost twice as effective as cork when used for heat insulation. Whereas in the earliest trawler cold stores a thickness of 20 cm of cork was necessary, a closed cell plastics insulation thickness of 10 cm can cope with a temperature gradient of 60°C or more; thus the internal volume of the store can be effectively increased. Closed cell materials are preferable to open cell ones, because they remain impervious to water and are virtually unaffected by leaks in the hull. Plastics that can be foamed in place have the advantage that they fill every awkward corner when properly applied, and can add to the structural strength of the cold store when bonded between hull and a lining. Loose and blanket insulating materials are of limited value for trawler cold store work, and their use is confined mainly to filling in awkward spaces, between frames for example, when rigid slab is being used for the main installation. Slabs should always be applied in more than one layer, so that joints can be staggered. A good vapour seal on the warm face of the insulation is essential. It is not necessary to seal the inner face of the insulation; if the cold face permits the passage of water vapour, any moisture that accidentally penetrates the insulation will then pass through the walls to end up as frost on the grids, rather than remain within the insulation to cause damage.

Blocks of frozen fish may enter the cold store through openings in either the roof or the walls of the store, but any such openings should be kept as high in the structure as possible in order to reduce the exchange of warm and cold air when they are open. The size of an opening can be as small as the cross sectional dimensions of a single block on a conveyer or chute, but a much larger deck hatch is required when mechanical hoists are used to move batches of frozen blocks. Handling of blocks within the cold store can be improved by using mechanical equipment, whether it be simply a portable length of roller conveyer or, in a very large hold, a more elaborate system of chutes and conveyors, possibly power driven.

Calculation of refrigeration load

It is not possible to do more here than indicate by example how estimates of refrigeration requirements are arrived at. A summary of the calculations for a vertical plate freezer installation and a cold store serves to show roughly what is typical for a freezer stern trawler. The great difference between the refrigeration requirements for freezing and for cold storage should be noted, and the example also shows the relative importance of the various sources of heat.

The following facts are assumed in the calculations. The product is to be a block of whole gutted white fish 10 cm thick and weighing 45 kg. The fish come aboard at a temperature of 10°C, and 35 tonnes of fish have to be frozen each day, using refrigerant at $-40°C$ in a bank of vertical plate freezers. The refrigerant is circulated by a 15 kW pump, and the known freezing cycle time for blocks of the size specified is 3 hours 40 minutes. The cold store is $20 \times 10 \times 5$ m in size, running at $-30°C$, and is insulated with the equivalent of 0.25 m of cork. The maximum outside air temperature is 27°C and the refrigerant pump for the cold store absorbs 3.75 kW.

There is no accurate method of predicting freezing time for many of the products handled in freezer stern trawlers. It is possible to make a reasonably accurate estimate for regular shapes like blocks of fillets without wrappings, but, generally speaking, it is necessary either to assume a freezing time based on experience of similar products or, better still, to make direct measurements on the product concerned. In this example, the freezing time is well known from experience; a time of 3 hours 20 minutes is a practical figure for a block of whole fish 10 cm thick being reduced in temperature from 10 to $-30°C$ in a vertical plate freezer carrying refrigerant at $-40°C$. Twenty minutes are added for loading and unloading the freezer, to give a cycle time of 3 hours 40 minutes. In practice, the cycle time is often rounded off to four hours, partly to make timekeeping easier for the freezer operators, and partly to give some safety margin. The cycle time must not be extended too much, however, or output will be unnecessarily reduced.

Heat is removed from the fish much more rapidly when they are first put into the freezer than when the freezing cycle is almost complete; half the freezing is done during the first quarter of the time in a vertical plate freezer. Thus the demand on the refrigeration machinery from one freezer falls throughout the freezing cycle. Correct loading practice in a freezer trawler requires that freezers be filled in rotation so that at any time during freezing the total load on the machinery remains roughly the same, and the machinery is normally designed to cope with the average load; simultaneous loading of all the freezers would grossly overtax the capacity of the machinery.

The largest component of the refrigeration load is the heat to be removed from the fish. The amount of heat to be removed from 1 kg of white fish in order to reduce its temperature from $10°$ to $-30°C$ is 340 kJ. When the initial temperature of the fish is higher, say at $15°C$, the amount of heat to be removed is higher, 360 kJ/kg, and when the fish are cooled before freezing, for example to $2°C$, the heat to be removed is reduced to 300 kJ/kg. Initial fish temperature is therefore important when designing the installation and, where the temperature is unknown, the likely maximum should be allowed for.

The refrigeration machinery also has to remove heat generated by refrigerant pumps, heat leaking in through insulation on freezers and pipework, and heat produced during defrosting of the freezers. Although the amount of heat introduced during defrosting is quite large, it can usually be extracted gradually during the time between defrosting operations, so that only a modest increase in plant capacity is required to cope with this duty. In this example it is assumed that there is a 20-minute interval between successive defrosts.

The refrigerant has to enter the freezers at $-40°C$. It is assumed that, as in many freezer trawlers, this is a secondary refrigerant, for example trichloroethylene, which is cooled in a heat exchanger by the primary refrigerant. There has to be a temperature difference of about $5°C$ between the primary and secondary refrigerants for efficient heat transfer, and there will be a loss of about $1°C$ in the piping system, so that the primary refrigerant has to be delivered at about $-46°C$. The lower the operating temperature, the smaller the capacity of the compressor so that, when a secondary refrigerant is used, there is a penalty; a larger compressor of greater power is needed for a given output. If the freezers were cooled directly by the primary refrigerant, the compressor could operate at $-41°C$ and would have about 30 per cent more capacity. However, leaks are much easier to contain by using a secondary refrigerant in the freezers, and loss of secondary refrigerant is less expensive than primary refrigerant 22 for example.

There is often very little insulation on the plate freezers; for example, the tops of vertical plate freezers are not usually insulated. This demand on the machinery is small however in comparison with the total load, and complete insulation is not vital. The figure used in the calculation is a rough estimate.

It is normal practice to introduce a safety factor by making the assumption that the freezer compressor is to run only 18 hours in 24, thereby giving a margin of standby capacity. A smaller safety factor of 10 per cent is added to the capacity of the cold store compressor, because the full demand on it is less likely to be a continuous one, and the machinery may often be running for much of the time below its designed capacity. The cold store refrigeration machinery has to remove the heat coming in through the insulation, heat generated by refrigerant pumps and by store lights, and heat from a number of intermittent sources such as open doors or hatches, men working in the store, and products that are warmer than the cold store air.

In this example, the loading hatch is assumed to be in the roof structure and, for a shipboard store of this size during normal operation, there would be about 2.7 air changes a day. The heat produced by crew working in the store is about 500 W/man hour at $-30°C$. Although the frozen fish should be reduced to store temperature before being put into the cold store, there is inevitably some warming of the product during and after discharge from the freezer. In addition, faulty freezer operation may at times result in blocks that are too warm when unloaded. It is important therefore to make some allowance for extra intermittent loads of this kind when deciding the size of cold store machinery, in order to keep temperature fluctuations to a minimum; quality of frozen fish is adversely affected by high temperature storage and by temperature fluctuations.

Example calculations

1. Freezing plant

    Specification:

    > Product – blocks of whole white fish 10 cm thick, 45 kg weight
    > Output – 35 tonnes fish/day
    > Refrigerant temp. $-40°C$ at freezer = $-47°C$ at compressor
    > Fish initial temp – $10°C$
    > Freezing time – 3 h 40 min including loading & unloading
    > Refrigerant pump – 15 kW

    Calculation:

    > A. Number of freezers required:
    > Output to be 35 tonnes/day = 35 000 kg/day
    > Each block weighs 45 kg, so

$\dfrac{35\,000}{45} = 785$ blocks/day

freezing cycle is $3\tfrac{2}{3}$ h, so there are

$\dfrac{24}{3.66} = 6.55$ cycles/day

therefore blocks/cycle $= \dfrac{785}{6.55} = 120$

Therefore freezer installation is
10 twelve-station freezers

B. Heat to be removed from fish:
to reduce 1 kg fish from 10°C to −30°C
requires removal of 340 kJ

35 000 kg fish/day $= \dfrac{35\,000}{24 \times 3600}$ kg/s

heat to be removed/second $=$
$\dfrac{35\,000}{24 \times 3600} \times 340\,000 = $ *136 000 J/s*

C. Heat generated by pump:
heat flow from 15 kW pump $= $ *15 000 J/s*

D. Heat produced during defrosting:
the heat produced when defrosting a 12-station freezer is estimated to be 24 000 kJ; this has to be removed in the period between defrosts, which is $\dfrac{3\text{ h }40\text{ min}}{10\text{ freezers}}$
$= $ about 20 min;
therefore heat to be removed/second
$= \dfrac{24\,000}{20 \times 60} = 20$ kJ/s $= $ *20 000 J/s*

E. Heat through freezer insulation is estimated to be *3 000 J/s*

Total heat load on freezer compressor =
136 000 J/s from	B
15 000	C
20 000	D
3 000	E

174 000 J/s

But the compressor is to run only 18 h in 24 h, therefore full required rating =

$174\,000 \times \dfrac{24}{18} = 230\,000$ J/s $=$

230 kW at an operating temperature of −47°C

2. Cold store plant

Specification:
Volume $= 20 \times 10 \times 5 = 1\,000$ m³ to hold about 600 tonnes frozen fish

Surface area $= (2 \times 20 \times 10) + (2 \times 20 \times 5) + (2 \times 10 \times 5)$
$= 700$ m²
Store temp $= -30°C$
Outside air $= 27°C$
Insulation thickness $= 0.25$ m cork or equivalent in other material
Refrigeration pump $= 3.75$ kW

Calculation:
A. Heat flow through the insulation:
thermal conductivity of cork $=$ 0.043 W/m°C
temperature difference across cold store wall $= 27° - (-30°) = 57°C$
thickness of cork $= 0.25$ m
store surface area $= 700$ m²

total heat leak $= \dfrac{\text{area} \times \text{temp difference}}{\text{insuln thickness}}$
$\times$ thermal conductivity
$= \dfrac{700 \times 57}{0.25} \times 0.043 =$
7 000 J/s

B. Heat introduced by air changes:
on average there will be 2.7 air changes a day in a trawler cold store volume of store $= 1\,000$ m³
1 m³ will introduce about 75 kJ of heat
therefore heat from air changes $=$
$1\,000 \times 2.7 \times 75\,000$ J/day $=$
$\dfrac{1\,000 \times 2.7 \times 75\,000 \text{ J/s}}{24 \times 3600} = $ *2 000 J/s*

C. Heat produced by lights of 1 000 W
$= $ *1 000 J/s*

D. Heat from men working in store, generating 500 W/man hour at −30°C assuming two men continuously in store, load $= 2 \times 500 = $ *1 000 J/s*

E. Heat introduced by warm products:
If fish enter store at −25°C, the heat to be removed from 1 kg to reduce the temperature to −30°C is about 12 kJ.
weight of fish entering store
$= 35\,000$ kg/day
heat to be removed/day
$= 35\,000 \times 12\,000$ J/day
heat to be removed/second
$= \dfrac{35\,000 \times 12\,000}{24 \times 3600} = $ *5 000 J/s*

F. Heat introduced by refrigerant pump:
pump power is 3.75 kW, rounded off to 4 kW, producing *4 000 J/s*

Total heat load on cold store compressor
= 7 000 J/s from A
   2 000   B
   1 000   C
   1 000   D
   5 000   E
   4 000   F
 20 000 J/s
Adding a 10% contingency factor,
  2 000
22 000 J/s

The full requirement for the cold store compressor is therefore 22 000 J/s, that is *22 kW at an operating temperature of $-47°C$*

It can be seen that the refrigeration requirement for freezing about 1½ tonnes of fish an hour is more than ten times that required to keep 600 tonnes of fish at $-30°C$.

THE QUALITY OF SEA FROZEN FISH

Stern trawlers can and do produce frozen fish that on thawing is equal to and sometimes better than the freshest of the chilled fish landed from the same fishing grounds, but there are problems in handling and freezing very fresh fish. The difficulties are more often associated with the appearance of the product rather than with eating quality; the flesh may become discoloured or show signs of breaking up. These changes may sometimes be accompanied by toughening and loss of flavour, but fish of good eating quality may be rejected solely because of defects in appearance; therefore care in selection of the raw material and in handling and processing can greatly enhance the value of the finished product.

The effect of initial quality

Spent fish, that is fish that have recently spawned, are almost always in poor condition and do not stand up well to freezing and cold storage. Spent fish after freezing and thawing are generally of poorer quality than they were in the unfrozen state, and yield soft and ragged fillets. Since the spawning season for particular species varies from ground to ground, it is often possible by judicious selection of grounds to pursue the fishery for a considerable part of the year without capturing large quantities of spent fish.

Parasites can affect the initial quality of certain species such as cod and hake, making those fish unacceptable for freezing. Cod from certain fishing grounds for example may be found to be infested with worms. The cod grounds most affected are mainly inshore, usually in the vicinity of large colonies of seals which act as hosts to the parasite at one stage in its life cycle. In the North Atlantic, wormy cod are found at times off the Scottish coast, off the west coasts of Iceland and Newfoundland, in the southern part of the Gulf of St Lawrence and on the Nova Scotia and St Pierre banks.

The larval worms found in cod are usually about the diameter of thick cotton thread, up to 3 cm long and varying in colour from creamy white to very dark brown. The coiled worm is found embedded mainly in the liver but also in the flesh. There is no evidence to suggest that cod worms are harmful to man, and they are killed by the freezing process, but they are aesthetically objectionable; consumers are understandably put off when they encounter worms in the flesh.

Grounds known to yield infested fish should be avoided, but some stragglers will inevitably be caught from time to time on other grounds and crews should watch for signs of infestation. A heavily infested cod liver does not always mean the flesh is affected, but wormy livers are a warning; the membrane should be removed from the belly flaps of a suspect fish, and the flesh beneath inspected. When worms are revealed, a dozen or more fish from the same haul should be closely examined, by cutting open the flesh. If worms are found in the body flesh, the fishing ground should be changed.

Discoloration

Thawed sea frozen fish whose flesh is badly discoloured is usually less acceptable to the buyer than whose flesh is white. The discoloration may be due to spoilage as a result of delays or poor handling before freezing, but in stern trawlers which handle the catch quickly and efficiently the defect is most likely to be due to blood trapped in the flesh, either as a result of physical damage or as a result of inadequate bleeding before freezing.

Isolated blood marks in the flesh are usually bruises, caused when blood vessels are ruptured during rough handling; bruises can generally be avoided by taking care to handle the fish gently, and by providing mechanical aids which obviate the need for throwing fish about or walking on them.

Widespread discoloration throughout the flesh is usually attributable to inadequate bleeding. There are wide physiological variations in fish which determine the ease with which they can be bled, but generally the blood in white fish from Arctic and temperate waters remains reasonably fluid for up to six hours after death when kept at a temperature close to 0°C. After that time the blood begins to thicken and, once clotted, is extremely difficult to remove from the flesh; washing, for example, will have no effect on a blood-stained fillet taken from a thawed frozen fish that was inadequately bled.

The fish can be bled either by cutting the throat or tail as a separate operation, as soon as it comes aboard, or by gutting, an operation which causes the fish to bleed. In some trawlers, notably Norwegian ones, bleeding is done as a separate operation, but equally white fillets can be obtained from fish that have been gutted and bled at the same time, provided the fish are kept chilled after capture and dealt with within about six hours.

The blood usually takes about 30 minutes to drain from the flesh at chill temperature; thus when fish are moved to the freezers too quickly after gutting, some of the remaining blood may be trapped by the freezing process. Adequate washing and bleeding time is very important, and some processing deck layouts now include post gutting tanks in which the fish remain long enough in chilled storage to allow the bleeding to be completed. A brief description of the system is given later in the chapter. Fish conveyed through continuous washers of the kind described earlier for handling chilled fish are often delivered to the freezers long before bleeding is complete.

The effect of rigor

The handling of newly caught fish in freezer stern trawlers has introduced a number of problems associated with the changes that take place in the fish immediately after death. Some explanation of what happens, and how the changes can affect the methods of handling the catch, is appropriate at this point.

Rigor, or, to give it its full name, *rigor mortis*, means the stiffening of the muscles of an animal shortly after death. Immediately after death, the muscles of fish are soft and limp, and can easily be flexed; the muscles will still contract when stimulated, for example by an electric shock. The flesh is said to be in the pre-rigor condition at this time. Eventually the muscles begin to harden and stiffen, and the fish is then said to be in rigor. The hardened muscles will no longer contract when stimulated, and they never regain this property. After some hours or days the muscles gradually begin to soften and become limp again; the fish has now passed through rigor, and the flesh is described as being in the post-rigor condition.

Rigor usually starts at the tail of a fish, and the muscles harden gradually along the body towards the head until the whole fish is quite stiff. The length of time a fish remains rigid can vary from an hour or so to as much as three days, and depends on a number of factors described below. The complicated chemical changes that cause rigor are not completely understood, but briefly what is thought to happen is this. The substances that keep the muscle pliable when the fish is alive, rather after the manner of a lubricant, are no longer produced when the energy reserves are used up after death. The two main protein components of fish muscle then interact and bond together so that when the muscle attempts to contract it eventually becomes hard and rigid.

The factors affecting the time a fish takes to go into and pass through rigor include the species, its physical condition, the degree of exhaustion before death, its size, the amount of handling during rigor and the temperature at which it is kept.

Some species take longer than others to go into and pass through rigor because of difference in chemical composition. Whiting for example go into rigor very quickly and may be completely stiff one hour after death, whereas redfish stored under the same conditions may take as long as 22 hours to develop full rigor. Trawled codling take two to eight hours to go into rigor when gutted and chilled in ice.

A poorly nourished fish takes less time than a well nourished one to go into rigor; spent fish for example go quickly into rigor because there is very little reserve of energy in the muscle to keep it pliable. In the same way, fish that have used up their energy resources by struggling in the trawl go into rigor faster than fish that have entered the net just before hauling. Small fish go into rigor faster than large fish of the same species.

Handling of pre-rigor fish does not appear to affect the onset of rigor, but flexing of the fish while it is stiff can shorten the time it remains in rigor.

Temperature is the most important factor governing the time a fish takes to go into and pass through rigor, at least in so far as handling the catch is concerned, because the temperature of the fish after capture can be controlled. The warmer the fish, the faster it will go into and pass through rigor. For example, cod kept at 0°C take about 60 hours to pass through rigor, whereas the same fish kept at 30°C take less than two hours.

The following table gives an indication of the rigor time observed for different species; times outside the limits given are possible in practice, for instance when fish have gone into rigor before they

Fig. 11. British wholefish freezer trawlers in port in Hull.

are landed on deck, either because they have completely exhausted themselves by struggling in the net, or because they have died from asphyxiation several hours before the trawl was hauled.

Table 2 Species	Temperature °C	Time from landing on deck to entering rigor hours	Time from landing on deck to end of rigor hours
cod	0	2–8	20–65
	3	4–9	54–64
	6	5	45
	17	2–6	16–20
	30		1–2
redfish	0	22	120
whiting	0	1	20
plaice	0	7–11	55
saithe	0	18	110
haddock	0	2–4	37
	12	2	24

The effect of rigor on frozen whole fish: rigor can affect the quality of whole frozen fish in three main ways, by causing gaping, toughening and excessive drip loss on thawing.

A fillet is said to gape when the individual flakes of muscle come apart, giving the fillet a broken and ragged appearance. This happens when the connective tissue that binds the flakes together breaks down. Rigor is only one cause of gaping, but other causes, often more dependant on the initial condition of the fish, are perhaps less amenable to control by the processor.

When a fish goes into rigor, the muscle attempts to contract but, because the skeleton and connective tissue prevent this, tension increases within the muscle. As long as the connective tissue can withstand the increased pull, the flesh does not gape, but once the tension becomes greater than the strength of the connective tissue, some gaping occurs. The temperature of the whole fish when it goes into rigor has a marked effect on the degree of gaping; the higher the temperature the greater the tension and the weaker the connective tissue. Thus the higher the temperature, the more the fish will gape. Furthermore there is a critical temperature, for example 17°C for cod, above which the contractions become so strong and the connective tissue so weak that the tissue breaks down completely, resulting in a fillet so ragged that it is totally unacceptable. Below the critical temperature, the cooler the fish is the less the damage done on going into rigor. Freezing and thawing accentuate the damage, but the full extent of the harm done by keeping newly caught fish too warm while awaiting freezing is not seen until perhaps months later when the fish are filleted.

When the temperature of the newly caught fish is lowered so much that they start to freeze while going into rigor, the connective tissue is again weakened, mainly by formation of ice, and gaping occurs. Gaping caused by the freezing of fish that are going into rigor occurs most in well nourished fish, because the contractions are stronger than in spent ones.

Rough handling of whole fish while they are in rigor can also cause gaping, because any attempt to bend a rigid fish will break either the muscle or the connective tissue. Damage of this kind occurs mostly when the fish are being loaded into the freezer, when attempts are made to straighten bent fish while they are stiff. Pressure from the freezer plates can also damage rigid fish lying in distorted positions in the freezer.

To sum up the effect of rigor on gaping in whole fish, gaping is most likely to occur when well-nourished fish are kept warm and then frozen after they have started to go into rigor, or when fish already in rigor are roughly handled.

When fish go into rigor while they are warm, there can also be a toughening effect, particularly with well-nourished fish. The higher the temperature at which the fish go into rigor, the greater will be the loss of drip on thawing, and the tougher and stringier will be the cooked flesh. Rigor is not the only cause of toughness and high drip loss from the thawed product; the flesh may be inherently tough or it may have been toughened by incorrect cold storage or thawing. Whole fish frozen before rigor tend to have a higher drip loss than similar fish frozen in rigor or after rigor, but this may be due to what is known as thaw rigor, which is explained later.

The effect of rigor on frozen fillets

Rigor can have much more effect on sea frozen fillets than on whole fish, and proper control of rigor on fillet freezing stern trawlers is essential. Unless precautions are taken, fillets cut from a fish before it goes into rigor will shrink; the shape of the fillet becomes distorted, and the surface of the flesh takes on a corrugated appearance. These defects remain throughout subsequent freezing and thawing.

When a whole fish goes into rigor, the muscle tries to contract but is prevented from doing so by being anchored to the skeleton, thus setting up the stresses that lead to gaping, but, as soon as the fillet is cut off, the restraint of the skeleton is removed and the fillet shrinks. The extent of the shrinkage depends on the condition of the fish and on the temperature at which it is kept. A fillet cut from a well fed fish before rigor and then kept at a high temperature before freezing may shrink as much as 30–40 per cent of its original length; on the other hand, a fillet taken from a fish in poor condition and frozen at once will shrink hardly at all.

Since the catcher will normally work fishing grounds where fish are known to be in good condition, it is very important to freeze fillets immediately after they have been cut from pre-rigor fish. When delay between filleting and freezing is unavoidable, the fillets must be kept chilled to avoid shrinkage, but even at 0°C some fillets will shrink after a time. Immediate freezing is the only safe way to avoid shrinkage. Fresh water or freshwater ice should not be used for chilling fillets; shrinkage is increased by contact with fresh water.

The cut surface of a pre-rigor fillet is different from that of a fillet taken from a post-rigor fish; it is dull, rough and corrugated, with a feel like crêpe rubber, caused by exposure of the cut ends of individual muscle fibres. Pre-rigor fillets cannot be satisfactorily smoke cured because the rough dull surface will not take on a good gloss.

When whole fish are kept at a low temperature until they go into rigor, fillets cut from them do not readily shrink but there are other problems. Mechanical filleting of fish in rigor is often difficult, and hand filleting may give a lower yield from fish in rigor than from fish that are soft and flexible. In addition, gaping may be caused by forcibly straightening bent fish in order to fillet them. Chilled buffer storage has to be provided in the trawler to accommodate the whole fish while they go into rigor.

Fillets cut from whole fish that have passed through rigor are normally of uniformly good quality when frozen, provided the whole fish have been carefully handled and properly chilled; the main disadvantage is the long time in buffer storage, up to three days, which makes extra demands on space and labour in the ship.

Rigor affects the toughness of frozen fillets in the same way as with whole fish; the warmer the fish when it goes into rigor, the greater will be the drip loss and the tougher will be the cooked fillet. Just as with frozen whole fish, pre-rigor frozen fillets will lose more drip than comparable fillets frozen during or after rigor.

Controlling the effects of rigor

The safest and most reliable way of avoiding the undesirable effects of rigor is to keep the fish chilled at every stage before freezing. Provided the fish pass through rigor at a low temperature, the effect of rigor on quality will not be serious. This implies the installation in freezer stern trawlers of pre-gutting and post-gutting chilling tanks.

It might be thought sensible to accelerate rigor, and thus reduce buffer storage space, by keeping fish warm on the processing deck. This cannot be recommended because, although the time through rigor will be shortened, there will be some loss of quality due to the higher temperature, and possibly some increase in gaping. Since there is a maximum temperature above which damage is irreparable (17°C for example for cod) it is safer on the whole not to attempt acceleration of rigor, but to keep the fish chilled until they enter the freezer.

Thaw rigor

When fish muscle is frozen before rigor and kept for only a short time in cold storage, it can still contract and go into rigor after thawing; this effect is known as thaw rigor and, when thawing is done rapidly at a high temperature, the muscle can then suffer all the defects associated with high temperature rigor. Thaw rigor is rarely a problem in whole fish, but when pre-rigor fillets are thawed they shrink and become corrugated, and lose a great deal of drip. The effects are most severe when the fillets are cooked from the frozen state, as for example with consumer packs of fillets or fish fingers; this is one of a number of difficulties likely to be encountered when making consumer packs at sea. The effects are much less marked with large blocks of fillets. Thaw rigor is not a serious problem in present commercial practice, but may become so should there be an attempt to use the factory trawler for making small retail packs. The ill effects of thaw rigor can be overcome by thawing slowly at about 15°C so that rigor is completed in the semi-frozen state, thus preventing severe contraction of the muscle.

When to freeze, before or after rigor

The three stages of rigor are not clear cut. The process is a gradual one, beginning from the moment a fish dies, and the effects are therefore very much a matter of degree. In the freezer stern trawler, the processing system has to be sufficiently flexible to handle fish properly in any stage of rigor and, perhaps more important, there has to be a reliable labelling system that will enable the processors ashore to identify the state of the fish when it was frozen at sea. The following tables list some of the advantages of freezing whole fish and fillets in all three stages of rigor.

TABLE 3

Frozen	Whole Fish Advantages	Disadvantages
Pre-rigor	No buffer store. No gaping, except perhaps from thaw rigor.	High drip loss possible. Large processing capacity needed to cope with high catching rate.
In rigor	Uniformly good quality possible.	Buffer store needed. Gaping when fish are forcibly straightened or are kept too warm. Fish pack badly in freezer.
Post-rigor	Uniformly good quality possible. Damage by contraction avoidable.	Buffer store needed. Gaping when fish are kept too warm or too long.

Frozen	Fillets Advantages.	Disadvantages.
Pre-rigor	No buffer store. Machine or hand filleting.	Fillets shrink when awaiting freezing or after thawing. Rough cut surface. Unsuitable for smoking. High drip loss possible. Large processing capacity needed to cope with high catching rate.
In rigor	Excellent quality possible. No shrinkage.	Buffer store needed. Difficult to fillet by hand or machine. Low yield. Usually unsuitable for smoking. Gaping when fish are forcibly straightened.
Post-rigor	Uniformly high quality. No shrinkage. Machine or hand filleting.	Large buffer store needed for up to three days. Usually unsuitable for smoking.

Summarising the advice on the effects of rigor, the changes occurring in fish before they are frozen may affect the quality of the catch in three main ways:

1. Toughening of frozen whole fish or fillets, accompanied by high drip loss.
2. Gaping in fillets taken from whole fish.
3. Shrinkage of frozen fillets.

These undesirable effects can be reduced or prevented by:

1. Keeping the fish chilled, particularly before they go into rigor.
2. Handling them carefully while in rigor.
3. Freezing fillets from pre-rigor fish as soon as they are cut.

Careful treatment of fish before and during rigor will inevitably result in a better quality frozen product with a correspondingly higher market value.

RECOMMENDATIONS FOR HANDLING FISH
IN FREEZER STERN TRAWLERS

Much of what has been said earlier about handling before chilled stowage is equally applicable to handling before freezing, but the advice on pre-treatment is repeated here because incorrect practice can have an even more marked effect on the quality of frozen fish. Advice is also given on correct use of freezers and cold store. Quality is everyone's responsibility, from skipper to deckhand; earnings and indeed the future of the industry may depend on it.

On the fishing deck.

As soon as the cod-end comes up the ramp, the fish should be dropped to the factory deck below; fish left lying about in the net or in deck pounds will quickly become crushed and bruised, and will spoil rapidly when warm. The bag and its contents should be handled as carefully as possible.

On the processing deck.

Ungutted fish should be kept chilled. Ideally, pre-gutting tanks should be provided, in which the fish can be held in refrigerated sea water until they are gutted.

Where chilling tanks are not provided, some other means of cooling the fish should be employed. Cold water sprays should be fitted over the pounds, or ice should be readily available for sprinkling on the fish. Use of a deck hose will help, provided the water temperature is not above 5°C.

Holding pounds should have sufficient dividers to stop excessive movement of the fish in rough weather; when fish slide about too much they become chafed and damaged.

The pounds should be so arranged that it is difficult to put newly caught fish on top of older fish awaiting gutting. The fish should be fed to the hand gutters or the gutting machines in the order in which they came aboard.

Gutting should always start immediately fish come aboard. Delays before gutting, especially when the fish are not chilled, result in rapid spoilage, and it becomes increasingly difficult if not impossible to bleed the fish properly. Fish that have been kept ungutted for more than six hours should be inspected by the factory deck manager, and should be specially labelled when they are frozen.

Gutting machines are now available for most sizes of round white fish, and their use can do much to reduce delays, ensure a uniform standard of gutting and eliminate a great deal of unnecessary handling, lifting and throwing of fish.

Prompt gutting is vital not only because the guts in the dead fish accelerate spoilage but also because bleeding starts when the fish are cut open. Unbled fish yield discoloured and unattractive fillets.

Where gutting is done by hand, gutting benches should be fitted together with conveyors or containers for carrying guts and livers away from the fish. The fish should be fed to the gutters at waist level, and the gutted fish should be carried away by mechanical handling equipment, so that physical damage and contamination are reduced to a minimum. It should never be necessary for crew to walk on fish or kick them about.

Hand-gutted fish should be double naped, and every trace of gut and liver should be removed; belly cuts should not go beyond the vent or into the flesh. Ragged cuts into the muscle will reduce the value of the fish.

Crews should be instructed to look out for parasites, and to report heavy infestations, of cod worms for example, to the factory deck manager. When inspection of the flesh under the belly flap membrane shows a number of fish to be affected, the skipper may wish to consider changing grounds. In any case, blocks of suspect fish should be specially labelled.

Large numbers of spent fish or unusually soft fish should also be reported to the factory manager; again it may be necessary to change fishing grounds, and fish of initially poor quality should be labelled as such when they are frozen. Crushed and damaged fish should be discarded.

The crew should be instructed to gut small fish before big ones of the same species, and to select carefully for size. Blocks of frozen fish of mixed sizes are less valuable to the buyer who has an outlet for a particular size range. The more perishable species should be gutted first; haddock for example should be gutted before cod, and cod before flatfish.

The gutted fish should be transferred to the washer or the bleeding tank as gently as possible; where a conveyer is not provided, the distance should be as short as possible to reduce the effort of throwing and to prevent unnecessary bruising caused by inaccurate throws.

In some freezer trawlers the fish are washed in equipment of the kind described in the section on handling fish for chilling; washing removes traces of gut and slime, and some of the bacteria that make fish go bad, but the fish also need adequate time to bleed before being frozen. Passage time through most continuous washers is far too short; ideally the fish should be allowed to bleed for at least 30 minutes at chill temperature in order to give a white fillet. It is recommended that post-gutting chilling tanks be provided for this purpose, and a brief description of the kind of equipment envisaged is given later in the chapter.

After washing and bleeding, there should be no need to manhandle the fish again until they are loaded into the freezers. The bled fish should be taken by conveyor to loading bins adjoining the freezers. The bins should each hold just enough fish to fill the minimum number of freezer stations that can be defrosted at one time. If the fish have been completely bled, residence time in the loading bins should be as short as possible; alternatively the fish should be chilled in the bins until bleeding is completed.

Fish should never be left lying in the holding bins when they can be loaded into the freezer. Even when there are not enough fish to completely fill a freezer, they should still be loaded and frozen rather than left in a warm factory area. New fish should never be dropped on top of old fish lying in the bottom of a bin; the oldest fish should always be frozen first. The holding bins should be washed out each time they are emptied; clean fish should never be put into a dirty bin. Different sizes and different species should not be mixed in the same holding bin; the flow of fish should be diverted to another bin whenever there is a change of type.

There should be proper arrangements for telling freezer operators about any quality defects reported at the gutting stage, so that batches of fish of poor quality can be kept separate and appropriately labelled when they are loaded into the freezer; for example, soft or spent fish, wormy fish or fish that have suffered long delay or been subjected to high temperature storage should all be identifiable when frozen into blocks. Mixing of bad fish with good ones may result in the whole catch being classed as of poor quality; the reputation of the ship and the price of future catches could thus be affected.

Crews should be instructed in the proper use of vertical plate freezers. The freezer plates should always be completely defrosted before loading begins; when fish are loaded between cold plates, they may stick to the plates before they are properly in position, thus forming loosely packed blocks which will freeze slowly, break more easily and stow badly.

Large fish should be stowed carefully between the plates, head to tail alternately with heads to the ends of the block and with as few gaps as possible. Positioning of very small fish like herring or whiting is less important, and it is possible to devise mechanical filling arrangements for freezers that operate only on fish of this size.

The fish should never be stowed higher than the top of the freezer plates; when the freezer is overfilled the top fish do not freeze properly, and the frozen block may be difficult to remove.

Sorting for size and species should be done at the gutting stage, but when fish are mixed in the loading bins, they should be sorted as they are loaded into the freezers. Small fish among large ones get crushed or distorted in the freezer. There should be a simple measuring board available at the loading point for checking length when fish within a rigid size range have to be frozen together.

Crew should be warned not to straighten fish that have gone stiff in a bent position; as explained earlier, the muscle structure will be damaged and the resultant fillets will tend to fall apart. Bent fish should be kept back until they have passed through rigor before attempting to freeze them.

Very large fish should not be forced into freezers; where heading is permitted this will make them much easier to load, but fish that are much too big for the freezer should be diverted to the air blast freezer room.

The freezer loading sequence must be strictly adhered to. It has been pointed out that the refrigeration plant is designed to cope with an average load, and that a small number of freezers should be filled at short intervals; when too many freezers are loaded at once, the initial demand is very high and the machinery may become overloaded. Freezing may then be inefficient and blocks will either be discharged before they are completely frozen or they will have to be left in longer, thus disrupting the freezing cycle. The rotation of loading should be such that when the last freezers have been filled the first ones are just ready for discharge and reloading.

Freezing time for a particular product should never be cut. There should be a dummy clock on every freezer or some other simple means of recording the time of loading. When blocks are removed too soon, even though they feel hard, they will not be properly frozen. The middle of the fish will still be soft, and this means the cold store has extra work to do for which it is not designed. The store temperature will rise, the fish will be frozen very slowly, and fish already in store will be subjected to fluctuating temperature. On the other hand, blocks should not be left in the freezer longer than necessary when other fish are waiting to be frozen; too long a freezing time reduces output and delays unfrozen fish unnecessarily.

The freezer plates should be defrosted before unloading just long enough to free the blocks from the plates. The defrost valve should then be closed. When the hot fluid is left flowing for too long, the blocks will be partially thawed before they are released and the next lot of fish to be frozen will be warmed too much when loaded. The freezer plates should never be forced apart during unloading; this may damage the freezer. The operator must wait until defrosting has freed the blocks before attempting to remove them. It should never be necessary to use force on the blocks or on any part of the freezer during unloading. Hooks should not be used for moving frozen blocks but, where their use is permitted, only the heads of fish should be spiked; fillets with holes in them are of little value.

Temperature of the refrigerant entering the freezers should be checked every time fish are loaded. Manufacturer's recommendations should be followed carefully. In most freezer trawlers the temperature should be −40°C. Whenever it is higher than this, the engineers should be informed so that it can be corrected; the fish will not freeze properly if the refrigerant is not cold enough.

An accurate record of freezer operations should be kept, showing loading and unloading times, the number and kind of blocks produced, and the refrigerant temperature at the freezer inlet. The information on block labels should be as detailed as possible; ideally a label should record not only the kind and size of fish, but also the place and time of capture and the initial condition of the fish.

In addition to the plate freezer installation, some stern trawlers have a special room for freezing very large or awkwardly shaped fish that cannot be handled in the plate freezers. The fish (typically, large cod and halibut) are hung on hooks in a stream of cold air. Operators should be instructed in the proper use of this type of freezer which can be easily abused. The fish must be hung so that air can blow between them; they will freeze far too slowly if piled on the floor. The freezer should never be overcrowded; fish that have been frozen should be stowed in the cold store to make room for more. When the room is too full, the cold air cannot circulate properly, and fish left in too long will become dried. The fan openings should not be obstructed by fish.

The temperature of the air in a blast freezer should be checked at regular intervals; if the temperature starts to rise, this may be because there are too many fish in the freezer, or because excessive build-up of frost on the cooler is preventing the transfer of heat from the air to the refrigerant. Where the cooler is an enclosed space, it may be necessary to remove the room lining to brush the pipes clear of frost.

Blocks of frozen fish may be discharged from the vertical plate freezers either direct into the cold store or onto the factory deck, depending on the design of the freezer. Blocks unloaded onto the factory deck should be moved immediately to the cold store; any delay will warm the blocks and impose additional load on the cold store machinery. Mechanical aids should be provided to make movement of blocks into store as easy as possible. The blocks may be lowered through a hatch in batches by means of a mechanical hoist, or they can be slid singly through a small deck opening using roller conveyors and chutes. The blocks should always be handled carefully; damaged blocks waste stowage space and are a nuisance to discharge, and damaged fish are useless fish. Broken blocks and single fish should always be stowed separately in the cold store. Wherever possible, fish of the same kind and size should be stowed together, and their position recorded on a stowage plan, so that the catch can be discharged in an efficient manner.

Blocks of fish should never be jammed too tightly during stowage; this may damage the fish, and further damage may be done when trying to prise them loose during discharge. Hatches and doors into the cold store should never be left open longer than necessary, and there should never be more than one door or hatch open at a time.

The cold store air temperature should be −30°C or below at all times. The temperature should be checked continually, and any rise reported to the ship's engineers so that corrective measures can be taken. Each time the store temperature rises, quality is affected, and long periods at too high a temperature may make the fish unacceptable at a later stage in processing or distribution.

Fig. 12. Baader fillet line for fish stick blocks on the factory deck of the trawler "Coriolanus".

Unfrozen or partially frozen fish should never be put in the cold store. The store is not designed to freeze fish, and the extra work imposed on the store compressor in this way will result in a rise in temperature and thus a loss of quality.

Strict instructions should be given about safety in shipboard cold stores; men working in a low temperature space in a rolling ship are at risk. Crew members should never work alone in the cold store; a man unconscious, for example, as a result of a knock or a fall or a leak of refrigerant, will not survive for long at $-30°C$. Cold store lights should never be switched off without first making sure the store is unoccupied. People working in the store should leave immediately if they feel drowsy or dizzy, and all crew should be instructed in the use of any alarm system fitted.

Most of what has been said about handling and freezing of whole fish is equally relevant to fillet freezing, but there are some additional points to be considered. Initial quality of the fish is perhaps even more important when cutting fillets; if the incoming catch is found on inspection to be composed of soft or spent fish, the fillets must be labelled to indicate this when they are packed and frozen.

Chilling before and after gutting is very important when processing fillets. Chilling before rigor prevents the blood from clotting too quickly, and chilling after gutting allows the fish to bleed. The fish should be gutted as soon as possible after capture, and allowed to bleed for about 30 minutes.

When the fillets have been cut by hand or machine they should be inspected for imperfections; damaged or wormy fillets should be discarded, and any second grade fillets should be labelled accordingly.

It has been explained that fillets from pre-rigor fish shrink rapidly; it is therefore very important to process the fillets as soon as they have been cut. When they cannot be loaded into the freezer immediately, they must be kept chilled. Fresh water should not be used to wash the fillets at any stage. Since it is better practice to delay the whole gutted fish than to delay fillets, the filleting line should be stopped when there is a hold-up at the freezer.

Horizontal plate freezers for fillets should be loaded in strict rotation in the same manner as a vertical plate freezer installation, so that there is a steady demand on the refrigeration plant and to keep delays to a minimum. When a freezer is ready for loading, fillets lying waiting should be put in, even though there may not be enough to make a full load. It is better to adhere to the freezing cycle and freeze a part load than to risk leaving fillets lying for too long. When only part of a freezer shelf is filled, the fish should be spread out to prevent the freezer plate from becoming bent during compression.

Trays and moulds used for making fillet blocks should be kept scrupulously clean; the cut surface of a fillet is much more exposed to contamination than the whole fish protected by its skin. Freezer plates and trays should be kept free from lumps of ice so that there is good contact between fish and plate; good contact means faster freezing and this in turn results in a better product and higher output.

The need for good housekeeping in a fillet freezer trawler cannot be emphasised too strongly. Fillets are much more susceptible to damage and contamination than whole fish, and should be handled carefully and hygienically at all times. Blocks of fillets should be properly wrapped before being loaded into cold store; fillets with faulty wrappings will dry out, lose flavour and lose weight before they are landed. Machines, conveyor lines and benches must be cleaned at frequent intervals; the factory trawler is handling highly perishable food under modern conditions. Freezing and cold storage cannot improve the quality of fish that is already dirty, contaminated or spoiled when it goes into the freezer.

The above advice on handling whole fish and fillets in freezer stern trawlers can be summarised in the following six precepts:

1. Keep the catch cool from the time it comes on board until it reaches the freezer,
2. Gut and wash each haul before starting the next one,
3. Leave the fish to bleed for 30 minutes,
4. Never delay fillets,
5. Never cut short the freezing time,
6. Store the fish at $-30°C$ as soon as they are frozen, and keep them at this temperature until they are landed.

MECHANICAL AIDS ON THE PROCESSING DECK

A stern trawler with a shelter deck is particularly suitable for mechanisation. Whether the fish are being handled for subsequent storage in chilled or frozen form, most of the operations before stowage, and the movements between them, can be mechanised; the labour content is reduced, the remaining manual jobs are less onerous, and the fish are handled more carefully and quickly.

Pregutting chilling tanks

It is desirable in all freezer stern trawlers to chill the catch as soon as it comes aboard and to keep it chilled until frozen. There is normally sufficient room on the after part of the processing deck to keep the fish in refrigerated sea water while awaiting gutting. Chilling systems have been used in a number of stern trawlers in Eastern Europe and South Africa, and the use of refrigerated sea water (RSW) is likely to be introduced in the British fleet. It is preferable to have a number of tanks which can be used in rotation. A typical installation might have four pre-gutting tanks, each holding up to five tonnes of fish, so that successive hauls can be kept separate and worked on the first in, first out principle. Each tank would have its own hatch on the fishing deck and, since the fish may come out of warmer waters at temperatures between $10°$ and $15°C$, they should be left in the RSW for at least 30 minutes to ensure adequate chilling before gutting. The ratio of fish to sea water should not be higher than 4 to 1.

Discharge from the tanks should be at the level of the gutting benches or gutting machines, and the space below the tanks can be used for the RSW reservoirs. The RSW should be delivered by pump to the bottom of the pre-gutting tank so that the cold water is forced up through the fish as the tank is being filled. The headroom in the tank may not always be sufficient to allow a tank floor with a steep slope; once the tank has been drained and opened, the last of the fish may not slide naturally to the gutting stations. Various devices are possible; some ships have tanks with tilting floors for example, and high pressure water jets at the rear of the tank might be used to push the fish forwards. It should not be necessary for crew to enter the tank to throw fish out. The refrigeration load for each five-tonne tank will be in the region of 20 000 J/s for fish coming aboard at $15°C$, including some allowance for heat gains through the tank walls and from the pump, and assuming the fish are reduced to a temperature of $0°C$ in four hours. The tanks would require about 3 cm of expanded plastic insulation for an outside temperature of $20°C$.

Gutting machines

The gutting operation is often a bottleneck in the handling system for white fish. One man can gut three to four fish a minute when handling round species like cod; thus, for fish weighing about 2 kg he can move about 400 kg an hour. The man soon gets tired and, when he has to lift the fish from the deck and throw it into a washer, his output will fall as the work continues. When the fish are conveyed to the man at waist height and he can gut them on a bench before dispatching them by conveyor, his output can be increased to four to five fish a minute.

Prototype gutting machines have been tried at sea since the 1950s, and reliable commercial designs have been available from British and German manufacturers since the late 1960s. The two sizes of British machine handle fish 30–44 cm and 40–80 cm in length respectively, and the output for both sizes is 30–40 fish a minute. Thus, with two men feeding fish to one machine, the output of fish weighing 2 kg is 4,000 kg an hour; in other words, two men and a machine can produce five times as much fish as two men gutting by hand. There are two steps in the machine gutting process: the fish, lying belly upwards in a cradle, are presented first to a circular cutter which slits the belly wall and throws out the guts, and then to a revolving brush which in combination with a high pressure water jet cleans out the belly cavity. The livers are not recoverable, because they are broken up and mixed with the guts when they are cut out.

The more sophisticated German machines handle roughly the same size ranges of fish, and have the same output; the fish are passed belly downwards over fixed knives which open the belly cavity and pull the guts out, and are then passed over water jets and a revolving brush to clean the cavity. The machines probably require more expert maintenance, but have the advantage that the livers are preserved intact. The German machines occupy about twice the deck space of the British ones.

Post-gutting chilling tanks

The prime purpose of post-gutting tanks is to allow the fish time to bleed. The required residence time is 30 minutes for white fish like cod; therefore the unit size of tank can be smaller than for the pregutting installation. Each tank should hold enough fish to supply one or two freezers at a time. If the freezer installation is taken to be the same as in the example calculations earlier in this chapter, ten 12-station freezers are loaded every 220 minutes. Thus a reasonable size of tank would be one to hold fish for two freezers, to be emptied after about 40 minutes; the weight of fish in a tank would be about one tonne and a bank of five tanks would keep the freezers continuously supplied, in a ship freezing 35 tonnes a day. The tanks would be drained and emptied in strict rotation, and any delay before freezing would take place in the tanks under chill conditions; fish would not be released from the tanks until a freezer was ready to receive them. A continuous system for loading and emptying post-gutting tanks might be feasible.

Fig. 13. Baader 163 gutting machine.

The refrigerated sea water system should be similar to that for the pre-gutting tanks. RSW would be pumped from a reservoir below the tanks into the bottom of each tank, and the ratio of fish to water should again be not more than 4 to 1. The tank floor should be steeply sloped so that the whole of the contents can be gravity fed to the conveyor leading to the freezers. The refrigeration capacity required for post-gutting tanks will be small in comparison with that for the pre-gutting tanks; a capacity of about 6 000 J/s for each one tonne post-gutting tank should be sufficient to cope with fish that are already chilled before gutting.

Filleting machines

A freezer trawler that produces fillets has to depend very largely on filleting machines to maintain output; hand filleting requires a large labour force and is a difficult task in a moving ship. Machines are available for the common north Atlantic species of round white fish, but, as with the

Fig. 14. Baader machine fillet line for large cod in a factory trawler.

117

gutting machines, each model has only a limited size range, so that two or more types are usually necessary to cover all sizes from 30 to 80 cm. Provision for a limited amount of hand filleting is also required to deal with very large fish, and fish of species for which there is no suitable machine. Skinning machines will also be required when laminated blocks of fillets are being made for shore production of portions or fingers. One filleting machine taking 20–25 cod a minute will move about 2,500 kg of whole fish an hour with fish averaging 2 kg each, and produce about 1,000 kg of skinless fillets. Thus, one machine working 18 hours a day can cope with a catching rate of 45 tonnes a day of fish within its size range.

Grading and orienting machines

Fish of the right size have to be loaded by hand into gutting and filleting machines, and two men are often required to one machine to utilise its full capacity; equipment is now being developed to eliminate some of this labour. In the next few years machinery is likely to be available that will sort the fish into size ranges for particular machines and feed them to the cutters in the correct attitude, head first or tail first, belly up or belly down. Equipment of this kind is already available for smaller species like herring.

Weighing machines

Weighing is a difficult operation in a moving ship, and one which can usually be dispensed with for bulk cargoes of frozen fish destined for further processing ashore; consignments can be weighed on entry to the shore cold store. Thus the weight of blocks of whole fish and large blocks of fillets is often governed by the volume of the mould in which they are frozen.

Marine weighing machines suitably compensated for ship's motion are available for use in factory trawlers, but these are rather expensive and are probably of more use for weighing items in kilogrammes than in grammes; the weighing of small retail packs of frozen fish that have to meet the requirements of weights and measures legislation is still very difficult, and it may be necessary to give a disproportionately large amount of overweight in order to avoid charges of short weight at the point of sale.

Packaging equipment

Blocks of whole white fish do not normally require protective packaging in a ship's cold store. Cartons can be used to keep the fish clean and to give some protection against damage, but the skin of the frozen fish is usually sufficient protection in itself, and the complications introduced by adding a packing operation are probably not justified. Protection against dehydration in cold store may be thought desirable, but glazing by dipping or spraying with cold water would protect the frozen block just as well as an impervious wrapper and would be simpler to do at sea. Again, experience has shown that glazing of whole fish for the few weeks in the ship's cold store is hardly worth while and in British practice the blocks are glazed for long term storage on entry to the shore cold store.

Blocks of fillets require protective packaging mainly to keep the cut surface of the fillets clean. Packaging before freezing is more practicable with air blast and horizontal plate freezers than with vertical plate freezers, and some form of wrapper or carton can often be put into the mould or tray. Packing of fish and closing of wrappers or cartons is mostly done by hand; packaging machines in a few large factory trawlers have so far proved extremely difficult to maintain in working order at sea.

Large blocks of fillets can also be frozen without wrappers in frames or moulds and packed in outer cartons afterwards. The loading of several blocks into a single carton and then sealing it is an operation that can be mechanised more readily. A packaging operation of any kind requires a good deal of deck space; in general the pack should be as big as possible and the type of package as simple as possible. Protection against contamination and physical damage is desirable, but the use of more sophisticated materials to prevent the movement of water and oxygen is probably unnecessary for frozen products that are to be further processed ashore.

Mechanical handling equipment

A wide range of conveyors, chutes and hoists is available for moving fish swiftly and smoothly from one operation to the next until the product is stowed in the cold store or the fishroom. Apart from the effects of movement of the ship and the presence of salt water, the problems of moving the fish about are much the same as those in any large processing plant. Simplicity of design, robustness, and ease of cleaning and maintenance are important for shipboard operation; safety is also important, bearing in mind that men may fall or be thrown against moving parts by the movement of the ship. In many large factory decks the network of conveyors moving whole fish, fillets and offal is often so complex that crew have to move under or over belts and

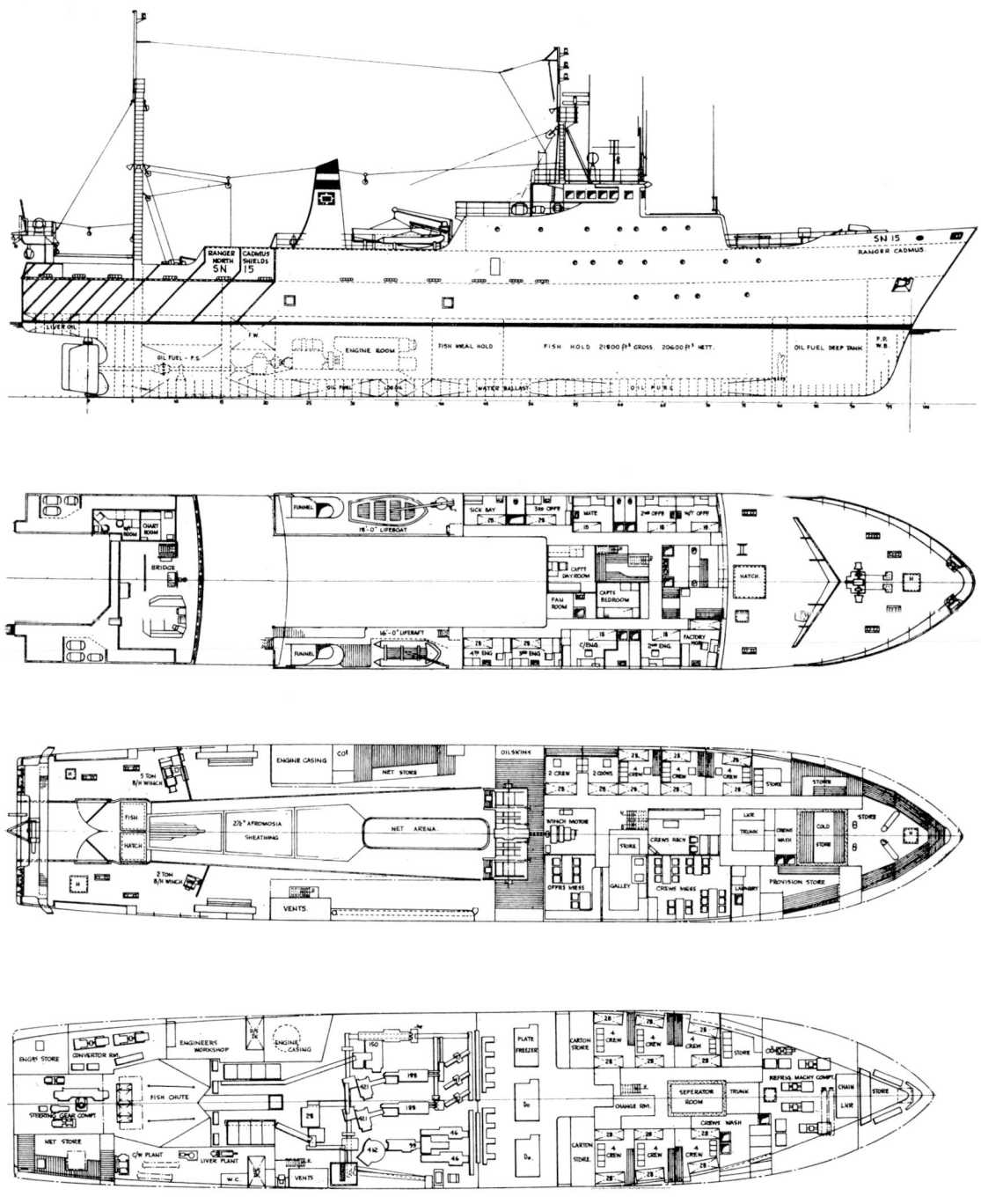

Fig. 15. Profile and general arrangement of a modern, small factory trawler. The "Ranger Cadmus" was built in 1971 and is the first of four similar ships for the Ranger Fishing Company. The numbers on the factory deck plan indicate the types of Baader machine installed.

chains in confined spaces; some otherwise productive deck space should be sacrificed in order to make it possible for crew to move freely without the risk of trapping fingers or clothing in moving machinery.

WHOLE FISH OR FILLETS

When a stern trawler is equipped with low temperature storage facilities, it might seem more sensible to fill the cargo space only with frozen edible material, that is fillets. About three times the weight of flesh can be stored as fillets than as whole fish in the same space, blocks can be thinner and therefore frozen more quickly, and the offal can be reduced to a fifth of its weight and carried as fish meal. The argument is not as simple as that, however, and some of the pros and cons of freezing whole fish or fillets will now be discussed.

Most British freezer trawlers have been designed to freeze whole white fish, and some other European countries, notably Spain and Portugal, have followed the same pattern. West German vessels, on the other hand, have nearly all been fitted for freezing fillets, while the fleets of the Eastern European countries include trawlers that can handle whole fish and fillets. The choice of product in each country has to a large extent been governed by the requirements of the existing marketing network shore. Spain for example chose to produce frozen whole fish because the fish trade and its customers were used to dealing in whole fish. In Britain also, the fish industry considered that sea frozen whole fish could, after thawing at the port, be reprocessed and distributed through all the usual outlets in much the same manner as the traditional chilled whole fish.

The arguments made in favour of freezing whole fish at sea are as follows. The thawed whole fish can be used in almost all of the ways in which chilled whole fish of high quality are used. The number of crew required in a trawler that is freezing whole fish is only a little larger than in a trawler of the same size icing the catch; British trawlers usually carry three or four extra men for the job. The vertical plate freezer is robust and simple to operate. The frozen blocks withstand a certain amount of rough handling without detriment to the quality of the product. Although the raw material requires handling with care before freezing, it is easier to ensure a finished product of high quality when handling whole fish than when handling fillets. Breakdowns are less frequent and maintenance at sea is easier on a processing line that does not include filleting, skinning and weighing equipment.

The arguments against the freezing of whole fish include the following. Use of shipboard cargo space for whole fish is wasteful; blocks of whole frozen cod have a stowage rate of about 550 kg/m³, based on a block density of about 800 kg/m³ with allowance for cold store structure, access space and broken stowage. Assuming a yield of 40 per cent by weight of fillets from whole fish, the stowage rate of edible flesh when freezing whole fish is about 220 kg/m³. The density of a large block of frozen fillets is about 900 kg/m³, giving a stowage rate in practice of about 700 kg/m³; thus, more than three times the weight of fillets can be carried in the same space. Whole fish take longer to freeze than fillets from the same fish; therefore the same weight of catch can be frozen more quickly as fillets than as whole fish. Whole fish take longer to thaw than fillets; blocks of whole fish usually have to be thawed by the port processors so that the fish can be filleted whereas fillets frozen at sea may not require thawing at the port.

The arguments against freezing fillets at sea include the following. It is almost always more costly to do a job at sea than on shore; the smaller the proportion of processing that has to be done in the ship, the more economic the operation. Because only 40 per cent of the whole fish is frozen, the cold store takes longer to fill; crewing problems are often greater when voyages are longer. More men and more equipment are required to handle fillets, but the ship does not necessarily catch any more fish. Discoloration and gaping of the flesh is much more difficult to avoid when processing fillets. The additional factory space and crew accommodation required for processing fillets make considerable inroads on the space available for cargo stowage. Fillets are fillets; the shore processor has to have a market for them more or less as they are; he cannot make a satisfactory smoked product from them for example. Laminated blocks for fish finger production can be made at sea, but this requires an extra operation to remove pin bones, and careful inspection to ensure the boneless standard is maintained.

The opportunity of making fish meal from filleting waste is sometimes regarded as an advantage in the fillet freezing vessel. If it is assumed that 40 per cent of the weight of the catch is processed as fillets, 60 per cent is available for reduction to meal. If a further 10 per cent is added to allow for fish that are normally discarded, then about one fifth of 70, that is 14 per cent of the catch, would be carried as fish meal. Thus for every 40 tons of fillets there would be about 14 tons of fish meal, but the value of the meal will be about one third that of the fillets, and it may well be worth considering filling 100 per cent rather than 75 per cent of the cargo space with frozen fish. Weight for weight, bagged fish meal takes up about the same space as frozen whole fish, and rather more room than frozen fillets.

It can be seen from the above that the choice of product is not a simple one. The economics of freezing whole fish or fillets will be different for different fisheries and different markets. From the British industry's point of view the early demise of the *Fairtry* class suggests that fillet freezing at least in that size of vessel is uneconomic, but the growth of the smaller *Ranger* class indicates that there is still room in the British market for sea frozen fillets in addition to the growing landings of sea frozen whole fish. The attractions of freezing fillets are likely to become stronger in the next decade as the technology improves and as trouble-free mechanisation becomes more of a reality.

Notable Small Stern Trawlers

LIEUT-COMMANDER JOHN BURGESS
(*Fishing News, Fishing News International*)

Interest in the viability of stern trawlers less than 100 ft. in overall length quickened in Europe in 1960 after the capabilities of a vessel called *Universal Star* had been demonstrated off Aberdeen in Scotland and Bergen in Norway.

Universal Star had been conceived at an informal gathering of trawler owners, builders and designers a few years before. Impressed by the performance of the world's first large stern trawlers, the *Fairtrys* operated by Chr. Salvesen in the North Atlantic, some of them got together and agreed to design, build and explore the potential of a much smaller vessel.

Prime movers in this scheme were Andrew Walker, an Aberdeen trawler owner; James Venus of Seawork Ltd., builders of trawlers and other vessels, and Dr. Corlett, managing director of Burness, Corlett and Partners, naval architects and designers of fishing vessels.

In developing the ideas of these three, Burness, Corlett and Partners, obtained the collaboration of the International MacGregor Organisation and also of the British White Fish Authority and the Torry Research Station. As a consequence of this a quarter full size mock-up of the stern of the proposed vessel was built at one of Seawork's shipyards—T. Mitchison Ltd. at Gateshead.

Trials with this mock-up were eventually so satisfactory that it was decided to go ahead and build. Thus the prototype of hundreds of small stern trawlers came to be built on the Tyne in England.

Universal Star was completed in the Mitchison yard at Gateshead towards the end of 1959. She measured 104 ft. overall, had a moulded breadth of 25 ft. 3 in. and mean draught of 11 ft., and was the first trawler ever to be fitted with a Unigan hydraulic stern trawling gantry. She was powered by two Lister diesels which gave her a speed of just over 11 knots. The port engine developed 495 hp at 750 rpm and the starboard engine 330 hp at the same revolutions. She had a 168 hp Lister diesel for driving the trawl winch generator and two other Lister auxiliary diesels for driving generators, compressors and pumps. Her engine room was situated below the accommodation forward of the bridge and her twin screws, which were driven through Hindmarch-MWD reverse-reduction gearboxes, were tucked away as far forward as possible from the stern to minimise the risk of their being fouled.

The Unigan gantry was a large steel arch of such a strength that it would support many times the load ever likely to be put on it. Blocks to take the trawl warps were slung from brackets fitted on the outer sides of the arms of the gantry and further blocks to take quarter ropes and recovery lines were slung inside it at the top.

Like a stern door which ran practically the width of the vessel, the gantry was hydraulically operated. Pivoting forward and aft at its base, it could be swung out over the stern so that the trawl doors could be lowered into the water or recovered, and it could be swung in again so that the doors could be lowered into their inboard stowage positions. It could be swung out to enable a bag of fish to be hoisted into it and then swung in again to allow the fish to be released from the cod-end on to the working deck.

The stern door lowered outwards to a horizontal position to enable the trawl and its gear to be shot away. Used in conjunction with the gantry, it enabled the gear to be handled at what was then considered to be an astonishingly high speed – up from 120 fathoms and back again in 16 minutes – with only two or three hands aft to handle it.

During the summer of 1960, *Universal Star* was sent over to Bergen in Norway to demonstrate her capabilities at the Fisheries Exhibition. There she created an enormous amount of interest both among Norwegian fishing vessel owners and among representatives of many important fishing countries from all over the world. As a consequence of these, and previous demonstrations from Aberdeen in Scotland, trawler-owning concerns in Norway, Germany, Spain and other countries commenced to build stern trawlers both large and small.

One of the most interesting among those under

100 ft. (30.48 metres) overall was the *Hessatraal* built by Aukra Bruk for Fredr. Hessen of Aalesund. This vessel was 25.85 metres long overall with a moulded breadth of 6.20 m. and depth of 3.40 m. She was powered by three 180 h.p. Scania Vabis diesels coupled by belt drive to a Liaaen reduction gear and thence to a controllable pitch propeller. She had a 7-ton Hydraulik A/S winch just aft of a forward superstructure, a stern ramp and a fixed gantry over it. She was probably the first small stern trawler to have a ramp and fixed gantry instead of arrangements like those in *Universal Star*.

Another unusually interesting small stern trawler was built in 1962 at Risor in Norway by Lindstols Skips and Batbyggeri for Myrefisk A/S. She was designed by the same firm of naval architects that had designed *Universal Star* – Burness, Corlet and Partners of Basingstoke – and had a hydroconic hull.

Named *Myrefisk*, she was of all-welded steel construction and was 91 ft. overall with a beam of 23 ft. and draught of 12 ft. 3 in. She was powered by a Wichmann 5ACA diesel which gave her a speed of over 10 knots and her deck machinery included a split trawl winch with a total pull of $13\frac{1}{4}$ tons and a hydraulically driven Unigan stern gantry Type 2. She proved to be a successful little vessel and her owners later had another built on more or less the same lines.

In 1962 Bathurst Marine commenced building three small steel stern trawlers in New Brunswick, Canada to designs by the Norwegian shipbuilders Aukra Bruk A/S. The first of them was for the Fishermen's Loan Board and was 84 ft. overall with a beam of 22 ft. and draught of 12 ft. She was powered by a 450 h.p. Bergen diesel driving a Hjelset controllable pitch propeller in a nozzle and had a top speed of over 10 knots. She was laid out more or less on the lines of a side trawler and had a Norwinch hydraulic trawl winch fitted on the foredeck. But right aft she had a fixed gantry and a steep stern ramp for getting the gear on board.

In 1963 it began to become apparent that trawler owners in most of the principal fishing countries in the world, while agreeing that stern trawling had many advantages over side trawling, differed to an astonishing extent in their ideas of how small stern trawlers should be laid out and equipped. Vessels of more or less the same size but entirely different in almost every other respect began to make their appearance in Europe and the USA.

In the USA that year the Blount Marine Corporation of Warren, Rhode Island completed a stern trawler of advanced design for the Narragan-

Fig. 1. The "Universal Star", 104 ft. long, built in 1959.

sett Trawling Corporation. And she was claimed to be the world's first automated stern trawler.

Named *Narragansett*, she was built of steel and measured $83 \times 21\frac{1}{2} \times 9$ ft. She was powered by a 385 hp Caterpillar diesel which drove, by means of a gear belt stern drive, a Hustad c.p. propeller to give a speed of over 11 knots. The drive allowed the engine to be installed over the propeller, thus making plenty of room for accommodation and fish holds in the rest of the vessel.

Blount 'Trawlmatic' split winches were fitted on the after deck and were powered by a 130 hp Caterpillar diesel. A net drum, capable of completely winding a net with 7 in. ground rollers was also fitted and, like the winches, could be controlled from the wheelhouse. Two Gearmatic winches were fitted at the base of the vessel's derrick and these could also be remotely controlled.

The *Narragansett* was unique in being the first stern trawler in the world to use a trawl handling system adaptable to remote and automatic control.

Fig. 2. The "Narragansett", 83 ft. long, built in 1963.

Fig. 3. The "Ross Daring", 99 ft. long, built in 1963.

She had a central area for navigation and deck gear control with 360 deg. observation, overlooking the deck and operable from one point by one man. To shoot the trawl, a mechanical locking system could be switched on from the control panel so that both winches would start paying out warp. The desired length could be veered and then the winches would stop automatically. To haul, the skipper had only to push a button and the warps would be automatically hauled.

In England in 1963 the Ross Group had another type of highly automated stern trawler built by Cochrane's at Selby. She was named *Ross Daring* and was 99 ft. overall with a moulded breadth of 23 ft. and depth of $12\frac{1}{2}$ ft. She was designed for short range work in the North Sea and to be operated by a crew of five, including the skipper, only. Her propulsion machinery consisted of a 450 h.p. Paxman diesel driving a Hindmarch/Berg c.p. propeller through a reduction gearbox to give a top speed of $10\frac{1}{2}$ knots.

Of particular interest in this vessel were the hydraulic winches, which were specially designed and developed for installation in her, and the fish handling and gutting arrangements. There were two trawl winches installed amidships, one on either side of the working deck under cover of the boat deck. They could be remotely controlled from a console in the wheelhouse. Drum speed synchronization was achieved by so arranging the hydraulic drive that excessive strain on either winch automatically slowed down the other. If required, the winches could be operated independently.

A few feet aft of the trawl winches a hydraulic twin-drum warping winch was installed and it, like all the other hydraulic deck machinery, was powered by an 87 hp auxiliary diesel. It could also be controlled from the console on the bridge which was so positioned that the skipper had a clear view of the winches and the whole of the after deck when operating its levers. Included in this view were a twin tackle derrick on the after mast, gallows on either quarter, a transom stern roller and a unique type of tray for stowing the trawl bobbins.

The fish pounds in *Ross Daring* were fitted on the starboard side of the working deck aft. Fish were transferred from them through a hatch in the after bulkhead straight into a waist high, aluminium gutting trough. When cleaned, they were placed in a washing trough, the exit of which led to a chute to the fish room below. On return to port, they were landed through a large hatch in the foredeck.

The *Ross Daring* and the *Narragansett* were much more complicated vessels than a new stern trawler built in France in 1963. This vessel, named *Jecrisa-Marie*, was built by C. & A. de la Perriere in Lorient for the Aubert-Jan Henriques Co. of Concarneau. She was 30 metres long overall and powered by a 475 hp Crepelle diesel which gave her a speed of 11 knots. The engine was installed aft and the fish room was forward of the engine room as was the practice in conventional side trawlers operating from Concarneau. Otherwise she differed from them radically in most respects.

She had a 30 square metre working deck forward with crew's accommodation aft of it. And she had a large after deck on which were installed a mast and derrick, gallows on either side and a trawl winch. Along the starboard side was a wide alleyway leading to the sheltered working deck and a little forward of amidships on this side were fitted another set of gallows. No stern door, stern ramp or stern gantry were fitted and a gilson on the derrick was used to hoist the trawl out and inboard. Arrangements for handling it, in fact, were as simple as those in the *Narragansett* were complex.

By 1964 small stern trawlers with all sorts of different layouts and gantries were being built in considerable numbers all over the world. One of the most unusual among them was a 94 ft. vessel built by NV Scheepswerf Appingedam in Holland for the Shamrock Shipping Company of Dalkey in Ireland. Named *Clearwater*, she was powered by a 520 hp Brons diesel, which gave her a speed of 11 knots, and fitted with a Lister auxiliary engine for powering a 90 hp Norwinch hydraulic winch pump. She had goalpost masts at the break of the deck with a derrick on them for handling the net, a removable gantry with gear handling blocks on it at the stern, and a roller across the transom.

Also built in Holland at this time was the first cutter designed to operate a beam trawl over the stern. She was not a twin-beam shrimp trawler, hundreds of which have been built in Holland and the USA both before and since the appearance of the *Universal Star* and which I am not including in this survey because they are a specialized type of vessel, not specifically designed to work their gear over the stern. She was a unique type of vessel with wheelhouse and accommodation forward, a winch just aft of the superstructure, and a mast and derrick installed in the middle of the after deck to operate the gear.

Named *Tiny Cornelia*, she was built by Gebr. Van de Sande at Breskens for J. Melesteeg of Ouddorp. Her overall length was 21.20 m., beam 5.60 m. and draught 2.60 m. and she had accommodation for a crew of seven. She was powered by a 320 hp Cummins diesel, fitted with the most up-to-date equipment, and must have proved a successful vessel as her owner later had a similar trawler with the same name built. Details of the latter are given towards the end of this chapter.

A small stern trawler of quite a different type was built by Herd and Mackenzie in Buckie, Scotland, in 1964 for the Government of Aden. She was named *Rizq-al-Bahr* and designed to be used for purse seining as well as trawling in the Arabian Gulf. Her overall length was 67 ft. and she was powered by a 320 hp Kelvin diesel driving a Friedenthal propeller through a reverse-reduction gear to give a speed of 9¼ knots. She had gallows on either quarter but no gantry or stern ramp. Her winch was made by J. Swan in Vancouver, Canada and her power block by Marco in Seattle, USA.

Other remarkable small stern trawlers were built that year both in the USA and New Zealand. The *Narragansett*, described before, having proved successful, Blount Marine built another similar vessel for her owners – the Narragansett Trawling Corporation. The new vessel was named *Canyon Prince*. She was 64 ft. long and powered by a 340 hp General Motors diesel which gave her a speed of over 11 knots. She was highly automated like her predecessor and experience in the latter enabled her deck machinery and controls to be so arranged that shooting and hauling her trawl on to a net drum could be carried out at high speed by one man.

The New Zealand trawlers were built by A. & G. Price Ltd. in Auckland for Marine Packers and Exporters Ltd. They were 67 ft. long and each was powered by a 200 hp Gardner diesel with an auxiliary 50 hp Gardner diesel to act as prime mover for the vessel's hydraulic system. Both vessels were fitted with hydraulic winches made by the builders and with fixed stern gantries. They provided further

Fig. 4. The "Canyon Prince", 64 ft. long, built in 1964.

evidence that swinging stern gantries were not likely to be utilized to any great extent in stern trawlers under about 100 ft. long.

What you might call very small stern trawlers started to be built in Britain between 1961 and 1964, and I don't suppose that swinging gantries were ever even contemplated for installation in them. Typical of such craft was the *Kay B* built by J. Samuel White at Cockenzie in Scotland for J. H. Booth of Fleetwood. She was 45 ft. long and powered by a 110 hp Gardner diesel which gave her a speed of about eight knots. She had a bipod mast forward to carry the derrick topping lift tackle and another right aft to carry two gilson hook tackles. She also had a small steel chute – a sort of miniature stern ramp in her transom.

About the beginning of 1965 the first Ocean type stern trawler was completed in Felix Amiot's shipyard in France – Constructions Machaniques de Normandie – for L'Armement Kuhn-Ballery of Concarneau. She was of exceptional interest as she was constructed to the builder's own patented design – one very different from that of any other stern trawler at the time.

The builder's aim when designing Ocean class stern trawlers was to incorporate the trawl and fish handling decks (placed one over the other in large stern trawlers) side by side and to have them both completely under cover. The lay-out was planned so that the trawl could be hauled inboard without effort and without risk to the crew; so that the net could be spread out as in a side trawler for examination and mending; and so that the crew would be able to gut, wash and stow fish under cover. Addi-

Fig. 5. The catamaran stern trawler "Caribbean Twin", built in 1965.

tional aims were that the vessels would have a conventional lay-out below the main deck – accommodation aft, engine room amidships and fish holds forward; wheelhouses with an all-round view; maximum automation to reduce crew fatigue; and maximum possible protection for the crew.

Lutece was the name of the first of these trawlers. She was 29 metres on the waterline with a moulded breadth of 7.96 m. and depth to the main deck of 4 m. On the main deck right forward there was a net and boatswain's store; and then, on the port side, a refrigerated provision store, mess and galley. On the starboard side, aft of the net store, was a tunnel freezing compartment. Aft of this and the galley, a bulkhead with a scuttle amidships traversed the hull, and on the after side of the bulkhead, split winches were installed – one to port and one to starboard.

There were clear decks under cover, with a combined total area of 100 square metres, running right aft from the winches. The port side deck was for examining and mending the trawl while the starboard one was for gutting and washing the catch. The port side deck led to a stern ramp; the starboard one to the fish pounds. Between them were located hatches to the fish holds on the lower deck; engine room casing; and, near the stern, the crew's washplaces.

On the lower deck, right forward, there were fuel oil tanks followed by two fish holds, engine room, crew's accommodation and steering engine compartment. Traversing the whole of the stern was a swinging gantry for hoisting the cod end inboard and for handling the trawl doors.

Lutece was called a 'Polythermic' trawler by the builders because fish could be carried at any temperature in her down to minus 25 deg.C in two fish holds. Capacity of the forward hold was 40 cubic metres and that of the after hold 91 cu.m.

Propulsion machinery consisted of a 600 hp Sulzer diesel driving a Lips c.p. propeller through a Hindmarch/Messian reduction gear. It gave her a service speed of about 11 knots.

A small stern trawler of unusual interest was completed in J. & J. Forbes & Company's yard at Fraserburgh in Scotland at the beginning of 1965. She was named *Constellation* and was of entirely different design from the traditional type of vessel used for trawling or seine netting around the Scottish coast. Her overall length was 65 ft. and she was powered by a 240 hp Kelvin diesel which gave her a speed of over 10 knots. She had a forward wheelhouse with a Sutherland winch just aft of it and at the stern a small swinging gantry, an entirely novel feature in a vessel of this size.

Later in the year two small steel stern trawlers with some unusual features about them were built at Ramsey in the Isle of Man. Named *Zulu Warrior* and *Massai Warrior*, they were 47 ft. long and powered by a 144 hp Rolls Royce diesel driving propellers shrouded in steering nozzles to give them a top speed of nine knots. Each was fitted with a Fifer hydraulic winch just aft of a forward wheelhouse, portable gallows aft (to enable scallop dredging to be carried out) and a roller across the transom.

Another stern trawler which created a great deal of interest that year was a catamaran built by The Twin Hull Boat Co. at the Keasby Shipbuilding Yard, New Jersey, USA. Named *Caribbean Twin*, she was 70 ft. long and powered by twin General Motors diesels each developing 350 hp to give her a speed of $12\frac{1}{2}$ knots. She had a forward wheelhouse with a 1,100 sq. ft. working deck aft of it. On the latter were fitted hydraulic winches and two hydraulic cranes for handling the gear. Between the hulls aft she had an 8×18 ft. steel stern ramp.

No great success seemed to be achieved with the *Caribbean Twin* and owners in the USA and elsewhere continued to have single hulled stern trawlers of all kinds built. Notable among these were three small stern freezer shellfish trawlers built by Hijos de J. Barreras in Vigo, Spain for three different owners.

The vessels were named *E. Rodriguez Pelayo*, *Juana Costas* and *Lolita Gomez*. They were 92 ft. long and powered by 510 hp Stork diesels which gave them a speed of 11 knots. They were fitted with Barreras/Brusselle electric winches on the after deck and each had the most unusual type of fixed gantry at the stern yet seen in any small stern trawler.

By this time every principal fishing country in the world seemed to be building small stern trawlers and Finland was among them. There, at the Turku shipyard of Oy Laivateollisuus A.B. a 23½ metre vessel named *Aniara* was built for E. Lildeberg of Helsinki. She was powered by a 500 hp Wartsila diesel driving a Liaaen c.p. propeller and had a top speed of 11½ knots. She was of unusually compact design with accommodation for a crew of five in a superstructure just forward of amidships. For her size, however, she had quite a large working deck aft with a Lidans winch at the forward, and small fixed gantry at the after, end.

Designers in Holland seemed to be as imaginative as any, and owners as venturesome. As a consequence the first shelter decked stern trawling cutter shortly made its appearance. The vessel was built in the Hakvoort Shipyard at Monnikendam, to a design by Ingenieursbureau Propulsion of Leiden for Jac. Yanis of Goedereede. She was 73 ft. long and powered by a 390 hp Deutz diesel which gave her a speed of nine knots.

Her engine room was forward of the crew's quarters and the fish room aft of them. The latter – and the fuel tanks – were so positioned as to make it unlikely for any trim alterations to have to be made during a voyage. She had a long forecastle in which there was a roomy net store, a combined galley and mess. The maindeck amidships was sheltered by a steel deck with hinged side panels, only the after deck being unsheltered. A Maaskant of Bruinisse winch was installed under the shelter deck and a mast with derrick for handling the gear on the after deck. No gantry of any kind was installed.

Early in 1966 what was to prove to be a very successful small stern trawler was completed by J. Samuel White and Co. at Cockenzie in Scotland for owners in Bridlington, England. She was named *Flamborough Light* and was 58 ft. long with accommodation for a crew of four. She was powered by a 240 hp Kelvin diesel which gave her a speed of 10 knots and her forward wheelhouse was exceptionally well equipped with the latest electronic navigating and fish finding devices.

Immediately aft of the wheelhouse she was fitted with a Norwinch hydraulic trawl winch which had had an extra barrel fitted to make three barrels and two warping drums in all. Above the stern towered a fixed four-legged gantry and the stern itself was raked forward with portable bulwarks stretching about 9 ft. across it. These were removable to enable the gear to be shot and hauled with a minimum of effort.

Yet another successful small stern trawler was

Fig. 6. The "Al Sabr", built for Aden in 1966.

built in a British shipyard that year. Named *Manxwood*, she was built of steel on the hydroconic principle, to the design of Burness, Corlett & Partners, at the Ramsey Shipbuilding yard in the Isle of Man for Manxwood Trawlers Ltd. She was one of the designer's Mannin Veg class and was specifically intended to operate around the coast of Scotland. Special consideration had been given to ensuring ability to maintain a steady working platform in adverse conditions.

The vessel was 53 ft. long and powered by a 240 hp Kelvin diesel driving a c.p. propeller. She was arranged with an all-round view wheelhouse forward, stepped down on its forward side to a sunken forecastle. A Smallwood hydraulic winch was installed immediately abaft the wheelhouse with the warping ends extended to allow the wings of the trawl to be hauled right forward to facilitate net repairs. A fixed goalpost gantry was also installed just aft of the wheelhouse with derricks on the centreline and on the starboard side. Gallows were fitted on either quarter.

A very small stern trawler was completed in 1966 for the Fisheries Department of the Government of Aden. Named *Al Sabr*, she was built by the Porthleven Shipyard in Cornwall, England, of plywood on oak frames and her hull was sheathed to the waterline with nylon cloth impregnated with resin. She was 40 ft. long and powered by a 90 hp Kelvin diesel which gave her a speed of 8¼ knots. She was fitted with a Fifer winch on the after deck but no gantry of any kind. She had, however, a Marco power block slung from her derrick.

Fig. 7. The Nigerian trawler "Akasa Bar", built in 1966.

Another, only slightly larger, was built by James N. Miller & Sons in Scotland for Nigerian owners who proposed to use her mostly for prawn trawling. She was 50 ft. long and named *Akassa Bar*. She was fitted with a 150 hp Gardner diesel, which gave her a speed of nine knots, and Fifer friction clutch winch. Near the stern she had a four-legged, fixed gantry. Her hull was also sheathed to the waterline with Cascover resin impregnated nylon cloth.

A larger and more complex stern trawler than either of these two was built in 1965 by the Barens Shipbuilding Co. in Durban for John Ovenstone Ltd., a firm which then operated trawlers from Port Nolloth on the Cape north west coast. Named *Dunblane*, she was 75 ft. long and powered by a 280 hp Burmeister & Wain diesel driving a c.p. propeller made by the same firm. In appearance, she resembled to some extent the Dutch shelter deck stern cutter previously described but instead of a mast and derrick aft she had a unique type of gantry.

This was an exceptionally high fixed structure. On its cross arm was fitted, in line with the slope of the vessel's transom, a net roller designed to simplify the job of hoisting the cod end of the trawl into the ship and over the fish pounds. For hauling and hoisting purposes one Hydraulik Brattvaag and two King hydraulic-drive winches were installed on the after deck. Two stern trawlers of similar design to that of the *Dunblane* were built in 1966 by the Globe Engineering Works in Cape Town. Some years later, however, these three vessels were lengthened and converted into purse seiners.

In Holland in 1966 another stern trawling cutter was built by the Van der Sande Shipyard in Breskens for a company in Scheveningen. She was named *Aleida Theodora* and was about the same size as the majority of small cutters operating off the Dutch

Fig. 9. The "Argo", designed by a parish priest and built in 1966.

coast. She was 21.20 metres long and powered by a 350 hp Kromhout diesel which drove a Van de Voorde propeller to give a top speed of ten knots. In this vessel the wheelhouse and accommodation were forward and she had a high goalpost gantry just aft of them with a Van der Sande three drum winch was installed below it. Across the transom was fitted another small fixed gantry.

In France a highly automated stern trawler, similar in many respects to the *Lutece*, was built by C. & A. de la Perriere at Lorient. She was named *Cezembre* and was 28.3 metres between perpendiculars with a moulded breadth of 7.3 m. and depth of 3.9 m. She was powered by a 600 hp Baudouin diesel, which gave her a speed of 12 knots, and fitted with a Bopp electrohydraulic winch. She was

Fig. 8. South African stern trawler "Dunblane", later lengthened and converted into a purse seiner.

Fig. 10. The "African Bounty", a small stern trawler built in Durban in 1967.

a shelter deck vessel with a long enclosed foredeck to the bridge which was situated aft. Astern of the bridge she had a gantry which, unlike that in the *Lutece*, was fixed.

I don't suppose that many small stern trawlers have been designed by parish priests and so a vessel called *Argo* built by James Noble in Fraserburgh, Scotland in 1966 for R. Smith and Partners of that port was notable for this as well as other reasons. She was designed by the Reverend Eric Milton of Rosehearty and was 64 ft. long with a steel whaleback and a small wheelhouse forward. Aft of the wheelhouse, directly above the engine room in which a 200 hp Gardner diesel was installed, was fitted a Sutherland winch; above it, a high goal post gantry. Astern of these the after deck was clear, neither a stern gantry nor gallows for hanging off the trawl doors being fitted.

A revolutionary type of small wooden stern trawler made the headlines in French newspapers that year after some remarkably successful trips. She had recently been built at Concarneau for Yvon David and had later been operated from Cherbourg. She was called *Precurseur*, was 20.20 m. long and was powered by a 360 hp Baudouin diesel which gave her a speed of $10\frac{1}{2}$ knots.

She had been built to her experienced owner-skipper's special requirements and was of semi-shelter deck design with an enclosed foredeck into which was built, on the port side, the bridge superstructure. The starboard side was left open for working space. A Brusselle trawl winch was installed on the port side of the working deck just aft of the superstructure and gallows were fitted on either quarter. Traversing the top of the transom stern was a roller to facilitate hoisting the cod end inboard with the aid of a derrick.

Research fishing vessels, both large and small, began to be arranged for stern trawling soon after the technique had been developed. And one of the first to appear was the *A. E. Verrill*, built at Blount Marine's Warren yard on Rhode Island for the Marine Biological Research Laboratory, Woods Hole, Massachusetts. She was 65 ft. long and powered by a 240 hp General Motors diesel. The engine was installed in the same way as that in the *Narragansett*; a belt drive on its forward end operated the propeller shaft which ran aft below the engine,

In this vessel Blount 'Trawlmatic' deck machinery, similar to that fitted in the *Narragansett* and *Canyon Prince*, was installed. It included a winch on the after deck and a swinging gantry at the stern, both of which could be controlled from the wheelhouse.

One of the first small stern trawlers to be put into service in 1967 was the *African Bounty*, built by the Barens Shipbuilding Corporation in Durban

Fig. 11. The Belgian stern trawler "Zeepaard", built in 1967.

for the African Line Fishing Co. of Port Elizabeth. She was 65 ft. long and powered by a General Motors diesel driving a Hundested c.p. propeller to give a speed of 10 knots. She had a Norwinch hydraulic trawl winch fitted immediately abaft a forward superstructure and a fixed gantry at the stern.

She had what you might call conventional deck arrangements aft but a small stern trawler that commenced operations in the North Sea about the same time had just the opposite. The latter was named *Zeepaard* and was built by Jos. Dewert at Ostend for Rene Vandierendonck of Zeebrugge. She was 82 ft. long and fitted with an MDX diesel. She had a Maaskant winch aft of a superstructure amidships and a pair of swinging gantries – one on either side – at the stern. In addition she had a unique type of stern ramp with a semi-circular gutter at the top of it for stowing the trawl bobbins.

American fishing vessel owners were not slow to appreciate the advantages of stern trawling and they had started to build both large and small ones in considerable numbers by 1967. One of the latter was the *Smaragd*, built of steel by the Sturgeon Bay Shipbuilding Co. to a design by John W. Gilbert and Associates for the Ellingsen Fishing Corporation of New Bedford, Mass. She was $94\frac{1}{2}$ ft. long and powered by an 850 hp Caterpillar diesel which gave her a top speed of $11\frac{1}{2}$ knots.

She was fitted with a Hathaway winch, powered by a separate General Motors diesel, and somewhat unusual deck arrangements aft. She had a stoutly-built fixed gantry installed just aft of the boat deck, gallows on either side of the after deck, two large booms or derricks constructed in similar fashion to those in an American twin-beam shrimp trawler and a light rail spanning the stern a few feet above the transom.

Quite a number of small stern trawlers were being built in Australia and New Zealand by this time. Typical of the very small ones built in Australia was the *Saltfiord*, a 32-ton wooden vessel completed by Burnett Boatbuilders Ltd. in Bundaberg, Queensland for Jan Lunde. She was 50 ft. long and powered by a 90 hp Kelvin diesel which gave her a speed of eight knots. She was fitted with a fixed goalpost gantry just aft of the wheelhouse and derricks both forward and aft for handling the gear.

Typical of those being built in New Zealand was the *Kaiti*, a product of the A. & G. Price yard in Auckland. This steel-built vessel was 69 ft. long and fitted with a 320 hp Paxman diesel which gave her a speed of 10 knots. She had two single drum hydraulic winches fitted in the middle of the working deck aft, a tripod mast and derrick at its forward end and a small fixed gantry of unusual shape at the stern. Gallows of equally original design were fitted on either quarter for hanging off the trawl doors.

Stern arrangements of quite a different sort were made in a small vessel built by Appledore Shipbuilders in Devon, England, for owners in the West Indies. In addition to a ramp she had a comparatively large fixed gantry on which blocks for handling the trawl doors were slung. This vessel's name was *Lundy Gull*. She was 42 ft. long and fitted with twin General Motors diesels, each of which developed 85 hp and drove a separate propeller. A Smallwood winch operated by a constant speed power pack was installed immediately abaft the wheelhouse.

Fig. 12. The US vessel "Smaragd", $94\frac{1}{2}$ ft. long and built in 1967.

Fig. 13. The New Zealand stern trawler "Kaiti", built in 1967.

The year 1968 saw something like a flood of small stern trawlers built in the UK and a steady increase in their numbers elsewhere. Early that year one of the most advanced of all was completed by Jones Buckie Shipyard in Scotland for Alan and Norman Morse of North Shields, England. Named *Conduan*, she was designed by G. L. Watson & Co. of Glasgow in collaboration with her owners who were pioneering the use of twin engines driving twin controllable pitch propellers in small stern trawlers.

The *Conduan* was 70 ft. long with accommodation for a crew of eight forward. She was powered by twin Gardner 6 L3B diesels, each developing 150 hp at 1000 rpm, driving twin 44 in. diameter Slack & Parr c.p. propellers through Slack & Parr $2\frac{1}{2}$:1 reduction gearboxes. A 42 hp Gardner diesel was installed on the main deck below the forward wheelhouse to drive a Sutherland winch fitted between the wheelhouse and the mast. Two derricks were fitted on the latter and a small fixed gantry across the stern.

A slightly smaller stern trawler was built in Scotland about the same time by J. Samuel White Ltd., for owners in Stornoway, Named *Loch Erisort*, she was 60 ft. long and powered by a 240 hp Kelvin diesel which gave her a speed of nearly 10 knots.

She was fitted with a Norwinch hydraulic trawl winch on the after deck, a tubular four-legged stern gantry and gallows on either side of a transom stern.

A steel stern trawler named *Kathleen* was built by J. & G. Forbes at Sandhaven near Fraserburgh for another owner in Stornoway in the Outer Hebrides. She was 65 ft. long and was also fitted with a 240 hp Kelvin diesel which gave her a top speed of between nine and ten knots. On the after deck she had an Andreas & Jensen 'Skagen' winch and two fixed gantries – a low one across the stern and a high one amidships.

The low gantry across the stern in this vessel and another Forbes trawler called the *Maritan*, was in many ways unique. Some called it a 'curtain rail' gantry as it would allow the two warp blocks to be moved independently from one side of the stern to the other, thus enabling both warps to be brought quickly to one quarter for making a turn. It consisted of a heavy girder running from one set of gallows to the other. The warp blocks were hung from a fixture which was mounted on the girder by means of two rollers on either side, thus allowing it to move freely across the girder. It could be held in position at one end but quickly freed to run

Fig. 14. The "Conduan", 70 ft. long and built in 1968.

across. In addition to this novel arrangement, the *Kathleen* had a ramp. She was, in fact, the first true, small stern ramp trawler to be built in the UK.

An even smaller trawler with a ramp was built by Frost and Drake at Tollesbury in Essex, England that year for an owner in Kent. Named *Kerrigan*, she was 38 ft. long and powered by an 86 hp marinised Ford diesel to give a speed of eight knots. She had a winch installed immediately abaft a forward wheelhouse, a fixed goalpost gantry amidships and a wishbone derrick fitted to its legs.

One of the few stern trawlers under 100 ft. long to be fitted with a swinging gantry was completed in 1968 by the Ramsey Shipbuilding Company in the Isle of Man for the University of North Wales. She was a fisheries research vessel, named *Prince*

Fig. 15. The "Loch Erisor", 60 ft. long, built in 1968.

Madog, designed by Burness, Corlett & Partners. Her overall length was 94 ft. and she was powered by a 600 hp Lister diesel driving a Liaaen c.p. propeller to give a top speed of $10\frac{1}{2}$ knots. On deck she had three winches made by Hydraulik of Brattvaag and at the stern a hydraulically operated gantry.

Other small stern trawlers completed in the UK during 1968 included the 54 ft. *Wavecrest* with a goalpost gantry amidships and a 'curtain rail' gantry at the stern; the 50 ft. *Janeen* with a fixed bipod gantry near the stern; the 54 ft. *Compass Rose* with a forward wheelhouse and stern arrangements similar to those of the *Loch Erisort*; and the 54 ft. *Mystic* with a wheelhouse aft and a 'curtain rail' gantry across the stern.

In Poland the Gdynia Shipyard built the prototype of a series of small stern trawlers intended to replace the standard 24 metre side fishing cutters

Fig. 16. The British stern trawler "Maritan", built in 1968.

that had been in use until 1968. She was called *Sola* and she was 29.15 m. long with a moulded breadth of 7.50 m., depth of 4.0 m. and mean draught of 3.00 m. She had accommodation for a crew of nine and a fish hold capacity of 140 cu.m. She was powered by a 450 hp Paxman 8RPHM diesel coupled to a Liaaen propeller shrouded in a Kort nozzle and had a top speed of about ten knots.

She was equipped with split hydraulic winches and had a fixed gantry spanning a ramp at the stern. Two warp blocks on the gantry were capable of being moved from the outer sides of the gantry to the middle, directly above the ramp. These blocks were reported to be hydraulically powered in a similar way to the blocks in large Polish stern trawlers.

Another particularly interesting small stern trawler completed in 1968 was the *Theresa R 2* from Atlantic Marine's yard at Fort George Island,

Fig. 17. The research trawler "Prince Madog", 94 ft. long and built in 1968.

Florida. She was basically one of the company's standard 87 ft. shrimp trawlers but instead of outriggers for twin beam shrimp trawling, was fitted with a stern gantry and a hefty derrick. She was powered by a 425 hp Caterpillar diesel and soon after her trials left for New Bedford, Mass. to engage in bottom trawling from that port.

Early in 1969 a most sophisticated, shrimp fishing freezer stern trawler, built by the Stader Schiffswerft in West Germany for Stahlunion Export of Iran commenced operations. Named *Matragh*, this vessel was 32.00 m. over all with a moulded breadth of 7.50 m. and depth of 3.65 m. She had accommodation for a crew of 14 and two fish holds, a 94 cu.m. refrigerated hold for frozen fish and a 42 cu.m. hold for fresh fish in ice. Propulsion engine was a 515 hp Deutz diesel.

In Canada a stern trawler, specifically designed to be less than 100 ft. (30.48 metres) long and therefore permitted to fish within the limit lines, was built at Marine Industries' Paspebiac shipyard for Canapro of the Magdalen Islands. The latter firm is a subsidiary of the Gorton Corporation of Gloucester, Mass. and because of the connection the vessel was named *G. C. Gorton*. She was 30.21 m. over all with a moulded breadth of 7.5 m. and depth of 4.26 m., and she was powered by a 565 hp Caterpillar diesel.

She was one of the comparatively few vessels built up to then both for stern trawling and purse seining. For this reason her deck arrangements and lay-out were somewhat unusual. A combined trawl and seine winch was installed at the forward end of the after deck and an Aukra Bruk power block was mounted on a pedestal on the starboard side of the deck. A tall fixed gantry spanned the stern and trawl gallows were fitted on either quarter each side of a stern ramp.

One of the smallest stern trawlers ever to be fitted with a hydraulic swinging gantry was built during 1969 for the Kenya Government's Department of Fisheries at the African Marine and General Engineering Company's yard at Mombasa. Named *Shakwe*, she was constructed to Burness, Corlett & Partner's hydroconic design and was 72 ft. over all with accommodation for 15 and a refrigerated fish hold capacity of 1,650 cu.ft. She was powered by a 320 hp Kelvin diesel and two 70 hp Kelvin auxiliary diesels, and fitted with a four-ton Robertson trawl winch and an Izui line hauler on the after deck.

Although an increasing number of sturdy little stern trawlers were built in Scotland in 1969, owners continued to differ widely in their ideas about the best type of lay-out and arrangements aft. There was no hint of progress towards adoption of standard fittings and lay-out as ultimately became customary in side trawlers.

Fig. 18. The small 54 ft. long stern trawler "Compass Rose".

Fig. 20. Canadian stern trawler "G. C. Gorton", 30.21 metres long.

The 50 ft. *Kildinguie*, for instance, built by J. Anderson at Stromness, Orkney for a local owner, had a forward wheelhouse with a stout goalpost gantry immediately abaft it and a rail joining the tops of gallows on either quarter by way of a gantry at the stern. She was powered by a 240 hp Volvo Penta diesel which gave her a top speed of $10\frac{1}{2}$ knots and had a Norwinch hydraulic trawl winch installed on the after deck.

The 66 ft. trawler *Artemis* also had a forward wheelhouse but her fixed gantry was a comparatively high one amidships and she had no gantry of any kind at the stern. She was built by J. & G. Forbes & Co. at Sandhaven for John Watt and Partners of Fraserburgh and was powered by a 320 hp Kelvin diesel which gave her a speed of 10 knots. She had a mechanically operated winch immediately abaft the wheelhouse with a canopy over it supported by the midships gantry.

By contrast, the 70 ft. *Morning Star*, which was also built by J. & G. Forbes at Sandhaven, had a wheelhouse aft and a rail joining gallows on either quarter by way of a stern gantry. This vessel was designed to be able to be used for seine netting as well as stern trawling, hence the seine derricks on either side of the wheelhouse. She was powered by a 345 hp Caterpillar diesel and had a Mastra hydraulic winch installed forward of the wheelhouse. Also installed on the foredeck was a hydraulically operated Shetland Type 17 fish gutting machine.

Fig. 19. The Polish vessel "Sola", 29.15 metres long, built in 1968.

Fig. 21. The "Kildinguie", 50 ft. long, built in 1969.

Two smaller stern trawlers were laid out in somewhat similar fashion but their deck fittings and arrangements differed considerably. One of them was the *Islander*, a 56 ft. steel stern trawler built by the Newport Shipbuilding and Engineering Company in Wales for an overseas owner. This vessel had a forward wheelhouse with a conventional winch installed between it and a stout mast stepped a little forward of amidships. She had a low gantry at the stern for hauling the trawl up a steep ramp across the stern.

The other was the *Providence*, a 49 ft. wooden stern trawler built by R. J. Prior at Burnham-on-Crouch for Peter French of West Mersea, Essex. She had an exceptionally high, stoutly-built gantry fitted across the after end of a forward wheelhouse, and another high gantry spanning a steep stern ramp. The reason for the exceptional height of the latter was because it was intended often to use the vessel on grounds littered with weed and rubbish. It was considered that an almost vertical lift would be necessary to get the bag inboard up the ramp.

Instead of a single winch like that installed in the *Islander*, the *Providence* was fitted with split winches on either side of the deck just abaft the wheelhouse. These were hydraulically operated from a pump on the vessel's 112 hp main engine and, in addition to a standard sized warping drum on the inner side, each had a large drum on the outboard side for the purpose of speeding up operations when unloading. Another special feature about the *Providence* was that she was fitted on either side of the steering gear compartment aft with ballast tanks which could be filled or emptied to adjust trim.

In Holland, early in 1970, Peters Scheepsbouw N.V. completed the third of three 62 ft. steel stern trawlers which were unusual for this size of vessel in that they had refrigerated holds. Otherwise they approached the conventional as closely as any small stern trawlers could be said to do at that time. Each had a wheelhouse at the after end of a raised deck forward with a mast and derrick immediately aft of it. Then came a winch and a clear after deck with a low gantry at the stern. Propulsion units were 200 hp Gardner diesels.

Later in the year another small stern trawler of exceptional interest was built in Holland. She was called the *Accord* and was constructed at the K. Hackvoort shipyard at Monnickendam for Jim Duthie of Peterhead, Scotland. Her overall length was 86 ft and she was powered by a 565 hp Caterpillar diesel driving a Van Voorden propeller in a Hodi nozzle. In addition to stern trawling, this vessel was capable of being used for side trawling,

Fig. 22. The British trawler "Morning Star", 70 ft. long, built in 1969.

pair trawling, Danish and purse seining. She was fitted with a Jensen hydraulic winch amidships and a Rapp Marco power block with hydraulic transport roller aft.

Creating great interest too at about this time was one of the first small stern trawlers to be constructed of ferro-cement. Named *Mascot*, she was built for Skipper Blowers of Lowestoft, England by Seacrete Ltd. at Wroxham, Norfolk. She was 38 ft. overall and her hull, three bulkheads, transverse floors, engine beds, decks, hatch coamings and superstructure were constructed in one piece. She was powered by a 95 hp Perkins diesel installed below a wheelhouse forward and had winch and gantry on the after deck.

On the other side of the world, New Zealand was busy building small stern trawlers with all sorts of different deck arrangements. Notable amongst these

Fig. 23. The "Accord", 86 ft. long and built in the Netherlands in 1969.

Fig. 24. The 38 ft. long ferro-cement hull trawler "Mascot".

at this time was the *Jay Maree*, the second of two sister ships to be built by A. & G. Price Ltd. in Auckland for the Seafoods Division of J.B.L. Consolidated Ltd.

This vessel was 73 ft. overall and was powered by a 330 hp Lister diesel which gave her a top speed of 10 knots. She was designed to be worked by a crew of four and had a hold capacity for 50 tons of fish on ice. Her layout was conventional in that she had a wheelhouse forward with a winch immediately aft of it and a gantry aft, but the latter was unusual as it had a forward swing derrick fitted to it. This was probably because it was intended that she could be adapted for purse seining if necessary.

She was, however, arranged entirely differently from another vessel of about the same size built for stern trawling and possibly purse seining in New

Fig. 25. A small Scottish trawler – the "Crimson Arrow", 50 ft. long.

Zealand waters. A comparison of these two vessels serves to illustrate how widely the ideas of experienced fishing vessel owners can differ when it comes to designing a small stern trawler, even if the vessel is to be used for catching the same species in the same waters.

The other vessel was the *Marine Countess*, built by Sims Engineering Ltd. in Port Chalmers for J. Wattie Canneries of Gisborne in the North Island. She was designed by D. Alexander of Auckland and was the first of two sister ships built for the company. Her overall length was 76 ft. and she was powered by a 425 hp. Caterpillar diesel driving a Liaaen controllable pitch propeller.

Her layout was most unusual for a small stern trawler. Her wheelhouse was amidships with a boat deck running the length of the vessel aft of it. Her winch was installed forward of a two tiered deckhouse and wheelhouse. And she had quite a big stern ramp. The trawl blocks, instead of being slung from a gantry or gallows aft, were suspended from the outer edges of the boat deck which had sturdy supports under them.

A large number of small stern trawlers and seiner-trawlers, notable for novel arrangements aft, were built in the UK – mostly in Scotland – during 1970.

One of the first to be put into service was the *Crimson Arrow*, a 50 ft. steel vessel built by the Campbeltown Shipyard for James Macdonald of Campbeltown. She was powered by a 142 hp. Dorman diesel driving a propeller shrouded in a Kort nozzle and had a transom stern with bulwarks raked forward above it. She had a forward wheelhouse and a fixed gantry across the stern unlike a stern trawler of similar size built by the yard and commissioned just before her. The later – the *Steadfast* – had her winch forward, the wheelhouse aft of amidships and gallows on either quarter.

Another completed early in the year was the 50 ft. *Anmara*, built by John Harker Ltd. of Knottingly, Yorkshire for its subsidiary fishing company. This little steel vessel had a stern ramp, stern gantry, 'midships gantry and a sizeable mast and derrick forward – quite an array for a vessel of her size. She was powered by a 180 hp Kelvin diesel and a Norwinch hydraulic trawl winch installed aft of a forward wheelhouse.

A third 50 ft. stern trawler was built – of wood – about the same time by Robsons of South Shields for Alan Strangeways of Amble, Northumberland. Named *Shulamit*, she was powered by a 172 hp Gardner diesel and was laid out in fairly conventional fashion. She had a wheelhouse forward with a mast and a Norwinch hydraulic trawl winch aft of it, and a fixed gantry across the stern. The latter was of the 'curtain rail' type with travelling towing blocks on it to enable warps to be brought together for making a turn.

One of the most notable of all small stern trawlers built in the UK in 1970 was completed by the Campbeltown Shipyard in Argyll, Scotland for David Tod of Anstruther, Fife. She was the first of her kind to be fitted with a combined winch and net drum for hauling and stowing the trawl.

Named *St. Adrian*, she was built of steel and was 49 ft. long between perpendiculars. She was powered by a six cylinder Cummins diesel driving a propeller in a Kort nozzle rudder, and had a wheelhouse and accommodation for a crew of four forward. The combined winch and net drum was installed on a raised platform aft of the wheelhouse. It was hydraulically operated and could be controlled from the wheelhouse. Procedure was to haul the trawl over two rollers through a 6 ft. opening in the stern bulwark. The warps passed through gallows blocks supported 7 ft. above the deck by two booms pivoting on a stern gantry.

Another unusually interesting vessel completed during the year was a twin-screw, freezer stern trawler built by W. R. Cunis Ltd. to a design by the Fairmile Construction Company for a fishing concern with headquarters in the Persian Gulf. She was the first trawler of her type ever to be built in a Thames shipyard.

Named *Farid*, she was built of steel and was 93 ft. long over all with accommodation for a crew of ten. The living quarters, galley and mess were on the main deck forward, easily accessible from the working deck aft. There was a sheltered space dividing living from working quarters where fish could be gutted. Here, at the head of net coamings running the length of the after deck to a stern ramp, a winch with two warping ends was installed. Below the main deck were two refrigerated fish rooms and the engine room.

There was a bridge across the stern of the vessel with towing blocks suspended below it and also a fixed gantry at the forward end of the working deck from which outriggers for beam trawls could be worked if the vessel were to be used for shrimp trawling. On the boat deck there was a wheelhouse with both a main trawl and a shrimp trawl winch installed aft of it.

Propulsion machinery consisted of a pair of 220 hp Gardner diesel engines driving twin Slack & Parr controllable pitch propellers to give the vessel a speed of 9½ knots. A hydraulic pump driven from a

Fig. 26. The "St. Adrian", a 49 ft. 3 in. long b.p. boat fitted with net drum.

fore end extension shaft on the starboard engine powered the vessels deck machinery which was all supplied by Hydraulik Brattvaag, Norway.

Unique among small stern trawlers built in Scotland during the year was a vessel built by J. & G. Forbes & Co. at Sandhaven for Albert Wiseman of Macduff. Her fittings and layout aft were entirely original.

Named *Avenger*, she was built of wood and was 73 ft. overall with accommodation for a crew of six. She was powered by a 330 hp Lister diesel and her deck layout and hauling arrangements were specifically designed to reduce manual handling of the gear as much as possible.

She had two split winches fitted just abaft a forward wheelhouse and whaleback. They were specially designed and made for the vessel, and each was

Fig. 27. The "Farid", 93 ft. long, built for the Persian Gulf.

Fig. 28. The "Avenger", 73 ft. long, built in 1970.

driven by a separate hydraulic pump. There were two chutes or cradles, fabricated from steel plate and angle bar, fitted at the stern, also a stern roller made of four lengths of heavy steel pipe and a small grooved roller at each end, under the cradles. Procedure was for each warp to be hauled over a small grooved roller and, via three deck leads, to the outer barrel of each winch.

V-form steel trawl doors were employed. They were so designed that when they surfaced they automatically slid up the cradles and fell into place without further manoeuvre. A specially designed bracket on the front of each door, which took the end of the warp, projected downwards through the slot in each cradle so that the warp lay on deck. No more hauling of the warp was then needed as it was fixed to the bracket and not clipped to one end of a pennant wire.

The arrangement of backstrop and pennant on the back of the doors was such that, once they had

Fig. 29. The "Aquarius", 50 ft. long, built in 1971.

fallen into place, a wire could be taken aft from the inner barrel of each winch and clipped to the pennant. Then the latter together with the sweeps, bridles and wings of the net could be hauled over the stern roller until the net was lying along the deck. Only then was it the practice to lift the bag on board by means of the gantry. The cod end was prevented from swinging around by stays running between the midships and after gantries.

There was no let up in the building of small stern trawlers in 1971. Although varied ideas were still held about the best ways of laying them out, the technique of handling gear over the stern instead of over the side had in general proved to be more efficient. As, however, new methods are continually being evolved, there were signs at the beginning of the year that a not insignificant number of owners and operators tended to favour twin-beam, instead of what by this time might have been called conventional, stern trawling.

There were even some determined to get the best of both worlds. For instance, Roland and Guy Nowe, after a visit to Holland to study the technique of twin beam trawling, commissioned E. R. Gueroult to design, and Leon Landy of Arques to build, a trawler capable of being used for both twin beam and conventional stern trawling.

Named *Arches des Nowe*, this steel vessel was 61 ft. long and powered by a 300 hp Duvant diesel. She had a gantry amidships for operating beam trawls and a Travhoist gantry aft for working an otter trawl. Blocks on the stern gantry enabled the warps to be led to a four drum Padmos winch which was belt driven from the main engine. A crew of four men only was considered sufficient to carry out either form of trawling when she commenced operations from Dunkirk.

A more conventional small wooden stern trawler was built at Eyemouth in Scotland early in the year. Named *Norwood*, she was 48 ft. overall and was powered by a 210 hp Volvo Penta diesel. She had a fixed gantry over the wheelhouse aft and gallows on either quarter.

Another little vessel, built of steel, was completed at Campbeltown on the west coast of Scotland about the same time. She was called *Aquarius*, was 50 ft. overall and was powered by a 142 hp Dorman diesel. She had a forward wheelhouse with a Sutherland winch immediately abaft it and a fixed gantry at the stern.

A few months before the *Aquarius* was commissioned another *Tiny Cornelia* (OD.10) commenced operations for Mr. J. Molesteeg of Ouddorp in Holland. She was a larger, more powerful vessel

Fig. 30. An outstanding new British small stern trawler – the "Merrydale", 83 ft. long and built in 1971.

than her forerunner and capable of being used for twin beam and pair as well as stern trawling.

Thirty metres long and powered by a 900 hp MaK diesel, she was unique in having a winch divided into two parts – one in the engine room and one on deck. Its main components – an electromotor, gearbox and two drums for beam trawl warps – were installed in the engine room and the rest on a bridge deck abaft the wheelhouse. The latter consisted of two drums for topping lifts, two for gilsons and two for wires from which fishing blocks at the top of the booms were suspended.

Another novel feature about the second *Tiny Cornelia* were her booms. They were of completely new design, being constructed of heavy piping fitted perpendicular to the centreline and supported by smaller piping running forward. They were not guyed by wires as was usually the case in Dutch twin beam trawlers.

A firm which decided early in the 1960s to operate stern trawlers large and small instead of the side trawlers they had been employing successfully for many years, was J. Marr and Son Ltd. of Hull, England. It commenced building a series of freezer stern trawlers over 200 ft. long which included the *Kirkella*, *Swanella* and *Marbella*. And then it turned its attention to building vessels under 100 ft. long designed to carry fish chilled in ice.

In my opinion, J. Marr & Son's designers did a superb job from the very start. They did not chop and change, experimenting with very different arrangements in successive vessels as some seem to have done. They came up with a first class design initially, a design which has only needed refining here and there in their large trawlers. As a consequence they were able to repeat their performance when they turned their attention to designing vessels under 100 ft. long.

I have a hunch that the design of their recently built *Merrydale* will prove to be a classic; that when men look back a hundred years hence, they will say that this proved to be the supreme type of small stern trawler for short range operations from British ports. Although last in this somewhat lengthy list of vessels, she is, in my opinion, the best of them all so far.

The *Merrydale* was built of steel for J. Marr & Son by Richard Dunston at Thorne, Yorkshire. She is 83 ft. overall with a moulded breadth of 21 ft. and has accommodation for a crew of five. Fish room capacity is 3,200 cu. ft.

Propulsion engine is a 495 hp Lister Blackstone diesel which drives a controllable pitch propeller to give a top speed of $10\frac{1}{2}$ knots. Both winch and steering gear are hydraulically operated and wheelhouse equipment includes an echo sounder, radar, automatic helmsman, medium and high frequency radio telephones, and electronic position finder. A robust midships gantry and low, fixed stern gantry span the working deck aft of the wheelhouse.

Shelter-deck Stern Trawlers Built Since 1963

PETER HJUL
(Editor *Fishing News International*)

Examination of stern trawlers built around the world in the eight years since 1963 reveals a remarkable diversity of vessels. There are great differences in size of ship; in arrangements of the hull; in accommodation; and in the organisation of the trawl and processing decks. From this diversity, some standard types have evolved. But, as the following pages show, there is as yet no typical stern trawler.

The brief descriptions in this chapter are taken from the reports of the ships published in the monthly magazine "Fishing News International", which, since 1963, has recorded the construction of some 250 types of stern trawler representing more than 600 ships.

From about 30 countries, we have selected 13 which have participated most prominently in the development of the stern trawler – some as users, some as designers and builders, and others both as builders and users. The countries chosen are Canada, France, the German Democratic Republic, the Federal Republic of Germany, Italy, Japan, the Netherlands, Norway, Poland, South Africa, Spain, the United Kingdom and the USSR. We have also selected examples from 17 other countries using stern trawlers in commercial fisheries or as research or training ships.

Some of these countries, such as Cuba, Iceland, Denmark (with Greenland and the Faeroe Islands), Bulgaria, Portugal, Roumania, and the United Arab Republic are developing their stern trawler fleets, and will certainly rise to places among the main users.

Another significant application of the stern trawler type ship (usually as a combination vessel) is in the growing fleet operated under the aegis of the Department of Fisheries of FAO in various technical aid projects in the developing countries. Experience with these ships will, no doubt, encourage further interesting additions to our list of owning and building countries.

Canada

The Canadian fishing industry takes a yearly catch of about 1.4 million metric tons. Canada has a large fishery for salmon, herring and other species along its Pacific coast, but the major fishing developments of the past decade have been from its east coast Maritime Provinces into the waters of the North Atlantic.

Rich in cod and other demersal species and in herring, these waters have long attracted the distant water trawlers of Europe. They have also stimulated the design by Canadians and by naval architects from other countries of one of the most varied collections of stern trawlers to be seen in any one country.

This was noted at a conference in Montreal in 1970 by a senior naval architect in the Federal Fisheries Service. "Examination of our present fleet," he said, "reveals some amazing differences not only in acquisition cost per unit, but in style, layout, powering required for various mission modes, manpower, hold capacity, radius of action, and when in service the gear used and actual fishing performance."

It is no secret that a number of the ships fell far short of the expectations of designer and owner, and some were conspicuous failures. But from this experience some successful ships have emerged and the Canadian trawler fleet could be said to have now moved out of a prolonged prototype and test period.

With fish close by, the Canadian requirement is for landings chilled in ice taken over periods of not much longer than a week. Working in co-operation with the provincial and federal fisheries services, owners have adapted the German one-boat pelagic trawl to local ships and conditions. Depending on season, the modern Canadian stern trawler uses the bottom trawl for demersal species and is capable of taking substantial catches of herrings by mid-water trawl.

After years of being used as a testing area, Canada is now evolving a shelter deck 150 ft. long

The "Brandal", 136 ft. 6 in. long, built in 1965.

wet fish vessel which appears to meet her fishing requirements.

Six ships of this size were ordered in 1971 from three east coast yards by National Sea Products of Halifax. They were designed by Heatman and Endal of Halifax and will operate for a freezing plant acquired by National Sea Products at St. John's in Newfoundland. Each will have a crew of 16, will be powered by 2100 hp diesel engines and will fish with bottom and one-boat mid-water trawl. They will cost 12 million dollars, and half of this will be covered by Canadian and Newfoundland government subsidy and grant.

Another plant operator in Newfoundland has turned to Norway for the more or less standard type of 150 ft. wet fish stern trawler now operating for Norwegian freezing plants.

Brandal

Built in 1965 by Dosco Industries Halifax Shipyard for a Halifax owner. A wet fish stern trawler of 371 gross tons, the *Brandal* is 136 ft. 6 in. long overall, with a moulded breadth of 26 ft. 6 in. and depth of 13 ft. She has crew accommodation for 24.

The fish room is insulated with polyurethane foam and has a capacity of 8,500 cu. ft. The main engine is a 1200 hp Brons 16GV diesel turning a Liaaen controllable pitch propeller.

A similar ship, the *Atkinson* for H. B. Nickerson & Sons, was completed in 1966. The bridge superstructure is set well forward to give a full lenght trawl deck. A Van der Giessen main trawl is sited beneath the after end of the superstructure.

The vessels were described at the time as good examples of a simple alternative to a side trawler. No freezing or refrigeration equipment was installed as this was not considered necessary for their areas of operation.

Nathan Cummings

Built in 1966 by Marine Industries Ltd. of Sorel, Quebec, for Booth Fisheries Corporation. A wet fish stern trawler of 630 gross tons, the *Nathan Cummings* is 152 ft. long overall with a moulded breadth of 33 ft. and depth of 16 ft. She has crew accommodation for 18.

The fish room is insulated with styrofoam and sheathed with glass reinforced plastic, and has a capacity of 12,000 cu. ft. The main engine is a 1530 hp Deutz diesel turning a Lips c.p. propeller through a Lohmann & Stolterfoht reduction gearbox.

The Holmes Lektron trawl winch is powered by a 300 hp Thrige electric motor and has a capacity for 1,000 fathoms of 3 in. circ. wire on each of its two main drums.

Cape Nova

With sister ships *Cape Morrow* and *Cape Pictou*,

The "Cape Nova", 155 ft. long, built in 1966,

built in 1966 by Dosco Industries Halifax Shipyard for National Sea Products Ltd. A wet fish stern trawler designed by Conrad Birkhoff, the *Cape Nova* is a 617 gross ton ship, 155 ft. long overall with moulded breadth of 33 ft. and depth of 16 ft. She has crew accommodation for 20.

The fish room is insulated with 5 in. rigid foam polyurethane and lined with aluminium. It has a capacity of 10,000 cu. ft. The main engine is a 1080 bhp eight-cylinder Deutz diesel turning a Liaaen c.p. propeller to give the ship a speed of 12 knots.

The Van der Giessen 7T trawl winch is hydraulically powered.

Atlantic Ellen
With sister ships *Atlantic Marie*, *Atlantic Peggy* and *Atlantic Beatrice*, built in 1967 by the Geo. T. Davie Division of Canadian Vickers Shipyards Ltd. in Lauzon, Quebec, for Atlantic Sugar Refineries Ltd. A wet fish stern trawler of 624 gross tons, the *Atlantic Ellen* is 152 ft. 5 in. long overall with moulded breadth of $30\frac{1}{2}$ ft. and depth to the maindeck of $14\frac{1}{4}$ ft. She has crew accommodation for 19.

The fish room is insulated with styrofoam and lined with fibreglass. It has a capacity of 12,088 cu. ft. and is cooled by means of air ducts along the sides. The main engine is an Industrie diesel developing 1560 bhp at 300 rpm and turning a four-bladed Lips c.p. propeller shrouded in a Kort nozzel.

A Copeland 2730 btu/hr compressor is installed for maintaining the temperature in the fish room at 20°F,

The four-drum Brusselle GMC 3 trawl winch is powered by a Brusselle 175 hp electric motor.

Newfoundland Eagle
First of four sister ships built in 1967 and 1968 by Dosco Industries Halifax Shipyards for North East Fish Industries Ltd. of Newfoundland. A wet fish stern trawler of 834.6 gross tons, the *Newfoundland Eagle* is 169 ft. 3 in. long overall with a breadth of

The "Newfoundland Eagle", 169 ft. 3 in. long, built in 1967.

35 ft. and depth moulded to the shelter deck of 23 ft.

The fish room is insulated with $6\frac{3}{4}$ in. polyurethane foam and has a capacity of 14,000 cu. ft. which enables her to carry about 200 tons of fish in ice.

The main engine is a Ruston-Hornsby diesel developing 1670 bhp and turning an Escher Wyss c.p. propeller through a Lohmann & Stolterfoht reduction gearbox. The propeller is shrouded in a Kort nozzle.

Scotia Bay
With sister ships *Scotia Cape*, *Scotia Point* and *Scotia Port*, built in 1967 and 1968 by the St. John Shipbuilding and Drydock Company for Superior Sea Products Ltd. of Yarmouth, Nova Scotia. A wet fish stern trawler designed by Conrad Birkhoff,

The "Atlantic Ellen", 152 ft. 5 in. long, built in 1967.

The "Scotia Point", 118 ft. long, sister ship of the "Scotia Bay".

the *Scotia Bay* is 118 ft. long overall, with a moulded breadth of 28 ft., depth of $13\frac{1}{2}$ ft. and fish room capacity of 9,000 cu. ft.

The main engine is a Caterpillar D398 TAC diesel developing 765 hp and turning a Lips three-bladed propeller to give a speed of $11\frac{1}{4}$ knots.

Acadia Thunderbird

Built in 1968 by Ferguson Industries Ltd. for Acadia Fisheries of Nova Scotia. The first of a class of four wet fish stern trawlers, the 800 gross ton *Acadia Thunderbird* was designed after an earlier and slightly smaller stern trawler built in 1965 – the *Acadia Albatross* – had consistently outfished side trawlers in her company's fleet.

Acadia Fisheries was until 1971 a subsidiary of Boston Deep Sea Fisheries Ltd. of Hull, England, but the British company withdrew from Canada and the Canso plant and fleet was taken over by a Canadian fishing firm. A new class of wet fish stern trawler built in Britain for the Boston group in 1971 was influenced by the successful design of the *Acadia Thunderbird* class.

The *Acadia Thunderbird* is 151 ft. $9\frac{1}{2}$ in. long overall with a breadth of 33 ft. Accommodation is provided for a crew of 20.

The fish hold, placed forward, is polyurethane insulated with sheet aluminium lining. It is cooled by a Sterne refrigeration system with trunked air ducts and can carry up to 400,000 lb. of fish and ice.

The trawl winch is a Brusselle machine driven by Laurence Scott electrics.

Main engine is a Ruston 8-cylinder diesel developing 1650 hp and turning a c.p. propeller to give a speed of $11\frac{1}{2}$ knots.

Mattuna Mariner

Prototype herring trawler and herring and tuna purse seiner built in 1970 by Ferguson Industries Ltd., Nova Scotia, for Mattuna Fisheries Ltd. of New Brunswick. Three similar ships also built in 1970. Designed by Cove, Hatfield and Co. Deck and handling equipment is arranged for quick change from mid-water trawl to purse seine. The *Mattuna Mariner* is 114 ft. long overall with a breadth of 30 ft. and depth of $14\frac{1}{4}$ ft.

The "Acadia Thunderbird", 151 ft. $9\frac{1}{2}$ in. long, built in 1968.

The "Mattuna Mariner", 114 ft. long, built in 1970.

The engine room is situated amidships between two refrigerated holds forward and four aft. The six aluminium tanks are cooled by a chilled brine system and have a total capacity of 12,770 cu. ft.

The fishing deck extends about 80 ft. aft of the aluminium deckhouse to a stern tramp. Fishing equipment includes a powered net roller on the starboard bulwark and a starboard mounted hydraulic net drum – both for the trawl. The two-drum Hydema combination seine and trawl winch is equipped with automatic spooling facilities.

Main engine is a Caterpillar D399 Series B diesel developing 1125 hp and turning a Canadian Stone four-bladed propeller through a Reintjes 4:1 reduction gearbox.

France

French fishing vessel owners have turned to yards in their own country and to builders in Poland, West Germany and Belgium and the Netherlands for stern trawlers which range up from small coastal vessels to distant water freezers.

The total French catch is between 750,000 and 800,000 metric tons a year. In 1970 landings of food fish at 30 Atlantic coast ports amounted to 451,000 tons valued at nearly 960 million francs (£72 million). The main trawler ports such as Boulogne, Concarneu, Lorient and Bordeaux all make extensive use of stern fishing vessels which bring back their catches frozen, salted or chilled in ice, for the port markets.

In recent years, these modern stern trawlers have been among the top catchers and earners in the French trawler fleets. In Boulogne, for example, the Polish-built stern trawler *Sydero* (in her first full year in service) was top ship in 1970 with a catch of 3,333 tons which earned 4.3 million francs. In Lorient, the stern trawler *Capitaine Cook* – with 1,599 tons which earned 2.28 million francs – was top ship for the third year in succession.

Cap Nord

Built in 1965 by A.G. Weser Werk of Bremerhaven, West Germany, for Soc. Boulannaise d'Armement la Garrec & Cie. of Boulogne. A medium size wet fish stern trawler of 489 gross tons, the *Cap Nord* is 52.9 metres long overall with a breadth of 9.5 m. and a depth of 6.8 m.

Her insulated fish room for catches held in ice has a capacity of 275 cu. m. Accommodation is provided for a crew of 24.

The ship is diesel-electric powered with two Deutz 900 hp diesel engines as the prime movers.

In 1970, the *Cap Nord* was the second highest earner in the port of Boulogne with landings of 3,094 tons worth 4.1 million francs.

Two similar ships – the *Cap Gris Nez* and *Cap Blanc Nez* – were built by A. G. Weser in 1968 for the same owner.

Mandarin

Built in 1965 by the Dutch yard Scheeps. Gebr. Pot of Bolnes for Codepec of Paris for operation from Lorient. First of two ships and of the same basic design as four ships built shortly before by the same yard for Canada. A whole fish freezer stern trawler of 624 gross tons, the *Mandarin* is 52.17 m. long overall with a breadth of 9 m. and a depth of 6.4 m.

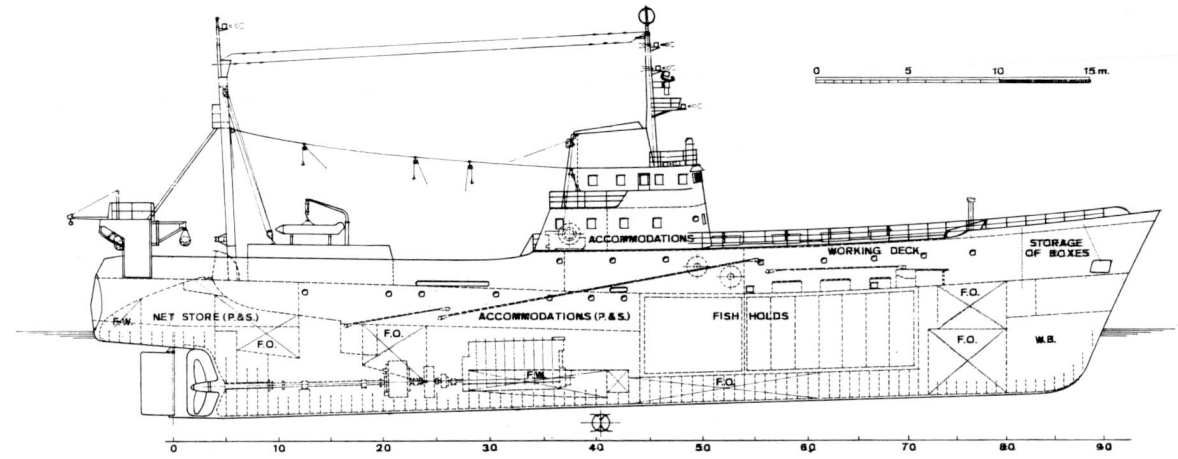

Profile drawing of the "Klondyke" class of stern trawler built in Belgium by Beliard Murdoch SA.

The engine room is sited amidships and there are two fish rooms fore and aft. The forward room has a capacity of 70 cu. m. and the after room a capacity of 190 cu. m. Two Jackstone Froster vertical plate freezers can handle 10 tons of blocks a day.

The wheelhouse superstructure is situated amidships and just aft of this is the Brusselle HMC 111 10-ton trawl winch with a drum capacity of 2,500 m. of 24 mm. warp and with a hauling speed of two metres a second.

Main engine is a SACM Mulhouse diesel of 1350 hp turning a c.p. propeller through a Messian 3.5:1 reduction gearbox to give a speed of 14 knots.

Pierre Vidal

Built in 1966 by Ateliers et Chantiers de la Rochelle-Pallice for La Pêche au Large of Bordeaux. A part-freezer trawler of 1,200 gross tons, the *Pierre Vidal* is 77 m. long overall with a moulded breadth of 12.4 m., depth to main deck of 5.5 m. and depth to upper deck of 7.9 m. Accommodation is provided for a crew of 50.

The *Pierre Vidal* was designed to use her catch partly for freezing and partly for salting. Her frozen fish hold has a capacity of 430 cu. m. and the salt fish hold a capacity of 520 cu. m. She was the sixth stern trawler to join the fleet of her owners.

Her 14-ton pull four-barrel Caillard main trawl winch is driven by a 420 hp electric motor.

Processing machinery on the factory deck includes two Baader 440 splitting machines, two 414 headers, a 38 skinner and two 47 skinners. Freezing plant includes two Jackstone 16-station vertical, top discharge plate freezers. A German Schlotterhose shipborne fish meal plant can process 12 tons of offal and waste fish in 24 hours.

Propulsion is by two MAN diesel engines of 2200 hp and 720 hp turning an Escher Wyss c.p. propeller through a Renk double reduction gearbox. Electrical power for all services is provided by two Chantiers d'Orleans 265 kVA alternators supplying 380–110 V a.c. and two Breguet-Sautter-Harle 350 kW generators which also supply the trawl winch. These are all driven from the reduction gear.

Klondyke

Built in 1966 by Beliard Murdoch SA of Ostend, Belgium, for the joint ownership of Nord Pecheries SA of Boulogne and Armement Leporc & Cie. of Fecamp. A similar ship to the *Le Matelot* completed earlier in the same year for S.A. Pecheries Manesse et Senechal of Boulogne.

A fresh fish stern trawler with provision for conversion to freezing, the *Klondyke* is a ship of 715 gross tons with a length of 58.26 m. overall, a moulded breadth of 10.1 m. and depth to main deck of 6.12 m. Accommodation is provided for a crew of 23.

The "Pierre Vidal", 77 metres long, built in 1966.

The "Klondyke", 58.26 metres long, built in 1966.

The ship was designed for both pelagic and demersal trawling. The fish hold has a capacity of 490 cu. m. enabling the *Klondyke* to carry about 200 tons of fish and 80 tons of ice. This hold is cooled to a temperature of 0° and 2°C. and is divided into two sections by a transverse bulkhead.

Her trawl winch is a three-barrel, electrically-driven Brusselle type HMC 111 unit with a 10-ton pull at a hauling speed of 2 m./sec.

From the fishing deck, the catch is dropped through a flush hatch into the pounds in the tween-deck space. A belt conveyor operating at two speeds carries the fish to a sorting table/conveyor. It then moves to the gutting area and to two washing machines.

The main engine is a nine-cylinder MAN diesel developing 1425 hp and turning a single propeller through a Renk reduction gearbox.

Ludovic Pierre

Built in 1967 by Beliard Murdoch S.A. of Ostend, Belgium, for S.A. Pecheries de Cornouaille of Lorient. A sister ship, the *Kerolay*, was built in 1966 for another Lorient owner but was wrecked as she arrived in the port. A part freezer stern trawler, the *Ludovic Pierre* is 48.9 m. long overall with a moulded breadth of 9.95 m. and depth to main deck of 5.95 m. Accommodation is provided for a crew of 19.

The factory deck includes a Baader 188 filleting line and two Jackstone Froster 16-station vertical plate freezers with a total freezing capacity of 7.5 tons a day. The frozen fish hold has a capacity of 135 cu. m. The wet fish hold has a capacity of 522 cu. m. and is kept at a temperature of 0°C.

The main engine is a Deutz 1320 hp diesel turning a single propeller through a Renk gearbox.

Pierre Pleven

Built in 1966 by Ateliers et Chantiers de Nantes Shipyard for the Pleven Company of Saint-Malo. This ship is a later version of the *Colonel Pleven-II* and also has her superstructure offset to port to give a long trawl deck. A part freezer stern trawler of 1,824 gross tons, the *Pierre Pleven* is 77.m. long overall with a moulded breadth of 12 m. and depth of 8.2 m. Accommodation is provided for a crew of 58.

The *Pierre Pleven* was designed to work in north-west Atlantic waters and when she came into service she was equipped with four Baader machine processing lines. Part of the catch is salted and is

The "Pierre Pleven", 77 metres long, built in 1966.

stored in a 490 cu. m. capacity hold. The freezing section can handle 40 tons a day and freezing is done in two Matal CVM16 vertical plate and two Sabroe PF12A horizontal plate freezers. The frozen fish hold has a capacity of 715 cu. m. and is refrigerated to $-20°C$. by means of Sabroe SMC 8/100 Freon 22 compressors.

The trawl winch is a Brusselle Neptune KMC-11 unit with a barrel capacity of 2,850 metres of warp and a pull of 14 tons at a hauling speed of 2 m./sec.

Main engine is an SEMT-Pielstick type 6PC2L diesel developing 2790 hp at 500 rpm and turning an ACN c.p. propeller through an ACN-Vulcan reduction gearbox to give a trials speed of 15.04 knots.

The "Orage", 43.2 metres long, built in 1967.

Alize
Built in 1967 by Chantiers et Ateliers de la Manche yard in Dieppe for the J. Gaury Company of La Rochelle. A similar ship, the *Saitonge 2*, was built in the same year for Association Rochelaise de Pêche a Vapeur, also of La Rochelle.

A wet fish stern trawler of 390 gross tons, the *Alize* is 38.2 m. long overall with a moulded breadth of 8.35 m. and depth to main deck of 6 m. Accommodation is provided for a crew of 14

The fish room has a capacity of 140 cu. m. and is cooled to 0°C. by means of two Matal Freon 12 compressors.

The trawl winch is a Fapmo F1300 unit with an 8-ton pull and a capacity on each main drum of 2,400 m. of 22 mm warp. It is powered by a Leroy 240 hp electric motor.

Main engine is a Deutz diesel developing 1060 hp and turning a single fixed propeller through a Messian reduction gearbox to give a speed of 13 knots.

Orage
Built in 1967 by the same yard, the *Orage* is similarly equipped but is larger than the *Alize*. She was also built for Jean Gaury of La Rochelle, is 495 gross tons, is 43.2 m. long overall, has a moulded breadth of 8.9 m. and depth to the main deck of 6.2 m. Accommodation is provided for a crew of 19.

The fish hold has a capacity of 250 cu. m. and is cooled to a temperature of 0°C.

Capitaine Cook
Built in 1968 by Beliard Murdoch S.A. of Ostend, Belgium, for Soc. d'Armement a la Pêche Jego-Quere of Lorient. This ship replaced the *Kerolay* which was wrecked on her delivery voyage in 1966, and is similar to her and to the *Klondyke*. Three other vessels to this successful design were ordered from the Beliard Murdoch yard in 1970 for delivery in 1971 and 1972. They will be powered by 1800 hp Crepelle diesel engines. One ship will be for the same owners as the *Capitaine Cook*. The other two will be for Soc. d'Armements des Pecheries d'Atlantique.

The *Capitaine Cook* is a wet fish stern trawler of 689 gross tons and is 58.12 m. long overall with a moulded breadth of 10.1 m. and depth to main deck of 6.12 m.

Provision has been made for later conversion of the ship into a freezer if this is required. The insulated fish room has a capacity of 280 cu. m. and 200 cu. m. of this space is cooled to 0°C.

Main engine is a Deutz diesel developing 1530 hp at 445 rpm and turning a four-bladed Lips propeller through a Renk reduction gearbox to give a speed of 14 knots.

Emile Joseph
Built in 1968 by the France-Gironde yard in Bordeaux for Pecheries Manesse et Senechal of Boulogne. A wet fish stern trawler of 774 gross tons, the *Emile Joseph* is 60.65 m. long overall with a moulded breadth of 10.9 m. and depth to main deck of 6.15 m. Accommodation is provided for a crew of 20.

Intended to operate for periods of up to 30 days, the *Emile Joseph* is similar in her basic design to earlier ships built in Belgium for French owners. She has engine room and accommodation amidships, but differs from the other trawlers in that her fish working area is situated forward on the main deck level and the catch is moved there from aft by conveyor.

The "Shetland", 60 metres long, built in Poland in 1969.

After the fish is hauled up, it is dropped through the hatch on the main deck down into sorting pounds. From them it is conveyed forward along the port side past the engine room casing and up to the main deck level into the working area. Here it is gutted on tables, taken by conveyor through the washer and then through the hatch into the holds.

There are two holds, one for boxed fish and the other for bulk stowage in ice. Total capacity is 500 cu. m. and the holds are cooled to at emperature of 0°C.

The trawl winch is a Brusselle Neptune IMC four-barrel unit of 12 tons pull and powered by a 360 hp electric motor. There are remote controls from two separate positions. The winch is located on the boat deck level in a sheltered position aft of the deckhouse. The bridle winches are down on the main deck level, again well under cover and as far forward as possible. This enables the trawl to be brought right under the shelter deck with the wings on either side of the casing.

There are two winches on either side, all hydraulically driven. Two are of 6 tons pull and the other two of 4 tons used for the bridles. There are also two Brusselle electric unloading winches located forward.

Main engine is a Crepelle V-form 12-cylinder diesel developing 1800 hp at 800 rpm and turning a four-bladed Lipsudest propeller through a Hindmarch-Messian reduction gearbox.

Shetland
Built in 1969 by the Gdynia Shipyard in Poland for Nord Pecheries of Boulogne. This yard has built trawlers for French owners since 1962 and attempts to develop a standard vessel design based on the requirements of the importing country. Thus the *Shetland*, the *Sydero* and similar ships – while resembling wet fish stern trawlers from Belgian and French yards – gain a price advantage from series construction methods.

The *Shetland* is designated by the Polish ship selling organisation Centromor as a Type B-411 trawler. The French ship *Bayard*, built in the Gdynia yard for Boulogne, is designated as a Type B-429 trawler; the *Saint Martin*, built in Gdynia for Glacieres Lejeune of Boulogne is a Type B-28 trawler.

A more recent delivery is the new Type B-421 factory stern trawler *Victor Pleven*, built in Gdynia for the Pleven Company of Saint-Malo. She was the 18th vessel built for French owners by this yard in nine years. The *Victor Pleven* is 90.55 m. long overall with a moulded breadth of 15 m. and a depth to trawl deck of 9.4 m. She has accommodation for a crew of 63.

Her refrigerated and wet fish rooms have a total capacity of 2,040 cu. m. The main engine is a Pielstick 2700 hp diesel which will give the ship a speed of about 14.5 knots.

During 1972 and 1973, the Gdynia yard is to

The Polish-built B-429 class stern trawler "Bayard".

The B-28 class trawler "Saint Martin".

build 13 Type B-423 stern trawlers for French owners.

The *Shetland* (and *Sydero*) is a wet fish stern trawler 60 m. long overall with a moulded breadth of 11.6 m. and a depth to the main deck of 5.85 m. Accommodation is provided for a crew of 23.

The ship has two holds, one for boxed fish and the other for bulk stowage in ice. Total capacity is 540 cu. m. The holds are cooled by air blast to 0°C. and they can be converted for the storage of frozen fish if this should be required.

Main engine is an 8-cylinder MAN diesel developing 1700 hp at 500 rpm and turning a fixed four-bladed propeller through a Renk gearbox.

Built to the highest class of the Bureau Veritas, the *Shetland* was the first fishing vessel classified AUT. This means that she meets the Bureau's requirements for an engine room not constantly manned. The main engine, trawl winch generator, reduction gear and other machinery can be remotely controlled from the wheelhouse.

Saint Louis II

Built by the Gdynia Shipyard, Poland, for Pecheries de la Morinie of Boulogne. A Type B-28/1 wet fish stern trawler with a length overall of 59.3 m., breadth of 11.3 m. and depth to main deck of 5 m.

Standard deck equipment on this type of vessel includes a 360 hp five-drum, electrically powered main trawl winch.

The factory room is on the main deck aft and installations include fish washing machines and

Built in Poland in 1971, the 90.55 metres long "Victor Pleven" is the largest factory trawler in the French fleet.

Main engines are twin MWM type TBRH 345 diesels developing 1700 hp at 514 rpm and turning a Lips c.p. propeller through a Renk gearbox.

East Germany

With a yearly catch of more than 300,000 metric tons, the German Democratic Republic has developed in the past 20 years both as an operator and as a builder of modern fishing vessels. Her particular contribution to the evolution of the stern trawler has been through the construction of large standard-type vessels built in considerable numbers for the Soviet Union, and providing the vast fishing fleet of that country with some of its most efficient catching and processing trawlers.

The GDR joined the stern trawler builders at the beginning of the 1960s when VEB Mathias Thesen Werft of Wismar produced a series of 11 Bertoldt Brecht class 3,000-ton freezer ships for the national fleet. Then large-scale production of stern trawlers began with the completion in 1962 of the first of 86 *Tropik*-class ships by VEB Volkswerft of Stralsund for the Soviet Union. These 79-metre long, 2,435-ton ships were followed from 1965 by 107 vessels of the much-improved *Atlantik* class. The *Atlantik* ships have gone through several modifications since the first was delivered and what may have been the ultimate in the design – the *Atlantik III* super trawler – was completed in 1972, again for the Soviet Union.

The GDR's own requirements for stern trawlers are being met by her shipbuilding industry with several designs of smaller cutter, by the *Nordsee* class stern freezer trawler and by the *Arthur Becker* class of catcher trawler for factory mother ship fleets.

The 59.3 metre long type B-28/1 trawler "Saint Louis II".

gutting tables linked by a conveyor system. Fish is held in ice in a 530 cu. m. capacity hold.

Main engine is an MAN type V7V30/45 four-stroke diesel developing 2080 hp and turning a Lips c.p. propeller through a reduction gearbox to give a speed of 14 knots.

Victoria
Built in 1970 by Constructions Industrielles et Navales de Bordeaux for Soc. Pêche au Large. A factory stern trawler 77 m. long overall with a breadth of 12.4 m. and depth to main deck of 5.5 m. Accommodation is provided for a crew of 54.

Total fish room capacity is 1,160 cu. m. Two large holds amidships and forward of amidships are refrigerated for the carriage of frozen fish and fish fillets and have a capacity of 940 cu. m.; a smaller 220 cu. m. hold in the aft section of the ship is for salted fish.

The *Victoria* is designed to operate on distant water trips of up to 80 days and she is fitted out with a range of Baader machines for heading, filleting and skinning her catch. Freezing is done in four Jackstone Froster plate machines – one horizontal freezer with a daily capacity of 10 tons and three 5-ton capacity vertical freezers.

Atlantik class
Although originally a trawler-type developed for export to the Soviet Union, the *Atlantik*-class whole fish or fillet stern trawler is now being offered to other fishing industries by DDR Schiffbau through its sales organisation, Schiffscommerz.

The *Atlantik II* is a stern trawler of 2,657 gross tons and is 82.2 m. long overall with a moulded breadth of 13.6 m. and depth to main deck of 9.55 m. Accommodation is provided for a crew of 81.

The ship is designed for bottom trawling and for one-boat mid-water trawling and can be adapted for operation in various fisheries in different climates. Propulsion plant in the ships built for the Soviet Union consists of twin SKL 8-cylinder four-stroke

The "Atlantik" class 82.2 metre long stern trawler, built by DDR Schiffbau for the Soviet fleet.

type 8NVD diesel engines, each developing 1160 hp at 375 rpm, and coupled through an induction coupling and reduction gearbox to a single c.p. propeller. Service speed is about 13 knots.

Trawl winches can be either electric or hydraulic powered and consist of a two-drum main winch with a pull on each drum of 6.3 tons at a hauling speed of 100 m/minute, two auxiliary 5-ton winches and two fleeting and cargo winches.

Catches brought aboard are sent first through a hydraulically operated trawl deck hatch down to four holding bunkers where 48 tons of fish a day can be chilled from 26°C. to 2°C.

For filleting her catch, the *Atlantik II* vessel is equipped with machine cutting lines. When processed whole, it is sent after gutting through two GDR designed and manufactured belt-type LBH25 freezers with a total daily output of 48 tons.

The LBH unit consists basically of a blast freezing tunnel with two lines of trays moving through it and it freezes whole fish in 10-kilo blocks. From an automatic weighing machine, the fish drop into the trays and the lids are closed. The freezing time is about four hours.

Frozen fish is held in refrigerated holds with a total capacity of 1,040 cu. m., and there is a fish meal hold with a capacity of 163 cu. m.

Meal is produced from waste fish and offal in a Volkswerft model VF/MO2 shipborne plant able to handle up to 35 tons of raw material in 24 hours.

From the successful *Atlantik I* and *Atlantik II* classes, VEB Volkswerft has developed the larger *Atlantik III* class, or *Super Atlantik*. The first ship in this class was launched in January 1971 and will be completed later this year. She is named *Prometey* and was built for the Soviet Union. A *Super Atlantik* is also being built for Cuba.

Laid down in March 1970, the *Prometey* is 102 m. long overall with a moulded breadth of 15.2 m. and depth to the main deck of 9.7 m. Deadweight capacity is 2,016 tons and the refrigerated fish holds have a capacity of 1,800 cu. m.

This is considerably larger than in the previous *Atlantiks* and is probably the maximum which can be reached within the general parameters of this class.

Main engine is two-stroke type NZD.A-2, 8-cylinder diesel engine which develops 4000 hp and is supplied complete with shaft and c.p. propeller by

Profile drawing of the new "Atlantik III" class stern trawler.

The "Nordsee" class 48.96 metre long trawler.

VEB Dieselmotorenwerk of Rostok. Effective power at the 3.4 m. dia. propeller of 3680 hp gives the ship a speed of 14.6 knots. The engine room can be run unmanned for up to 16 hours.

The *Super Atlantik* is designed for bottom and mid-water trawling and it is claimed that catching capacity is increased by about 30 per cent over earlier *Atlantik* ships through the use of electrical trawling gear and by working trawls down to depths of 1,500 metres.

Another feature of the ship is that the gear handling system on the trawl deck can maintain almost continuous fishing by shooting one trawl as the other is hauled up.

Processing capacity is 120 tons of raw material a day. Incoming fish can be held in cooling bunkers. Machine filleting plant is installed and freezing capacity is about 54 tons of fillets a day. A GDR-made meal plant can handle 60 tons of waste fish and offal in 24 hours.

Nordsee class
A medium size freezer stern trawler extensively used in the East German fleet for the catching and processing of herrings. Series production started in 1966 in the yard of VEB Elbewerften in Boizenburg. A ship of 644 gross tons, the *Nordsee* stern trawler is 48.96 m. long overall with a breadth of 10 m. Accommodation is provided for a crew of 23.

Main engine is an SKL model 8NVD 48-AU diesel developing 1000 hp at 375 rpm and turning a propeller in a nozzle to give a speed of 12 knots. Refrigerated hold capacity is 540 cu. m.

The 23 m. long trawl deck and remote-controlled four-drum winch permit very quick handling of the gear. Fish is discharged into the receiving hopper tanks where it is pre-cooled with chilled seawater. It is removed from the hoppers by air-lift pumps and passed on to conveyors for sorting.

From the conveyors, the fish moves into buffer storage bins and then, as required, to vertical plate freezers which have a capacity of 21 tons a day and are loaded mechanically.

After freezing, the blocks are released by hot gas and drop into a carriage from which they are pushed individually by a lazy-tongs on to a conveyor. This takes them through a glazing and packaging machine to another conveyor system leading to the hold via a paternoster-type hoist.

The blocks are stored automatically in the hold, layer by layer, using a fore-and-aft conveyor on the centre-line and a side to side pusher above the conveyor. As stowage proceeds, the conveyor is raised layer by layer.

In port the conveyor and paternoster hoist can be reversed and speeded up for discharging the cargo automatically at a rate of up to 15 tons an hour. The whole preparation, freezing and packaging sequence is controlled by two men.

Another very interesting ship from the VEB Elbewerften yard is the *Habana*-class fish meal cutter. This is a stern trawler equipped to reduce her catch into meal at the rate of 35 tons of raw material a day. Fifteen of these ships have been built for Cuba.

Arthur Becker
This class of stern trawler is designed to maintain a very high catch rate to supply the GDR factory mother ships *Junge Welt* and *Junge Garde*. The factory ships are vessels of 10,130 gross tons and are 141.4 m. long overall. They work in the North Atlantic and can process up to 320 tons of raw material a day.

The *Arthur Becker* class ships have been built since 1967 in the VEB Peenewerft Wolgast yard and 21 were delivered to the GDR fleet and two to the Soviet Union. They are wet fish stern trawlers of 991 gross tons with a length overall of 62.2 m. and a breadth of 10.6 m. Accommodation is provided for a crew of 19.

In the *Arthur Becker* class, the bridge and other superstructure is offset to the port side to give a trawl deck 33.5 m. long, or 54 per cent of the ship's length. The vessel can be used for bottom or mid-water trawling and shooting and hauling is claimed to take only about 30 minutes.

The catch is carried for periods of up to about three days in six chilled water holding tanks with a total capacity of 120 cu. m. Fish is transferred from these tanks, in cod ends, to the mother ship.

The "Arthur Becker" class 62.2 metre long catcher stern trawler in GDR factory mother ship fleets.

Main engine is a VEB Dieselmotorenwerk unit developing 1750 hp at 225 rpm and turning a c.p. propeller in a nozzle to give a speed of 12½ knots.

West Germany

The Federal Republic of Germany takes a yearly fish catch between 650,000 and 700,000 tons and a large share of this is now being supplied by a sea-freezing fleet of some 60 ships which contains many of the world's finest and most efficient frozen fillet producing stern trawlers.

If it was the British who pioneered the fillet trawler and the Russians who developed its large-scale use, it was the owners working from Bremerhaven, Cuxhaven and other West German fishing ports who demonstrated the great value in distant water fleets of the well-designed and well-equipped factory trawler.

Two other highly significant contributions to the progress of the stern trawler have also come from West Germany. One of them is the varied range of Baader fish cutting machines which made it possible to produce frozen fillets economically at sea; the other is the development of the German one-boat method of mid-water trawling. This was an inspired application by Federal government research workers and the industry of the improved towing power and gear handling provided by the stern trawler to a new fishing method.

One of the interesting characteristics of the West German stern trawler fleet is that the ships and their equipment have come almost entirely from German yards and manufacturers. It is a home-grown fleet meeting a domestic requirement for quality frozen fish. But in the past few years there have been indications that there is still a need in the high seas fleet of 108 ships for efficient wet fish trawlers.

This is to be met by converting some of the earlier fillet freezers into wet fish stern trawlers and replacing them with a new-generation series of 15 vessels.

Orders for these new fillet freezers were placed with German yards in 1971. Each will be able to freeze 40 to 50 tons a day and will be able to carry about 800 tons.

Othmarschen
Built in 1965 by Rickmers Werft, Bremerhaven, for Ernest A.P. Koch of Hamburg-Altona. A sister ship, the *Altona*, was completed later in the same year. A wet fish and freezer stern trawler of 1,400 tons, the *Othmarschen* is 76 m. long overall with a moulded breadth of 12.2 m. and depth to upper deck of 8 m. She has accommodation for a crew of 54.

Wet fish hold capacity is 295 cu. m., refrigerated

The "Othmarschen", 76 metres long, built in 1965.

hold capacity 512 cu. m. and meal hold capacity is 240 cu. m.

The *Othmarschen* is equipped with Baader processing machinery for large and small white fish and for redfish. Offal and waste fish is reduced to meal in a Schlotterhose plant.

The Achgelis four-drum trawl winch is electrically powered by a 360 hp electric motor.

Main engine is an 8-cylinder MAN diesel developing 2140 hp at 300 rpm and turning a KaMeWa c.p. propeller through a 2:1 Wulfel reduction gearbox.

Hamburg

Built in 1965 by the Seebeck yard in Bremerhaven for the Cranzer Fishing Company. A factory stern trawler of 1,800 gross tons, the *Hamburg* is 82.1 metres long overall with a moulded breadth of 13.6 m. and depth of 8.3 m. Accommodation is provided for a crew of 60.

The refrigerated fish rooms have a capacity of 870 cu. m. maintained at a temperature of −29°C.

The main engine is a Deutz type SBVM350 diesel developing 3000 hp at 350 rpm and turning an Escher Wyss propeller to give a speed of 15 knots.

Bonn

The first of a series of six "University" class factory stern trawlers built from 1964 to 1966 by A.G. Weser Werk Seebeck for "Nordsee" Deutsche Hochseefischerei of Bremerhaven, one of the world's largest fishing companies. Other ships in the class are the *Heidelberg, Erlangen, Freiburg, Marburg* and *Tubingen*. One of the features of this class is the Unigan-type swinging gantry aft for hauling the catch aboard.

The 2,557 gross tons *Bonn* is 87.7 m. long overall with a breadth of 14 m. and depth of 9 m.

The ship was designed to produce quick frozen fillets. The fish is machine cut and filleted in Baader lines and is frozen in eight plate freezers. The frozen product, packed in cartons, is held at −28°C. in a 1,000 cu.m. capacity refrigerated fish room. Waste fish and offal is reduced to meal in a plant capable of processing up to 30 tons a day.

Propulsion is by two MaK type MA582 diesels, each developing 1900 hp at 300 rpm, which are geared to a single shaft and turn an Escher Wyss c.p. propeller to give a speed of 15.5 knots.

The 87.7 metre long "Bonn" was built in 1964 and was the first of six "University" class factory stern trawlers.

Weser

Built in 1965 by Rickmers Werft for Hanseatische Hochseefischerei of Bremerhaven. A combined white fish and herring stern trawler of 2,176 gross tons, the *Weser* is 79.5 m. long overall with a moulded breadth of 13.6 m. and depth to upper deck of 8.5 m. Accommodation is provided for a crew of 55.

The *Weser* is equipped with Baader fish processing machinery and freezing is done in Jackstone vertical plate freezers able to handle up to 30 tons a day. She has two fish rooms with a total capacity of 860 cu. m. and one of these can be refrigerated down to $-30°C$. Fish meal storage capacity is 165 tons.

Main engine is a Deutz V-form model SBV12M-350 diesel developing 3000 hp at 350 rpm.

A similar ship, named the *Sagitta Maris*, was built in the same year for F. Busse & Company of Bremerhaven.

Wumme

Built in 1966 by Rickmers Werft for the Bremen-Vegesacker Fischerei Gesellschaft of Bremen-Vegesack. A similar ship, the *Hamme*, was completed later in 1966 for the same company by the Schiffbau Gesellschaft Unterweser yard in Bremerhaven.

At the time of her building the *Wumme* was the largest herring trawler to be delivered to a West German owner. A wet fish stern trawler of 846 gross tons, she is 56.7 m. long overall with a breadth of 10.6 m. and depth to main deck of 6.92 m.

She was designed to carry her herring catch packed in ice in layers or boxes in two fish rooms. The first of these, for fish packed in layers, has a capacity of 284 cu. m. The second, for boxed fish, has a capacity of 128 cu. m.

The trawl winch is an electric-powered Achgelis machine with a pull of 8.5 tons.

Main engine is a Deutz 8-cylinder diesel developing 1000 hp and turning an Escher Wyss propeller to give a speed of 13.8 knots.

Neufundland (Hildesheim)

Built in 1967 by the Schiffbau Gesellschaft Unterweser yard in Bremerhaven. This vessel operates under charter to "Nordsee" Deutsche Hochseefischerei of Bremerhaven and is now named the *Hildesheim*. A factory stern trawler 1,580 gross tons, the *Hildesheim* is 83.3 m. long overall with a moulded breadth of 13.6 m. and a depth to upper deck of 8.2 m. Accommodation is provided for a crew of 54 to 56.

The ship has two fish holds, one of which can be

The "Weser", 79.5 metres long, built in 1965.

used for carrying wet fish in ice. This hold has a capacity of 624 cu.m. and the second hold has a capacity of 322 cu.m. In the processing lines are Baader gutting and heading machines, Baader188 filleters for smaller white fish, Baader 99 filleter for larger white fish and a Baader 150 filleter for red fish. The ship is also equipped with a Walcker Waco 70/375 washer and a complete Waco conveyor system. Freezing is done in three Bergedorfer plate freezers with a total output of 45 tons a day.

Waste fish and offal is reduced to meal in a Schlotterhose plant with a capacity of 30 tons a day.

Main engine is a Deutz diesel developing 3000 hp at 350 rpm and turning an Escher Wyss c.p. propeller through a Wulfel reduction gearbox to give a speed of 15.7 knots.

Seydisfjord

Built in 1967 by Rickmers Werft shipyard in Bremerhaven for Hochseefischerei Carl Kemp of Bremerhaven. A wet fish stern trawler of 1,047 gross tons, the *Seydisfjord* is 63.6 m. long overall with a moulded breadth of 10.28 m. and depth to main deck of 5 m.

Designed for fresh fishing only, the *Seydisfjord* has a well-mechanised working deck equipped with

The "Seydisfjord", 63.6 metres long, built in 1967.

The "Seefahrt", 63.5 metres long, built in 1967.

Waco conveying, washing and distribution plant. Also installed is a Waco fish discharging plant and fish elevator.

The fish room has a capacity of 595 cu. m. and is fully insulated with cork slabs and mineral wool.

Superstructure is located about amidships and immediately aft of this is the Seebeck six-barrel 14-ton trawl winch. This has a main drum capacity of 1,400 fathoms of 3.5 in. circ. steel warp and hauling speed of 110 m/min. The winch has four auxiliary barrels and two warping heads and is powered by a 440 hp electric motor.

Main engine is a Deutz diesel developing 2140 hp at 320 rpm and turning a KaMeWa three-bladed c.p. propeller through a 1.6:1 reduction gearbox to give a speed of 15.35 knots.

Seefahrt
Built in 1967 by the Rickmers Werft yard in Bremerhaven for the Hanseatische Hochseefischerei of Bremerhaven. The *Seefahrt* was designed as a multi-purpose ship capable of fishing with bottom and mid-water trawls and purse seine. She is a vessel of 1,084 gross tons with a length overall of 63.5 m., a breadth of 10.8 m. and depth to upper deck of 7.48 m.

The first shelter deck commercial stern trawler to add purse seining to her fishing capabilities, the *Seefahrt* has an unusual layout. The bridge superstructure is located forward of amidships. This is continued aft along the port side and houses the funnel casing. The trawl deck extends along the starboard side with the eight-drum Brusselle winch just aft of the bridge superstructure. Aft over the stern ramp, the ship has a large platform for her purse seine net.

The fish room has a capacity of 605 cu. m., is insulated with cork and mineral wool and is lined with aluminium.

Propulsion is by two Deutz diesel engines, each developing 1300 hp at 500 rpm and coupled through a reduction gearbox to an Escher Wyss c.p. propeller. The ship has a speed of 15.5 knots. The engine room is designed to work without attention for 16 hours and is controlled by the officer on watch from a soundproof console room at the after end.

Österreich
Built in 1968 by Rickmers Werft for "Nordsee" Deutsche Hochseefischerei of Bremerhaven. A development of the earlier "University" class with an enclosed and extended fore-castle deck and without the Unigan-type gantry aft. The *München* is a sister ship from the same yard.

A factory stern trawler of 2,700 gross tons, the *Österreich* is 86.5 m. long overall with a moulded breadth of 14.2 m. and depth to upper deck of 9.3 m. She has accommodation for a crew of 73 in single and two berth cabins.

Four separate Baader machine cutting lines are installed on the spacious factory deck. Fish is fed in from the trawl deck above through twin chutes into four reception pounds and it passes from them by conveyor for gutting and machine filleting.

Large white fish are filleted by a Baader 99 machine, smaller white fish by two 188 machines and

The 86.3 metre long "Sonne", built in 1969 and among the most modern West German factory stern trawlers.

red fish by a 150 machine. Fillets are trimmed and packed at tables at the forward end of the machine lines and are then frozen in a battery of six Bergedorfer Eisenwerke horizontal plate freezers which have a total output of 40 tons a day. After freezing, the fillets are vacuum packed and sealed using Krame & Greme machinery and are then placed in master cartons for transfer to the refrigerated hold along a Waco conveyor system. The hold has a capacity of 1,050 cu. m. and can carry about 700 tons of packed fillets.

Waste fish and offal is reduced to meal in Schlotterhose plant which can handle about 35 tons of raw material a day.

The trawl winch is a Seebeck six-barrel machine powered by two 260 hp electric motors. The two main drums have a capacity for 1400 fathoms of steel warp. Like most of the larger and higher powered units in the West German stern trawler fleet, the *Osterreich* is equipped to take her fish by bottom or mid-water trawl.

The ship has a diesel-electric propulsion system consisting of four MaK model 281AK diesel engines, each developing 1000 hp at 750 rpm and each coupled to a BBC 810 kVA generator. This system powers two BBC 1000 kW propulsion motors which are geared to a single shaft turning an Escher Wyss c.p. propeller at 200 rpm to give the ship a top speed of 15.5 knots.

Fuel oil tanks have a capacity of 1,200 cu. m. allowing an endurance of about 100 days. Double bottom freshwater tanks have a capacity of 50 cu. m. and two Atlas freshwater generators can produce 30 tons a day.

A similar ship to the *Osterreich* was built in 1969 by the same yard for Nordstern Rederei of Bremerhaven and was named the *Sonne*. On her first voyage, which lasted 65 days, the *Sonne* caught more than 1,600 tons of fish to produce 625 tons of frozen fillets. She improved on this on her $2\frac{1}{2}$-month second voyage when she produced 725 tons of fillets from a catch of about 2,000 tons.

Italy

Deepsea distant water trawlers account for only a small proportion of Italy's total yearly catch of around 350,000 metric tons. But construction by Italian yards during the 1960s of a number of imaginatively designed and efficient stern trawlers contributed both to the progress of this vessel type and to the productivity of the section of her fleet working outside the Mediterranean.

The main distant water area fished by Italian ships is the middle Atlantic off the coast of West Africa. Catches there have helped to reduce Italy's dependence on imports for supplies of frozen fish.

Aspa Terzo
With a sister ship *Aspa Quarto*, built in 1965 by Cantieri Navale Apuania S.A. for "Aspa" Armatoriale Sarda Pesca Atlantica SpA of Olbid. At the time of her building the largest and most powerful Italian stern trawler, the *Aspa Terzo* is a ship of 1,600 gross tons with length overall of 74.5 metres, a moulded breadth of 12 m. and depth to upper deck of 8.3 m. Accommodation is provided for a crew of 38.

The "Aspa Terzo", 74.5 metres long, built in 1965.

The fish hold has a capacity of 1,200 cu. m. and the ship can carry up to 570 tons of frozen fish and 70 tons of meal.

The main trawl winch is hydraulically powered and recovery of the cod end is assisted by a Unigan-type moveable gantry.

The ship is diesel-electric powered by three 900 hp Deutz diesel engines driving three 730 kVA three-phase alternators. Two 950 hp electric motors are geared to a single shaft which turns a KaMeWa c.p. propeller.

Andrea Speat
Built in 1965 by Cantiere Navale di Pesaro for Societa Pesca Atlantica of Palermo in Sicily. A freezer stern trawler of 630 tons, the *Andrea Speat* is 63.3 metres long overall with a moulded breadth of 9.4 m. and depth of 5.5 m. Accommodation is provided for a crew of 30.

Fish is air-blast frozen in a freezing tunnel which can handle 18 to 20 tons a day. Two fishrooms are refrigerated down to −20°C. and have a total capacity of 640 cu. m.

The main engine is a Deutz type RBV6M 358 diesel developing 1500 hp and turning a Zeise four-bladed fixed propeller to give the ship a speed of 15 knots.

A similar but slightly larger ship was built by the same yard in 1967 for Societa Pesca Atlantica. Named *Luca Speat*, she is a freezer stern trawler of 780 gross tons with a length overall of 63.9 metres, a moulded breadth of 9.6 m. and depth of 5.3 m.

Nembo
Built in 1967 with a sister ship, the *Pelagos*, by Soc. Esercizio Cantieri SpA of Viareggio for Frescogel SpA of Cagliari. The ships were the first units built to a standard design developed by the yard, and were delivered for operation off the coast of West Africa. A freezer stern trawler of 850 gross tons, the *Nembo* is 63.5 metres long overall with a moulded breadth of 10.4 m. and a depth of 7.05 m. She has accommodation for a crew of 40.

The main winch is a Hydraulik type 2A8U unit with four barrels and was manufactured in Italy by San Giorgio. The winch is mounted on a platform above the level of the trawl deck and the wings of the trawl are taken forward on either side of the superstructure by means of two Hydraulik type A8 winches. The wings pass through tunnels beneath the raised platform of the winch and the trawl is pulled right up to the platform. This system of working enables more than two-thirds of the length of the ship to be used.

On the main deck below the fish are washed in a Walcker Waco cross current type 70-375 washing machine. Freezing is done in four Jackstone Froster horizontal plate freezers which can handle a total of 28 tons a day.

The main engine is a Deutz SBV6M 358 diesel developing 1500 hp at 285 rpm and coupled direct to a Lips c.p. propeller to give a speed of 13.5 knots.

Storione
Built in 1967 by Cantieri Navale M. & B. Benetti of Viareggio for Fratelli Cefalu of Palermo. A freezer stern trawler of 1,233 gross tons, the *Storione* is 67 metres long overall with a moulded breadth of 11.5 m. and depth to upper deck of 7 m.

Her trawl winch is a Hydraulik six-barrel machine with the two main drums having a pull of 16 tons. At the fore end of the main engine is a power take-off of 450 hp which drives five pumps powering hydraulic motors to drive the trawl winch.

The "Nembo", 63.5 metres long, built in 1967.

The fish hold has a capacity of 1,000 cu. m. and is insulated with rigid polyurethane (plastifoam) and lined with glass polyester. A Frick-Barbieri refrigeration system using ammonia as a refrigerant serves the holds and the air-blast freezing tunnels. These tunnels can handle about 20 tons a ton but when fishing is heavy a stand-by compressor can be brought into use to boost capacity to 25 tons.

The main engine is an MAN type G8V30/45 diesel developing 1700 hp at 500 rpm and turning a Lips c.p. propeller through a Rademakers gearbox. The propeller is shrouded in a Kort nozzle. Another feature of the *Storione* is that she has been built with a bulbous bow. On trials she attained an average speed of 14.75 knots.

A similar ship, named the *Airone*, was built for the same owners in 1969.

Tontini Pesca Terzo

Built in 1969 by Soc. Esercizio Cantieri SpA of Viareggio for Tontini Pesca SpA of Anzio. A freezer stern trawler of 1,500 gross tons, the *Tontini Pesca Terzo* is 73.2 metres long overall with a breadth of 12 m. and a depth of 7.9 m. Accommodation is provided for a crew of 35.

Her trawl winch is a hydraulically powered two-drum unit made by Norwinch.

Equipped with eight Aermarelli plate freezers, this trawler can freeze up to 30 tons a day. Her refrigerated fish hold has a capacity of 1,300 cu. m. It is insulated with polyurethane plastifoam and a temperature of $-25°C$. is maintained by five Carrier-Marelli type 5H 120 compressors using Freon 22 as the refrigerent.

The main engine is a Deutz RBV8M 358 diesel developing 2250 hp at 305 rpm and turning a four-bladed propeller to give a speed of 14.5 knots.

De Giosa Guiseppi

Built in 1971 by Soc. Esercizio Cantieri for the Meridion Alpesca company of Bari. This trawler is

The 67 metre long "Airone", sister ship of the "Storione".

The "De Giosa Guiseppi", 66.7 metres long, built in 1971.

One of the world's largest trawlers, the 5,295 gross ton "Tenyo Maru" was built in 1971 for the Taiyo Fishery Company. She is 111.45 metres long overall and is powered by a 5,700 hp diesel engine. The ship is one of a number of this size built in 1970 and 1971 to operate in Northern Pacific pollack fishery.

a slightly larger and improved version of a series of six ships built by the yard and which started in 1967 with the *Nembo* and *Pelagos*. A freezer stern trawler of 900 gross tons, the *De Giosa Guiseppi* is 66.7 metres long overall with a breadth of 10.4 m. and a depth of 7.1 m. Accommodation is provided for a crew of 33.

Freezing capacity is 32 tons a day of whole fish in four Samifi Babcock air-blast tunnels. The ship is also equipped with two Amerio-Samifi plate freezers. The frozen fish is kept at −25°C. in a 1,050 cu. ft. hold.

The main engine is an Atlas-MaK type 6 Mu 551 AK diesel developing 2000 hp at 250 rpm and running an Ansaldo-Lips four-bladed propeller to give a top speed on trials of 15 knots.

The seventh ship in this series, the *Carlo di Fazio*, is powered by a Deutz RBV8M diesel engine.

Japan

The world's greatest fishing nation with a catch in 1970 of more than nine million tons, Japan took over the stern trawler concept when it was being pioneered in Europe, adapted it to the particular requirements of her fishermen and industry and has developed her own distinctive type of vessel.

This was well described by Tasuo Shimizu, an engineer with the giant Taiyo Fishery Co., in a paper given at the FAO Third Fishing Boats Technical Meeting in Gothenburg in 1965. When the Japanese trawler industry was searching for new overseas fishing grounds, he explained, a study of European stern trawling techniques was first undertaken. This was in the 1950s and Japan's deepsea trawler owners had up to then been taking good catches in nearby waters. But they expected that they might eventually have to follow the tuna vessel owners in an ocean wide search for stocks.

The stern trawler, with its potential for improved gear handling and for the processing and freezing of fish at sea, seemed the most promising type of vessel for working far distant waters. In 1955 the stern trawler type training ship *Umitaka Maru* was built for Tokyo's University of Fisheries. She followed the design of the European stern trawler as did the prototype commercial vessel *Taiyo Maru No. 51*, which was built in 1957.

These two ships obtained impressive results and led to a rush of building by Japanese yards. During the years 1960 to 1963 about 30 stern trawlers from 1,500 to 2,500 tons were built, and by 1964 some of the new ships were from 2,500 to 3,000 tons. Most of them were whole fish freezers but, with the *Zuiyo Maru* and a few other vessels, the first fillet producers also came into the fleet, equipped, as were their European counterparts, with Baader cutting machinery.

From the earliest ships following the prototypes up to the very big trawlers now being built, the Japanese stern trawler has a layout that derives from the whale factory ship. The engines are in the after part with the holds forward of amidships. To avoid obstructing the shelter deck or the trawl deck, the engine casing is reduced to a minimum or, the casing and funnel (or funnels) is divided longitudinally and sited at the sides of the deck. Wheelhouse superstructure is concentrated well forward and in many Japanese trawlers the heavy gantries, and not the superstructure, are the most prominent profile feature.

One of the strongest recent influences on Japanese stern trawler size and design has come from the huge fishery for Alaska pollack in the Bering Sea. This species is sought for the production of minced fish or surimi which is in increasing demand for the production of fish paste, cakes and sausages. Processing is a complex operation and moved from shore plants to sea first in large factory mother ships. By 1968 more than half of an output of 105,000 tons of surimi was being produced at sea.

The companies involved in this were also taking a closer look at the vessels to be employed and in the past three years up to 1971 they have tended to turn away from the mother ship and feeder catchers to the processing "super" trawler of 4,000 and now more than 5,000 gross tons. In 1970 the catch of Alaska pollack had increased to more than two million tons. In volume this is the most important species now being caught by the Japanese industry and the factory stern trawler has moved up to a top place as a producer in her fisheries.

The *Yamato Maru*, first of the 5,000-ton ships, was delivered in the autumn of 1970. She was followed in January 1971 by the *Rikuzen Maru*, a ship 109 metres long overall with a beam of 17 m. built by Hitachi. In February 1971 the Maizuru Heavy Industries yard completed the 5,000-ton *Ohtori Maru*. This ship is 105 m. long overall with a beam of 17.6 m. and a depth of 11 m. She is powered by a 5,900 hp diesel engine. The *Ohtori Maru* has a freezing capacity of 70 tons and can produce about 40 tons of surimi a day. Her meal plant can handle 125 tons of raw material in 24 hours.

Two 5,300 gross ton ships, the *Tenyo Maru* and the *Chikubu Maru*, were completed in April and October 1971.

Mikami Maru
Built in 1964 by Nippon Kokan Kabushiki Kaisha for Hoko Suisan. The first stern trawler to be built by this yard, the *Mikami Maru* is a flush deck type vessel with long trawl deck and low and compact wheelhouse superstructure forward of amidships. The 2,538 gross ton trawler is 84.9 metres long overall with a moulded breadth of 13.5 m. and depth to upper deck of 9 m. She has accommodation for a crew of 75.

Freezing equipment consists of tunnel and plate freezers. A direct-expansion semi air blast system has a capacity for 6.66 tons a day and plate freezers handle 42.5 tons. The refrigerated fish hold has a capacity of 2,353 cu. m.

The diesel-electric powered trawler "Sankichi Maru No. 51" built in 1964.

The main engine is an Akasaka diesel type 6NET 45/75 developing 2800 hp at 235 rpm to give a speed of 15 knots.

Sankichi Maru No. 51.
Along with the development of the large stern trawler, Japanese owners and yards between 1962 and 1965 introduced several interesting types of smaller trawler. These included some 10 vessels of about 300 gross tons. The *Sankichi Maru No. 51.* was unusual in that she had diesel-electric propulsion. The 299 gross ton trawler was built in 1964 by the Niigata yard of Niigata Engineering Co. for the Koyo Fishing Co. She is 37.6 m. long overall with a breadth of 8 m. and depth of 3.6 m. She has accommodation for a crew of 32.

She is equipped with automatic heading and fish washing machines on her working deck and three freezers have a capacity of 16 tons a day. The refrigerated fish room has a capacity of 310 cu.m.

Propulsion is by two 172 kW three-phase electric motors (powered by two Niigata diesel-driven alternators) geared to a single shaft turning a c.p. propeller.

Hakurei Maru
Built in 1966 by the Miho Shipyard in Shimizu for the Ishikawa Prefecture Deep Sea Trawl Company. A similar ship, the *Kaiko Maru No.1.*, was built in 1966 by the same yard for Chuo Fisheries Bureau. After delivery both vessels were sent to grounds off the north-west coast of Africa.

A freezer stern trawler of 991 gross tons, the *Hakurei Maru* is 62 metres long b.p. with a moulded breadth of 11.2 m. and depth to main deck of 5 m.

The refrigerated fish room has a capacity of 1,000 cu. m. Fish is frozen in three Mitsubishi Denki plants.

The "Hakurei Maru", 62 metres long b.p., built in 1966.

The "Toyo Maru", 62 metres long, built in 1967.

The main engine is a Akasaka diesel developing 2220 hp at 250 rpm and turning a five-bladed propeller to give a speed of more than 14 knots.

Toyo Maru
Built in 1967 by the Yamanishi Shipbuilding & Iron Works of Ishinomaki City for the Toyo Fisheries Company. A freezer stern trawler of 549 gross tons designed to operate in the Atlantic Ocean, the *Toyo Maru* is 54.5 metres long overall with a moulded breadth of 9.3 m. and depth of 4.2 m. Accommodation is provided for a crew of 33.

Her main trawl is a hydraulic unit with a 10-ton pull and has a hauling speed of 80 m/min.

Freezing is done in four Maekawa plate freezers, with a total capacity of 16.6 tons a day.

The main engine is a Hanshin type Y6YCSH diesel developing 1500 hp at 315 rpm and direct coupled to three-bladed c.p. propeller to give a top speed of 14.3 knots.

Daiko Maru No.2
Built in 1967 by Miho Shipyard Company for Daiko Fisheries. A freezer stern trawler of 1,497 gross tons, the *Daiko Maru No.2* is 72 metres long overall with a moulded breadth of 12.5 m. and depth to upper deck of 8.3 m. Accommodation is provided for a crew of 57.

Freezing is done in Kyodo plate machines able to turn out 40 tons of frozen blocks a day. Also installed on the working deck is a Kishino heading machine, a Tokai Kogyo washer and a Kishino glazing machine. The 1,600 cu.m. fish room can be kept at a temperature of $-25°C$.

The main engine is an Akasaka 6UET 45/75 diesel developing 2800 hp at 240 rpm to give a service speed of 13 knots.

The "Daiko Maru No. 2", 72 metres long, built in 1967.

Shirane Maru

Built in 1967 by the Shikoku Dockyard Company for Nippon Suisan Kaisha. A freezer stern trawler of 2,529 gross tons, the *Shirane Maru* is 84 metres long overall with a moulded breadth of 13.5 m. and depth of 8.75 m. She has accommodation for a crew of 65.

Her trawl winch is an electrically powered Tokyo Kikai 20-ton unit with three drums and a hauling speed of 80 m/min.

The ship is equipped with Nihon-Sabroe plate freezers with a daily output of 45 tons of frozen blocks. These are stored at $-20°C$. in a 2,327 cu.m. fish hold.

The main engine is a Mitsui-Burmeister & Wain type DE 742VBF-75 diesel developing 2750 hp at

The "Shirane Maru", 84 metres long, built in 1967.

Eikyu Maru No.52

Built in 1967 by the Niigata Engineering Company for the Hamaya Fishing Company. A 300 gross ton freezer stern trawler designed for operation in the Pacific or the Atlantic, the *Eikyu Maru* is 42.88 metres long overall with a moulded breadth of 8 m. and a depth of 3.6 m. She has accommodation for a crew of 28.

Freezing is done in a Nisshin air blast tunnel with an output of 12 tons a day. The refrigerated fish hold has a capacity of 285 cu.m.

The ship's trawl winch is a hydraulically powered unit with a pull of six tons at a hauling speed of 60 m/min.

The main engines are twin Niigata type 6MMGP 20HS diesels each developing 430 hp at 900 rpm and turning a three-bladed c.p. propeller through a reduction gearbox to give a service speed of 10.5 knots.

The "Eikyu Maru No. 52", 42.88 metres long, built in 1967.

240 rpm and turning a four-bladed fixed propeller to give a service speed of 12.9 knots.

Oshika Maru No.2

Built in 1967 by the Niigata Engineering Company for the Ojika Fisheries Company of Tokyo. A freezer stern trawler of 999.7 gross tons, the *Oshika Maru No.2* is 60.4 metres long overall with a moulded breadth of 11.4 m. and depth of 5.1 m. She has accommodation for a crew of 52.

Her freezing plant consists of plate machines made by Nisshin Kogyo and having a total output of 25 tons a day. The frozen product is held at $-23°C$. in a 1,006 cu.m. capacity fish hold.

The trawl winch is a 13-ton electrically powered unit with a hauling speed of 60 m/min.

The main engine is a Niigata type M8F43CHS diesel developing 2200 hp at 275 rpm and turning a five-bladed fixed propeller to give a speed of 12 knots.

Zuiyo Maru No.2

Built in 1968 by the Hayashikane Shipbuilding & Engineering Co. for the Taiyo Fishery Company. A factory stern trawler of 3,339 gross tons, the *Zuiyo*

The "Oshika Maru No. 2", 60.4 metres long, built in 1967.

The "Koyo Maru No. 2", 88 metres long, built in 1968.

Maru No.2 is 99.5 metres long overall with a moulded breadth of 15.5 m. and depth to main deck of 7.4 m. Accommodation is provided for a crew of 129.

On her large factory deck the ship has four machine processing lines producing fillets which are frozen by 18 Maekawa plate freezers, with a total output of 60 tons a day. The frozen fillets are held at temperatures down to $-30°C$. in a fish hold with a capacity of 3,069 cu.m. Her refrigeration plant includes four Maekawa high-speed, multiple-cylinder ammonia compressors.

For meal and oil production the ship is equipped with a De Laval Centrifish plant capable of handling 50 tons of raw material a day. The fish meal hold has a capacity of 342 cu.m.

The trawl winch is an electrically powered Hayashikane unit with a pull of 18.5 tons at a hauling speed of 70 m/min. It is powered by a 335 kW Kawasaki electric motor.

The main engine is a Mitsubishi 8UET 45/75 diesel developing 4000 hp at 240 rpm and turning a five-bladed fixed propeller to give a speed of nearly 16 knots.

Auxiliary plant includes three Niigata 600 hp diesels each coupled to a 490 kVA alternator.

Koyo Maru No.2

Built in 1968 by the Fujinigata shipyard at Osaka of the Mitsui Shipbuilding & Engineering Company for Hokuyo Suisan. A freezer stern trawler of 3,456 gross tons, the *Koyo Maru No.2* is 88 metres long b.p. with a moulded breadth of 16 m. and depth to upper deck of 9.8 m.

Fish handling and processing plant on her factory deck includes two washing machines, nine conveyors, six gutting machines and one filleting line. Whole fish and fillets are frozen in five 15-station and ten 14-station plate freezers with a total daily output of 48 tons. Refrigeration is provided by Sabroe ammonia compressors and the refrigerated fish hold has a capacity of 2,723 cu.m.

For meal and oil production the ship has a De Laval Centrifish plant with a capacity of 50 tons a day. A Sasakura-Atlas AFGU freshwater plant can produce 20 tons a day for ship and factory use.

The trawl winch is a Tokyo Kikai electrically-powered unit with a pull of 25 tons at a hauling speed of 80 m/min.

The main engine is a Mitsui-Burmeister & Wain nine-cylinder type 942VBF75 diesel developing 3900 hp at 248 rpm and turning a four-bladed propeller to give a top speed of 15.9 knots.

Niitaka Maru

Built in 1968 by the Hitachi Shipbuilding & Engineering Company in Mukaishima for Nippon Suisan Kaisha of Tokyo. A factory stern trawler of 3,914 gross tons, the *Niitaka Maru* is one of two similar ships for the same owner. She is 96.68 metres long overall with a moulded breadth of 16 m. and depth to upper deck of 9.8 m. A flush deck type vessel, the *Niitaka Maru* has a low profile wheelhouse structure well forward to give a long trawl deck. The engine exhausts are taken up on either side of the factory and trawl deck from the engine room and up through the posts of her aft gantry. The ship has accommodation for a crew of 99.

Gutting, heading and filleting machinery on her factory deck process the catch into fillets for freezing in a battery of plate machines which have an output of 60 tons a day. Waste fish and offal is reduced to meal in a De Laval Centrifish plant.

The fish room has a total capacity of 3,210 cu.m. and there is a 250 cu.m. capacity hold for fish meal.

The trawl winch is a Tokyo Kikai machine electrically driven by a 300 kW Mitsubishi motor. It has a pull of 25 tons at 80 m/min.

The main engine is a Hitachi-Burmeister & Wain diesel developing 4400 hp at 248 rpm and turning an Ichihachi four-bladed propeller to give a service speed of 14.5 knots.

Katata Maru
Built in 1968 by the Usiki Iron Works for Hoko Suisan of Tokyo. At the time of her completion in August 1968, the 4,251 gross ton *Katata Maru* was the largest ship of her type in the Japanese fleet and the largest factory stern trawler outside the USSR. One feature of particular interest was that the ship was built with an eye on the growing fishery for Alaska pollack in the Bering Sea and her factory plant included machinery for producing about 15 tons of surimi (minced fish) a day.

Commenting on his company's new trawler, Seikichi Fukao, president of Hoko Suisan said: "In addition to our tuna and salmon activities, our company has been increasing its trawling operations in the Atlantic Ocean off West Africa. But we are also aware of the advantages of developing fishing in the nearer Bering Sea. Knowing the conditions in this area, we have come to believe that we can succeed there using a trawler so large that she can work down to the deeper levels, and so well equipped that she can make the best possible use of the fish she catches. Some companies operate a mother ship system or other group system in conjunction with transports. But we prefer a single-ship system."

This forerunner of the giant trawlers now engaged in the Alaska pollack fishery is 103 metres long overall with a moulded breadth of 16.6 m. and depth to main deck of 7.4 m. She has accommodation for a crew of 115.

The factory deck is well-equipped with continuous processing plant consisting of Toyo machinery for conveying, washing, gutting, heading and filleting the catch. A battery of plate freezers has a total capacity of 75 tons a day. The frozen product is held at temperatures down to $-30°C$. in a fish hold with a capacity of 3,288 cu.m. Waste fish and offal is reduced to meal and oil in a De Laval Centrifish plant.

An electrically-powered trawl winch has a pull of 25 tons at a hauling speed of 80 m/min.

The main engine is a Kobe 7UET 45/75C diesel developing 4400 hp at 240 rpm and turning an MAU four-bladed propeller to give a service speed of 12 knots. Auxiliary plant includes three 1000 hp diesel engines each coupled to an 850 kVA alternator.

Haruna Maru
The *Katata Maru* was soon followed by other "super" trawlers designed to work in the Alaska pollack fishery. Among them were the *Haruna Maru* and the *Kongo Maru*, built in 1969 in the Mukaishima yard of the Hitachi Shipbuilding & Engineering Company for Nippon Suisan Kaisha of Tokyo. Designed by the builders, these 4,040 gross ton factory stern trawlers are of flush deck construction with the engine room well aft and the engine exhaust trunked through the posts of the stern gantry. The *Haruna Maru* is 102.26 metres long overall with a moulded breadth of 16 m. and depth to upper deck of 10 m. She has accommodation for a crew of 103.

Her factory deck is equipped throughout with a Konishi conveyor system. Other plant includes a Bibun Kikai washer, three Wakamatsu headers and six Takubo gutting and filleting machines. A Nippon Suisan minced fish plant has an output of 30 tons a day. Freezing is done in a battery of plate freezers with a daily output of 57.7 tons. The fish meal plant is a De Laval Centrifish shipborne unit able to handle 50 tons of raw material a day.

The trawl winch is electrically powered on the Ward Leonard system by a 390 kW Mitsubishi motor and has a 40-ton pull at a hauling speed of 40 m/min.

The main engine is a Hitachi-Burmeister & Wain type 9M42CF single acting two-stroke diesel developing 4400 hp at 248 rpm and turning a four-bladed fixed propeller to give a top speed of 16.5 knots and a service speed of 13.75 knots. Auxiliary plant includes three Mitsui-B. & W. 900 hp diesels each coupled to a 787 kVA alternator.

Shunyo Maru No. 18.
Interesting developments were also taking place around this time at the lower end of the size scale. Built in 1969 by Narazaki Shipbuilding Company of Muroran City for the Kanefuji Fisheries Company of Hakodate, the *Shunyo Maru No. 18* is a wet fish stern trawler of 500 gross tons and is 54.5 metres long overall with a moulded breadth of 9.5 m. and a depth of 4.1. m.

The "Shunyo Maru No. 18", 54.5 metres long, built in 1969.

Her insulated main fish hold has a capacity of 446 cu. m. and there is also a refrigerated hold of 43 cu. m.

A Setozaki 10-ton trawl winch is driven by two Meiden 110 kW electric motors on the Ward Leonard system. Hauling speed is 90 m/min.

The main engine is an Akasaka model UZ63S diesel developing 1600 hp at 280 rpm and turning a Kawasaki three-bladed c.p. propeller to give a top speed of 13.7 knots.

Kaiiun Maru No. 38.
Built in 1969 by Narazaki Shipbuilding Company for the Komatsu Fisheries Company of Iwaki. A wet fish stern trawler of 350 gross tons, the *Kaiiun Maru No. 38* is 50.54 metres long overall with a moulded breadth of 8.7 m. and a depth of 3.9 m.

The "Kaiiun Maru No. 38", 50.54 metres long, built in 1969.

The insulated fish hold has a capacity of 383 cu. m. and there is also a refrigerated hold of 35 cu. m.

The Ebara electrically-powered trawl winch has a pull of 10 tons and a hauling speed of 80 m/min.

The main engine is a Fujii model 6SD37BH diesel developing 1600 hp at 325 rpm and turning a Kamone three-bladed c.p. propeller to give a top speed of nearly 13 knots.

The Netherlands

The main contribution of the Netherlands to the development of the stern trawler has been through several interesting designs of medium-size and small vessels built by Dutch yards for local owners or for export to France, South Africa, Canada and West Germany and other countries.

With cod and related demersal species making up about 70,000 tons of a yearly catch of 320,000 tons the trawler is an important fishing unit in the Dutch fleet. The possibilities of the stern trawler were soon evident to Dutch owners and fishermen. Medium-size ships such as 46-metre long *Rijnmond*, built by N.V. Scheepsbouwerk "De Dageraad" and using a swinging type gantry instead of a ramp on a short trawl deck, were among the early successful stern trawlers. There were several versions of this type of ship and they were introduced into the fleets of two or three countries outside the Netherlands.

The medium-size ramp stern trawler was also built, including the four *Pionier*-class trawlers for

The "Yke", 48.4 metres long, built in 1966.

South Africa and a later factory freezer ship, the *Prima 1*. And in 1971 N.V. Sleephelling of Scheveningen completed the first of four new ships built to a standard design evolved from experience with two earlier ships – the 50-metre long *Cornelius Vrolijk* class built in 1966 and the 61-metre long stern trawler type research ship *Tridens*.

These standard ships have a moulded breadth of 30.2 metres with a depth of main deck of 4.2 m. Each has accommodation for a crew of 19. Plate and tunnel freezers have a total capacity of 27 tons a day. The fish are stored in a 505 cu. m. capacity hold, 235 cu. m. of which is refrigerated.

Each of the first three ships is powered by an Industrie diesel engine developing 2000 hp and turning a Lips c.p. propeller. The fourth ship is powered by a Deutz diesel of 2000 hp.

Yke

Built in 1966 by the Firma S. Seijmonsbergen shipyard in Amsterdam for N.V. Rederij Jaczon of Scheveningen. A wet fish stern trawler of 540 gross tons, the *Yke* is 48.4 metres long overall with a moulded breadth of 8.5 m. and depth to main deck of 4.25 m.

Her two fish holds have a capacity of 132 cu. m. and 260 cu. m. and are cooled to 1°C. using Grenco plant. Waste fish and offal is reduced to meal in a De Laval plant with a capacity of 24 tons of raw material in 24 hours.

The main engine is a Deutz RBV8M545 diesel developing 1200 hp at 380 rpm and turning a Van Voorden propeller in a Hodi nozzle to give a speed of 13 knots.

Cornelis Vrolijk Fzn

Built in 1966 by the N.V. Sleephelling 'Scheveningen' yard for N.V. Cornelis Vrolijk Visserij. A part freezer stern trawler of 606 gross tons, the *Cornelis Vrolijk Fzn* is a shelter deck vessel with engine room and superstructure just aft of amidships, a short trawl deck aft and a fixed gantry over a roller system at the stern.

She is 50 metres long overall with a moulded breadth of 8.52 m. and depth to main deck of 4.2 m. She has accommodation for a crew of 21.

When she entered service the ship was designed to freeze only part of her catch. For this she has two Sabroe plate freezers with a total output of 18 tons a day. Frozen fish are held in a 150 cu.m. capacity hold refrigerated down to $-28°C$. The other hold is for wet fish in ice. It has a capacity of 220 cu. m. and is cooled to 2°C.

An electrically-powered trawl winch is sited immediately aft of the bridge superstructure. It is a Bodewes six-drum machine with a pull of 9.5 tons at a hauling speed of 115 m/min. Each of the two main drums has a capacity of 2,200 m. of steel warp. The winch is driven by a 310 hp electric motor and can be controlled from the wheelhouse.

The main engine is a Deutz RBV8M545 diesel developing 1320 hp at 380 rpm and turning a Van

The "Zeehaan", 49.1 metres long, built in 1966.

Voorden four-bladed propeller through a Lohmann and Stolterfoht reduction gearbox and Vulkan flexible coupling to give a speed of 14.6 knots.

Zeehaan

Built in 1966 by N.V. Scheepsbouwerk "De Dageraad" for N.V. Visserij Maatschappij Batavia of Ijmuiden. A part freezer stern trawler of 559 gross tons, the *Zeehaan* is 49.1 metres long overall with a moulded breadth of 8.5 m. and depth to main deck of 4.3 m. She has accommodation for a crew of 20.

Her fish freezing plant consists of three Jackstone Froster vertical plate machines capable of handling up to 18 tons a day. Frozen fish is stored in a refrigerated hold with a capacity of 160 cu. m. and wet fish is stored in ice in a 260 cu. m. hold.

A four-drum Van de Giessen hydraulic winch has a capacity for 2400 m. of warp on each of its main drums. Hydraulic motors are powered by a 315 hp Deutz diesel engine.

The main engine is a Deutz RBV8M-545 diesel developing 1320 hp at 370 rpm and turning a nozzle-shrouded propeller to give a speed of 13 knots.

The "Clara", 49.84 metres long, built in 1967.

Clara

Built in 1967 by T. van Duijvendijk's Scheepswerf N.V. for N.V. Rederij Jaczon of Scheveningen. A part freezer stern trawler, the *Clara* is 49.84 metres long overall with a moulded breadth of 8.5 m. and depth to main deck of 4.34 m. She has accommodation for a crew of 19.

Her freezing plant consists of three plate freezers with a total capacity of 15 tons a day and frozen fish is stored at $-20°C$. in a 160 cu. m. capacity hold. The wet fish hold is cooled to a temperature of $2°C$., has a capacity of 275 cu.m. and is insulated with polyurethane foam and lined with aluminium.

The main engine is an Industrie diesel developing 1200 hp at 380 rpm and turning a Van Voorden propeller in a Hodi nozzle.

Johanna Maria

Built in 1968 by the T. van Duivendijk yard at Lekkerkerk for N.V. Rederij Jaczon. A part freezer stern trawler, the *Johanna Maria* marked a departure from the up-to-then usual arrangement in Dutch vessels of her type by having her bridge superstructure placed well forward. Her six-barrel Bodewes electrically-powered trawl winch is placed just aft of the bridge superstructure and the warps are taken round either side of the funnel casing aft. The ship can fish with bottom or mid-water trawls and is equipped to freeze her catch or to carry it in ice or in barrels.

The *Johanna Maria* is 52 metres long overall with a moulded breadth of 9.5 m. and depth to main deck of 4.24 m.

A large hold of 332 cu. m. capacity is situated about amidships just forward of the engine room. It is lined with aluminium and insulated with polyurethane foam for the carriage of wet fish in ice. Forward of this is a 131 cu. ft. hold for fish frozen in three Jackstone Froster 20-station vertical plate freezers which have a capacity of 19 tons a day.

The main engine is an Industrie model 8D7HDN diesel developing 1240 hp at 400 rpm and turning a Lips three-bladed c.p. propeller through a Kuypers reduction gear. The propeller is shrouded in Kort nozzle.

Norway

The introduction of the stern trawler in Norway has been a long, uphill struggle against strong prejudices shaped by the coastal nature of the country's huge fishing industry and against government regulations which seem designed to restrict the flow of capital into the industry for larger, higher capacity ships.

The 850 gross ton "Havstrand", built in 1971, is a standard type factory trawler developed by the A.M.Liaaen yard in Aalesund. She is 60 metres long overall.

Since the pioneering vessel *Hekktind* (working for a freezing plant in the Vesteraalen) demonstrated the capabilities of the shelter-deck stern trawler in the early 1960s, Norwegian trawler operators and builders have persevered against the obstacles placed in front of them and have made some extremely useful contributions to the development of stern fishing.

Norwegian developments have been in two main directions and have resulted in two basic vessel types. There is a small, but efficient fleet of factory stern trawlers numbering eight or nine ships; and there is a much larger fleet of medium-size wet fish stern trawlers built by three or four yards to a more or less standard design. The size of these ships is determined by a regulation which permits them to fish, subject to certain controls, within the 12-mile limit and up to four miles from the coast. They have to be of less than 300 gross tons and are ingeniously designed to meet this requirement. The ships are usually owned by trawler companies associated with the freezing plant supplied by the ships. This form of ownership was made possible by a relaxation in the regulations when freezing plant operators succeeded in convincing the government that trawlers were essential to provide regular supplies.

A wet fish ship of 300 tons takes the bulk of her catch within the limits and may bring in from 1,500 to 2,000 tons of cod and other fish a year – heads off and packed in ice in plastic or aluminium boxes. By mid-1971 some 50 medium-size trawlers were in operation or building or on order. But their future and that of the plants they supply was being threatened by a new regulation which may eventually force all trawlers to work outside the 12-mile limit. Existing vessels or those approved before the passing of the regulation have been allowed a phase-out period up to July 1974.

This could stop the expansion of the Norwegian stern trawler fleet, but the yards building the standard-type vessels have received their first export orders and are looking outside Norway to what they hope will be an expanding market in the world's trawler fleets.

When they began to think about factory trawlers, Norwegian owners looked first at the British *Fairtry* vessels but decided that they lacked the capital to finance ships of that size. The first Norwegian factory trawler was the 200 ft. *Longva* completed in 1963. She has been followed by the *Ole Saetremyr* (1966), the *Longva II* (1967), *Gadus I* (1967), *Ottar Birting* (1968), the *Labrador* (1969), *Nordstar* (1969), *Gadus II* (1970), *Havstrand* (1971). In 1971 a 247 ft. long ship was ordered from the Soviknes yard for delivery in 1972.

Speaking in Trondheim in 1969, Norwegian trawler owner Reidar Saetreymyr said that one reason for this slow growth of a factory fleet is that those who had the initial capital and had received permits to build had been stopped when they applied to the only Norwegian bank able to finance fishing craft. Those who had the capital and could finance the ships through other sources were stopped by the permit system.

In 1970 a shipowning company behind the two *Gadus* trawlers, in association with a Canadian con-

The "Roeggen", 47.15 metres long, built in 1965.

cern, was unable to get permission for a three-ship project. The ships are being built in Norway but, when they are delivered in 1972 they will sail under the British flag from a port in the United Kingdom.

Vesttind

With sister ship *Nordtind*, built in 1965 by the Fredriksstad mek. Verksted yard for A/S Havfisk of Melbu in the Vesteraalen. This owning company is associated with the freezing plant company in Melbu which processes about 10,000 tons of cod and other species a year and is the largest single supplier to the Frionor marketing group. The Melbu company helped to pioneer the stern trawler in Norway with the *Hekktind*. In 1971 it had a fleet of five trawlers which supplied more than four-fifths of the fish handled by the freezing plant.

The *Vesttind* is a stern trawler of 296 gross tons with an overall length of 137 ft. 1 in., a moulded breadth of 26 ft. 11 in. and depth to main deck of 20 ft. 8 in. She has accommodation for a crew of 23.

The fish rooms have a capacity of 16,520 cu. ft. and 7,900 cu. ft. is refrigerated down to a temperature of $+20°C$.

Propulsion is by two Caterpillar diesel engines, a type D398TES unit of 800 hp and a type D353TES of 400 hp. Both engines are coupled to a twin input, single output Renk gearbox and drive a Liaaen c.p. propeller to give a speed of 13 knots.

Roeggen

Built in 1965 by Storvik mek. Verksted of Kristiansund North for Olaf Roeggen & Co. to supply the large Findus freezing factory at Hammerfest in northern Norway. A ship of just under 300 gross tons, the *Roeggen* is 47.15 metres long overall with a moulded breadth of 8.4 m. and depth to main deck of 4.35 m. She has accommodation for a crew of 23.

Her fish room has a capacity of 280 cu. m. and can be refrigerated down to a temperature of $-25°C$. by Lemkuhl refrigeration plant.

The main engine is an MWM four-stroke diesel developing 1200 hp at 375 rpm and turning a Hjelset c.p. propeller.

Haaja

Built in 1966 by Fredriksstad mek. Verksted for A/S Hammerfest Havfisk, a company in the Findus group. This ship was designed to operate around Spitzbergen and in the Barents Sea and bring her fish back to the Findus factory in Hammerfest. The *Haaja* is a stern trawler of 465 gross tons with a length overall of 165 ft., a moulded breadth of 29 ft. 6 in. and depth to upper deck of 22 ft. She has accommodation for a crew of 24.

She was designed to bring back her fish frozen or chilled and boxed in ice. Her refrigerated fish room has a capacity of 260 cu. m.

Propulsion is by twin Normo LSMC6 diesels each developing 780 hp at 750 rpm and driving a four-bladed Hjelset c.p. propeller through a Modern Wheel Drive twin input, single output reduction gearbox. The propeller is shrouded in a Kort nozzle.

Ole Saetremyr

Built in 1966 by the A.M. Liaaen yard in Aalesund to a design by Reidar Saetremyr for the Saetremyr Brothers of Maaloy. A factory stern trawler of 499 tons when she was built, the *Old Saetremyr* originally had a length of 50.5 metres long overall with a moulded breadth of 9.6 m. and depth to main deck of 4.1 m.; she had accommodation for a crew of 38; and was equipped to produce frozen and salted fish. She was later lengthened, became a full fillet pro-

The "Haaja", 165 ft. long, built in 1966.

The "Gadus II", 80.27 metres long, built in 1970.

ducer and her hold capacity was increased from 450 to 600 tons.

On deck the ship has two Hydraulik Brattvaag trawl winches.

The main engine is an MaK diesel developing 1300 hp at 340 rpm and turning a Liaaen c.p. propeller to give a speed of 13 knots.

Gadus I

Built in 1967 by Trondheims mek. Verksted for Gadus A/S of Aelesund. A factory stern trawler of 1,530 gross tons, the *Gadus I* is 80 metres long overall with a moulded breadth of 13.3 m.

The *Gadus I* was designed for a high rate of production of semi-finished fillet to be landed for further processing, mainly in the United Kingdom. The unsorted, unskinned fillets were simply boxed as they came from the freezers and then stored in the refrigerated hold.

Described in *Fishing News International* at the time of her first landing at the British port of Hull as one of the most sophisticated and lavishly equipped trawlers afloat, the *Gadus I* cost the equivalent of about £900,000 to build. She was then worked by a crew of only 40 but provision was made in her accommodation for 60 men.

Her fillet cutting lines consist of Baader machines and freezing is done in a battery of Kvaerner horizontal plate frezers. To reduce roll, the ship is fitted with flume stabilisation tanks.

The *Gadus I* is able to carry up to 1,300 tons of frozen fillets in her refrigerated fish holds.

She is powered by four Wartsila high-speed diesel engines, two developing 1000 hp and two 800 hp. They are all connected to a common gearbox and, with their total power, the ship has a speed of about 17 knots. But normally she uses only two 1000 hp engines for propulsion and the two 800 hp units provide auxiliary power supplies. Under this arrangement she has a speed of 14 knots. The engine room can be operated unmanned for long periods.

Gadus II

Built in 1970 by Trondheims mek. Verksted for A/S Gadus of Aalesund. Like her sister ship, the *Gadus II* is designed to operate in the North Atlantic and off northern Norway or in tropical waters to the south. She can use bottom or pelagic trawls.

A factory stern trawler of 1,600 gross tons, the *Gadus II* is 80.27 metres long overall with a moulded breadth of 13.3 m. and depth to upper deck of 8.25 m. She has accommodation for a crew of 60 but normally her complement does not exceed 36.

The main difference between the two ships is in the factory deck. The first ship was designed to produce mainly unsorted, unskinned industrial fillets. The *Gadus II* concentrates on more directly marketable products without necessarily aiming at consumer packs.

Her processing line, which includes three Baader filleting machines, feeds to a battery of Kvaerner horizontal plate freezers with a total output of 50 tons of frozen fillets a day. These are stored in a 1,780 cu.m. capacity refrigerated hold.

The "Ottar Birting", 51.25 metres long, built in 1968.

The propulsion system is similar to that of the *Gadus I*.

Vagakall
Built in 1967 by Trondheims mek. Verksted for A/S Vagafisk of Svolvaer in the Lofoten Islands. The *Vagakall* is the prototype vessel in a class of three ships for this owner, and was the first small trawler to be fitted with flume stabilisation tanks.

A wet fish stern trawler of 278 gross tons, the *Vagakall* is 38.8 metres long overall with a moulded breadth of 9 m. and depth to main deck of 4.05 m. She was designed to fish off the coast of northern Norway and has accommodation for a crew of 17, but is normally operated by 13 men. She delivers her fish boxed in ice to local freezing plants.

Her catch is dropped through a hatch into sorting pens on the working deck. Here a Vega washing machine is installed and two Vega conveyors for transporting the fish to the hold. The hold has a capacity of 28 cu.m. and is cooled to 1°C. by plant which includes a Kvaerner compressor using Freon 22 as the refrigerant.

The vessel uses almost her entire deck length for handling her trawl. Exhausts from the engine room aft are trunked up through funnels placed on either side of the deck. The trawl winch, consisting of two Hydraulik Brattvaag DIA1OU units is mounted further aft, where there are also two Hydraulik A8 gilson winches. The wings of the trawl are hauled right forward beneath the bridge superstructure by means of a combined windlass and winch mounted at the forecastle.

The main engine is a Wichmann model 7ACAT two-stroke diesel developing 1120 hp at 375 rpm and turning a Wichmann three-bladed c.p. propeller to give a speed of 12 knots.

Ottar Birting
Built in 1968 by Aukra Bruk A/S for the Huse-Sporsheim company. This ship was originally to have been a purse seiner but, with the decline in herring fishing, it was decided to complete her as a combination vessel, with stern ramp, bulbous bow and a factory deck for producing frozen fillets and salt fish. Eventually she came into service as a trawler.

A ship of 609.3 gross tons, the *Ottar Birting* is 51.25 metres long overall with a moulded breadth of 9.6 m. and depth to main deck of 5.1 m. She has accommodation for a crew of 36 and is fitted out with a flume stabilisation tank system.

The factory deck has two processing lines – for fillets and for salt fish. The freezing section includes

The factory stern trawler "Labrador", 56 metres long, built in 1969.

The "Nordstar", 75.5 metres long, built in 1969.

a Baader 163 gutting machine, Baader 188 filleter and Baader 47 skinners. Freezing is done in two Kvaerner horizontal plate machines with a total output of 16 tons. The frozen fish hold, situated forward, has a capacity of 300 cu.m. and is refrigerated to a temperature of −25°C. The saltfish hold amidships has a capacity of 350 cu.m.

This ship also uses almost all the length of her upper deck for handling the trawl. The Hydraulik D2A8U four-barrel trawl winch is mounted above the level of the deck just aft of the amidships bridge superstructure. Bridles and the wings of the trawl are taken along the deck through tunnels in the superstructure up to a combined anchor and bridle winch on the foredeck. Two auxiliary barrels are used for hauling the cod ends.

The main engine is an eight-cylinder MWM diesel developing 1650 hp at 375 rpm and turning a Hjelset c.p. propeller to give a trials speed of 14.45 knots.

Labrador
Built in 1969 by A.M. Liaaen mek. Verksted for the Ervik brothers and the Stoylen brothers of Bringsinghaug, Aalesund. This ship follows the design of the successful *Longva* and *Longva II* built by the same yard. A factory stern trawler of 675 gross tons, the *Labrador* is 56 metres long overall with a moulded breadth of 10 m. and depth to upper deck of 6.5 m.

The processing line for large fish consists of a Baader 164 gutting machine, a Baader 99 filleter and two Baader 46 skinners. The line for smaller fish includes a Baader 188 filleting machine and two Baader 47 skinners. Freezing is done by two Kvaerner horizontal plate machines each with an output of 12 tons a day. The two fish holds have a capacity of 687 cu.m. and can carry about 540 tons of frozen fish.

The Hydraulik split winch consists of two identical units each with a main drum capacity of 2,400 metres. The ship is equipped to handle bottom and mid-water trawls.

The main engine is a Deutz model SBV8M 545 diesel developing 1500 hp at 375 rpm and turning a Liaaen c.p. propeller to give a loaded speed of 12.5 knots.

Nordstar
Built in 1969 by Aukra Bruk A.S. for A/S Ibestad Havfiske of Harstad. A factory stern trawler of 1,584 gross tons, the *Nordstar* is 75.5 metres long overall with a moulded breadth of 13 m. and depth to upper deck of 8.18 m. She has accommodation for a crew of 57 in 13 single and 22 double berth cabins.

The trawl deck extends 20 metres forward from the ramp. The Hydraulik Brattvaag split winch is placed in a well-sheltered position beneath the midships gantry.

Three of the R/155 type standard stern trawlers built by A/S Storviks yard to supply fish freezing plants in northern Norway. The ships are 46.5 metres long and are just under 300 gross tons.

Fish emptied from the cod-end pass through a hatchway with hydraulically operated doors down to the processing deck, which has three lines, one for large fish and two for smaller fish. Cutting machinery includes a Baader 164 gutting machine, a Baader 99 filleter for large fish and two Baader 188 filleters for smaller fish. Four Kvaerner horizontal plate freezers can handle up to 32 tons of fish a day. The frozen fillets are stored in a 1,468 cu.m. capacity fish hold refrigerated down to −30°C.

The main engine is an MaK type 6M551-AK diesel developing 2300 hp at 300 rpm and turning a Hjelset c.p. propeller to give a service speed of 13 knots.

Kjolnes

Built in 1970 by A/S Storviks mek. Verksted of Kristiansund North for Norkap Havfiskeselskap A/S of Honningsvaag on the Finnmark coast of northern Norway. This ship is one of the Storvik yard's well-tried R/155 class of standard stern trawler. Ships of her size or very similar include the *Stamsund*, *Myrefisk III*, *Varøy*, *Ballstad*, *Helnes*, *Lofottral III*, *Persfjord* and *Hakøy*. The *Kjolnes* is a wet fish stern trawler with two full length decks, engines aft and fish hold amidships. The bridge structure is placed well forward. She is 46.5 metres long overall and 40 m. long b.p., with a moulded breadth of 9 m. and depth to upper deck of 4.3 m. In some of the ships accommodation is provided for crews of up to 20 but mechanisation of gear handling and the use in several of the ships of gutting machines enables them to be worked efficiently by crews of 13 to 15 men.

Although the hulls are standard, the equipment and machinery can be varied from ship to ship as the owners require. The *Kjolnes* has a Hydraulik Brattvaag three-drum trawl winch placed just aft of the bridge superstructure and this winch has a capacity on the main drum for 1,000 fathoms of three-inch warp. The vessel has sufficient winch and engine power to use pelagic as well as bottom trawls.

Fish are washed, headed and gutted on the working deck and conveyors move it to a 280 cu.m. fish hold. The ships can be equipped for freezing their catches but usually hold it boxed in ice and the fish is seldom more than seven or eight days old when delivered to the freezing plant ashore.

The main engine in the *Kjolnes* is a Wichmann type 8ACAT eight-cylinder diesel developing 1200 hp at 350 rpm and direct coupled to a Wichmann propeller to give a speed of 12.5 knots.

In the R/155 class trawler *Lofottral III*, the main engine is an MWM type TBD 484–8 diesel developing 1500 hp at 375 rpm and turning a Hjelset propeller. The trawler *Varøy* has an MaK model 8M451 diesel developing 1500 hp at 375 rpm and turning a Hjelset c.p. propeller. The *Myrefisk III* has a Deutz model SBV BM545 diesel developing 1200 hp at 380 rpm and turning a Hjelset c.p. propeller.

Nord Rollnes

Built in 1968 by Sterkoder mek. Verksted of Kristiansund North for Ytr Rolloya Fiskarsamvirke of Harstad. A wet fish stern trawler of 299.5 gross tons, the *Nord Rollnes* was the prototype of what has since become this yard's successful class of standard stern trawler. She is 44.5 metres long overall and 38 m. long b.p. with a moulded breadth of 9.16 m. and depth to upper deck of 6.5 m. Accommodation is provided for a crew of up to 20.

The "Andenesfisk III", a standard type stern trawler built by the Sterkoder yard.

At the time of her completion, the *Nord Rollnes* was described in *Fishing News International* as "an extremely well designed vessel, allowing for good living standards for her crew and safe and practical working conditions". The design of the working area was very advanced. From the chute bringing the fish from the trawl deck above, there is a transverse sorting and cutting table. Forward of this is a series of bleeding tanks. Hydraulic ramps to these tanks move the fish forward to a second transverse working table with a washer in the centre. Here the fish are gutted, sent through the washer and then moved to the hold on a Haahjem conveyor.

The vessel has two separate fish holds. There is an upper hold on the working deck forward of the washing and gutting area. This has a capacity of 140 cu.m. The main hold below and forward of this has a capacity of 295 cu.m. Kvaerner refrigeration plant keeps the fish holds cooled to 1°C.

In the *Nord Rollnes* the trawl winch is an Achgelis machine electrically driven by a 240 hp motor which is powered by a 195 kW REM generator driven from the main engine.

This is a Deutz model SBV8M545 diesel developing 1500 hp at 375 rpm and turning a Liaaen c.p. propeller to give a speed on trials of 13 knots.

Another trawler of this class, the *Andenesfisk III*, has a Norwinch hydraulically-powered trawl winch and her main engine is an MaK diesel developing 1500 hp.

The Sterkoder yard late in 1969 completed the first of ten standard-type stern trawlers to supply the Findus factory at Hammerfest. This ship, the *Rairo*, was built for A/S Hammerfest Industrifiske.

She is a wet fish trawler of 298.5 gross tons and is 47 metres long overall with a moulded breadth of 9 m. and depth to main deck of 4.28 m.

The engine room is designed to run unattended for long periods and fish and gear handling is extensively mechanised. Because of these improvements, the ship can be efficiently worked by a crew of only 13 men.

The 300 cu.m. fish hold is cooled by a Finsam ice blowing machine and the catch is kept boxed in ice at a temperature of 0°C.

The main engine is a Wichmann 8ACAT diesel developing 1200 hp at 350 rpm and turning a c.p. propeller in a nozzle.

Bötral–I

Built in 1969 by Kaarbos mek. Verksted of Harstad for Bö Havfiskeselskap on Langøy in the Vesteraalen. This ship is the successful prototype which launched her builders into the series construction of stern trawlers. Other ships in this class include the *Bötral–II* completed in the same year and the *Kaagtind* for Skjervøy Havfiskeselskap in 1970. A third ship for the Bö owners was among the standard trawlers building in the Harstad yard in 1971.

The *Bötral–I* is a wet fish stern trawler of 299 gross tons with a length overall of 37.9 metres, a moulded breadth of 9 m. and depth to main deck of 4.3 m. She has accommodation for a crew of 21 but, as in the other Norwegian-built standard trawlers, this number is considerably reduced by mechanisation aboard.

Deck machinery includes a Kaarbos-Norwinch main trawl winch with a capacity on each of two

The "Kaagtind", a 37.9 metres long standard type stern trawler built by the Kaarbos yard in Harstad.

main drums of 2,200 m. of three-inch warp. Maximum pull with empty drum is 24 tons at 56 m/min. and hauling speed with full drum is 120 m/min. The winch is split and is hydraulically powered from a Framo pump gear take-off of 490 hp from the main engine.

The ship has two fish holds both cooled to 0°C. With the engine room sited about amidships, the main hold is built aft and has a capacity of 280 cu.m. A second hold forward has a capacity of 65 cu.m.

The main engine is a Wichmann model 8ACAT diesel developing 1200 hp at 350 rpm and turning a Wichmann c.p. propeller to give a speed of 12 knots.

Poland

Poland began building her first stern trawler in 1958. At that time her fishing industry was only just venturing out beyond the Baltic and into the North Sea and North Atlantic. The shelter-deck stern trawler has since become one of the most important types of vessel in the Polish fleet and its effective use in distant waters by comprehensive fishing enterprises such as the Dalmor and the Gryf organisations has helped to raise her catch from only 145,000 tons in 1958 to a record 470,000 tons in 1970.

Reporting this rise in catch of 62,600 tons in 1970, the *Polish Maritime News* noted that the Gryf fishing enterprise had fulfilled its plan for the year by 212 per cent. This success was attributed to the introduction in the Gryf fleet of the new type B-29 freezer stern trawlers. In 1970 alone Polish shipyards delivered two B-22 factory trawlers, a B-418 trawler and five B-29 trawlers to the national fishing fleet.

It is exports, however, which have taken up the bulk of Polish fishing vessel production. These are handled through the central ship selling organisation, Centromor. During the past 20 years more than ten countries have bought fishing vessels from Poland, and nine-tenths at least of all these exports have been to the USSR.

Poland's first stern trawler for the Soviet Union was supplied in 1960 and the ship was the B-15 stern trawler *Leskov*. She came from the Gdansk yard which from about 1963 shared production with the Gdynia yard of the later B-26 class developed from the prototype vessel *Kosmos*. Between 1960 and 1970 these two yards delivered 54 stern trawlers of the B-15 and B-26 class to the USSR.

From their experience in the design and large-scale construction of these vessels, the yards have developed a range of series-built shelter deck stern trawlers both for the Polish fleet and for owners in France and the United Kingdom.

Foka

A B-18 class freezer stern trawler built by the Gdynia yard for the ODRA deepsea fishing enter-

A B-15 class standard factory stern trawler operating in the Polish fleet.

The 75.5 metres long "Laskara", built in 1969 and the prototype of the B-29 class stern trawler.

prise at Swinoujscie in 1965. The yard built about 10 of the class for this concern and they included the *Foka, Finwal, Pletwal* and *Orka* (built in 1965) and the *Homar* and *Langusta* (built in 1966).

A ship of 3,090 gross tons, the *Foka* is 87.25 metres long overall with a moulded breadth of 14.14 m. and depth to upper deck of 9.75 m. She has accommodation for a crew of 82 in single and double berth cabins, all fully air-conditioned.

The trawl winch is electrically driven using the Ward Leonard system and has a pull of 12 tons at a hauling speed of 72 m/min.

The factory deck is equipped for heading, gutting, washing, freezing and packing the catch, and can also be fitted out with filleting machines. When the ship is operated in tropical climates, the pounds are filled with chilled seawater which is kept at about $-5°C$. Freezing is done in two tunnel freezers and three plate machines and the total throughput of this plant is about 30 tons a day. There are four holds with a total capacity of 1,680 cu.m. – two for storing frozen fish at $-25°C$. and two which can be temperature regulated between $5°C$. and $-25°C$. Waste meal and offal is reduced to meal in a compact shipborne plant.

The main engine is a Zgoda-Sulzer type 6TAD 48 diesel developing 2250 hp at 225 rpm and turning a c.p. propeller to give a speed of nearly 14 knots.

Laskara

A B-29 class factory or whole fish freezer stern trawler built by the Gdynia shipyard in 1969 for the Gryf deep sea fishing enterprise. Research preceding the building of this prototype of what has become a very successful class of stern trawler included the use of a computer to find the optimum design for efficiency and productivity.

A B-18 stern class trawler, 87.25 metres long, built in 1966.

A B-22 class 88 metre long stern trawler.

The *Laskara* has two continuous decks and a three-tier superstructure. The length of the trawl deck from stern ramp to winch is 36 metres. Two generators are driven from the main engine gearbox – one for the ship's mains and the other for the trawl winch. This machine is powered on the Ward Leonard system, has two drums and has a pull of 12 tons at a hauling speed of 110 m/min.

A ship of 1,885 gross tons, the *Laskara* is 75.5 metres long overall with a moulded breadth of 12.7 m. and depth to upper deck of 8 m. She can be worked by a crew of 58 but has accommodation for 62.

Ships of this class have the capability of working bottom or pelagic trawls in the North, Middle or South Atlantic. They have an endurance of around 60 days and reach grounds 4,000 miles from their home port without refuelling. The trawl deck and the factory deck are highly mechanised, and the ships can be equipped for producing whole fish or fillets.

After being dropped down chutes through a hydraulically opened hatchway in the stern, the catch goes first to two reception tanks with a capacity of 38 cu.m. From there the fish is passed to a "buffer" section consisting of three tanks filled with iced water. By mixing flake ice with the catch, the reception tanks can also be used as chilling tanks. The *Laskara* has two flake ice plants with a total output of 16 tons in 22 hours. A special ice storage hold has a capacity of 10 tons.

A special conveyor system sorts the fish into different size groups. Baader 33 herring filleters are installed for when the ship is catching this species. Freezing of pelagic or demersal fish is done in four Jackstone Froster vertical plate freezers with an output of about 30 tons of frozen blocks a day.

Waste fish and offal are reduced to meal in a plant which can handle 25 tons of raw material a day.

The refrigerated holds for frozen fish have a capacity of 1,058 cu.m. and they are cooled down to $-20°C$.

The main engine is a Fiat-Cegielski type B3012-SS diesel developing 2500 hp at 500 rpm and coupled through a reduction gearbox to a c.p. propeller to give a speed of 14.5 knots.

B-22 class

A factory or whole fish stern trawler of 2,700 gross tons with a length overall of 88 metres, a moulded breadth of 14.5 m. and depth to upper deck of 9.75 m. The ship can accommodate a crew of up to 103 and has an endurance of 90 days.

The *B-22 class* ship can be used for bottom or pelagic trawling. The winch is an electrically powered two-drum unit with a rated pull of 12.5 tons at 110 m/min.

After the cod-end is hoisted on deck, the fish is dropped through chutes into 20 cu.m. capacity bins. From these it passes to one of four machine processing lines. Fillets from these lines (or whole fish) is frozen in two tunnels with a total capacity of 60 tons a day. The frozen products are glazed, packed in cartons and stored in refrigerated holds with a capacity of 1,553 cu.m. A meal plant is installed to process waste fish and offal.

The main engine is a Fiat-Cegielski B3012SS 12-cylinder diesel developing 2500 hp at 500 rpm and turning a c.p. propeller through a reduction gear which reduces the speed at the shaft to 175 rpm.

Kalmar

A B-418 class factory stern trawler built in 1970 by the Gdynia shipyard. Designed for bottom or pelagic trawling, the *Kalmar* is 89 metres long overall with a moulded breadth of 15 m. and depth to upper deck of 9.4 m. She has accommodation for a crew of 72.

Trawl handling gear includes an electrically driven 15-ton pull four-drum main winch and two single-drum auxiliary winches.

The catch in the receiving tanks on the factory deck is held before processing in water cooled to $2°C.$ in four 14 cu.m. tanks. Fish processing lines consist of headers, filleters and skinning machines. Freezing capacity is 38 tons a day in four plate machines and in a tunnel for larger fish. The frozen product is stored in refrigerated holds with a capacity of 2,060 cu.m.

Waste fish and offal is reduced to meal in a plant with a capacity of 25 tons of raw material a day.

The main engine is a Fiat-Cegielski B3012SS diesel developing 2700 hp at 500 rpm and turning a c.p. propeller through a reduction gearbox to give a speed of about 14 knots.

Otter Bank

Built in 1971 by the Gdynia shipyard for Nord Pecheries of Boulogne, France. This ship is the prototype in a series of 13 type B423 wet fish stern trawlers ordered from Poland by French owners for delivery from 1971 to 1973. The *Otter Bank* is 54.25 metres long overall with a moulded breadth of 11 m., and depth to trawl deck of 7.8 m. She has accommodation for a crew of 22.

The eight-drum trawl winch has a pull of 10 tons at an average speed of 120 m/min. The capacity on each of the two main drums is 2,900 m. of 24 mm. dia. warp.

Fish is dropped by chute from the trawl deck aft to the processing section below where it is held in pounds and then sorted, gutted, washed and moved by conveyor to the fish hold forward. This hold has a capacity of 510 cu.m. and is cooled down to −4°C. for the carriage of boxed or bulk stowed fish.

The main engine is a Crepelle type 12PSN-SR diesel developing 2000 hp at 800 rpm and turning an Escher Wyss c.p. propeller at 178 rpm through a reduction gear box to give a speed of 14.3 knots.

South Africa

The South African deepsea trawling industry consists of one large integrated fishing company – Irvin & Johnson Ltd. with its head office and processing base in Cape Town – and two or three smaller concerns operating from Hout Bay, Saldanha Bay and from Walvis Bay in South West Africa. Trawling was one of the early commercial fisheries in Southern Africa and Irvin & Johnson was founded in the early part of this century.

In the years since World War II the major development in Southern African fisheries has been in the exploitation of huge resources of pelagic fish, such as the pilchard, the anchovy and the mackerel.

The catch exceeded two million metric tons in 1969. For many years the demersal catch by deep-sea trawlers has ranged from about 100,000 to 135,000 tons a year. Until the early 1960s this was taken by wet fish side trawlers around 130–150 ft. in length on trips of about one week. More than four-fifths of the demersal catch is made up of hake, which is the predominant bottom species in the area.

The "Otter Bank", first of 13 B-423 class 54.25 metre long trawlers for French owners is launched at the Gdynia yard in 1971.

This rich hake resource has attracted distant water fleets of several other countries to the south-east Atlantic and heavy fishing during the past 12 years led to a decline in the catch rates of the small South African ships. Falling catches and the evidence around them of the efficiency of the modern stern trawlers from Japan, Spain, the USSR and other countries encouraged South African operators to consider this type of ship for their own fleets.

The first locally-owned stern trawlers were delivered in 1964. They were wet fish ships, but a few years later they were followed into service by whole fish and fillet freezers. It was then decided that the requirements of the main markets for Cape hake would be met by freezer trawlers producing a well-prepared, glazed and packed whole fish block at sea. Six freezers were ordered by Irvin & Johnson in 1968 and a further six were ordered early in 1971. Seven of the ships are being built in the United Kingdom and five by South African yards.

Pionier 1.

With sister ships *Pionier 2* and *Pionier 3*, built in 1964 and 1965 by N.V. Ijsselwerf of Rotterdam for Friedman & Rabinowitz (a company in the Kaap-Kunene group) of Cape Town. Following merger arrangements, these ships were later absorbed into the Irvin & Johnson fleet.

A wet fish stern trawler of 577 gross tons, the *Pionier 1* is 45.75 (150 ft.) metres long overall with a breadth of 8.8 m. (28.9 ft.) She has accommodation for a crew of 22.

Her trawl winch is a hydraulically powered Van der Giessen unit driven by a 200 hp motor.

The "Pionier 4", 45.75 metres long, built in 1966.

The fish hold has a capacity of 370 cu.m. (14,000 cu.ft.) and is cooled to a temperature around 33°F.

The main engine is a Deutz RBV6 M 545 diesel developing 900 hp at 380 rpm and turning a Lips c.p. propeller to give a speed of 13 knots.

A fourth ship in this series, the *Pionier 4*, was completed by N.V. Ijsselwerf in 1966 and was fitted out as a freezer trawler. The factory deck has an extensive conveyor system and freezing is done in four Jackstone Froster vertical plate machines. The refrigerated fishroom has a capacity of 305 cu.m.

Hawthorn

Built in 1964 by Hall, Russell & Co. of Aberdeen, Scotland, for Irvin & Johnson Ltd. of Cape Town. A wet fish stern trawler of 589 gross tons, the *Hawthorn* is 140 ft. 6 in. long overall with a moulded

The "Hawthorn", 140 ft. 6 in. long, built in 1964.

breadth of 31 ft. and a depth of 14 ft. 3 in. A sister ship, the *Hibiscus*, was built in 1965.

The ship has two complete decks and the bridge superstructure is placed well forward to give a long clear deck for handling the trawl. The four-barrel electrically driven trawl winch is situated under the boat deck to give maximum weather protection to the operator.

Fish are dropped through a chute aft to the working deck where they are headed and gutted, washed and then moved by conveyor chute in the hold below.

The "Corvina" (sister ship of the "Sea Horse"), 130 ft. long b.p., built in 1965.

The main engine is a W. H. Allen diesel developing 1250 hp and turning a Liaaen c.p. propeller through a Lohmann & Stolterfoht reduction gear. The *Hawthorn* averaged a speed of 13 knots on trials.

Sea Horse

Built in 1964 by Brooke Marine Ltd. of Lowestoft, England, for Amalgamated Fisheries of Hout Bay. A sister ship, the *Corvina*, was built by the same yard in 1965.

A wet fish trawler of 420 gross tons, the *Sea Horse* is 130 ft. long b.p. with a moulded breadth of 30 ft. and a depth of 14 ft.

She has an electrically powered Elliot and Garrood trawl winch. This is installed on the trawl deck abaft the bridge superstructure and is driven by a Laurence Scott 200 hp motor.

The fish room is insulated with foamed-in-place polyurethane and has a capacity of 9,500 cu.ft.

The main engine is a W. H. Allen diesel developing 1100 hp at 550 rpm and turning a Seffle c.p. propeller through a Lohmann & Stolterfoht reduction gear. The *Sea Horse* has a service speed of 10½ knots.

Marlin

In 1967 Brooke Marine completed two larger wet fish trawlers for the same owners. Named the *Marlin* and the *Redfin*, these are ships of 698 gross tons with a length overall of 150 ft., length b.p. of 127 ft., moulded breadth of 32 ft. 6 in. and depth to main deck of 22 ft. 9 in. Each has accommodation for a crew of 18.

The trawl winch is a Clarke Chapman unit electrically powered on the Ward Leonard system comprising a 205 kW generator driven from the main engine gearbox and a 250 hp motor driving the winch.

The fish hold has a capacity of 11,000 cu. ft.

The propulsion system is similar to that in the first two ships, with each of the newer vessels powered by a W. H. Allen 1100 hp diesel engine.

Prima 1

Built in 1966 as a factory and whole fish freezer stern trawler by N.V. Ijsselwerf of Rotterdam for Friedman & Rabinowitz of Cape Town. Like the earlier *Pionier* stern trawlers, this vessel was eventually taken into the fleet of Irvin & Johnson Ltd. Experience in operating her indicated that filleting at sea was not the most economical method of processing her hake catch. The ship was later converted into a whole fish freezer only. Experiments aboard her with buffer stages for the fish and the production

The "Marlin", 150 ft. long, built in 1967.

of a high quality "dressed" whole fish block led to the design of the processing system in the 12 *Protea*-class trawlers built and building for the Irvin & Johnson fleet.

A ship of 1,184 gross tons, the *Prima 1* is 221 ft. long overall with a moulded breadth of 36 ft. 3 in. When operating as a factory trawler, she carried a crew of 62.

The trawl deck is 80 ft. long and the four-drum trawl winch is electrically driven by two independently coupled 180 hp Hansa motors. The winch has an average pull of eight tons on each of its two main drums which take 1,500 fathoms of warp.

When hauled aboard, her catch is dropped through chutes into six chilled seawater tanks which have a total capacity of 30 tons. Like all refrigeration in the ship, the seawater is cooled by Grenco plant. The smaller fish are gutted by a Baader 163 machine. Freezing is done in Jackstone Froster plate machines. Waste fish and offal is reduced to meal in an Atlas Stord packaged plant able to handle 15 tons of raw material a day.

The fish hold is fed by conveyor and can take 425 tons of fish, keeping it at $-30°C$.

Propulsion is by two Deutz type SBV6 M 545 diesels each developing 1000 hp at 380 rpm and turning a single Lips c.p. propeller through a Lohmann & Stolterfoht gearbox. This gearbox has two power take-off shafts each able to transmit 240 bhp at 1500 rpm.

Harvest Sun

Built in 1969 by the Barens Shipbuilding & Engineering Corporation of Durban for Sea Harvest Corporation (Pty.) Ltd. The first large freezer trawler from a South African yard, the 756 gross ton ship is 52.1 metres (170 ft. 11 in.) long overall with a moulded breadth of 10 m. (32 ft. 10 in.) and depth to main deck of 4.3 m. (14 ft. 2 in.). She has accommodation for a crew of 35.

The "Harvest Sun", 52.1 metres long, built in 1969.

Her electrically powered trawl winch is a Brusselle Neptune with a pull of eight tons at a hauling rate of 365 ft./min.

Equipment on the processing deck includes a washer, five conveyors for fish, one for empty trays and four gutting tables. Two tunnel freezers have a daily capacity for 31,680 lb. of fish in three seven-hour charges. Two Jackstone Froster vertical plate freezers are also installed.

The frozen blocks of whole fish, headed and gutted, are stored at −13°F. in a 450 cu.m. capacity hold.

The main engine is an MAN type G8V 30/45AT diesel developing 1325 hp at 375 rpm and turning a Zeise-Liaaen c.p. propeller to give a speed of 11½ knots.

Protea

Built in 1970 by Hall, Russell & Co. of Aberdeen, Scotland, for Irvin & Johnson Ltd. of Cape Town. A whole fish freezer stern trawler of 950 gross tons, the *Protea* is a prototype ship of a series of 12 similar vessels. The first six were ordered in 1968 and orders for six more vessels were placed in 1971. Seven are building or have been completed by the Aberdeen yard and five by yards in Cape Town and Durban. When the last of the 12 trawlers is completed in 1973, this large scale fleet replacement programme will have cost Irvin & Johnson about £10 million.

For this investment they will have some of the most advanced whole fish freezer ships afloat. Following experience with the trawler *Prima 1*, each of the new ships has been designed with two sets of chilled water buffer stage tanks to hold the catch in good condition just after catching and during processing.

The ships produce heads-off whole fish which are frozen in vertical plate freezers, are glazed and then the 25 kilo polythene-wrapped blocks are cartoned. This product is sent direct into the Irvin & Johnson fish distribution network through South Africa.

First ship in series of 12 wholefish freezer stern trawlers, the 200 ft. long "Protea" was built in Scotland in 1970.

The *Protea* is 200 ft. long overall with a moulded breadth of 38 ft. 6 in. She has accommodation for a crew of 44.

The trawl winch is a 350 hp six-drum Robertson unit which is electrically driven by a Laurence Scott motor.

When the catch is dropped through the chute down to the factory deck, it goes first into the tanks of the first buffer stage. From them it moves on to a conveyor system and all trash fish is removed. The good fish goes on through a descaler to two Baader 423 headers and is then gutted. After this it is washed on to an elevator which takes it to the chilled water bleeding tanks of the second buffer stage where it is left for about an hour.

The fish is then graded into four sizes before it is packed into aluminium trays for freezing. This is done in four large Jackstone Froster horizontal plate machines which can handle about 36 tons in 24 hours.

From the freezers, the blocks are taken out of the trays and are glazed, polythene wrapped and cartoned before being sent down to the hold in a pneumatic lowering platform. This hold has a capacity of 18,000 cu. ft. and is cooled to $-20°F$. Grenco of the Netherlands supplied the refrigeration system for each of the *Protea*-class ships.

The main engine is a Ruston 8ATCM diesel developing 1800 hp at 600 rpm and turning a Lips c.p. propeller through a Modern Wheel Drive gearbox to give a speed of 14.5 knots.

Spain

With a yearly catch around 1.5 million metric tons, Spain is the second largest fishing country in Western Europe and her development of the stern trawler during the 1960s has made her one of the world's leading builders and operators of this type of vessel.

Her fishing industry turned to fish freezing on a large scale and then to the stern trawler, which made it possible to accomplish this at sea, just over ten years ago. At the beginning of the 1960s increasing domestic demand began to exceed supplies from traditional areas in the middle and north Atlantic. Hake (merluza) is a popular fish in Spain and her industry was aware that there were abundant resources of this species thousands of miles away in the south-east and south-west Atlantic. But it was unable to reach to these resources with the small side trawlers, pair trawlers and coastal fishing boats which then made up its fleets.

In 1961 a Vigo company called Pescanova SA fitted out two side trawlers with refrigeration plant. It sent one of these ships on the long voyage south to the hake grounds off Southern Africa while the other ship went down the other side of the South Atlantic to the hake grounds of the Patagonian shelf off South America.

Both ships found abundant stocks of the type of fish in demand in Spain and the Southern African fishery was regarded as particularly promising. The first supplies came from refrigerated side trawlers. Pescanova also embarked on an even more ambitious venture when it converted a former passenger liner into the factory mother ship *Galicia* and had ten small stern trawlers built as catcher vessels. The *Galicia* venture fell below expectations and, when Pescanova became associated with a South African company in a shore freezing plant, most of the catcher fleet was placed under South African register to supply this plant.

However, Pescanova had also decided that the side trawler was not the most suitable vessel for taking hake from the depths it was found on the Southern African shelf; nor could it provide the processing and freezing capacity which would be needed to make such a long range operation profitable. The type of vessel required was indicated by the large Soviet and Japanese stern trawlers which were also recent arrivals in the area.

Pescanova, and soon other Spanish companies, decided the distant water South Atlantic fishery was worth developing; that it would be worked by ships which could stay in the area for long periods and would send their catches home, whole frozen in refrigerated carriers; and that the catching ships would be whole fish freezer stern trawlers.

The first such ship was the 1,604 gross ton *Villalba*, built by Astilleros Construcciones and delivered in June 1963 to Pescanova. In December 1961, the Spanish government had enacted a law for the Protection and Renovation of the Fishing Fleet and substantial state support was eventually provided for one of the largest programmes of new trawler construction outside the centrally planned countries.

From 4,000 tons in 1962, Spain is now producing about 180,000 to 200,000 tons of frozen fish a year. Almost all of this is done at sea; the basic product is fish frozen in the round (although there are some fillet trawlers now in service) and hake provides around 80 per cent of the raw material. But massive building resulted in over capacity for grounds whose yield has declined as a result of intensive fishing. In 1970 some trawlers were sold to Cuba, and there has been little state aid available for more hake freezers. As a result, most Spanish trawler construction in 1971 was of ships for export or of Spanish vessels with applications outside whole fish freezing.

Mar Austral

This ship was the first of a class of nine built between 1963 and 1965 and represents one of the early attempts by designers and a large yard to introduce a standard type of stern trawler. Built by Astilleros Construcciones SA for distant water operations in Southern African or South American hake grounds, the *Mar Austral* was the prototype of this yard's ACSA53 and ACSA 53A classes. Other ships built were the *Ribera Gaditana*, *Ribera Andaluza*, *Dionisio Tejero*, *Virgen del Cabo*, *Monteaya*, *Benigna Montenegro* and *Vigo*. The *Mar Austral* was delivered in August 1963 to Pesquerias Oceanicas SA.

She is a whole fish freezer stern trawler of 929.25 gross tons with a length overall of 61.12 metres, a moulded breadth of 9.5 m. and depth to upper deck of 7.4 m. She has accommodation for a crew of 34.

The ship was designed to use the German Rickmers Werft system for shooting, hauling and emptying the trawl, thus introducing West German experience in stern trawling to the Spanish industry. The 250 hp electrically powered trawl winch has four drums and two outer warping drums.

Arranged with engine room amidships, the *Mar Austral* has refrigerated fish holds fore and aft and the bridge superstructure well forward gives a long trawl deck. Her catch is frozen in Grasso air blast

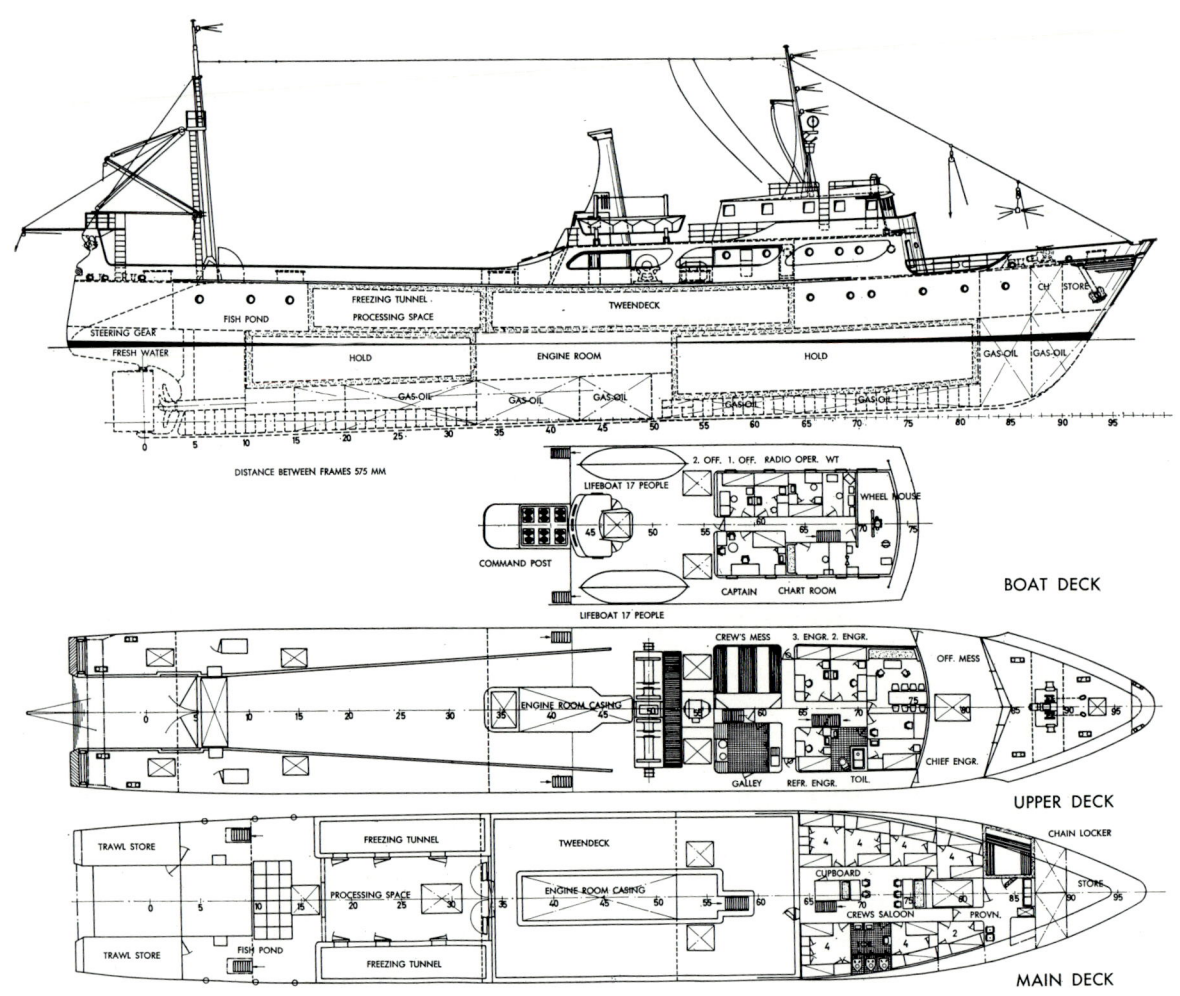

Profile drawing of the 61.12 metre long "Mar Austral", first of a class of nine freezer stern trawlers built between 1963 and 1965.

freezing tunnels with a throughput of 25 tons a day and the holds have a total capacity of 929 cu. m.

The main engine is an MWM type TbRHS 356 AU diesel developing 2000 hp at 500 rpm and turning a fixed propeller at 250 rpm through a Lohmann & Stolterfoht reduction gear to give a service speed of 13.5 knots.

Juan de Urbieta

Built in 1965 by Hijos de J. Barreras of Vigo for Jose Maria Urbieta Vizcay of Huelva for operation off the African coast. A freezer stern trawler of 754 gross tons, the *Juan de Urbieta* is 54.38 metres long overall with a moulded breadth of 10.4 m. and depth to upper deck of 7.4 m. She has accommodation for a crew of 40.

Bridge superstructure and engine room are amidships with fish holds forward and aft. The trawl winch is a Brusselle HMC-111 electrically powered unit with a pull of 10 tons.

The catch is frozen in five Jackstone Froster vertical plate freezers with an output of 25 tons a day. The fish holds have a capacity of 458 cu. m. and are cooled to −25°C.

The diesel-electric propulsion system consists of MWM diesels driving Siemens generators to power two Siemens type MPA 2196 propulsion motors, each of 440 kW, and turning a KaMeWa c.p. propeller through a Renk reduction gear. The propeller speed is 250 rpm to give the ship a speed of 12 knots.

Alvican

Built in 1965 by Astilleros Construcciones SA of Vigo for Lloret y Llinares SA. Following the nine ACSA 53 class ships, this yard developed a larger ACSA 56 class of more than 1,100 gross tons and an operating range of 12,000 miles. The *Alvican*, *Maris Stella* and *Nuevo Odiel* were built in 1965 and in 1966 two ships slightly different – the *Guasa* and the *Biajaiba* – were built for Cuba.

A freezer stern trawler of 1,112 gross tons, the *Alvican* is 64.7 metres long overall with a moulded breadth of 11.4 m. and depth to upper deck of 7.4 m. She has accommodation for a crew of 41.

Ships of this class are equipped with Grasso or Vizcaino blast freezing tunnels with an output of 25 tons a day. The refrigerated holds are cooled to temperature of −25°C. and have a total capacity of 1,200 cu. m.

The main engine is a Barreras-Werkspoor type TMABS-398 diesel developing 1950 hp at 280 rpm and turning a fixed-blade propeller to give a speed of 13.5 knots.

The whole fish freezer trawler "Mar Austral".

Marcelina de Ciriza

Built in Vigo in 1965 by the Factorias Vulcano shipyard of Enrique Lorenzo y Cia for Pesquera Vasco-Gallega SA. This diesel-electric powered ship marked a further significant stage in the rapid evolution of the Spanish stern trawler. At the time of her completion she was by a long way the largest vessel of this type to join the Spanish fleet. A whole fish freezer stern trawler of 2,625 gross tons, the *Marcelina de Ciriza* is 90.87 metres long overall with a moulded breadth of 13.m. and depth to upper deck of 9.2 m. She has accommodation for a crew of 60.

This trawler was actually planned well before the first ships went south for hake. She was launched in 1959 at the Bilbao yard of Astileros de Cadagua and was intended for north-west Atlantic grounds. But her completion was delayed so that she could incorporate new equipment and design features and the hull was towed to the Vigo yard to be fitted out.

Fish passes down a chute to the factory deck where it is hand gutted, and then headed by two Baader 414 machines. After washing it is frozen in plate or tunnel freezers. This freezing plant is made by Sabroe-Moller. The blast freezing tunnels each have an output of 15 tons a day and the two horizontal plate freezers can each handle 10 tons a day. The frozen product is held at −28°C. in fish holds

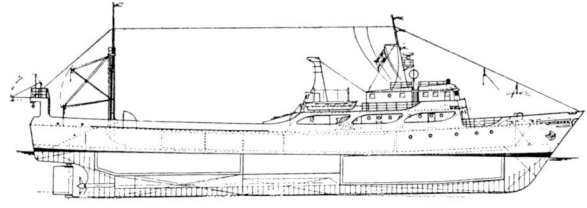

The 64.7 metre long "Alvican" and her sister ships were a development of the smaller "Mar Austral" class.

forward and aft of the engine room and these holds have a total capacity of 2,300 cu. m.

The Yarza trawl winch is a split drum type with a pull of 12 tons at a hauling speed of 120 m/min. Each of the two main drums has a capacity of 2,200 m. of 22 mm dia. steel warp. The winch is electrically powered by two 240 hp Siemens motors.

Propulsion is by two Siemens electric motors of 880 kW each and turning a four-bladed Escher Wyss c.p. propeller through a Renk twin input, single output reduction gear. Power is generated by three Mercedes-Maybach 975 hp diesel engines each driving a Siemens 850 kVA alternator. The ship has a service speed of 14 knots.

Mar del Cabo

Built in 1966 by Astilleros Construcciones of Vigo for Mar SA of Vigo. This was the prototype ship of the yard's ACSA 67-B class. Other ships of the same type followed her for Spanish owners and three were built in 1967 for the United Arab Republic. A whole fish freezer stern trawler of 1,413 gross tons, the *Mar del Cabo* is 75.9 metres long overall with a moulded breadth of 12 m. and depth to upper deck of 7.3 m. She has accommodation for up to 76 crew, and has an operating range of 21,500 miles.

Her catch is frozen in four Sabroe blast freezing tunnels which have a total output of 30 tons a day. The engine room is aft and the superstructure placed well forward gives an extended trawl deck. The fish holds forward of the engine room space are cooled to −25°C. and have a total capacity of 1,700 cu. m.

The trawl winch is a Brusselle HMC 111/4G electrically powered 10-ton unit.

The main engine is a Barreras-Werkspoor type TMABS-398 diesel developing 2000 hp at 398 rpm and turning a fixed-blade propeller to give a speed of 13.5 knots.

Isla Montana Clara

One of four whole fish freezer stern trawlers built in 1966 by the Hijos de J. Barreras yard in Vigo for the Cooperativa del Mar de Lanzarote in the Canary Islands. The other three ships are the *Isla Lanzarote*, *Isla Graciosa* and *Isla Alegranza*. A ship of 494 gross tons, the *Isla Montana Clara* is 49 metres long overall with a moulded breadth of 9.5 m. and depth to upper deck of 7 m. She has accommodation for a crew of 30.

The ship has her engine room aft and the bridge superstructure is well forward to give a long trawl deck. The trawl winch is a Barreras-Brusselle type GMC-111 six-drum machine with a capacity on each of the two main drums of 1,900 m. of 23 mm. dia warp. It is powered by a 180 hp electric motor.

Freezing is done in two Grasso-Iberico blast tunnels with an output of 12 tons in 18 hours. The fish hold has a capacity of 420 cu. m. and is cooled to −25°C.

The main engine is a Barreras-Werkspoor type TMABS-278 diesel developing 1100 hp at 380 rpm and turning a four-bladed fixed propeller to give a speed of about 12.75 knots.

Mar de Vigo

Built in 1967 by Astilleros Construcciones for Mar SA of Vigo. One of the largest stern trawlers to be built in or for a Western European fishing country, this vessel is to the yard's ACSA-95 design for operation in distant waters either as a single unit or as a mother ship to a fleet of smaller vessels. A whole fish freezer stern trawler of 2,938 gross tons, the *Mar de Vigo* is 105 metres long overall with a moulded breadth of 13.8 m. and depth to upper deck of 8.25 m. She has accommodation for a crew of 66.

The trawl deck is 52 metres long from the stern ramp to the bridge superstructure situated far for-

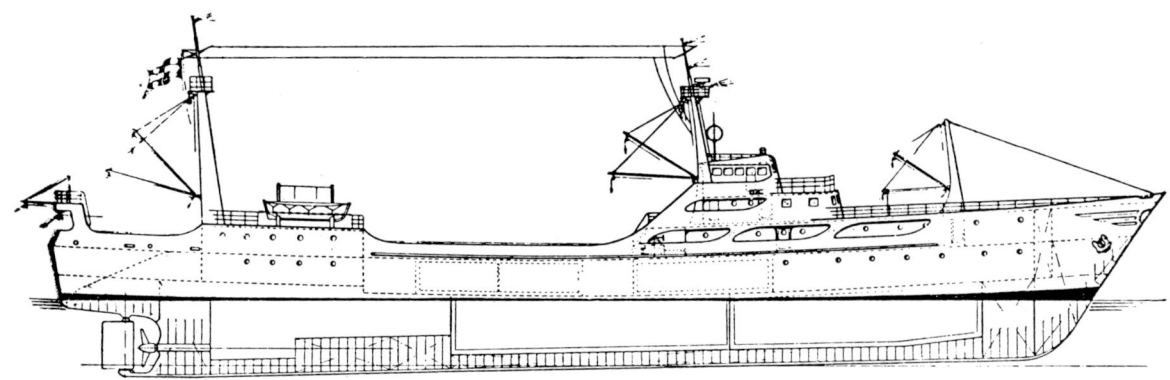

Profile drawing of the "Mar del Cabo", 75.9 metres long, built in 1966.

The "Mar de Vigo", 105 metres long, built in 1967.

ward. The trawl winch is a Brusselle Neptune type KMC-11 four-drum unit with a capacity on each of the two main drums of 2,500 m. of 28 mm. steel warp. It is powered by a 420 hp motor on the Ward Leonard system.

Six blast freezing tunnels equipped with hydraulic loading devices have a total output of 45 tons a day of headless whole frozen fish blocks. These are stored at $-25°C$. in fish holds with a capacity of 3,000 cu. m.

Waste fish and offal is reduced to meal in a Schlotterhose plant with an output of six tons a day. The meal is carried in a hold with a capacity of 350 cu. m.

The *Mar de Vigo* is powered by two Barreras-Werkspoor type TMABS-398 diesel engines each developing 2000 hp at 288 rpm and each turning a fixed blade propeller to give a trials speed of 14.75 knots.

Principado de Asturias

Built in 1967 by Astilleros Construcciones of Vigo for Justo Ojeda Perez. This was the prototype vessel of the yard's ACSA-62 class and was designed for distant water operations off the coast of Southern Africa. A whole fish freezer stern trawler of 1,312 gross tons, the *Principado de Asturias* is 71.8 metres long overall with a moulded breadth of 11.8 m. and depth to upper deck of 7.6 m. She has accommodation for a crew of 63.

The trawl winch is a Barreras-Brusselle type HMC-111 unit with four drums. Capacity of each of the two main drums is 2,500 m. of 25 mm. warp and the winch has a pull of 10 tons at a hauling speed of 120 m/min. The 300 hp electric winch motor is operated on the Ward Leonard system.

The processing deck is equipped with a Baader 423 header, a Waco washing machine and a Baader conveyor system. Six Astra blast freezing tunnels

The "Principado de Asturias", 71.8 metres long, built in 1967.

The "Notos Segundo", 48 metres long, built in 1967.

have a total output of 28 tons of frozen whole fish blocks a day. These frozen blocks are stored at −25°C. in fish holds with a total capacity of 1,480 cu. m. Provision was made in the design of this class for the installation of filleting plant, including horizontal plate freezers.

The main engine is a Naval-Stork-Werkspoor type TMABS-398 diesel developing 2000 hp at 288 rpm and coupled directly to a fixed-blade propeller to give a speed of 12.5 knots.

Notos Segundo
Built in 1967 by Astilleros y Talleros del Noroeste for owners in Huelva. One of a series of four freezer stern trawlers designed by Birkhoff-Iberica SA for operation on the middle Atlantic grounds off Senegal. The ships are named *Notos 2, 3, 4* and *5*.

A ship of 498 gross tons, the *Notos 2* is 48 metres long overall with a moulded breadth of 9.8 m. and depth to upper deck of 7 m. She has accommodation for a crew of 31.

Engines and bridge superstructure are amidships and the fish processing area is along the starboard side of the factory deck. After gutting, heading and washing, the fish are frozen in four Jackstone Froster plate freezers with a total daily output of 20 tons. The fish hold has a capacity of 452 cu.m. and is cooled to −25°C.

The trawl winch is an electrically driven Barreras-Brusselle Neptune GMC-111 four-drum unit with a pull of 12 tons.

The main engine is a Deutz type RBV8M 545 diesel developing 1200 hp at 380 rpm and turning a four-bladed propeller to give a trials speed of 12.86 knots.

Ciclon
Built in 1967 by Hijos de J. Barreras of Vigo for Pesquerias y Secaderos de Bacalao de Espans (PYSBE) of San Sebastian. This ship was one of two prototypes – of 56 metres long b.p. and of 46 m. long b.p. – built by the yard to operate in the cod grounds off Labrador and Newfoundland and to produce saltfish aboard. A stern trawler of 999 gross tons with engine room and bridge superstructure amidships, the *Ciclon* is 67.75 metres long overall with a moulded breadth of 11.4 m. and depth to upper deck of 7.25 m.

The smaller prototype was completed in 1968 and was named the *Sierra Paz*.

For the preparation of her catches for salting, the *Ciclon* is equipped with Baader heading and splitting machines. She has two fish holds, one forward of the engine room with a capacity of 685 cu. m. and one aft with a capacity of 171 cu. m.

The trawl winch is a Brusselle type HMC-111 ten-ton unit powered by a 300 hp electric motor.

The main engine is a Barreras-Werkspoor type TMABS-398 diesel developing 2000 hp at 288 rpm and turning a fixed-blade propeller to give a speed of 14.15 knots.

Castelo
With sister ship *Acorsa*, a pair trawler built in 1968 by the Astilleros Luzuriaga yard at Pasajes San Juan for F. Acebal y Cia and Echevarria y Cia of San Pedro. These ships were the first cod fishing pair trawlers built by the yard and were designed to operate on the grounds off Newfoundland.

A salt fish stern trawler of 575 gross tons, the *Castelo* is 52.5 metres long overall with a moulded breadth of 10.2 m. and depth to upper deck of 7.1 m. She has accommodation for a crew of 32.

The ship has her engine room well aft and a large fish hold forward with a capacity of 600 cu. m. Her trawl winch is electrically powered and has a pull of 10 tons at a hauling speed of 120 m./min.

The main engine is Deutz diesel developing 1600 hp at 300 rpm and coupled directly to a fixed-blade propeller to give a speed of 14 knots.

Gondomar
In 1968 and 1969 the Vigo shipyards Astilleros Construcciones and Hijos de J. Barreras, working in a consortium, built the first large factory trawlers for the Spanish fishing fleet. The ships were designed

The factory stern trawler "Mino", 110 metres long, built in 1969.

by Tecnaco SA and were built for the firm Pescanova SA.

First two completed of the four vessels were the *Gondomar* and the *Gelmirez* and they were built in the Astilleros Construcciones yard. The second two ships, named the *Mino* and the *Sil*, have a slightly larger capacity and were built in the Barreras yard.

A factory stern trawler of 2,506 gross tons, the *Gondomar* is 110 metres long overall with a moulded breadth of 14 m. and depth to upper deck of 8.25 m. She has accommodation for a crew of 87.

The engine room is located aft and immediately forward of it are two fish meal holds, one on either side of an Atlas-Stord meal plant able to process 50 tons of raw material a day. Further forward are the two fish holds which have a total capacity of 3,000 cu. m. and can carry up to 2,000 tons of frozen fillets or whole fish at a temperature of −25°C.

Fish awaiting processing is chilled by flake ice from two plants capable of making 20 tons a day. One of the ship's three processing lines on the factory deck is for fish below 40 cm. long which is sent through a Baader 188 filleting machine, skinning machines and a Baader 510 fillet washing machine. Fish between 40 and 70 cm. is headed and gutted by a Baader 163 machine and is either sent through for freezing whole or is filleted in another 188 machine. Fish larger than 70 cm. is headed by a Baader 423 machine, is hand gutted and then frozen whole.

Freezing is done in two blast tunnels with a capacity of 40 tons a day of whole fish, and in two horizontal plate freezers which can handle 20 tons of fillets a day. The refrigeration plant was supplied by Ramon Vizcaino.

The trawl winch is a Barreras-Brusselle type KMC-11-4 unit of 14 tons pull and driven by a 420 hp motor electrically-power on the Ward Leonard system.

The main engine is a Barreras-Deutz type RBV-13-M350 diesel developing 4000 hp at 430 rpm and turning a fixed-blade propeller through a Lohmann & Stolterfoht 2:1 reduction gear to give a speed of 14 knots.

Mino

With her sister ship *Sil*, built in 1969 for Pescanova SA of Vigo. These ships are basically similar to the *Gondomar* and the *Gelmirez*, described above, but are of 3,000 gross tons with an overall length of 110 metres, moulded breadth of 15.75 m. and depth to upper deck of 9 m.

The refrigerated fish holds have a total capacity of 3,750 cu. m. and there are two fish meal holds with a capacity of 600 cu. m.

As in the other two ships, blast tunnels and plate freezers have a capacity for 60 tons of whole fish and fillets a day.

They are similarly powered by a Deutz diesel engine developing 4000 hp at 430 rpm.

Urquil

Built in 1967 by the Factorias Vulcano yard of Enrique Lorenzo y Cia for Pesquera Vasco-Galleg SL. A sister ship, the *Usurbil*, was built in 1968. A factory and whole fish freezer stern trawler of 1,490

The "Pescafria Cuarto", 106 metres long, built in 1969.

gross tons, the *Urquil* is 74.7 metres long overall with a moulded breadth of 12 m. and depth to upper deck of 7.6 m.

The factory deck is equipped with Baader filleting machines and the ship is able to freeze up to 26 tons of whole fish and fillets a day. Frozen products are stored in a fish hold with a capacity of 1,700 cu. m. and is cooled down to a temperature of $-25°$C.

The Yarza trawl winch is electrically powered and has a pull of 10.35 tons.

The main engine is a Barreras-Deutz RBV8M-358 diesel developing 2000 hp at 300 rpm and turning a fixed-blade propeller to give a service speed of 12.5 knots.

Aracena
Built in 1968 by Hijos de J. Barreras for Pesqueros Asociades del Suratlantico of Cadiz. A factory and whole fish freezer stern trawler of 2,396 gross tons, the *Aracena* is 106 metres long overall with a moulded breadth of 14.5 m. and depth to upper deck of 8.5 m.

Fish is held chilled in buffer tanks which are cooled by flake ice made by two plants each with a daily output of 10 tons. The factory deck is equipped with a Baader 510 fillet washing machine, two Baader 423 headers, a Baader 163 gutting machine, a Baader 188 filleter and Baader 47 skinners. Fish is washed in a Waco 70-500 machine.

The freezing plant supplied by Ramon Vizcaino consists of ten blast tunnels with a total output of 40 tons a day. A Jackstone Froster horizontal plate machine with a capacity of 10 tons a day is installed for the freezing of fillets.

The refrigerated fish holds have a capacity of 3,400 cu. m. and there is a fish meal hold with a capacity of 500 cu. m.

The trawl winch is an electrically-powered Barreras-Brusselle type KMC-11-4 four-barrel unit with a pull of 14 tons at a hauling speed of 120 m./min.

The main engine is a Barreras-Deutz type RBV12M-350 diesel developing 4000 hp at 430 rpm turning a fixed-blade propeller through a reduction gear to give a speed on trials of more than 14 knots.

Pescafria Cuarto
Built in 1969 by Astilleros Construcciones for Pesqueras Rodriguez SA to the design of Tecnaco SA. A factory and whole fish freezer stern trawler of 2,400 gross tons, the *Pescafria Cuarto* is 106 metres long overall with a moulded breadth of 14.5 m. and depth to upper deck of 8.5 m. She has accommodation for a crew of 82. This ship is the same size as the *Aracena* built by the Barreras yard and is similarly equipped and powered.

Meixueiro
With sister ship *Xaxan*, a pair trawler built in 1969 by the Factorias Vulcano shipyard of Enrique Lorenzo y Cia. for J. Molares Alonso of Vigo. A saltfish stern trawler of 557.56 gross tons, the *Meixueiro* is 52.1 metres long overall with a moulded breadth of 10 m. and depth to upper deck of 6.5 m. She has accommodation for a crew of 30.

Each ship is equipped with a Baader 415 heading and a Baader 440 splitting machine. Catches mainly of cod taken in the north-west Atlantic are salted

The "Meixueiro", 52.1 metres long, built in 1969.

The "Playa de Cadiz", 53 metres long, built in 1969.

and then stored in the 500 cu. m. capacity fish hold.

The trawl winch is a Barreras-Brusselle Neptune GMC 111-4 unit powered by a 265 hp electric motor.

The main engine is a Barreras-Deutz type RBV6M-358 diesel developing 1250 hp at 250 rpm directly coupled to a fixed-bladed propeller to give a service speed of 11.2 knots.

Playa de Cadiz
Built in 1969 by Hijos de J. Barreras for Pesquerias Cadiz SA. A freezer stern trawler of 659 gross tons, the *Playa de Cadiz* is 53 metres long overall with a moulded breadth of 10.4 m. and depth to upper deck of 7.1 m.

She can freeze up to 20 tons of fish a day and carries her catch in a 648 cu. m. hold which can be cooled down to $-25°C$.

The main engine is a Barreras-Deutz type RBV6M-358 diesel developing 1250 hp at 250 rpm and turning a four-bladed fixed propeller to give a speed of 13 knots.

Sara-Costas
Built in 1970 by the Factorias Vulcano yard of Enrique Lorenzo y Cia. for Atlantica de Pesca. A factory stern trawler of 1,500 gross tons, the *Sara-Costas* is 76.5 metres long overall with a moulded breadth of 12 m. and depth to upper deck of 8.16 m. She has accommodation for a crew of 50.

Her factory deck is equipped with Baader gutting, heading, washing, filleting and skinning machines and the frozen product is carried in fish holds with a capacity of 1,700 cu. m.

The main engine is a Werkspoor type TMABS-3910 diesel developing 2440 hp at 288 rpm and directly coupled to a four-bladed fixed propeller to give a speed of 13 knots.

The factory trawler "Sara-Costas", 76.5 metres long, built in 1970.

The "Victory" 244 ft. 9 in. long, built in 1965.

United Kingdom

By the end of 1972 more than 50 large and medium-size stern trawlers will be operating out of the United Kingdom ports of Hull, Grimsby, Aberdeen, Fleetwood and North Shields. The growth of this fleet has taken place over the past ten years with a particularly active period of building during 1965, 1966 and 1967 when it seemed that stern trawler development in the UK would concentrate on the ship producing heads-on whole frozen fish. These vessels provide the bulk of some 75,000 tons of sea-frozen fish products landed each year by British trawlers. But in the past three years there have been indications of renewed interest in the fillet-producing trawler, pioneered by the *Fairtry* ships in the 1950s and carried on in the UK during the 1960s mainly by the Ranger Fishing Company of North Shields.

This company placed an order for four more such ships in 1969 and when these are all delivered by 1972 it will have a fleet of nine factory trawlers. The large British United Trawlers group of Hull in 1971 ordered two factory ships to join the *Coriolanus* built some years ago. A Canadian-Norwegian company is having three factory ships built in Aalesund. These ships will operate from a port in England and will be managed by a British trawler owner.

Another significant development is taking place in the replacement of ageing side trawlers with stern trawlers which bring back their catches chilled in ice. One owner had a large wet fish stern trawler built in Poland but later converted her into a freezer.

But the distant water trawler *C.S. Forester*, working out of Hull, has been an outstanding success and her owners have ordered a similar ship. In 1971 three or four ships in what could be a growing fleet of 140 ft. and 150 ft. wet fish stern trawlers entered service and have quickly demonstrated their fishing capacity. In only six months of operation out of Fleetwood, for example, the trawler *Gavina* earned more than £100,000 and her second landing set a new record in the port.

Victory

Built in 1965 by John Lewis & Sons Ltd., Aberdeen, for Northern Trawlers Ltd. of Grimsby (now a company in the British United Trawlers group). A whole fish freezer stern trawler of 1,800 gross tons, the *Victory* is 244 ft. 9 in. long overall with a moulded breadth of 41 ft. and depth to upper deck of 27 ft. 3 in. She has accommodation for a crew of up to 31.

The ship has a long, clear working deck protected by high bulwarks. The trawl winch was specially built for the ship by an associate company, James Robertson & Sons of Fleetwood. It is a four-drum unit with a capacity of 1,500 fathoms of $3\frac{1}{4}$ in. circ. wire rope on each of the two main drums. The winch is driven by a constant current force-ventilated electric motor of 350 hp.

For freezing her catch whole and heads-on after gutting and washing, the *Victory* is equipped with 10 top loading, side unloading vertical contact plate freezers designed for the ship by L. Sterne & Co. These can freeze about 31 tons of fish in 24 hours.

The frozen product, in 100 lb. blocks, is held at

−20°F in fish rooms which can hold more than 500 tons.

The propulsion system is diesel-electric with three English Electric generating plants developing a total of 2700 hp. A 2100 hp propulsion motor turns a single propeller.

Conqueror

Before the end of 1966, Northern Trawlers had taken delivery of two more freezer stern trawlers for its Grimsby-based fleet. The *Conqueror* was built in 1965 by Hall, Russell & Co. of Aberdeen and the *Defiance* by John Lewis & Sons.

A whole fish freezer stern trawler of 1,664 gross tons, the *Conqueror* is 232 ft. 6 in. long with a moulded breadth of 41 ft. and depth to upper deck of 26 ft. 6 in. She has accommodation for a crew of 29, with provision for a larger crew if required.

A feature of the hull form is the bulbous bow below the waterline and the "tulip" shape bow above. This form was developed by the builder to give improved sea keeping.

The trawl winch is an electrically powered Robertson five-drum unit. Clutches and brakes can be remotely controlled from the bridge.

On the factory deck the fish is held in pounds for gutting and washing. It is then conveyed to bins. These hold a full load for each of the 10 vertical plate freezers which have a total capacity of 35 tons a day. The refrigeration plant was supplied by L. Sterne & Co. and operates with Freon 22 as the primary refrigerant and with trichlorethylene as the secondary refrigerant.

On completion of the freezing cycle, the 100 lb. fish blocks are moved on rollers to a pneumatic lift which lowers them into the refrigerated fish hold, which has a capacity of 27,000 cu. ft. and is maintained at a temperature of −20°F.

Each of the two ships is powered by a Mirrlees National type KLSSMR eight-cylinder diesel engine developing 2350 hp at 400 rpm. This engine turns a Stone KaMeWa three-bladed c.p. propeller through a Modern Wheel Drive gear with a reduction ratio of 1.67:1. There are two power take-offs from this gearbox, one driving a 300 kW ship's service generator and the other a 280 kW trawl winch motor generator.

Kirkella

Built in 1965 by Hall, Russell & Co. of Aberdeen for J. Marr & Son of Hull. The development of the whole fish freezer stern trawler was taken a significant step forward in 1962 when J. Marr & Son took delivery of the 240 ft. long diesel-electric powered

The "*Defiance*" (sister ship of the "*Conqueror*"), 232 ft. 6 in. long, built in 1966.

vessel *Junella* from Hall, Russell & Co. This was the first British stern trawler designed to freeze all her catch in the round at sea and to bring it back in the form of frozen blocks to be thawed and filleted ashore.

The success of this pioneer ship gave her owners an early lead in the operation of distant water freezers, and it encouraged them to plan ahead for a fleet of these ships. The second vessel was built by Hall, Russell & Co. in 1964. Named the *Northella*, she is also diesel-electric powered and, with an overall length of 254 ft. 6 in., is larger than the *Junella* and she incorporated other changes in design based on her owners' experience with the first ship.

The *Kirkella*, built by Hall, Russell & Co. the following year is 245 ft. 6 in. long overall with a moulded breadth of 40 ft. 6 in. and depth to upper deck of 26 ft. 6 in.

Her hull form was based on tank tests carried out by the builders and includes a bulbous bow. As in the earlier ships, engine room and bridge superstructure are placed well forward to give a long and clear trawl deck. The trawl winch is an electrically

The "*Northella*", 254 ft. 6 in. long, built in 1964.

The "Kirkella", 245 ft. 6 in. long, built in 1965.

powered Holmes-Lekton type unit with a capacity of 1,500 fathoms of $3\frac{1}{8}$ in. circ. warp on each of the two main drums.

The freezing plant consists of vertical plate freezers by L. Sterne & Co. and can handle 37 tons of fish a day. The frozen product is stored at $-20°F$. in the fish holds amidships and aft which have a capacity for more than 500 tons.

The English Electric diesel-electric propulsion system powers a 2100 hp electric motor which turns a single propeller.

Marbella
Built in 1966 by the Goole Shipbuilding & Repairing Co. of Goole, Yorkshire, for J. Marr & Son of Hull. The *Marbella* is similar in most respects to the *Kirkella*. A sister ship, the *Swanella*, was built by the same yard in 1967.

A whole fish freezer stern trawler of 1,786 gross tons, the *Marbella* is 245 ft. 6 in. long overall with a moulded breadth of 40 ft. 6 in. and depth to upper deck of 26 ft. 6 in. She has accommodation for a crew of 34.

The ship has a Robertson four-drum trawl winch with a capacity of 1,500 fathoms of $3\frac{1}{8}$ in. circ. warp on each of the two main drums. The winch is powered by a 350 hp Laurence Scott electric motor.

Freezing of the catch is done in 14 Stern twelve-station vertical plate freezers with each station able to produce a four-inch thick 90 lb. block of frozen fish in four hours. These are stored at $-20°F$. in a 30,000 cu. ft. capacity hold.

The diesel-electric propulsion system consists of two English Electric 12CVSM diesels driving tandem type main and auxiliary generating sets. Each engine is rated at 1800 hp at 750 rpm. The electric propulsion motor develops 2100 hp at 204 rpm and turns a four-bladed Stone propeller to give a top speed of more than 15 knots.

Criscilla
Built in 1966 by Hall, Russell & Co. of Aberdeen for J. Marr & Son. A smaller ship than the Hull-based Marr freezers, the *Criscilla* was built to operate from the English west coast port of Fleetwood. A whole fish freezer stern trawler of 952 gross tons, she is 185 ft. 6 in. long overall with a moulded breadth of

The diesel-electric powered stern trawler "Marbella", 245 ft. 6 in. long, built in 1966.

36 ft. and depth to upper deck of 23 ft. The ship is worked by a crew of 21 and has accommodation for 23.

The Robertson trawl winch is an electrically powered four-drum unit with a capacity of 1,200 fathoms of 3¼ in. circ. warp on each of the two main drums.

Seven Sterne vertical plate freezers have an output of 20 tons of frozen blocks of whole fish a day. The frozen product is stored at −20°F. in a hold with a capacity for 300 tons.

The main engine is a Mirrlees National type KSSMR 7 diesel developing 1680 hp at 400 rpm and turning a Liaaen four-bladed c.p. propeller through a Modern Wheel Drive reduction gear to give a top speed of more than 13.5 knots.

Southella
Built in 1969 by Hall, Russell & Co. of Aberdeen for J. Marr & Son. This ship was developed from the

The "Criscilla", 185 ft. 6 in. long, built in 1966.

smaller *Criscilla* and differs considerably from the earlier diesel-electric powered trawlers built for the Marr fleet between 1962 and 1967. A whole fish freezer stern trawler of 1,144 gross tons, the *Southella* is 246 ft. long overall with a moulded breadth of 41 ft. 8 in. and depth to main deck of 26 ft. 7 in. She has accommodation for a crew of 26.

Early in 1972 J. Marr & Son had three similar ships under construction in British yards.

The six-drum Robertson trawl winch is electrically powered by a Laurence Scott motor on the Ward Leonard system. The two main drums each have a capacity of 1,350 fathoms of 3¼ in. circ. steel warp.

Eight Jackstone Froster 20-station vertical plate freezers have an output of 50 tons of frozen whole fish blocks a day. These are stored in a fish hold with a capacity of 31,000 cu. ft.

The "Southella", 246 ft. long, built in 1969.

The main engine is a Mirrlees National diesel developing 2880 hp at 450 rpm and turning a Lips c.p. propeller through a Modern Wheel Drive reduction gear to give a top speed of 16.5 knots.

Ross Intrepid
Built in 1965 as the *Cape Kennedy* by Cochrane & Sons of Selby, Yorkshire, for Hudson Bros Trawlers of Hull. Then a member of the Ross group, this company (with Ross Trawlers) is now a member of the British United Trawlers group formed in 1969 by the merger of the fleets of Ross and Associated Fisheries. The *Ross Intrepid* is a sister ship of the *Ross Valiant* built for Ross Trawlers in 1964 by the same yard.

A whole fish freezer stern trawler of 1,156 gross tons, the *Ross Intrepid* is 227 ft. long overall with a moulded breadth of 36 ft. and depth to upper deck of 24 ft. 6 in. She has accommodation for a crew of 29.

The trawl winch is a four-drum Holmes Lektron unit powered by a 300 hp electric motor. The winch

The "Ross Valiant", 227 ft. long, built in 1964.

The "Ross Vanguard", 234 ft. long, first of four sister ships built between 1966 and 1970.

has a capacity of 1,500 fathoms of $3\frac{1}{8}$ in, circ. warp on each of its two main drums.

Freezing is done in 10 Jackstone Froster vertical plate machines which have an output of more than 30 tons a day. The frozen product is stored at $-20°F$. in a fish hold with a capacity for more than 400 tons of whole fish frozen in 100 lb. blocks.

The diesel-electric propulsion system consists of three Mirrlees National diesel engines developing 925 hp at 700 rpm and driving three General Electric 375 kW, 330 v. d.c. generators. The propulsion motor develops 1950 hp at 175 rpm and turns a Stone fixed-blade propeller.

The factory trawler "Ranger Ajax", 171 ft. long, built in 1965.

Ross Vanguard
Built in 1966 by Cochrane & Sons of Selby for Ross Trawlers. This ship is one of four whole fish freezer stern trawlers built by the Cochrane yard between 1966 and 1970 and now operated by companies in the British United Trawlers group. The *Ross Illustrious* was built in 1966, the *Ross Implacable* in 1968 and the *Invincible* in 1970.

A ship of 1,488 gross tons, the *Ross Vanguard* is 234 ft. long overall with a moulded breadth of 39 ft. 6 in. and depth to upper deck of 26 ft. She has accommodation for a crew of 28.

The trawl is a Holmes Lektron five-drum unit powered by a Laurence Scott 300 hp electric motor and with a capacity of 1,500 fathoms of warp on each of the two main barrels.

Refrigeration is by Sterne compressors and the catch is frozen in 12 Jackstone Froster vertical plate machines with an output of about 30 tons a day. Two fish holds, one forward and one aft of the engine room have a total capacity of 30,500 cu. ft.

The main engine is a Ruston type 9ATCM diesel developing 2160 hp at 520 rpm and turning a Stone KaMeWa four-bladed c.p. propeller through a Wiseman reduction gear to give a trials speed of 14.5 knots.

Ranger Ajax
Built in 1965 by Brooke Marine of Lowestoft for the Ranger Fishing Company of North Shields. This

ship was the first of a class of three small factory stern trawlers. The other two ships, the *Ranger Apollo* and *Ranger Aurora*, were built in 1966. While trawler owners in Hull and Grimsby were developing the whole fish freezer, the Ranger company (a subsidiary of the P & O shipping group) decided to venture into ships able to produce quality fillets at sea.

The company encountered considerable initial technical and marketing problems, but eventually built up a factory trawler operation. In 1969 and 1970 it bought two factory trawlers second-hand from West German owners, naming them *Ranger Boreas* and *Ranger Briseis*. In 1969 it placed an order worth £3.2 million for four new factory trawlers and the first of these, the *Ranger Cadmus*, was delivered in 1971.

A ship of 779 gross tons, the *Ranger Ajax* is 171 ft. long overall with a moulded breadth of 32 ft. She has accommodation for a crew of 23.

Machine processing plant on her factory deck includes Baader heading machines, a Baader 188 filleter and Baader 46 and 47 skinners. Freezing of the fillets is done in Jackstone Froster horizontal plate machines. The refrigerated fish hold has a capacity of 13,000 cu. ft.

The main engine is an English Electric 12CVSM diesel developing 1338 hp at 600 rpm and turning a Hindmarch/Berg c.p. propeller (in a Kort nozzle) at 250 rpm through a Modern Wheel Drive reduction gear to give a speed on trials of 11.8 knots.

Arctic Freebooter

Built in 1966 by the Goole Shipbuilding & Engineering Co. for the Boyd Line of Hull. A whole fish freezer stern trawler of 1,633 gross tons, the *Arctic Freebooter* is 242 ft. 7 in. long overall with a moulded breadth of 41 ft. and depth to upper deck of 26 ft. She has accommodation for a crew of 26.

The trawl winch is a Holmes Lektron electrically powered four-drum unit with a capacity on each of the two main drums of 1,500 fathoms of 3¼ in. warp.

The catch is frozen in 10 twelve-station Jackstone Froster vertical plate freezers (with bottom unloading) with a total output of about 40 tons a day. The refrigerated fish hold has a capacity of 28,250 cu. ft.

The main engine is a Mirrlees type ALSSM6 Monarch diesel developing 2380 hp at 275 rpm and turning a Liaaen c.p. propeller through a Modern Wheel Drive 1:1 gearbox from which power take-offs drive generators for ship's mains and the trawl winch motor. The ship has a top speed of more than 15 knots.

The "Arctic Freebooter", 242 ft. 7 in. long, built in 1966.

Sir Fred Parkes

With sister ship, the *Lady Parkes*, built in 1966 by Hall, Russell & Co. of Aberdeen for Boston Deep Sea Fisheries of Hull. These two ships have the builder's tulip form bulbous bow and are also fitted with flume passive water stabilisation tanks.

A whole fish freezer stern trawler of 1,737 gross tons, the *Sir Fred Parkes* is 240 ft. 3 in. long overall with a moulded breadth of 41 ft. and depth to upper deck of 26 ft. 6 in.

When she entered service the *Sir Fred Parkes* was equipped with a Baader machine processing line to fillet part of her catch. But this was later removed and she is now used only for whole fish freezing. Her freezing plant consists of 12 Jackston Froster twelve-station vertical plate machines and her fish hold has a capacity of 27,000 cu. ft.

The trawl winch is a Brusselle Neptune type KMC 2 four-drum unit with a pull of 15 tons and a hauling speed of 310 ft./min. The winch is powered by a Laurence Scott 350 hp electric motor.

The main engine is a Mirrlees National KLSSMR diesel developing 2350 hp at 400 rpm and turning a Stone KaMeWa three-bladed c.p. propeller through a Modern Wheel Drive 1.67:1 reduction gear.

Othello

Built in 1966 on the Clyde by Yarrow & Co. for Hellyer Bros. of Hull (now a member of the British United Trawlers group). The first British freezer stern trawler to be built with engine room aft and with engine exhausts trunked through two funnels

The "Lady Parkes" (sister ship of the "Sir Fred Parkes"), 240 ft. 3 in. long, built in 1966.

on either side of the trawl deck. The *Cassio* and *Orsino*, two sister ships built by the same yard in 1966 and 1967, were also whole fish freezers, but a fourth ship of similar dimensions and design – the *Coriolanus* – is a factory trawler and has been operated with such success from the port of Hull that British United Trawlers have now placed an order for two more factory trawlers.

The *Othello* was badly damaged by fire while she was off the Norwegian coast in 1969. Much of her original equipment was destroyed and was replaced when she was repaired.

A ship of 1,570 gross tons, the *Othello* is 224 ft. long overall with a moulded breadth of 39 ft. and depth to upper deck of 25 ft.

The trawl deck is 85 ft. long from the top of ramp roller to the five-drum Robertson winch placed just aft of the bridge superstructure. This winch is powered by a 350 hp electric motor and each of its two main drums has a capacity of 1,500 fathoms of $3\frac{1}{4}$ in. circ. warp.

In the *Othello* when she came into service and in her two whole fish freezer sister ships the factory deck was laid out for conversion for filleting if this

The 224 ft. long "Othello", first of a class of four ships built in 1966 and 1967.

was required. Freezing is done in 10 Sterne vertical plate freezers with an output of nearly 30 tons a day and the blocks are stored at −20°F. in two refrigerated holds with a total capacity of 27,000 cu. ft.

The factory trawler *Coriolanus* was designed to maintain a catch rate of about 37 tons a day when on the grounds. She is equipped with Baader gutting machines. The fish are washed in a holding stage before filleting in a Baader 99 and two Baader 188 machines. The Baader 188 filleters are fitted with a device for removing pinbones. This, together with other labour saving equipment, enables the ship and factory to be worked by a crew of only 37 men. Freezing is done in two Jackstone Froster eleven-station horizontal plate machines with an output of 24 tons a day.

The main engine in each of the four *Othello*-class trawlers is a Mirrlees National type KLSSMR8 diesel developing 2350 hp at 400 rpm and turning a Stone KaMeWa three-bladed c.p. propeller through a Modern Wheel Drive reduction gear.

St. Jason

Built in 1967 by the Clyde Shipyard of Ferguson Brothers (Port Glasgow) Ltd. for Thomas Hamling Ltd. of Hull. In 1964 this yard built the *St. Finbarr* for the same owners. She was a new type of design of whole fish trawler in that an attempt was made to provide similar capacity to ships then built or building in a smaller hull. The *St. Finbarr* was operated successfully in north-west Atlantic waters but was badly damaged by fire in December 1966 and sank while being towed to Newfoundland. Before this, however, her owners had decided that her results

The 224 ft. long factory stern trawler "Coriolanus".

were sufficiently encouraging to continue and improve her design in further ships. The *St. Jason* was followed into service in 1967 by her sister ships *St. Jasper* and *St. Jerome*, built by the same yard.

A whole fish freezer stern trawler of 1,137 gross tons, the *St. Jason* is 231 ft. long overall with a moulded breadth of 39 ft. and depth to upper deck of 24 ft. 6 in. She has accommodation for a crew of 31.

When the cod end is hauled up the ramp, it is discharged through a hydraulically operated Cargo-speed hatch to the factory deck below and the fish are assisted by water jets to slide down an internal

The 231 ft. "St. Jason", first of a class of three wholefish freezer trawlers.

The 212 ft. long, "Boston York", built in Poland in 1968.

Boston York

Built in 1968 by the Gdynia Shipyard in Poland for Boston Deep Sea Fisheries of Hull. This was one of four ships built in 1968 by this Polish yard for two Hull trawler owners. The first ship completed was the *Boston Lincoln* which came into service as a wet fish stern trawler. But Boston Deep Sea Fisheries decided after she had been in operation for about 18 months that she was too large to operate as a wet fish ship and she was taken out of service, lengthened by 25 ft. 7 in. and fitted out as a whole fish freezer.

Two other ships, the *Arctic Raider* and the *Arctic Privateer*, were delivered as whole fish freezers to the Boyd Line.

A whole fish freezer stern trawler of 846 gross tons, the *Boston York* is 212 ft. long overall with a moulded breadth of 38 ft. 4 in.

Her electrically powered trawl winch is a Gdansk shipyard unit with two main drums and an offset auxiliary drum.

Freezing of the catch is done in five Jackstone Froster vertical plate machines with an output of about 30 tons a day. The fish holds have a total capacity of 21,200 cu. ft.

The main engine is a Mirrlees National type KLSSMR8 series II diesel developing 2500 hp at 400 rpm and turning a Liaaen c.p. propeller through an A.G. Weser 2:1 reduction gear to give a top speed of more than 15 knots.

ramp to a transverse gutting table. Freezing is done in four Jackstone Froster 20-station vertical plate freezers and the frozen blocks are stored in refrigerated fish holds with a capacity of 32,000 cu. ft.

The trawl winch is a hydraulically powered four-drum unit manufactured by the Norwegian firm Hydraulik Brattvaag; it has a capacity on each of the two main drums of 1,200 fathoms of $3\frac{1}{4}$ in. circ. wire warp.

The main engine is a British Polar type M66T diesel developing 1920 hp at 225 rpm and directly coupled to a Liaaen four-bladed c.p. propeller.

The "Arctic Privateer", one of two ships built in Poland in for the Boyd Line of Hull.

C.S. Forester

Built in 1969 by Charles D. Holmes & Co. of Beverley, Yorkshire, for Newington Trawlers of Hull. This ship was ordered by her owners as a wet fish stern trawler for operation in distant waters. She has been a very successful ship and has earned more than £200,000 for her owners in each of her first two years of operation. Newington Trawlers have a second similar ship on order.

The *C.S. Forester* is 185 ft. long overall with a moulded breadth of 36 ft. and depth to upper deck of 24 ft.

Her trawl winch is a Holmes Lektron four-drum unit powered by a 300 hp Laurence Scott electric motor. It has a capacity on each of the two main drums of 1,200 fathoms of 3¼ in. circ. warp.

This ship was the first British deepsea trawler to install a Type 28 Shetland gutting machine. Her catch, after gutting and washing, is stored in ice in an insulated fish room with a capacity of 16,500 cu. ft. Cooling grids in this fish room maintain a temperature of 0°C.

The main engine is a Stork-Werkspoor type TMABF 398 diesel developing 1950 hp at 288 rpm and turning a Stone KaMeWa c.p. propeller to give a speed of 14 knots.

The wet fish stern trawler "C.S. Forester", 185 ft. long, built in 1969.

Ben Lui

Built in 1971 John Lewis & Sons for Richard Irvin & Sons of Aberdeen. This was the first shelter deck stern trawler to operate from Scotland's largest fishing port. Two more stern trawlers for the same owners, each 153 ft. long, have been ordered from a French yard and will be delivered in 1972.

A wet fish stern trawler of 650 gross tons, the *Ben Lui* is 160 ft. (48.8 metres) long overall with a moulded breadth of 33 ft. She has accommodation for a crew of 19.

The ship was the first new British trawler to come into service already fitted with two Type 28 Shetland gutting machines linked to a conveyor system. She carries her fish boxed or shelved in ice in a 13,000 cu. ft. capacity fish room situated slightly forward of amidships.

The main engine is a British Polar type SF112 VS-C diesel developing 1650 hp at 750 rpm and turning a single propeller through a Modern Wheel Drive reduction gear to give a speed of 13.5 knots.

Gavina

Built in 1971 by the Small Ship Division of the Swan Hunter Group for J. Marr & Son. This ship is the first of five wet fish stern trawlers designed to replace her owners' 140 ft. class of side trawler. She operates from the port of Fleetwood.

The *Gavina* is 151 ft. 3 in. (46.12 metres) long overall with a moulded breadth of 32 ft. and depth to upper deck of 20 ft. She has accommodation for a crew of 16.

Her trawl winch is a Robertson three-drum unit with a capacity on each of the two main drums of 1,350 fathoms of 3¼ in. circ. warp. The winch is powered by a 300 hp Laurence Scott electric motor.

Her fish room is aft of the engine room amidships and has a capacity of 12,400 cu. ft.

The main engine is an English Electric type 12CVSM diesel developing 1900 hp at 750 rpm and turning a Liaaen c.p. propeller through a Liaaen reduction gear.

Boston Beverley

Built in 1971 by Richard Dunston (Hessle) Ltd. for Boston Deep Sea Fisheries. A sister ship, the *Boston Blenheim*, was also completed in 1971.

A wet fish stern trawler operating in distant waters from Grimsby, the *Boston Beverley* is 149 ft. long overall with a moulded breadth of 33 ft. and depth to upper deck of 22 ft. 9 in. She is worked by a crew of 15 men.

A British trawler of this size would normally require a crew of about 20. But the use of two Shetland Type 28 gutting machines dispenses with two crew; a saving of another two is achieved through automation in the engine room, and the vessel has no galley boy.

The *Boston Beverley* is designed to bring her

The wet fish stern trawler "Gavina", 151 ft. 3 in. long, built in 1971.

catch back chilled in ice in plastic boxes in a 10,500 cu. ft. capacity fish room.

The main engine is an English Electric 12CVSM diesel developing 1950 hp at 750 rpm and turning a three-bladed Stone/Seffle c.p. propeller through a Modern Wheel Drive 3:1 reduction gear to give a speed on trials of 13½ knots.

Ranger Cadmus
Built in 1971 by Brooke Marine of Lowestoft for the Ranger Fishing Company of North Shields. The first of four ships for delivery in 1971 and 1972. The other ships are the *Ranger Calliope*, *Ranger Callisto* and *Ranger Castor*.

A factory stern trawler of 1,106 gross tons, the

The "Boston Beverley", one of two 149 ft. wet fish trawlers built in 1971.

The "Ranger Cadmus", 216 ft. 9 in. long, first of four factory stern trawlers built in 1971 and 1972. For profile and general arrangement plan, see page 119.

Ranger Cadmus is 216 ft. 9 in. (66.08 metres) long overall with a moulded breadth of 40 ft. and depth to upper deck of 25 ft. 6 in. She has accommodation for a crew of 50.

The ship is designed to work bottom and midwater trawls. Her trawl winch is a six-drum unit made by Clarke Chapman & Co. and powered by a 300 hp Laurence Scott electric motor. Each of the two main drums has a capacity of 1,200 fathoms of $3\frac{1}{4}$ in. circ. warp, while the four auxiliary drums can each take 250 fathoms.

The catch, after gutting by hand or by a Shetland Type 28 machine, is washed and sent through three white fish and/or one red fish filleting lines. These are equipped with Baader machinery, including one type 412 header, two type 421 headers, one type 99 filleter, two type 188 filleters, two type 46 skinners, three type 47 skinners and one type 150 filleter/header for red fish.

Freezing of the fillets is done in three APV Clarke-Built horizontal plate machines with a total throughput of 20 tons a day. The frozen fillet blocks are stored at $-20°F$. in a fish hold with a capacity of 21,000 cu. ft.

Waste fish and offal are reduced to meal in an Atlas Stord plant capable of handling 25 tons of raw material a day.

The main engine is an English Electric type 16RK3CM diesel developing 2600 hp at 750 rpm and turning an Escher Wyss four-bladed c.p. propeller in a Kort nozzle through a Lohmann & Stolterfoht 3.5:1 reduction gear.

USSR

The use of the large shelter deck whole fish freezer or factory stern trawler by the fishing industry of the USSR began with the introduction into its deepsea fleets of 24 *Pushkin*-class ships built between 1954 and 1956 by Kieler Howaldtswerke of West Germany. These ships of some 2,480 gross tons with a length overall of 85.5 metres were based closely on the design of the British *Fairtry* factory trawlers, whose introduction had coincided with the decision of the Soviet government to boost the country's fish production by extending the catching effort far out into distant waters.

Under the direction of Minister Alexander Ishkov (still in this post in 1972), the Soviet Ministry of Fisheries sensed the huge potential of the processing stern trawler well before the industries and governments of many other major fishing countries. The USSR had been persuaded by Mr. Ishkov and others in its fishery organisations that a desire to raise the dietary standards of the Soviet people might be accomplished faster and at less cost by joining the hunt on the world's oceans than by investing heavily in livestock projects on the land. The result was the

USSR-built stern trawlers on show at the Leningrad fishing exhibition in 1968.

incorporation in development plans of funds necessary to fit out distant water fleets with the latest and best ships available.

When the first of these ships came into service, the industry had already been operating an elaborate investigation service which had sent scout and test fishing ships thousands of miles to probe possible new fishing areas. By today's standards the *Pushkin* trawlers – with a crew of 102 and a frozen product capacity in two blast freezers of only 20 tons a day – were crude ships and the larger *Mayakovski* trawlers of 3,170 tons with a capacity of 30 tons a day (introduced in 1958) were not much better.

But the areas they went to fish had been well-surveyed and some of the grounds – such as those in the south-east and south-west Atlantic – had not been heavily fished until then. Many of the ships achieved remarkably high catch rates and the gamble of series building from unproved prototypes appeared to have been justified. From 2.5 million metric tons in 1954, the Soviet catch has increased to around seven million tons. The latest Five-year Plan requires a catch of about nine million tons by 1975.

Much of this rise has come through the operation of stern trawlers – the large BMRT's familiar now in most parts of the world. While yards in the USSR turned out the *Mayakovski* ships, Poland became a supplier with her B-15 class ships pre-

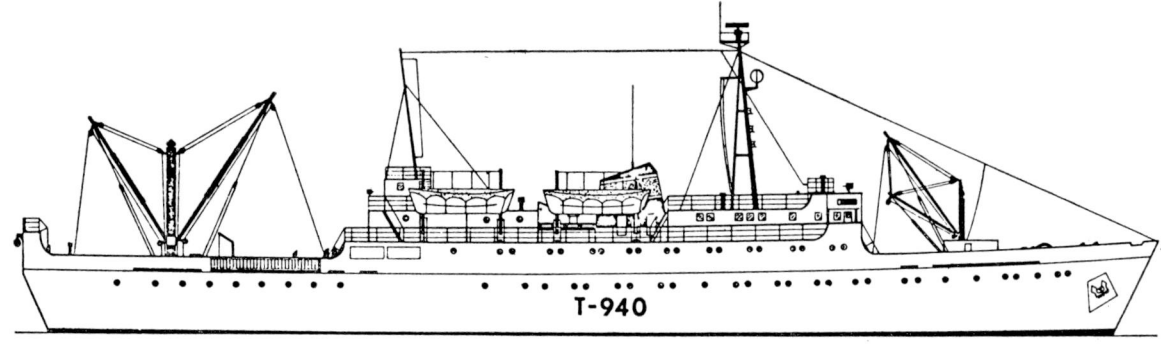

Profile drawing of the USSR-built "Mayakovski" class stern trawler.

ceded in 1960 by the prototype trawler *Leskov* and in 1963 with the *Kosmos* class B-26 ships. Altogether 54 of these B-15 and B-26 trawlers had been built for the USSR by 1971.

Experience of operating *Pushkin* and *Mayakovski* trawlers indicated the need for a ship specially designed for fishing in tropical waters. The East German yards met the requirement with their *Tropik* class ships. Of 2,435 gross tons and 79 metres long, the *Tropik* trawler was designed to hold its fish in tanks chilled by flake ice produced aboard so that it did not deteriorate before processing. The ship could be equipped for producing whole frozen fish or fillets. Freezing plant has an output of about 30 tons a day and the crew requirement had been brought below 80.

A total of 86 *Tropik* trawlers were built before a new, and much improved, *Atlantik* class of 2,650 gross tons was introduced. The Soviet industry was sufficiently impressed by the performance of the prototype to place an order for 107 ships. These have been built since 1966 on an efficient production line system in the VEB Volkswerft yard in Stralsund where up to 16 ships have been in various stages of construction at the same time. They have gone through three classes since 1966 and the latest is the new *Super*-Atlantik III class (see East Germany).

Other stern trawlers have been built in smaller numbers in Denmark, the Netherlands and France. They have all helped to give the USSR a stern trawler fleet which must now number well over 500 large shelter deck vessels. But we are unlikely to see a return of the days of the massive orders for series built ships.

While the USSR was building up production, other fishing countries had also reached out to the remoter areas. The large, cumbersome ships designed to work anywhere the fishing was promising must have found it hard to compete for dwindling stocks with the later much more sophisticated vessels brought out by Japan, West Germany, Spain, the United Kingdom and other countries. The later *Atlantiks* and Polish vessels such as the B-29 class *Laskara* compare well with the latest trawlers joining Japanese and Western European fleets. But, while most fishing countries had moved cautiously and had been left with few of the pioneer ships (the *Fairtrys*, for example, were withdrawn by their British owners about three years ago when it was decided they were not economic to operate), the Soviet industry has to meet a domestic demand it has created with hundreds of ships which a West German, British or Spanish owner would regard as

A "Mayakovski", class trawler at sea. This ship was built in 1959 and was sold in 1966 to Greek owners.

obsolete and inadequate for present highly competitive conditions on the grounds.

Their intensive experience as they built up the world's largest fleet of stern trawlers has, however, given Soviet operators and builders a clear idea of the ships they now require. Several interesting new designs are being planned or have been built and are under test.

In a paper given at a technical conference held in conjunction with the fishing exhibition in Leningrad in 1968, Mr. E. V. Kamensky of the State Designing Institute for Fishing Vessels reviewed his country's experience in the large scale use of processing stern trawlers. Thirteen years of operating these ships had, he explained, provided a mass of information, on the basis of which it had been possible to design and now to build technically improved vessels of this type.

From the original BMRTs of the first five to seven years, there had evolved a fleet of large-

This UN National Marine Fisheries Service photograph shows an East German built "Tropik" class trawler. The ship, the "Volopas", was built in 1963.

A Soviet "Tropik" class stern trawler berthed in the fishing base at Havana in Cuba.

tonnage trawlers comprising a whole range of factory stern fishing ships which varied in their dimensions, their propulsion plant, their system of fishing and their general construction.

He categorised these vessels according to their processing systems as:

1. Large freezer factory trawlers for working in the middle and high latitudes, producing mainly frozen processed fish and by-products. These were represented by the *Mayakovski*, *Pushkin* and Polish-built *Leskov* and *Kosmos* types.

2. Freezer trawlers for work in the tropics, producing mainly frozen unprocessed fish and by-products. These were represented by the *Tropik* and *Atlantik* types.

3. Freezer super-trawlers with increased endurance which enabled them to work without interruption of production in middle distance waters where weather conditions were difficult. These were represented by the *Grumant* and *Rembrandt* types (built in Denmark and the Netherlands) and by a diesel-electric *Altai* type trawler (with freezing plant capacity of 50 tons a day) then under construction.

4. Part freezer trawlers, which refrigerated their catch during the first part of a trip and brought the later catch back chilled in ice. The trawler under development for this was the diesel-electric powered *Sever* which was one of the vessels shown at the Leningrad exhibition.

5. Canning factory trawlers. This type was represented by the world's largest trawlers – the ships of the *Natalia Kovshova* type built in France.

6. Freezer-fish meal trawlers. This type was under development in a ship called the *Mintai* which had increased capacity for meal from lower value fish but could also process the higher value food fish. The *Mintai* had a freezing plant capacity for 30 tons a day and a meal plant able to process 60 to 70 tons of raw material in 24 hours.

Soviet trawlers, Mr. Kamensky explained, varied in design and in the arrangement of holds, engine room space and superstructure. Thus ships of the *Pushkin*, *Mayakovski*, *Grumant*, *Rembrandt* and *Mintai* series had the engine room and superstructure amidships, while the *Natalia Kovshova* and *Altai* types had superstructure forward and engine room amidships. The *Sever* diesel-electric vessel had her superstructure well forward and the engine room was in two sections, one forward and the other aft.

Despite the variations, the trawlers all had the same system for handling their fish on deck. The catch was hauled up a ramp to the after trawl deck where it was emptied from the cod-end into a pound space on the factory deck below. From the pound space, fish was conveyed to a section for sorting, gutting and washing. It was then either processed into fillets, or canned or sent for freezing in the round. The finished products were packed and transferred by lifts or conveyors into the holds.

Details of new-generation stern trawlers planned for the Soviet fleet were given at the end of 1969 in the publication *Sudostroyeniye* (Shipbuilding). These included a BMRT vessel, the *Meridian*; a combination stern trawler-purse seiner, the *Rumb*; and a medium-size SRTM combination vessel, the *Zhelyezniy potok*.

During the 1960s, it was noted, large trawlers for the Soviet fleet had been acquired from the GDR and Poland, while yards in the USSR had built "several hundreds" of *Mayakovski* class ships.

But over the years the grounds to be exploited had become more and more distant, the kinds of fish to be caught from them had become much more varied and the consumers had become more sophisticated and exacting as regards quality, preparation and packing. It had, therefore, become necessary to develop a vessel on completely new lines to meet all the changed requirements. This had led to the development of the *Meridian*-type trawler which would be followed by super-trawlers with much more powerful winches that would enable them to work depths down to 1,000 to 1,500 metres.

The *Meridian* was designed for year-round operation in middle or high latitudes and could carry fuel and supplies to reach grounds 7,000 miles from her base and work there until her holds were full.

In view of the long periods the ship would be away from her home port, crew quarters are well planned and comfortable with single and double-berth cabins, mess rooms, lounges and other amenities.

Fish are either filleted or whole frozen and stored at −28°C. Freezing capacity is 50 tons in 24 hours. Waste fish and offal is reduced to meal in a shipborne plant able to handle 30 to 35 tons of raw material in 24 hours.

The main engine is a 3500 hp diesel turning a c.p. propeller through a reduction gear with power take-off to drive the generators for ship's mains. The ship has speed of about 15 knots and can tow a deep trawl at six knots.

The first SRTM (medium size refrigerated trawler) of the stern trawler type was the *Zhelyezhyakov*, which was shown at the Leningrad exhibition. This vessel has her superstructure and accommodation amidships and the trawl winch is far forward near the forepeak. The trawl warps pass through tunnels under the superstructure. Fish is sorted and washed in pounds and on conveyors on the port side. It then passes forward into hoppers amidships on the deck below where it is kept chilled by flake ice. Freezing is done in four air blast tunnels, each with a capacity of about three tons a day, and frozen blocks are stored in a 205 cu. m. capacity hold.

Next design for a medium-size stern trawler was that of the *Zhelyezniy potok*, which is 54.8 metres long overall with a moulded breadth of 9.8 m. As can be seen from the profile drawing of this ship, the stern ramp leads up straight to the deck of the superstructure which serves as an upper working

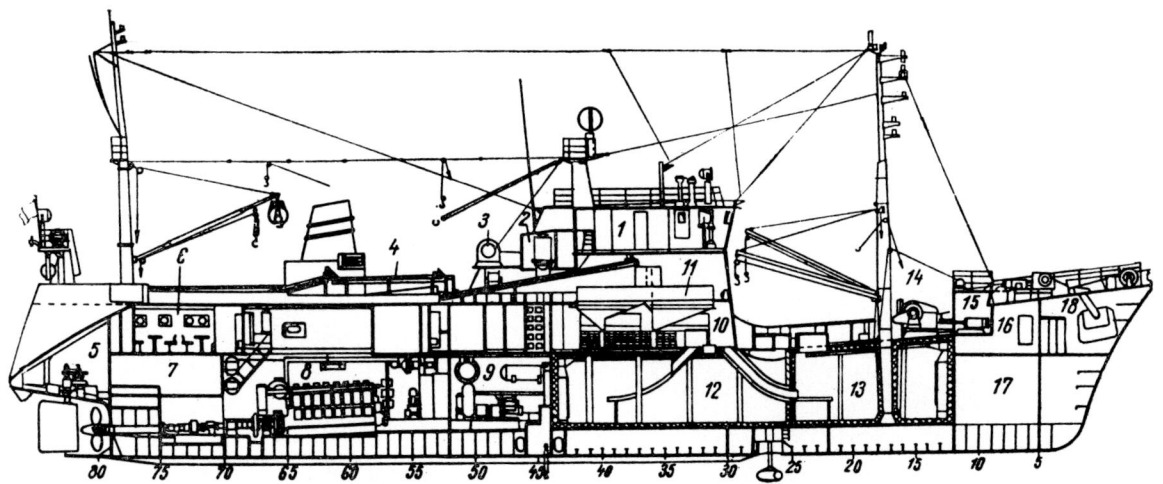

Profile drawing of the new SRTM medium-size trawler "Zhelyezniy potok". Key to numbers. 1. Wheelhouse 2. Ice-making plant 3. Gilson winch 4. Transporter 5. Steering engine compartment 6. Messroom 7. Fresh water tank 8. Engine room 9. Refrigeration plant 10. Freezers 11. Chilling tanks 12. After fish hold 13. Forward fish hold 14. Trawl winch 15. Winch motor room 16. Bos'un's store 17. Sanitary water tank 18. Forepeak.

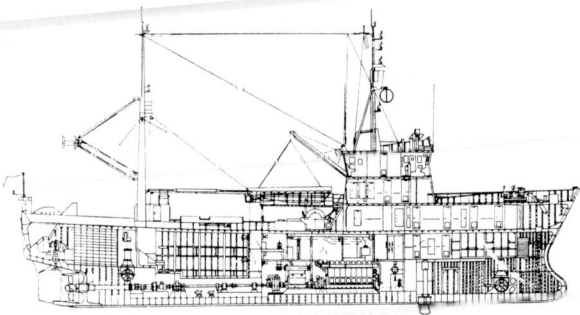

Profile drawing of the combination trawler "Rumb".

processing deck. When the ship is trawling (she can also be used for purse seining), fish from the cod end are emptied into pounds along the port side of the upper processing deck. From these it is moved amidships by conveyor to four holding tanks below the bridge superstructure where it is held in water chilled by flake ice. From these tanks, it is gravity fed to packing tables in the freezing section below where it is put into trays and then goes into blast tunnels with a capacity for 12 tons in 24 hours.

Frozen blocks are glazed, packed in cartons and then gravity fed by chute into the fish holds which have a total capacity of 400 cu. m.

The ship is powered by a 1000 hp diesel turning a c.p. propeller. There are four diesel generators each with a nominal rating of 100 kW.

The combination seiner-trawler of the *Rumb* class is designed to work with a factory mother ship. This vessel is 49.2 metres long overall with a breadth of 10.5 m. and depth to main deck of 6.5 m. She has a 318 cu. m. capacity hold which is cooled to $-5°C$. Accommodation is provided for a crew of 23.

The ship is powered by diesel engine developing 1320 hp at 428 rpm and turning a nozzle-shrouded c.p. propeller through a reduction gear to give a speed of 13 knots.

Although not a shelter deck trawler, the *Nadyezhda*-class feeder combination boat marks another interesting stage in the development of the stern fishing method in the USSR. Fourteen of these RP-hull boats will be carried to the grounds – seven on either side – by the giant factory ship *Vostok*. The prototype of this class was built on the Black Sea coast in 1965, has been under intensive test in distant waters and was shown at the Leningrad exhibition. The trawler-purse seiner is 17.2 metres long with a breadth of 5.26 m. The boat will work from the *Vostok* with a crew of five men and has four holding tanks for her catches. She will handle her trawl using a high-powered hydraulic winch and a swinging gantry.

The vessel is powered by two Soviet-built 12-cylinder vee-type diesel engines each developing 300 hp and turning twin-screws in nozzles. Also in the engine room is a 150 hp auxiliary diesel power plant.

The contribution by the German Democratic Republic and Poland to the growth of the Soviet trawler fleet is referred to in the sections on those countries. Stern trawlers from other countries have included the following:

Grumant
Built in 1964 by the Burmeister & Wain yard in Copenhagen, Denmark. The first ship in a class of 11 vessels designed to operate as stern trawlers or as mother ships to a fleet of catcher boats. A ship of 4,700 gross tons, the *Grumant* is 91 metres long b.p. with a moulded breadth of 16 m.

The main engine is a Burmeister & Wain type 50-VBF-90 diesel developing 3530 hp at 200 rpm to give a speed on trials of 14 knots.

Rembrandt
Built in 1965 by N.V. Koninklijke Maatschappij "de Schelde" of Flushing, the Netherlands. With the *Van Dijk*, *Frans Hals* and *Van Gogh*, one of a class of factory stern trawler/mother ships. Later vessels include the *Zarechensk*, *Zodiac* and *Tkvarcheli*.

The *Rembrandt* is 103.59 metres long overall with a moulded breadth of 16.6 m. and depth to upper deck of 11.3 m. She has accommodation for a crew of 102.

Freezing of the fish is done in two air blast tunnels of "de Schelde" design and each has a capacity of 25 tons in 22 hours. Waste fish and offal is reduced to meal in an Atlas Stord compact plant able to handle 30 tons of raw material in 24 hours.

A "Rembrandt" class ship, 103.59 metres long, built in the Netherlands.

The factory ship "Natalia Kovshova", 128 metres long and the world's largest stern trawler.

The main engine is a Schelde Sulzer diesel developing 3000 hp at 225 rpm and directly coupled to a Lips-Schelde four-bladed c.p. propeller to give a speed of 14 knots.

Natalia Kovshova
Built in 1965 by Ateliers et Chantiers de Nantes in France. The first of three canning factory ships for the USSR and still the largest stern trawler in the world. Her sister ships, built in 1966, are the *Maria Polivanova* and *Anotoly Khulin*.

A ship of 8,425 gross tons, the *Natalia Kovshova* is 128 metres long overall with a moulded breadth of 19 m. and depth to upper deck of 12 m. She has accommodation for a crew of 232 men and women.

The ship was designed to fish with bottom or midwater trawls and is equipped to deal quickly with large catches taken in tropical waters. A temporary storage hold on the factory deck feeds fish on to a conveyor where it can be sorted at the rate of a ton a minute. Fish for canning is transferred from this stage to chilled sea water storage tanks from where it is pumped to the cannery where 166 workers are able to pack up to 100,000 cans a day. To reduce roll, the ship is fitted with flume stabilisation tanks.

Additional processing plant includes a blast freezing tunnel with a capacity of 20 tons a day and a meal plant able to handle 20 tons of raw material in 24 hours.

Three holds for canned fish have a capacity of 2,000 cu. m. There is also a 740 cu. m. capacity refrigerated hold, and a 300 cu. m. fish meal hold.

The trawl winch is electrically powered and is a five-drum unit with a pull of 18 tons at 120 m./min.

The *Natalia Kovshova* is equipped with diesel-electric power plant. Electrical power for propulsion and factory requirements is generated by three SEMT-Pielstick type 6PC2L diesels each developing 2520 hp at 500 rpm and driving a 2100 kVA alternator. Two electric propulsion motors of 2000 hp each turn a c.p. propeller to give a service speed of 14 knots. The ship is also equipped with a 400 hp active rudder and a 400 hp bow thruster.

Research ships

The many advantages of the stern trawler design have influenced more than the operators of commercial vessels. Stern trawlers – in various arrangements and sizes, and for several different duties – have been designed and built for fisheries research work, for training, for experimental fishing and for the development of fishing gear and techniques.

In some cases, such as the Soviet ship *Akademik Knipovich*, the research and training ship has been adapted from a standard trawler design. This vessel has done valuable work for the Soviet industry and (in co-operation with the Department of Fisheries of FAO) as a training ship for scientists from the developing countries.

The *Akademik Knipovich* is a modified *Mayakovski*-class stern trawler of 3,200 gross tons. She was built at the Nikolayev shipyards on the Black Sea in 1964. Some of her most important research voyages have been in Antarctic waters, and these have included investigations (including processing tests) into the huge and still barely used krill resource.

One of the first large stern trawler type research ships to be built for a Western European fishing

The Soviet "Mayakovski" type research trawler "Akademik Knipovich".

country was the West German vessel *Walther Herwig*. A product in 1963 of the A.G. Weser yard in Bremerhaven, she is a diesel-electric powered ship of 2,000 gross tons with a length overall of 83.33 metres and a moulded breadth of 12.5 m. At the time of her completion she was regarded as the most advanced stern trawler type vessel afloat, setting new standards even in a country which had been no laggard in the progressive use of this design.

Using the *Walther Herwig*, the Institut für Fangtechnik of Hamburg was able to accelerate its development of the one-boat mid-water or pelagic trawl. She is a ship designed specifically for fishing investigations. In 1963 she had all the equipment necessary to indicate the way ahead and she did this

The West German research ship "Walther Herwig".

so well that by 1970 she was out of date. This was explained by Dr. Joachim Schärfe, the German gear technologist, now with FAO, at a White Fish Authority conference in London in December 1970.

Suggesting that it was highly desirable that a ship for fishery research and development work should be superior to and also more flexible than the standard of the fishing fleet to be served, he added that ships with this quality could not be planned for a useful lifetime of more than five to ten years, "because by then they will probably be outmoded and should be replaced".

The *Walther Herwig* had, he said, been overtaken by the commercial trawlers even faster than had been anticipated. After she had been in service only four years planning started for a new "super" stern trawler of double her fishing capacity.

This ship is now being built by Schlichting-Werft of Travemunde and will be delivered in 1972 when the *Walther Herwig* will be modernised and will replace an earlier and smaller research ship. The "super" trawler will be powered by two diesel engines developing more than 4000 hp and will be equipped with a high powered trawl winch with a pull of 40 tons.

The *Professor Siedlecki*, now building at the Lenin Shipyard in Gadansk, Poland, is another research ship due for delivery in 1972 and planned with "super" trawler capabilities. She will work initially for a joint Polish and FAO/UNDP £5½

The Dutch vessel "Tridens", 61 metres long, built in 1968.

million project, which will include research into trawl gear and fish abundance surveys.

Designated a B-424/1 type ocean-going research vessel, the *Professor Siedlecki* is 89.4 metres long overall with a moulded breadth of 15 m. She will be diesel-electric powered with three Fiat engines as the prime movers and a 2,300 hp propulsion motor turning a single propeller.

Anticipation of fisheries research and gear technology requirements for many years ahead has been attempted in other new-generation ships which have been brought into service for state marine laboratories during the past four years.

Tridens

Built in 1968 by N.V. Sleephelling Maatschappij 'Scheveningen' for the Netherlands Ministry of Agriculture and Fishery. A stern trawler type ship designed for marine biological, gear and methods and processing research, the *Tridens* is 61 metres long overall with a moulded breadth of 9.8 m. and depth to upper deck of 7 m. She has accommodation for a crew of 25 and for 13 research staff.

This ship is equipped with a refrigerated hold and with other equipment to enable her to study various systems of fish preservation.

She has a trawl deck 14 metres long aft but has no stern ramp, and a bulwark roller assists hoisting of the cod-end. Her Bodewes eight-drum trawl winch is powered by two 200 hp electric motors. The two warp drums have a capacity of 2,200 metres of wire on each drum and the hauling speed is 120 m/min. at a pull of eight tons.

The propulsion system consists of two Bolnes diesel engines of 1200 and 600 hp providing normal propulsion power of 1200 hp with 600 hp reserve. These engines turn a Seffle c.p. propeller through a Brevo twin gearbox.

Delaware II

Built in 1968 by the South Portland Engineering Co. in Maine for the United States National Marine Fisheries Service. A ramp stern trawler type combination fishing vessel, the *Delaware II* was designed for exploratory fishing and gear research. She is 155½ ft. long overall with a moulded breadth of 30 ft., is powered by a 1000 hp diesel engine and has accommodation for a crew of 14 and six scientists.

The committee planning the *Delaware II* made a close study of stern trawling methods and decided that their main advantage was their ability to bring the trawl with its catch aboard in the shortest time and with the least labour.

To achieve this in the *Delaware II*, it was decided that there would be sufficient space available on deck to haul the trawl aboard in one continuous pull. For this, it was necessary to use almost the entire length of the ship. The trawl winch is near the bow section and it pulls up the wings of the trawl through a passage under the bridge superstructure.

G.O. Sars

Built in 1970 by Mjellem & Karlsen for the Norwegian Institute of Marine Research in Bergen. This ship and her complex array of electronic fish resource survey equipment were described in considerable detail in the fishing technical press at the time of her entry into service. She was planned by a committee of three marine scientists and a naval

Norway's 70 metres long "G.O. Sars", built in 1970.

ship was planned to match the efficiency and catching power of a modern trawler or a purse seiner, but she does not have the deck space nor the carrying capacity to carry out continuous fishing. For trawling she has a Norwinch hydraulic split winch with a capacity of 2,400 metres of 24 mm. dia wire on each drum.

The main propulsion plant consists of a Normo four-engine arrangement of type LSM6 diesels, each developing 835 hp. These engines turn a four-bladed c.p. propeller through a 4.3:1 A.G. Weser reduction gearbox. Only three of the engines are required for the 2500 hp output through the gear box to the shaft. The forward two engines also power two 575 kVA alternators, while the two aft engines have auxiliary power take-offs for driving the pumps for the hydraulic machinery aboard.

Cirolana

Built in 1970 by Ferguson Brothers (Port Glasgow) Ltd. for the Ministry of Agriculture, Fisheries and Food to serve the Fisheries Laboratory in Lowestoft, England. Like the *G.O. Sars* and the Scottish research ship *Scotia* (completed in 1971), the *Cirolana* has been fitted with highly advanced electronic fish location devices for surveying and sampling fish stocks and plankton. She also carries out research into gear development, using bottom and mid-water trawls.

A shelter deck stern trawler type ship of 1,594 gross tons, the *Cirolana* is 229 ft. 8 in. (71 metres) long overall with a moulded breadth of 46 ft. and depth to upper deck of 26 ft. She has accommodation for 43 crew and scientists.

When the ship is working her trawl gear, the cod end is brought aboard over rollers using a conventional stern ramp and emptied into deck pounds and fish bins. A flush hatch on the trawl deck gives access to a 1,650 cu. ft. capacity fish hold which is refrigerated down to $-20°F$.

The trawl winch is a C.D. Holmes 11-ton four-drum unit with a capacity of 1,200 fathoms of $3\frac{1}{4}$ in. warp on each of the two main drums. The winch is powered by a 400 hp Laurence Scott electric motor.

The diesel-electric propulsion system was supplied by Laurence Scott and Electromotors Ltd. and this consists of three 1100 hp W.H. Allen diesel engines each driving a constant current generator. An alternator for the auxiliary load is coupled in tandem on two of the sets. A 2200 hp Laurence Scott propulsion motor is in a separate compartment immediately aft of the engine room and turns a four-bladed propeller in a Kort nozzle to give a speed of 14 knots.

architect and was designed by the shipyard Bergen Mekaniske Verksteder.

In addition to her studies of fish and their environment, the *G.O. Sars* is equipped to carry out test fishing using trawl or purse seine gear; she searches for and studies fish stocks using the most advanced Simrad sonar and echo sounding instruments; and she has an on-line computer system to assist in processing the mass of information she is capable of collecting.

A stern trawler type research ship of 1,500 gross tons, the *G.O. Sars* is 70 metres long overall with a moulded breadth of 13.3 m. and depth to upper deck of 7.45 m.

For the fishing side of her research work, the

The British research trawler "Cirolana", 71 metres long, built in 1970.

Bjarni Saemundsson

Built in 1970 by Gesellschaft Unterweser of Bremerhaven for the Icelandic Government. A shelter deck stern trawler type combination fishing vessel designed for resource research, exploratory fishing and gear and methods development, the *Bjarni Saemundsson* is equipped for bottom or mid-water trawling and for purse seining. She is a ship of 777 gross tons with a length overall of 49 metres and a moulded breadth of 10.6 m. She has accommodation for a crew of 14 to 16 and normally carries four to five scientists, with bunk space for up to 17.

Her winches are hydraulically powered and were manufactured by A/S Hydraulik Brattvaag.

The propulsion system is diesel-electric with three generators each driven by an MAN 600 hp diesel engine. Two 700 hp electric motors are geared to a single Zeise fixed-blade propeller.

Scotia

Built in 1972 by Ferguson Brothers (Port Glasgow) Ltd. for the Department of Agriculture and Fisheries for Scotland to serve the Marine Laboratory, Aberdeen. Although basically a resource research ship, the *Scotia* will also assist the investigations being carried out by the Marine Laboratory into improved gear for bottom trawling. Like the other new research ships built in Europe in recent years, she is capable of using the largest and heaviest types of commercial gear for bottom and mid-water trawling.

The *Scotia* is 225 ft. (68.6 metres) long overall with a breadth of 44 ft. Her trawl winch is electrically powered but all other deck machinery is powered by high pressure hydraulic systems.

Propulsion is by a constant-current diesel-electric system. This consists of three British Polar diesel engines, each developing 1200 hp and driving a d.c. generator for the constant-current loop, and a three-phase alternator of 435 kVA. The main propulsion motor is designed to deliver 2000 hp to a four-bladed propeller in a Kort nozzle to give a speed of 13 knots.

Other countries

In this section we briefly describe shelter deck stern trawlers operated in the fleets of some other major fishing countries. Some mention should also be made of the distant water high seas operations now being carried out by Bulgaria and Roumania. With the exception of the trawler *Constanta* and her sister ship built in Japan in 1964 for Roumania, the large shelter deck ships used by these countries are *Tropik*, *Mayakovski* and other series-built stern trawlers from yards in East Germany, the USSR and Poland.

Some years ago Greece also introduced series-built *Mayakovski*-class trawlers, acquired from the USSR, into her distant water fleet; she has since added other stern trawlers built in her own yards and in Italy.

ARGENTINA

Puerto Madryn

With sister ship *Bahia Camarones*, built in 1966 by Astilleros de Cantabrica y de Riera of Gijon, Spain, for Juan D'Ambra y Cia (COPEMAR SA) of Mar del Plata. These ships were designed to catch and freeze octopus (pulpo) off the coast of north-west Africa, and also to operate for hake and other fin fish off Argentina. A freezer stern trawler of 248 gross tons, the *Puerto Madryn* is 30.5 metres long b.p. with a breadth of 7.5 m. and depth to upper deck of 3.7 m. She has accommodation for a crew of 16.

The *Puerto Madryn* is equipped for stern trawling with a Unigan swinging gantry and has a 150 hp Norwinch hydraulic winch.

At the time of her building the freezing system of this ship was described as "an interesting example of how to fit comparatively high-capacity plant in a remarkably small space". This refrigeration and freezing plant was designed by the British firm J. & E. Hall Ltd. and consists of three Hall 95 bu 76 mm six-cylinder compound compressors using Freon 22 as the refrigerant. The plant operates on the simple direct expansion pump circulation system.

Freezing is done in two Jackstone Froster 20-station vertical plate machines with a total maximum capacity on fish fillets of nearly 15 tons a day. Each freezer station is fitted with four removable dividers to that when octopus is being processed five evenly-shaped 5.12 kilo blocks are produced. On octopus, the freezing capacity is 14.1 tons.

After freezing the blocks of octopus are packed five blocks to a cardboard carton and are passed through a small hatch into the forward end of the frozen fish hold. This hold has a capacity of 180 cu. m. and is cooled down to $-25°C$.

The *Puerto Madryn* is powered by a Deutz SV6M536 diesel engine developing 375 hp at 500 rpm and turning a c.p. propeller to give a speed of 12 knots.

BELGIUM

Lans

Built in 1967 by Beliard Murdoch SA for the Lans Company of Ostend. A two-deck vessel from aft of

Belgian trawler "Lans", 42.7 metres long, built in 1967.

the midships superstructure, the *Lans* is 418 gross tons with a length overall of 42.7 metres, a moulded breadth of 8.9 m. and depth of 5.9 m. She has accommodation for 14 but was designed to be worked by a crew of only 10 men.

Her winch (mounted at the forward end of a 22 m. long trawl deck) is a Brusselle Neptune GMC 11/3 unit of eight tons pull and with three drums. The main drum capacity is 2,100 metres of 22 mm. dia. steel warp and mean hauling speed is 2 m./sec. It is powered by a 240 hp ACEC electric motor on the Ward Leonard system.

The *Lans* is a wet fish trawler designed to bring back her catch chilled in ice in a 245 cu. m. capacity hold which is cooled by Sabroe refrigeration plant to a temperature 0°C.

The main engine is a Deutz type SVBGM585 diesel developing 980 hp at 380 rpm and turning a Zeise-Liaaen propeller through a Renk 2:1 reduction gear to give a speed of 13 knots.

CUBA

During the past five or six years Cuba has been developing a substantial distant water fishing fleet which includes a number of large, modern shelter deck stern trawlers built in Spain and in East Germany.

At the beginning of 1971, the Flota Cubana de Pesca, based on Havana, operated more than a dozen large stern trawlers. These included five *Atlantik*-class ships built in East Germany. Cuba was also to take delivery of one of the first of the new *Atlantik III*-class trawlers.

Earlier deliveries from Spanish yards to this fleet included the:

Tiburon. A ship of 1,305 gross tons and 69.48 metres long built by the Factorias Vulcano yard in 1966. She has two holds, one of 830 cu. m. capacity for salt fish and one of 250 cu. m. capacity for frozen fish.

Guasa and *Biajaba*. Two ACSA-56-C type ships built in 1966 by Astilleros Construcciones of Vigo. These ships, which are similar to the trawler *Alvican* (see Spain), are 64 metres long overall, have accommodation for a crew of 50, and have 1,200 cu. m. capacity fish holds cooled down to −25°C.

Manjuari and *Camaron*. Built in 1967 by Hijos de Barreras of Vigo. These are ships similar to the *Tiburon*. Each has accommodation for a crew of 50 and freezes its fish in air blast tunnels.

The "Playa Giron", an "Atlantik" class trawler built in East Germany for the Cuban distant water fleet.

Isla de la Juventad. Built in 1966 by Soc. Espanol de Construccione Naval. A shelter deck stern trawler of 1,556 gross tons, the *Isla de la Juventad* is 70.3 metres long overall with a moulded breadth of 12.5 m. and depth to upper deck of 7.95 m. She has accommodation for a crew of 54.

Freezing is done in Ramon Vizcaino air blast tunnels and the whole frozen product is held at −25°C. in a 1,200 cu. m. capacity fish hold.

The main engine is an MWM diesel developing 2200 hp at 500 rpm and turning a c.p. propeller to give a speed of 13 knots.

Mar Caribe

Built in 1968 by Astilleros Construcciones. This ship is one of three or four large 106 metres long overall factory stern trawlers supplied from Spain between December 1968 and 1970. She is one of her builder's TASBA-96T class of stern trawler. A similar ship, the *Mar de Plata*, was delivered in 1969. A smaller TASBA-67T trawler 76 metres long overall – the *Golfo de Tonkin* – was also built for Cuba in 1969.

A fillet and whole fish freezer stern trawler of 2,400 gross tons, the *Mar Caribe* has a length b.p., of 96 metres, with a moulded breadth of 14.5 m. She has accommodation for a crew of 82.

Her trawl winch is a Barreras-Brusselle model KMC-11 unit powered by a 450 hp electric motor.

As Cuban stern trawlers of this size and capacity are worked on the hake grounds of the South Atlantic, they are fitted with holding tanks where the fish are kept chilled before processing by flake ice made by two plants with a daily output of 10 tons each. Processing plant includes a Baader 163 gutter and 188 filleting machines. There is a horizontal plate freezer for fillets, and blast tunnels (with a total capacity of 40 tons a day) for whole fish. Waste fish and offal is reduced to meal in a compact shipborne plant.

The fish hold has a capacity of 3,400 cu. m. and there is an additional hold with a capacity of 500 cu. m. for fish meal.

The main engine is a Barreras-Deutz type RBV-12-M350 diesel developing 4000 hp at 430 rpm and turning a fixed-blade propeller through a Lohmann & Stolterfoht reduction gear to give a top speed of 15.5 knots.

Habana

During 1970 and 1971 VEB Elbewerften of the German Democratic Republic built 15 *Habana*-class fish meal cutters for the Cuba fleet. Although not shelter deck ships, these are interesting compact processing stern trawlers designed to reduce 35 tons

The "Manjuari" built in 1967.

of fish a day into meal and oil. They are ramp vessels, each equipped with a winch having a pull of eight tons at 35 m./min. and capable of working bottom and pelagic trawls from an 11-metre long deck.

The *Habana* trawler is 37.7 metres long overall with a moulded breadth of 8.2 m. and depth to main deck of 5.5 m. She has accommodation for a crew of 21 and has an endurance of 50 days.

The ship has her engine room aft, 332 cu. m. capacity meal hold amidships and superstructure well forward above the factory area containing the meal plant.

When the catch is brought aboard up the stern ramp, the cod end is emptied into a receiving bunker aft of the engine room where the fish is broken up before being pumped forward for processing and bagging in a type VF/M2 plant designed and manufactured by VEB Volkswerft of Stralsund.

The main engine is an SKL type 8NVD36 diesel developing 578 hp at 500 rpm and turning a single propeller through a reduction gear to give a speed of 10.5 knots.

One of 15 "Habana" class fish meal cutters built in East Germany for Cuba.

The factory stern trawler "Vesturvon", built in Norway for Faeroe owners.

FAEROE ISLANDS

Stella Kristina

Built in 1968 by Soviknes Verft Shipyard in Norway for P/f Stella of Klakksvik. One of four similar vessels, she was the first factory trawler to be built for the Faeroe fishing fleet. A shelter deck stern trawler of 834 gross tons, the *Stella Kristina* is 61.74 metres long overall with a moulded breadth of 10.21 m. and depth to upper deck of 7 m. She has accommodation for a crew of 48.

The ship can operate bottom or mid-water trawls and is equipped with Hydraulik Brattvaag deck machinery including a type MA10A trawl winch.

The factory deck has two processing lines – for small and large fish – and heading, gutting and filleting is done by Baader machines. Freezing is done in three Kvaerner horizontal plate machines.

The main engine is an MWM type TbRHS 345-A diesel developing 2200 hp at 500 rpm and turning a Liaaen c.p. propeller through a Renk gearbox to give a service speed of 14 knots.

Greenland wet fish trawler "Nuk", 50 metres long, built in 1969.

The third ship in this series was the *Vesturvon* which was built in 1969 by the Hatlo mek. Verksted yard in Norway for the firm P/f Vesturvon of Sorvaag.

Like her sister ships, this vessel has a full factory processing deck for the production of pre-packed frozen fillets. After passing through the two Baader machine lines, fillets are frozen in three Kvaerner plate freezers or a large blast freezer. This plant has a total capacity of 24 tons a day. The frozen product is stored in an 800 cu. m. capacity refrigerated fish hold.

Sjurdarberg

Built in 1971 by A.M. Liaaen A/S of Norway for J. Kjolbro of Klakksvig. A sister ship is being built for the same owner for delivery in 1973. A wet fish stern trawler, the *Sjurdarberg* is 60 metres long overall with a breadth of 11m. and depth to upper deck of 7.4 m.

The ship is equipped with Baader 165 gutting machine and 670 washer. The fish hold has a capacity of 930 cu. m.

The main engine is a Burmeister & Wain diesel developing 2160 hp and turning a Liaaen propeller through a Lohmann & Stolterfoht reduction gear to give a speed of 14 knots.

GREENLAND

Nuk

Built in 1969 by the Ankerlokken Verft yard for the Royal Greenland Trade Department of Copenhagen. She was the first deepsea fishing vessel to join the Greenland fleet and operates from Godthaab harbour. A shelter deck stern trawler designed by

Bergens Mekaniske Verksteder of Norway, the 433 gross ton *Nuk* is 50 metres long overall with a moulded breadth of 9.45 m. and depth to upper deck of 4.6 m. She has accommodation for a crew of 26.

The ship has her superstructure forward of amidships and her engine room aft. She can work bottom or mid-water trawls. The trawl winch is a two-drum Norwinch hydraulic unit.

Heading and gutting machines are installed on the factory deck. Fish can either be salted or kept chilled in ice for landing at ports in west Greenland. The insulated fish hold has a capacity of 300 cu.m.

Propulsion is by two Normo type LMS8 diesel engines each developing 1110 hp at 750 rpm and each coupled to Hjelset c.p. propeller to give a speed of 15 knots.

ISRAEL

Azgad III

Built in 1965 by the Akers Group in Norway for Atlantic Fisheries Company of Haifa. A freezer stern trawler with an overall length of 232 ft., the *Azgad III* has a moulded breadth of 37½ ft and depth to main deck of 18 ft.

She can freeze up to 24 tons of fish in 24 hours and this can be stored at a temperature of $-28°C$. in a 35,000 cu.ft. capacity fish hold.

The main engine is a Burmeister & Wain type 735 VBF-62 diesel developing 1960 hp at 300 rpm and turning a c.p. propeller to give a speed of 14 knots.

REPUBLIC OF KOREA

Kang Wha 601

Built in 1966 by the Dubignon-Normandie yard in France. One of two sister ships for the Korea Marine Industry Development Corporation, the *Kang Wha 601* is a freezer stern trawler of 1,500 gross tons with a length overall of 77 metres, a moulded breadth of 11.3 m. and depth to main deck of 5.3 m. She has accommodation for a crew of 48.

The vessel has a low bridge superstructure forward and a long trawl deck. Her trawl winch is a Brusselle Neptune HMC unit with a pull of 14 tons.

The catch is frozen in Samifi air blast tunnels with a total output of 18 tons a day. The frozen product is held at $-20°C$ in a 900 cu. m. capacity fish hold.

The main engine is a Fiat type B3012 SS diesel developing 2500 hp at 500 rpm and turning a single propeller through a Messian reduction gear to give a speed of 15 knots.

Israeli trawler "Azgad III", built in Norway in 1965.

PORTUGAL

Santa Isabel

Built in 1965 by Estaleiros Sao Jacinto of Aveiro for Empresa de Pesca de Aveiro Ltda. A saltfish and freezer stern trawler of 2,056 gross tons for fishing off Labrador and Newfoundland, the *Santa Isabel* is 80.3 metres long overall with a moulded breadth of 12.5 m. and depth to main deck of 8.6 m. She has accommodation for a crew of 68.

Her freezing plant consists of one Jackstone horizontal and two Jackstone vertical plate freezers with a total capacity of 10 tons in 20 hours. The frozen product is stored at $-25°C$. in a 223 cu. m. hold. The larger saltfish hold has a capacity of 1,350 cu. m.

The trawl winch is a Holmes Lektron type TWZP five-drum unit.

Propulsion plant consists of two Werkspoor type TEBF 296 diesels each developing 1260 hp at 450 rpm and turning a KaMeWa c.p. propeller through a Modern Wheel Drive twin input, single output gearbox to give a speed of 15 knots.

Mar de Hielo

Built in 1966 by Hijos de J. Barreras of Vigo, Spain, for Jose, Antonio and Salvador Juan Borras Esteva of Ceuta. The *Leiza*, a ship of similar dimensions but with slightly different appearance and equipment, was built in 1966 by the same yard for the Spanish owners Pesquera Vasco-Astur.

A freezer stern trawler of 1,034 gross tons, the *Mar de Hielo* is 65.85 metres long overall with a moulded breadth of 11.4 m. and depth to upper deck of 7.4 m. She has accommodation for a crew of 41.

The trawl winch is a Barreras-Brusselle Neptune HMC 111 unit with a pull of 10 tons.

Freezing is done in five Jackstone Froster vertical

plate machines and in one Vizcaino tunnel freezer with an output of 12 tons a day.

The main engine is an MAN type G8V 40/60 diesel developing 1950 hp at 273 rpm and turning a single propeller to give a service speed of 13 knots.

Praia de Ericeira
Built in 1967 by Estaleiros Navais de Viana do Castelo for Soc. de Pesca a Vapor 'Exportador'. The first of a series of five freezer trawlers for the Portuguese fishing fleet and designed to operate for long periods on the south-east Atlantic hake grounds, transferring catches at Southern African ports to refrigerated cargo ships for the market in Portugal.

The *Praia de Ericeira* is a whole fish freezer stern trawler of 1,138 gross tons and is 62.45 metres long with a moulded breadth of 10.5 m. and depth to upper deck of 7.3 m. She has accommodation for a crew of 33.

Bridge superstructure is forward of amidships, the engine room is amidships and there are refrigerated holds fore and aft. A third refrigerated fish room separates the working area on the factory deck. Fish are headed, gutted and washed before freezing in plant consisting of six vertical plate freezers (with a total output of 18 tons a day) and two air blast tunnels able to handle 10 tons a day. Refrigerated hold capacity totals 1,000 cu. ft.

The propulsion system is a "father and son" arrangement with an MaK diesel developing 1500 hp and a second MaK diesel developing 300 hp and available for propulsion or to power a generator for the electrically powered winch or ship's mains.

Luis Ferreira de Carvalho
Built in 1969 by Estaleiros Navais de Viana do Castelo for Soc. Nacional Armadores de Bacalhau. This ship was designed to work north-west Atlantic cod grounds and produce saltfish, but provision has been made for later adaption, if this is considered necessary, into a freezer for North or South Atlantic waters.

A shelter deck stern trawler of 2,389 gross tons the *Luis Ferreira de Carvalho* is 84.8 metres long overall with a moulded breadth of 14 m. and depth to upper deck of 8.9 m. She has accommodation for a crew of 71.

The factory deck is equipped with a WACO type 70/500 washer and Baader heading and splitting machines. It also has an Atlas type 71W fish meal plant. The hold has a capacity of 1,450 cu. m. It is situated forward of the engine room, while aft there is a 350 cu. m. fish meal hold.

Propulsion plant consists of two MaK type 8M-452AK diesels each developing 1500 hp at 500 rpm and turning a single propeller through a Lohmann & Stolterfoht reduction gear to give a speed on trials of 14 knots.

ROUMANIA

Constanta
With sister ship *Galati*, built in 1964 by the Sakurajima yard of Hitachi Zosen in Japan. A fillet or whole fish freezer stern trawler of 3,631 gross tons, the *Constanta* is 93.1 metres long overall with a moulded breadth of 15.6 m. and depth to upper deck of 9.1 m. She has accommodation for a crew of 80.

The ship is equipped to fillet her catch and for this she has four Baader machine processing lines which include a type 99 filleter for large white fish, a type 38 filleter, a type 150 header/filleter for red fish and a type 33 filleter for herrings.

Four horizontal plate freezers have a capacity of 20 tons a day and a further 20 tons capacity is pro-

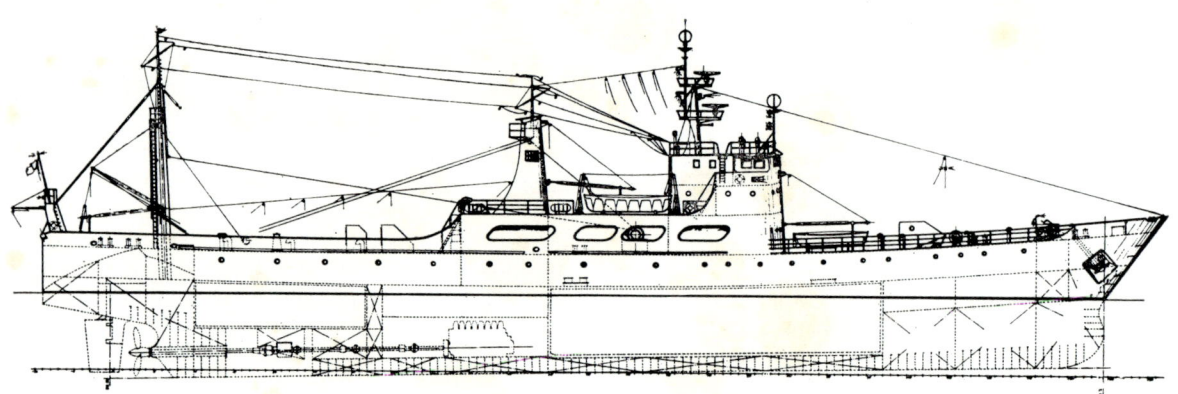

Profile drawing of the Portuguese trawler "Luis Ferreira de Carvalho", built in 1969 and 84.8 metres long.

vided by two air blast tunnels. Her main refrigerated hold has a capacity of 1,246 cu. m. and there is a smaller hold with a capacity of 389 cu. m. Waste fish and offal is reduced to meal in a Schlotterhose plant able to handle 35 tons of raw material a day.

Propulsion is by a Hitachi-Burmeister & Wain "father and son" arrangement with the first engine developing 1210 hp at 360 rpm and the second engine 1040 hp at 360 rpm. When both engines are used for propulsion, they turn a three-bladed c.p. propeller. On the grounds the smaller engine is used to drive an 800 kVA alternator to provide power for the electric winch motor.

TAIWAN

Golden Dragon No.1.

Built in 1967 by the Miho Shipyard Company of Shimizu, Japan, for the Chang Shing Ocean Enterprise Corporation of Kaohsing. This vessel was the first stern freezer trawler to join the Taiwan fleet and began her career fishing in the middle Atlantic off the coast of north-west Africa.

A ship of 1,900 gross tons, the *Golden Dragon No. 1* is 78.5 metres long overall with a moulded breadth of 12.5 m. She has accommodation for a crew of 67.

Her trawl winch is a Toyo Denki machine powered by a 135 kW electric motor and having a main drum pull of 14 tons at 80 m./min. on 22 mm. dia. warp.

Freezing is done in seven contact plate machines with a total output of about 40 tons a day.

Roumanian trawler "Constanta", 93.1 metres long, built in Japan in 1964.

Propulsion plant consists of two Kawasaki-MAN type V6V 22/30 ATL diesels each developing 1400 hp at 800 rpm and turning a Kawasaki c.p. propeller through a Kawasaki twin input, single output reduction gearbox to give a service speed of 13 knots.

UNITED ARAB REPUBLIC

Ras Banus

Built in 1967 by Astilleros Construcciones of Vigo, Spain, for the General Egyptian Organisation for Aquatic Resources (GEDAR). With the *Berenice* and the *Hurghada*, one of three freezer stern trawlers of the yard's ACSA-67B design for operation in the distant water fleet operated by the UAR in the Atlantic.

Taiwan stern trawler "Golden Dragon No. 1", 78.5 metres long, and built in Japan in 1967.

UAR stern trawler "Baltim", 106 metres long, and built in Spain in 1970.

A ship of 1,239 gross tons, the *Ras Banas* is 76 metres long overall with a moulded breadth of 12 m. and depth to upper deck of 4.55 m. She has accommodation for a crew of 75.

Her trawl winch is a Barreras-Brusselle type HMC-111 unit powered by a 360 hp Indar Electric motor on the Ward Leonard system.

The catch is whole frozen heads-off in three air blast tunnels with a total output of 30 tons a day. Refrigeration for these freezers and for the 1,700 cu. m. capacity fish holds is provided by five Sabroe Freon 22 compressors each powered by a 60 hp electric motor.

The main engine is a Naval-Werkspoor TMABS-398 diesel developing 2000 hp at 288 rpm and turning a fixed-blade propeller to give a speed of 13.5 knots.

Ras el Bar
With sister ship *Baltim*, built in 1970 by Hijos de J. Barreras of Vigo, Spain, for GEDAR and operated by the Egyptian High Seas Fisheries Company of Alexandria. These ships of about 2,400 gross tons are of a more or less standard design developed by the yard and they were built in just over a year.

A fillet and whole fish freezer stern trawler, the *Ras el Bar* is 106 metres long overall with a moulded breadth of 14.5 m. and depth to upper deck of 8.5 m.

Her trawl winch is a Barreras-Brusselle type KMC 111/5 electrically powered unit with five drums and a rated pull of 15 tons. It is driven by a 450 hp motor.

For processing her catch, the *Ras el Bar* is equipped with a Baader 163 gutter and header, two 423 headers, a 510 fillet washer and dryer, a 188 filleter and a 47 skinner. Fillet freezing is done in a Jackstone Froster horizontal plate machine with an output of 10 tons a day. Whole fish are frozen heads-off in Ramon Vizcaino blast tunnels with a capacity of about 30 tons. Waste fish and offal are reduced to meal in a reduction plant able to handle up to 30 tons of raw material a day.

The fish holds are cooled down to $-25°C$. and have a total capacity of 3,400 cu. m. The ship also has a 400 cu. m. capacity meal hold. She is able to carry 2,040 tons of frozen fish and meal.

Propulsion is by twin 2000 hp Barreras-Werkspoor type TMABAS-398 diesels each developing 2000 hp at 288 rpm and turning a single fixed-blade propeller to give a speed on trials of 15.6 knots.

UNITED STATES

Seafreeze Atlantic
Built in 1968 by the Maryland Shipbuilding & Drydock Company in Baltimore for American Stern Trawlers Inc. A sister ship, the *Seafreeze Pacific*, was completed early in 1969 and differs only in her processing plant which includes a line for filleting red fish. The first and so far the only ocean going factory stern trawlers built for an American owner, the two ships cost 5.3 million dollars each (half of it paid by the US Government under the Fishboat Subsidy Program). As their names imply, the first vessel was designed for operation in the North Atlantic and the second in the North Pacific.

The *Seafreeze Atlantic* is 295 ft. long overall with a moulded breadth of 44 ft. 3½ in. and depth to upper deck of 28 ft. 10½ in. She has accommodation for a crew of 56.

The bridge superstructure is placed well forward to give a trawl deck 140 ft. long. Her trawl winch is a

Seebeck "Gronland" type made by A.G. Weser of Bremerhaven, consisting of two separate parts driven through a double bevel spur gear by two 260 hp electric motors. Each winch part has a trawl warp drum, two auxiliary drums and one warping head. Each warp drum has a pull of 8½ tons at a hauling speed of 400 ft./min. and a capacity of 1,800 fathoms of 3½ in. circ. warp.

The ship is equipped with two Baader 163 machines for heading and gutting her catch. The fish are washed in a WACO cross current machine and then held in four bins through rigor. Larger fish are filleted in a Baader 99 machine fitted with a Baader 80 pin bone cutter. Smaller fish go through three lines of Baader 188 filleters. (The *Seafreeze Pacific* is equipped with a Baader 150 filleter for red fish in addition to the above lines.) All waste fish and offal is reduced to meal in an Atlas Stord reduction plant which can process 25 tons of raw material into five tons of bagged meal in 24 hours.

Freezing is done in three Amerio 20-station horizontal plate machines with a daily capacity of 48 tons. There is also a Jackstone Froster vertical plate freezer, with a capacity of 4½ tons a day of gutted whole fish and a blast freezer able to handle 6½ tons a day.

The fish hold is cooled down to $-20°F$. and has a capacity of 34,500 cu. ft. There is also a 'tween deck fish room with a capacity of 8,380 cu. ft.

Propulsion is by a diesel-electric system with electrical power for this purpose and for ship's services provided by two AEG 1000 kW constant current d.c. generators driven by two 1500 hp General Motors type 12-645-E2 diesel engines, and by an AEG 670 kW generator driven by a GM 975 hp diesel. Two AEG electric motors turn a single propeller through a reduction gear to give a service speed of 14.5 knots.

Old Colony
Built in 1968 by the Sturgeon Bay Shipbuilding and Dry Dock Company for the Old Colony Trawling Company of Boston. She was designed by Potter & McArthur Inc. A wet fish trawler of 311 gross tons with stern ramp and enclosed forecastle, the *Old Colony* is 131 ft. long overall with a moulded breadth of 28 ft. She has accommodation for a crew of 14. (A sister ship, the *Tremont*, was built in 1970).

The "Seafreeze Atlantic", one of two 295 ft. long factory trawlers built in the United States in 1968 and 1969.

Her trawl winch is a six-drum unit made by the New England Trawl Equipment Company. It is hydraulically powered and the drum line speed is 210 ft./min. at 36,000 lb. pull. The winch is placed on the superstructure deck and the trawl warps pass above the working deck with 9 ft. vertical clearance.

After gutting and washing, the fish is stored in an insulated fish hold with a capacity of 9,550 cu. ft.

The main engine is a General Motors type 1264E2 diesel developing 1275 hp at 800 rpm and turning a Columbian fixed-blade propeller through a Lufkin reduction gear to give a speed of 13.5 knots.

The wet fish trawler "Tremont" (sister ship of the "Old Colony"), 131 ft. long, and built in the United States in 1970.